Exclusion and Judgment in Fellowship Meals

Exclusion and Judgment in Fellowship Meals

The Socio-historical Background
of 1 Corinthians 11:17–34

LANUWABANG JAMIR

Foreword by Steve Walton

◥PICKWICK *Publications* • Eugene, Oregon

EXCLUSION AND JUDGMENT IN FELLOWSHIP MEALS
The Socio-historical Background of 1 Corinthians 11:17–34

Copyright © 2016 Lanuwabang Jamir. All rights reserved. Except for brief quotations in critical publications or reviews, no part of this book may be reproduced in any manner without prior written permission from the publisher. Write: Permissions, Wipf and Stock Publishers, 199 W. 8th Ave., Suite 3, Eugene, OR 97401.

Pickwick Publications
An Imprint of Wipf and Stock Publishers
199 W. 8th Ave., Suite 3
Eugene, OR 97401

www.wipfandstock.com

PAPERBACK ISBN 13: 978-1-4982-3337-8
HARDCOVER ISBN 13: 978-1-4982-3339-2

Cataloguing-in-Publication Data

Jamir, Lanuwabang

　　Exclusion and judgment in fellowship meals : the socio-historical background of 1 Corinthians 11:17–34 / Lanuwabang Jamir.

　　xxviii + 276 p. ; 23 cm. Includes bibliographical references.

　　ISBN: 978-1-4982-3337-8 (paperback) | ISBN: 978-1-4982-3339-2 (hardback)

　　1. Bible. Corinthians, 1st, XI, 11–34—Criticism, interpretation, etc. 2. Lord's Supper. 3. I.

BS2675.52 L23 2016

Manufactured in the U.S.A.　　　　　　　　　　　　　　　　　　　04/05/2016

This book is gratefully dedicated to
Dr. Montagu Gordon Barker

Contents

Foreword by Steve Walton | xi
Acknowledgments | xiii
Introduction | xv
Abbreviations | xix

CHAPTER 1
Fellowship Meals: Practices in the Ancient World | 1
   Introduction | 1
   Fellowship Meals in the Ancient World | 1
   Fellowship Meals in the Greco-Roman Milieu | 3
      Fellowship Meals in Different Settings | 6
      Fellowship Meals Customs and Practices | 10
      Moral and Social Response | 18
   Fellowship Meals in the Jewish Context | 21
      Fellowship Meals in the OT | 22
      Intertestamental Period | 34
      Eschatological Judgement and the Messianic Banquet | 56
   Conclusion | 59

CHAPTER 2
Fellowship Meals: Their Roles and Functions in the Ancient World | 62
   Introduction | 62
   Communal Bonding | 62
      Communion with the Gods | 64
   Social Division and Status | 69
   Social Identity | 76
   Morality and Ethics | 80
      Egalitarianism | 87

Social Politics | 90
The Sacred and Secular Dimensions | 93
Judgment Motifs and Fellowship meals | 97
    Divine Judgment | 97
    Human Judgment | 107
Greco-Roman Influences and Judeo-Christian Meal Practices | 109
Conclusion | 112

CHAPTER 3
Fellowship Meals in Corinth: The Abuse at the Lord's Supper | 114
  Introduction | 114
  The Christian Community in Corinth | 115
  Fellowship Meals in the Early Church | 124
  Fellowship Meals in Corinth | 125
    Analysis of the Corinthian Situation | 127
    Identity of the Groups | 136
  Paul's Response to the Corinthian Situation | 139
    Paul's Interpretation of the Lord's Supper Tradition | 143
    The Antecedent of the Lord's Supper | 148
    The Saying over the Bread (v. 24) | 152
    The Saying over the Cup (v. 25) | 157
    The Proclamation at the Lord's Supper (v. 26) | 159
  Conclusion | 163

CHAPTER 4
Judgment at the Lord's Supper in Corinth | 166
  Introduction | 166
    Judgment in Corinth | 167
  Judgment in the Lord's Supper | 170
    ἀναξίως | 171
    ἔνοχος | 173
  Causality and the Lord's Supper | 177
    Meal Traditions and Judgment in the Lord's Supper | 179
  ἀσθενεῖς, ἄρρωστοι, and κοιμῶνται | 184
    Restricted or Universal Judgment | 187
  The Lord's Supper and Final Judgment | 190
  Repentance and the Lord's Supper | 193
  Ordinances for the Lord's Supper | 201
    δοκιμαζέτω (v. 28) | 201

    διακρίνων (v. 29) | 203
    διεκρίνομεν (v. 31) | 209
    ἐκδέχεσθε (vv. 33–34) | 211
  Conclusion | 216

Final Conclusion | 218

Bibliography | 221
Index of Modern Authors | 251
Index of Ancient Sources | 257

Foreword

Dr. Lanuwabang Jamir is a fine scholar and this is a fine book. In it he offers fresh and helpful perspectives on perhaps the greatest puzzle in Paul's account of the Lord's Supper in 1 Corinthians 11:17–34: the warnings of God's judgment for those who participate unworthily in the meal, and how we should interpret them.

Dr. Jamir's approach is through identifying parallels with the ancient practice of fellowship meals, a practice which is widespread across a number of first-century cultures and societies. A notable contribution of his work is to bring this material together into two helpful chapters, looking at such meals in both Greco-Roman and Jewish settings. He draws out clearly the roles and functions of such meals, including: they bond a community together; their practice marks social divisions and status; they create and reinforce social identity; they have implications for ethical standards and morality in the society and community; they have socio-political implications; and they have "sacred" dimensions in the relationship with God/the gods they presuppose and promote. Most notably for this research, there are judgment themes—both human and divine—associated with such meals.

When Dr. Jamir turns to Corinth, he finds significant and illuminating parallels in Paul's discussions of communal meals, and the Lord's Supper in particular. He offers careful and well-balanced exegesis of the key passages in 1 Corinthians in identifying the nature of the abuse of the meal which the Corinthian believers were practising, and in examining the material on judgment in the context of the Supper (1 Cor 11:27–34). He recognises that the well-recognised socio-economic factors in the Corinthian practice of the Supper provide only a partial explanation of the judgment material, and he locates Paul's teaching in an eschatological context to illuminate the text. He also alerts us to the way Paul redefines fellowship meal practices familiar to his hearers into the context of the Christian gospel, which creates and shapes the body of Christ to which the believers belong. Dr. Jamir is sensitive to the Corinthian social and cultural context, and shows Paul to be a theologian and pastor who contextualises his theology into particular settings.

Dr. Jamir's central question not only addresses a fascinating aspect of the exegesis of Paul, but also has significant pastoral implications for Christian understanding of and participation in the eucharist today. Readers who engage with this book and grasp its central argument will find themselves gripped, informed and illuminated, as well as stimulated to reflect on its implications for Christian thinking and practice today—I commend it most warmly.

Steve Walton
Professor of New Testament, St Mary's University, Twickenham (London)

Acknowledgments

THIS RESEARCH WAS SUBMITTED for my PhD degree at London School of Theology, under Middlesex University in 2012. My supervisor was Dr. Conrad Gempf. His guidance and support throughout my research was outstanding. I am greatly indebted to him. His insightful criticisms were always given with sensitivity and kindness, making an overall positive impact on my life both personally and professionally.

I am grateful to my sponsors, the Langham Trust and the Church Mission Society. My study would not have been possible were it not for their generous financial support. I am especially indebted to Dr. Montagu G. Barker and Mrs. Rosemary Barker for their special support and contributions in my life. They have been a blessing to me in so many ways and their Christ-centered life is an inspiration to me always.

I express my appreciation to the faculty and staff at London School of Theology for their assistance; Tyndale House, Cambridge for their excellent library resources; Union Biblical Seminary, Pune for granting me study leave for the duration of my study. I am very thankful to Jacqueline Gray, Jon Harris, Dr. John Jeacocke and Dr. Jean Tyler who proofread my thesis. I remain indebted to Dr. John Jeacocke who has helped me in so many ways, especially in meticulously preparing the manuscripts for the publication of this book.

Further acknowledgement and gratitude needs to be expressed to the many friends and members of the different churches I am associated with whose prayers have strengthened and sustained me, and to my fellow research colleagues at Guthrie Centre who provided outstanding Christian fellowship and support throughout my study, and finally to my whole family for their support and encouragement not only during this time of research but throughout the years as I have sought to fulfill God's call in ministry. For all of these people and many more I give thanks to God. Let this humble work be for God's glory and the edification of his church, the Body of Christ.

Introduction

STUDIES ON THE ORIGIN of the Lord's Supper and its interpretation based on the accounts in the gospels and in Paul's letter to the Corinthians have resulted in a number of divergent views and theologies. Based on the synoptic accounts, the common view was that the Lord's Supper was based on the Passover meal.[1] But this view has been challenged on many grounds; the details will be discussed in chapter 4. Some scholars see its origin in some other prevalent Jewish meals and thus explain it on the basis of that relationship.[2] Another contentious study was that of Friedrich Spitta who proposed a double origin of the Lord's Supper.[3] But this view became better known through the monumental work of Hans Lietzmann who also disagreed with the originating of the Lord's Supper from the Passover and proposed two separate origins of the Lord's Supper in the tradition of the early church. He traced one tradition to Paul and the other to the early Jerusalem tradition.[4]

---

1. For example, based on the Synoptic gospels, J. Jeremias and A. J. B. Higgins identified the Passover meal as the original setting of the Lord's Supper and therefore as the source for the orthodox form and theology of the Lord's Supper. Jeremias, *Eucharistic*; Higgins, *Lord's Supper,* 56–57; This view was supported by many others including I. Howard Marshall and G. Feeley-Harnik. Marshall, *Last*; Feeley-Harnik, *Lord's Table*.

2. Box and Oesterley suggested that the Lord's Supper corresponds to the *kiddūsh* meal which was held before the Passover. Box, "Jewish Antecedent," 357–69; Oesterley, *Jewish Background,* 157–58. H. Lietzmann and G. Dix suggested that the Lord's Supper was similar to the *haburah* meal; Lietzmann, *Mass and Lord's,* 165–71; Dix, *Shape of the Liturgy,* 50–51; similarly, Otto, *Kingdom of,* 278. M. Black, sees the Pharisaic "Haburoth" meal as the prototype of the Eucharist; Black, *Scrolls and Christian Origins,*115. Some see the possible influence of "Joseph and Aseneth" in the Lord's Supper, Burchard, "Importance of Joseph and Aseneth," 121–22.

3. Friedrich Spitta, "Die urchristlichen Traditionen," 1.207–337.

4. According to Leitzmann, the origin of the Lord's Supper can be traced back through the liturgy of the church. He identifies two types of liturgies: the first is the liturgy of

XV

Introduction

On the other hand, some scholars see the antecedent of the Lord's Supper as some Hellenistic cultic meals, especially that of the sacred meals of the Mystery religions.[5] The phrase "Do this in remembrance of me" has led some to identify it with a memorial meal like those of the funerary banquets held in commemoration of a loved one.[6] The funerary meal tradition has some credence but such events were held only once a year, on the birthday of the deceased. Others are of the view that the Lord's Supper was based on a communal meal, a common Greco-Roman practice of those days, owing to the similarity between the Corinthian supper and Greco-Roman meal practices of that time. This is the view of E. Schweizer and others on the basis of NT text, and Jewish and other traditions.[7]

These scholars have postulated on the assumption that the Lord's Supper was based on a specific meal which in turn will help to interpret and develop the Lord's Supper theology. The problem here has to do with identifying which specific meal was the antecedent of the last supper of Jesus with his disciples. The above-mentioned debates show that there is no consensus among scholars on the origin and theology of the Lord's Supper. Nonetheless, the different theories proposing varieties of meals point to a fact that meal traditions did play an important role in ancient cultures and societies and this can be the key factor in understanding the Lord's Supper. Hence, this study will incorporate in its approach the theory that there was an ancient consensus that all meal practices were considered important and there was an existence of a meal tradition with features and significance common to different ancient cultures. In that respect all meal practices including the Lord's Supper partake of this common meal tradition. This will do away with the issue of the antecedent to the Lord's Supper which has been a contentious subject for many centuries.

Hippolytus, which he traces to Paul; the second is the liturgy of Sarapion, which he traces to the Didache. The Pauline tradition emphasizes the commemoration of the death of Jesus. The Didache tradition, which he also identifies with the early Jerusalem tradition, commemorated the table fellowship of Jesus with his disciples without reference to his death. Lietzmann, *Mass and Lord's Supper*, 172–215. This position has been reformulated in Mack, *Myth of Innocence*.

5. R. Bultmann and R. Reitzenstein conceived the Eucharistic meal as a representational rite like the "acted rites" of the mysteries; Bultmann, *Theology*, 149; Reitzenstein, *Hellenistic Mystery-Religions*, 77; Likewise Hyam Maccoby expresses the view that Paul was the originator of the Lord's Supper and it was based on the ritual meal of the Mystery religions, Maccoby, "Paul and Hellenism," 247–67.

6. Like the memorial meal of the Epicureans. Cf. Smith, *From Symposium*, 189.

7. Schweizer, *Lord's Supper*; Lampe, "Eucharistic Dinner Party," 1–15.

INTRODUCTION

This study will then investigate the background, roles, and functions of the meal traditions in both Greco-Roman and Jewish contexts based on the literature and traditions of meal culture from antiquity to the early formative Christian centuries. The aim of this study is to unravel the importance of meal practices in the ancient societies and study the Lord's Supper in that cultural context. The term "fellowship meal" will be used instead of the common term "table fellowship," for the study of these meal traditions. First, because it does not always involve tables or other furniture as such; in its earliest rudimentary form, an animal skin or a woven rug, or mat would have been used probably to keep the food away from sand. Second, in order to emphasize one of the most important functions of the meal practices in ancient cultures in creating bonding among the participants.[8] As the study will show these meal practices involved not merely associations limited to the sharing of communal meals, but involved greater roles and mutual responsibilities for the participants in the community. The definition of fellowship meal used here also pertains and is inclusive of all kinds of meal practices in the different settings and not only the formal meals eaten to observe special events.

This research will begin with a study on the fellowship meals in the ancient world, their structures, ideologies, functions in society. The purpose is to find how the meal traditions were understood and used by the different communities. The study will explore the link between fellowship meal practices and judgment both as a religious and social category. The term "exclusion" in the context of this research will refer to the discipline and punishment of offending members in the ancient societies through the fellowship meals. Likewise, the term "judgment" will be used to mean reward and blessing as well as retribution and punishment in the context of the wider fellowship meal tradition. Based on that, the study will investigate the Lord's Supper tradition, and how the meal traditions have shaped the origin and development of the Lord's Supper in the Early Church, especially in the multicultural Corinthian context. This will enable us to have a better understanding of the context in which Paul has expressed his view,

---

8. See the work of M. Douglas, who in her fundamental essay "Deciphering a Meal," 161–81, has shown that, dining was a socially structured gathering where sharing and consumption of food was a means of establishing a community or relationships. Secondly, to refer to the practice from its earliest rudimentary form, where an animal skin or a woven rug, or mat instead of a table, would have been used probably to keep the food away from sand.

xvii

INTRODUCTION

and thereby understand more clearly what he intended to say in 1 Corinthians 11:17–34.

This will also necessitate the study of the institution at the Last Supper by Jesus against the general background of the meal traditions, to the different levels of influences in the Gospel tradition as it was passed on to the believing community. The interrelationship between the Gospels' accounts and Paul's account will be investigated to help us in analysing how Paul's theology developed and the level of redaction that has taken place when he presents the theology of the Lord's Supper in 1 Corinthians 11, especially in regard to the judgment motif. Why does Paul connect judgment with the Eucharistic fellowship? How are those who are sick and dead connected with the abuse of the Lord's Supper? Is it based on Jesus' teaching or tradition? Or was Paul influenced by other Greco-Roman philosophies or traditions in Judaism to warrant such a teaching in Corinthians?

The meanings and values of the meal traditions in the different cultures can be a valuable aid to biblical exegesis and can shed light on the interpretation of the Lord's Supper and thereby understand its significance more fully.

Abbreviations

AB		Anchor Bible
ABD		Anchor Bible Dictionary. Edited by D. N. Freedman. 6 vols. New York, 1992.
ABR		Australian Biblical Review
Acts Pet.		Acts of Peter
Aeschylus		
	Suppl.	Supplices
AJSR		Association for Jewish Studies Review
ALGHJ		Arbeiten zur Literatur und Geschichte des hellenistischen Judentums
ANTC		Abingdon New Testament Commentaries
Apul.		Apuleius
	Metam.	Metamorphoses (The Golden Ass or Asinus aureus)
Aristophanes		
	Ach.	Acharnenses
	Vesp.	Vespae
Aristotle		
	Eth. Nic.	Ethica Nichomachea
	Pol.	Politica
Artemidorus Daldianus		
	Onir.	Onirocritica
ASOR		American Schools of Oriental Research
ATANT		Abhandlungen zur Theologie des Alten und Neuen Testaments

Abbreviations

Ath.		Athenaeus
	Deipn.	*Deipnosophistae*
AThR		*Anglican Theological Review*
b.		Babylonian tractate
BCH		*Bulletin de correspondance hellénique*
BDAG		Bauer, W., F. W. Danker, W. F. Arndt, and F. W. Gingrich. *Greek-English Lexicon of the New Testament and Other Early Christian Literature*. 3d ed. Chicago, 1999
BDF		Blass, F., A. Debrunner, and R. W. Funk. *A Greek Grammar of the New Testament and Other Early Christian Literature*. Chicago, 1961
BECNT		Baker Exegetical Commentary on the New Testament
BEvT		Beiträge zur evangelischen Theologie
BJS		Brown Judaic Studies
BNTC		Black New Testament Commentary
BSac		*Bibliotheca Sacra*
BZNW		Beihefte zur Zeitschrift für die neutestamentliche Wissenschaft
CBET		Contributions to Biblical Exegesis and Theology
CBQ		*Catholic Biblical Quarterly*
Cicero		
	Att.	*Epistulae ad Atticum*
	Cael.	*Pro Caelio*
	Cat.	*In Catalinam*
	Fam.	*Epistulae ad familiars*
	Mur.	*Pro Murena*
	Nat. d.	*De natura deorum*
	Off.	*De officiis*
	Phil.	*Orationes philippicae*
Cl. Al.		Clement of Alexandria
	Strom.	*Stromata*
CNT		Commentaire du Nouveau Testament
ConBNT		Coniectanea Biblica, New Testament Series
CRINT		Compendia rerum iudaicarum ad Novum Testamentum

ABBREVIATIONS

Did.	*Didache*
Dio C.	Dio Cassius
Hist. Rom.	*Historia Romae*
Dio Chrysostom	
Or.	*Orationes*
EKKNT	Evangelisch-katholischer Kommentar zum Neuen Testament
EMC	*Echos du monde classique/Classical Views*
EncyDSS	*Encyclopaedia of the Dead Sea Scrolls*, ed. L. H. Schiffman and J. C. VanderKam. 2 Vols. Oxford: Oxford University Press, 2000
Euripides	
Bacch.	*Bacchae*
El.	*Electra*
Eusebius	
Hist. eccl.	*Historia ecclesiastica*
EvT	*Evangelische Theologie*
ExpTim	*Expository Times*
FBBS	Facet Books, Biblical Series
FN	*Filologia Neotestamentaria*
Gell.	Aulus Gellius
Noct. att.	*Noctes Atticae (Attic Nights)*
Grimm-Thayer	Grimm and Thayer, *A Greek-English Lexicon of the New Testament*
GTA	Göttinger theologischer Arbeiten
HDR	Harvard Dissertations in Religion
Herm.	Shepherd of Hermas
Herm. Sim.	*Similitude*
Hesiod	
Op.	*Opera et dies*
Hippolytus	
Trad. ap.	*The Apostolic Tradition*
HNT	Handbuch zum Neuen Testament
Hom.	Homer

xxi

Abbreviations

	Il.	*The Iliad*
	Od.	*The Odyssey*
Horace		
	Carm.	*Carmina*
HTA		Historisch Theologische Auslegung
HUT		Hermeneutische Untersuchungen zur Theologie
IB		*Interpreter's Bible.* Edited by G. A. Buttrick et al. 12 vols. New York, 1951–1957
ICC		International Critical Commentary
IDB		*Interpreter's Dictionary of the Bible,* ed. G. Arthur. Nashville, TN: Abingdon, 1990.
IESS		*International Encyclopedia of the Social Sciences*
Ign.		Ignatius
	Eph.	*To the Ephesians*
	Rom.	*To the Romans*
ILS		*Inscriptiones Latinae Selectae,* ed. H. Dessau
JBL		*Journal of Biblical Literature*
JHS		*Journal of Hellenic Studies*
John Chrysostom		
	Hom. Matt.	*Homiliae in Matthaeum*
Jos.		Josephus
	J.W.	*Jewish War*
	Ant	*Jewish Antiquities*
Jos. Asen.		*Joseph and Aseneth*
	JRH	*Journal of Religious History*
	JSJ	*Journal for the Study of Judaism in the Persian, Hellenistic, and Roman Periods*
JSNT		*Journal for the Study of the New Testament*
JSNTSup		Journal for the Study of the New Testament: Supplement Series
JSOTSup		Journal for the Study of the Old Testament: Supplement Series
JSPSup		Journal for the Study of the Pseudepigrapha: Supplement Series

JSS		*Journal of Semitic Studies*
JTS		*Journal of Theological Studies*
Jub.		*Jubilees*
Juvenal		
	Sat.	*Satirae*
KEK		Kritisch-exegetischer Kommentar über das Neue Testament (Meyer-Kommentar)
LCL		Loeb Classical Library
LEC		Library of Early Christianity
Let. Aris.		*Letter to Aristeas*
Lucian		
	Dial. d.	*Dialogi deorum*
	Dial. meretr.	*Dialogi meretricii*
	Lex.	*Lexiphanes*
	Par.	*De parasite*
	Sat.	*Saturnalia*
	Symp.	*Symposium*
m.		Mishnah tractate
Mart.		Martial
Epig.		*Epigrams*
NAC		New American Commentary
NCB		New Century Bible
NICNT		New International Commentary on the New Testament
NICOT		New International Commentary on the Old Testament
NIDNTT		*New International Dictionary of New Testament Theology*. Edited by C. Brown. 4 vols. Grand Rapids, 1975–1985
NIGTC		New International Greek Testament Commentary
NJBC		*The New Jerome Biblical Commentary*. Edited by R. E. Brown et al. Englewood Cliffs, 1990
NovT		*Novum Testamentum*
NovTSup		Novum Testamentum Supplements
NTAbh		Neutestamentliche Abhandlungen
NTD		Das Neue Testament Deutsch

Abbreviations

NTS		*New Testament Studies*
Odes Sol.		*Odes of Solomon*
Origen		
	Cels.	*Contra Celsum*
OTL		Old Testament Library
Ovid		
	Fast.	*Fasti*
Paus.		Pausanias
	Descr.	*Graeciae description*
Petron.		Petronius
	Sat.	*Satyricon*
Philo		
	Contempl.	*De vita contemplative*
	Flacc.	*In Flaccum*
	Leg.	*Legum allegoriae*
	Post. Cain	*On the Posterity and Exile of Cain*
	Spec.	*De specialibus legibus*
Pindar		
	Isthm.	*Isthmionikai*
	Ol.	*Olympionikai*
Plato		
	Leg.	*Leges*
	Phaedr.	*Phaedrus*
	Resp.	*Respublica*
	Symp.	*Symposium*
	Theaet.	*Theaetetus*
Pliny the Younger		
	Ep.	*Epistulae*
Plut.		Plutarch
	Alex.	*Alexander*
	Cat. Maj.	*Cato Major*
	Conj. praec.	*Conjugalia praecepta*
	Mor.	*Moralia*

Abbreviations

Quaest. conv.		*Quaestiones convivales*
Sept. sap. conv.		*Septem sapientium convivium*
	Sera.	*De sera numinis vindicta*
	Vid. put.	*De vitioso pudore*

Porphyry

	Abst.	*De abstinentia*
Pss. Sol.		*Psalms of Solomon*
PTMS		Pittsburgh Theological Monograph Series
PW		Pauly, A. F. *Paulys Realencyclopädie der classischen Altertumswissenschaft.* 49 vols. New Edition. G. Wissowa. Munich, 1980
QS		Qumran Scroll
RAr		*Revue archéologique*
RB		*Revue biblique*
RefR		*Reformed Review*
RelSRev		*Religious Studies Review*
RevQ		*Revue de Qumran*
RNT		Regensburger Neues Testament
RTR		*Reformed Theological Review*
SANT		Studien zum Alten und Neuen Testaments
SBL		Society of Biblical Literature
SBLDS		Society of Biblical Literature Dissertation Series
SBLMS		Society of Biblical Literature Monograph Series
SBLSP		*Society of Biblical Literature Seminar Papers*
SBT		Studies in Biblical Theology
ScrHier		Scripta hierosolymitana
Sib. Or.		*Sibylline Oracles*
SIG		*Sylloge inscriptionum graecarum.* Edited by W. Dittenberger. 4 vols. 3d ed. Leipzig, 1915–1924
SJLA		Studies in Judaism in Late Antiquity
SJT		*Scottish Journal of Theology*
SNTSMS		Society for New Testament Studies Monograph Series
SPB		Studia Post-Biblica
SPCK		Society for Promoting Christian Knowledge

Abbreviations

STDJ		*Studies on the Texts of the Desert of Judah*
Strabo		
	Geogr.	*Geographica*
Str-B		Strack, H. L., and P. Billerbeck. *Kommentar zum Neuen Testament aus Talmud und Midrasch.* 6 vols. Munich, 1922–1961.
Suetonius		
	Aug.	*Divus Augustus*
	Claud.	*Divus Claudius*
	Dom.	*Domitianus*
	Jul.	*Divus Julius*
	Vesp.	*Vespasianus*
t.		Tosefta tractate
Tac.		Tacitus
	Ann.	*Annales*
	Hist.	*Historiae*
TDNT		*Theological Dictionary of the New Testament.* Edited by G. Kittel and G. Friedrich. Translated by G. W. Bromiley. 10 vols. Grand Rapids, 1964–1976.
THKNT		Theologischer Handkommentar zum Neuen Testament
TNTC		Tyndale New Testament Commentaries
TRu		*Theologische Rundschau*
TynBul		*Tyndale Bulletin*
WUNT		Wissenschaftliche Untersuchungen zum Neuen Testament
WW		*Word and World*
Xen.		Xenophon
	Anab.	*Anabasis*
	Hell.	*Hellenica*
	Mem.	*Memorabilia*
	Symp.	*Symposium*
y.		Jerusalem tractate
ZNW		*Zeitschrift für die neutestamentliche Wissenschaft und die Kunde der älteren Kirche*

ZTK	*Zeitschrift für Theologie und Kirch*

CHAPTER 1

Fellowship Meals
Practices in the Ancient World

INTRODUCTION

IN THIS CHAPTER WE shall look at fellowship meals in their different settings in the Greco-Roman societies and in the Jewish context. It will highlight the importance of the fellowship meals, the different customs and practices that are relevant to the study of the Lord's Supper in the Corinthian context. The specific roles and functions of the fellowship meals in the different traditions will be discussed later in chapter 2.

FELLOWSHIP MEALS IN THE ANCIENT WORLD

The importance and significance of sharing food among ancient people can be found throughout the extant ancient literature. The practice of fellowship meals appears to be a common trend in the ancient world. The Homeric poems illustrate a number of features of early archaic social life, and in particular the central role of feasting (*Od.* 1.225–226; 9.5–10).[1] Fellowship

---

1. Meal scenes are well depicted in poetry, art, vases, and paintings. See Schmitt-Pantel, "Sacrificial Meal," 17–18, 26–30.

Exclusion and Judgment in Fellowship Meals

meals were usually associated with social or religious events and celebrations in the family or community.[2]

Social scientific studies on meals have shed a lot of light on the role they played in the communities. Mary Douglas who has done extensive anthropological studies on the subject has given an insightful view and explanation on the matter.[3] Her views are clearly expressed in this statement:

> If food is treated as a social code, the messages it encodes will be found in the pattern of social relations being expressed. The message is about different degrees of hierarchy, inclusion and exclusion, boundaries and transactions across the boundaries. Like sex, the taking of food has a social component, as well as a biological one.[4]

Meal practices thus reflect society and culture on a microcosmic level. Discussing ritual purity and food laws in different cultures, she illustrates that dining together was simply not an act of satisfying one's hunger, but it goes well beyond that: "One cannot share the food prepared by people without sharing in their nature."[5] Food in itself constitutes a "code" which carries different social messages and is associated with different social events. Jack Goody shows some concrete examples in certain cultures in this regard:

> In looking at the cuisines of the Eurasian societies, we noted a set of specific characteristics: 1. The link between cuisine and "class," with social groups being characterized by different styles of life. 2. The contradictions, tensions, and conflicts connected with this differentiation. The various forms, include the contradictions between ideologies of equality . . . and ideologies of hierarchy . . . as well as the conflict, at the individual as well as the group level, between fasting acknowledged as "good" and feasting as "pleasurable."[6]

So through the ages the practice had become laden with social meaning and significance. Hence food becomes an embodiment of human interaction and relations. Once food is shared the bond between the participants is regarded in a realistic way. Thus in many ancient cultures when meals

---

2. Fellowship meals played a "central part" in both the Greek and Roman culture. Fisher, "Roman Associations," 2.1205. Cf. Smith, *From Symposium*, 1–2.
3. See Douglas, *Purity and Danger*; "Deciphering a Meal," 61–81.
4. Douglas, "Deciphering a Meal," 61.
5. Douglas, *Purity and Danger*, 126.
6. Goody, *Cooking, Cuisine and Class*, 191.

were shared even with strangers, it implied that the host was willing to protect and defend the guest in case of danger with his life. This prevails even today in certain societies.[7] Accordingly, food was considered as a means of creating special bond and community ties among the participants and carried with it a number of obligations. In this regard Robertson Smith observes:

> The value of the Arabic evidence is that it supplies proof that the bond of food is valid in and of itself, that religion may be called in to conform and strengthen it, but that the essence of the thing lies in the physical act of eating together.[8]

FELLOWSHIP MEALS IN THE GRECO-ROMAN MILIEU

The importance of fellowship meals in the Greco-Roman world cannot be overstated.[9] This is seen in the symposia traditions of the different clubs or associations which were central to life in the city-states in the Greco-Roman world.[10] One major indication of the importance of the fellowship meal is seen in its extensive coverage and focus by the Greek and Roman authors. Among many, some of the prominent authors are Plato, Xenophon, Aristotle, Lucian, Plutarch, Athenaeus, Catullus, Horace, Cicero, the younger Pliny, Petronius, Aulus Gellius and Macrobius who have written significantly on the subject. Architectural designs of houses and villas from

---

7. For example, this sort of practice is seen among the Bedouins. Hospitality (*diyafa*) is considered the highest Bedouin virtue. A complex code of manners regulates this and all other relationships. In Bedouin tradition, once they have shared food from the same table, guests including strangers were offered protection and the hosts would fight to their own death to defend their guest from any harm. See Jabbur, *The Bedouins*; Keohane, *Bedouin*; W. R. Smith, *Religion of the Semites*, 269–70. This desert code of hospitality may be the background to Ps 23:5. See, "Hospitality," in Ryken, *Dictionary of Biblical Imagery*, 403.

8. Smith, *Religion of the Semites*, 271.

9. Meal culture became quite prevalent and popular during the Hellenistic period, the very word *pergraecari* (to behave in a very Greek way) meant in effect the enjoyment of dinners, drinking parties, and women (e.g., Plautus, *Mostellaria*, 22ff.) Cf. Fisher, "Roman Associations," 2.1202.

10. For a detailed study on the importance of fellowship meals in the Greco-Roman society see Fisher's articles, "Greek Associations," 2.1167–1225 and "Roman Associations," 2.1199–1225. Dennis E. Smith, "Social Obligation," and many of his articles now summarized in, *From Symposium to Eucharist*. Corley, "Jesus' Table Practice," 444–59; and *Private Women*.

the Greco-Roman period with elaborate settings for dining further attest to the importance of fellowship meals among the inhabitants.[11] It was not only the public meeting places that had a pivotal role in conducting the meals but the private houses also.

Fisher in his analysis of the Greek and Roman societies summarizes that:

> In most, if not all, societies, social relationships of all sorts tend to be sanctified and solidified by a shared taking of food and drink; but in few societies have celebrations of shared eating and drinking been so highly valued, so idealized and stylized, so widely practiced at many levels, and so significantly used as occasions for philosophical, political, and moral discussions and their reflections in poetic and prose literature.[12]

The popularity of fellowship meals contributed to the development of the symposium as a literary tradition. This can be traced back to Plato who describes the gathering of the learned for a fellowship meal and the drinking sessions that followed where they discussed and debated on various subjects and issues.[13] This was followed by many of the philosophers, including those writers in Jewish and Christian literature.[14] Two Greek terms χάρις (*charis*) and εὐφροσύνη (*euphrosyne*), are used together frequently to describe the underlining principle of the symposium. They conveyed the value of the hospitality, reciprocal goodwill, fun, equality, friendship and loyalty that the symposium was meant to represent.[15] Plutarch, who follows in the Platonic tradition, describes the fellowship as: "A symposium

---

11. The placement of couches was done in such a way that the most privileged guests had the finest views of the surroundings. Pliny the Younger *Ep.* 2.17. See Fisher, "Roman Associations," 2.1208, 1216 and Crossan, "Who and What Controls your Banquet?" 306–316, for archeological findings and description of Greco-Roman houses.

12. Fisher, "Greek Associations," 2.1167 also see "Roman Associations," 2.1199.

13. Plato, whose work reflects a lot of Socrates's activities, through his work *Symposium* established the standard in the late fifth century BC, Plato, *Lysis*. *Symposium*. *Gorgias*, 77. Fisher indicates that it developed towards the end of the seventh century BC or earlier. "Greek Associations," 2.1170.

14. The influence of this literary tradition can be seen in both Jewish and Christian literature, for example in the Jewish *Letter of Aristeas* and in various sections of the New Testament where meals are referred to, such as in the Gospel of Luke. See D. Smith and Taussig, *Many Tables*, 29.

15. Cf. Fisher, "Greek Associations," 2.1170; Schmitt-Pantel, "Sacrificial Meal and Symposion," 23.

is a communion of serious and mirthful entertainment, discourse, and actions."[16] It was meant to further:

> a deeper insight into those points that were debated at table, for the remembrance of those pleasures which arise from meat and drink is ungenteel and short-lived . . . but the subjects of philosophical queries and discussions remain always fresh after they have been imparted . . . and they are relished by those who were absent as well as by those who were present at dinner.[17]

The extant data that portrays the meal practices in the early centuries were to a certain extent a literary form of expression of societal values and yearnings. A good example can be seen in the works of Plutarch in *Moralia*, where he explains his association in table talk with famous personalities and its recordings:

> . . . but also has the most famous of the philosophers to bear witness against it, Plato, Xenophon, Aristotle, Speusippus, Epicurus, Prytanis, Heironymus, and Dio of the Academy, who all consider the recording of conversation held at table a task worth some effort . . .[18]

Another example can be seen in his description of the meal of the legendary seven sages (*Dinner of the Seven Wise Men—Septem sapientium convivium*), which is described in a first-person account, which was a style of the symposium tradition.[19] This will explain certain themes and motifs that are recurrent in the literatures, one of which is the magnifying of a certain person or character.[20] Thus fellowship meal traditions even made an impact and contributed to literary development in the Greco-Roman world.

---

16. Plut. *Quaest. conv.* 7.6, 708D.

17. Ibid., 6.0.1, 686C. See Stein, "Influence of Symposia Literature," 18.

18. Plut. *Quaest. conv.* 612D–E.

19. Plutarch, *Moralia*. D. Smith argues for it in "Messianic Banquet," 69–70. Also see Aune, "Septem Sapientium," 79–80.

20. Smith who sees the Greco-Roman influences on NT literature summarizes that: "Meals were also part of the repertoire used to typify the life of a hero or great man. Thus when we come upon meals in the literature of early Christianity, we must be aware of the pervasiveness of literary and folklore motifs in the tradition." D. E. Smith, "Historical Jesus at the Table," 470.

Exclusion and Judgment in Fellowship Meals

Fellowship Meals in Different Settings

We now begin with a survey of the fellowship meal practices in the Greco-Roman context; this will enable us to see the varied forms of the fellowship meals in different settings and what significance they held for the communities.

Festivals and feasts featuring communal eating and drinking were the common activities central to the different groups in the Greco-Roman world. There were different types of specialized meals for different occasions and purposes. It was a sort of platform for them to get together for fun and entertainment as well as for serious business. So for all sorts of occasion they had meals associated with it, for instance the birthday banquet, wedding banquet, funeral banquets in memory of the deceased. Fellowship meals were associated with civic and business associations, trade guilds, funerary societies, philosophical schools, and religious associations in honour of a patron deity and to mark special events and rites of passage.[21] These indicate that different occasions culminated in or were centered on fellowship meals.

For instance, the funerary banquet περίδειπνον (*perideipnon*), held in honor of the deceased, was a common affair. S. R. F Price observes that:

> In the classical period a funerary banqueting scene was used only in connection with the relatively small number of official state heroes, while in the Hellenistic and Roman periods the imagery was employed of any deceased member of a private family.[22]

This was observed within the family and at times when important people were involved the whole city was part of it. It basically celebrated the death with sacrifices and feasts.[23] Probably the purpose was for the communal bonding between the family and the deceased symbolically realized and maintained through the meals. According to Etruscans' funerary reliefs, in these commemorative meals, the dead are depicted as participating in

---

21. For a detailed description, see Smith, *From Symposium*, 38–40; Klinghardt, *Gemeinschaftsmahl*, 35–40.

22. Price, *Rituals and Power*, 35.

23. Price explains that: "For this purpose the appropriate type of sacrifice was the *thysia* (or sacrifice commonly used in the cult of the gods), part of which could be eaten by those present, rather than the non-consumable heroic sacrifice (*enhagisma*), but the sacrifices were not directed to the deceased and did not deify them." *Rituals and Power*, 36.

Fellowship Meals: Practices in the Ancient World

the feast and enjoying the wine libation offered by the family.[24] Some of the trade guilds also functioned as funerary societies where the members usually from lower economic conditions could have provision for funeral rituals and memorial meals in honor of deceased members and patrons.[25] Egyptian associations differed in a number of ways from Greek or Roman associations in terms of its duration of existence and functions, but there were a number of similarities, one of which was the common practice of having monthly banquets.[26]

Clubs and associations were formed for various purposes and were one of the main features of Hellenistic social life. They were found to be sometimes formed for the sole purpose of having fellowship meals for the club members, paid in from the club funds raised for the purpose.[27] This is also noticed in the trade guilds formed by people in the same profession, and in the clubs formed in honor of some patron deities, where the fellowship meals were more religious in outlook. For example, this is seen in the society of Diana and Antinous[28] where the banquet was the main activity of the group. Fisher summarizes that: "Club dinners, held in their clubhouses with as much pomp, friendship, and luxury as members and patrons could provide, were no doubt for many the highlight of each month and a major feature of membership."[29] Aristotle states in this regard: "some associations appear to be formed for the sake of pleasure, for example religious guilds and dining-clubs, which are unions for sacrifice and companionship."[30] The central role of the meals in these groups is also manifested in the names of the clubs and associations. Some clubs even named their groups in accordance to their meal practices:

---

24. Avramidou, *Codrus Painter*, 45; Angus, *Mystery Religions*, 127. Also see Ascough, "Forms of Commensality," 14.

25. Fisher, "Greek Associations," 2.1195; Smith and Taussig, *Many Tables*, 28–29.

26. Ferguson, *Backgrounds*, 133–34.

27. Dunbabin, *Roman Banquet*, 94. Donahue, *Roman Community*, 85. Smith summarizes it as follows: "But in virtually every case where we have documented records of club activities, we find that the banquet emerges as one of their primary reasons for gathering." Smith, *From Symposium*, 87. For example, in the Arval Brethren, the Luperci, and the Salii, representing the priestly colleges of *sodales*, ancestral rituals and the shared common banquet were the main features. See Fisher, "Roman Associations," 2.1200.

28. A burial society dedicated to the goddess Diana and the deified Antinous. The lengthy inscription of its by-laws was found in Lanuvium, Italy and it is dated in the year 136 CE. Cf. Smith, *From Symposium*, 97; Fisher, "Roman Associations," 2.1223.

29. Fisher, "Roman Associations," 2.1223.

30. *Eth. nic.* 8.9.5.

for example, "college of messmates" (*collegium comestorum*), "drinking buddies" (*sodalex ex symposia*), and "table companions who customarily share banquets together" (*convictores qui una epula vesci solent*), "diners" (*comestores*) or "boon companions whose custom is to eat a feast together" (*convictor(es) qui una epulo vesci solent*).[31]

The fellowship meals in these clubs were commonly designated by two names, suggesting that there were two types of clubs, those clubs or guilds which were formed for religious purposes were designated as θίασοι (*thiasoi*: religious guilds) and all other clubs as ἔρανοι (*eranoi*: dining clubs).[32] But as Athenaeus states, there was in fact not much difference between the two and both are included under the category of "association" (κοινόν).[33] These clubs were formed for social, economic, political and religious purposes and most all their activities were centered on fellowship meals.[34] Thus some of the earliest associations which flourished in the mid-third century BC to imperial times, were called the societies of ἐρανισταί (*eranistai*), a term derived from ἔρανος—dinner.[35]

At religious festivals, feasting for all participants on the sacrificed meat was a common feature. A portion of an animal offering was burned on the altar, and portions were set aside for the deity and the priests. The worshippers ate the rest within the temple's precincts.[36] Thus many of the temples had a separate place for dining within their sacred precincts. The best-preserved example can be seen in the Corinthian *Asclepeion*, or shrine to Asclepius.[37] In religious sects and associations there were various sacrifices

---

31. Ascough, "Forms of Commensality," 2–3.

32. Cf. Aristotle *Eth. nic.* 8.9.5.

33. Ath. *Deipn.* 8.362: "The same kind of dinner may be called either eranus or thiasus, and the members who come together eranistae or thiasotae. . ." Smith adds: "In actuality, these terms . . . merely refer to the different dimensions of the club. As religious organisations, these clubs provide communal sacrifices. These sacrifices also include an emphasis on the sacrificial banquet; thus they provide 'social intercourse' (synousia)." *From Symposium*, 88. Also see, Aune, "Septem Sapientium Convivium," 71–72.

34. Fisher reiterates that: "These associations had in common a central and supportive religious element that, as expressed through sacrifices, banquets, and drinking parties, many then and now would see as their primary function." Fisher, "Greek Associations," 2.1195.

35. See Ferguson, *Backgrounds of Early Christianity*, 131. Aune, "Septem Sapientium Convivium," 74.

36. Kane, "Mithraic Cult Meal," 327.

37. See the description in Crossan, "Who and What," 301–2.

Fellowship Meals: Practices in the Ancient World

associated with patron deities and most of them involved feastings, as an inherent part of the rites.[38] Thus Dio Chrysostom's statement: "what sacrifice is acceptable to the gods without the participants in the feast?"[39] Nock indicates that "sacrifices" basically came to mean "dinner party" as early as Herodotus 8.99.[40]

Likewise the philosophical schools utilized the fellowship meals for their philosophical discourses and discussions. The popular description of the philosophical banquets in numerous ancient literatures indicates the popularity of these meals in the civilized societies. This led to a trend where the sophists were normally invited to banquets to be facilitators in the table-talk.[41]

The philosophical schools met for communal meals often under the patronage of poets, philosophers, or other thinkers. The philosophical tradition, of course, is especially associated with the classical definition of the symposium. This tradition goes back at least to Plato and the literary form which he helped to popularize, whereby philosophers partaking in a meal would be described. The main emphasis was on the philosophical dialogue that would take place during the drinking party. This literary form of the symposium became highly influential and it became a sort of literary reference whenever fellowship meals and their motifs were described. It was also influential in Jewish and Christian literature, as seen for example in the Jewish *Letter of Aristeas* and in various sections of the New Testament where meals are referred to, such as in the Gospel of Luke.[42] Fellowship meals of a philosophical nature became popular in the Greco-Roman society and were emulated. This is seen in the description of fellowship meals of philosophical nature which were held in different settings, like weddings or birthdays where philosophical discourses were carried out.[43]

---

38. Plato states: "when offering a sacrifice and feasting," describing the Homeric period, this phrase suggests that meals were integral to the sacrificial ritual (*Symp.* 174C).

39. Dio Chrysostom *Orations* 3.97. Cf. Lietzmann and Kümmel, *Korinther I, II*. Yerkes also comments that communal meals were an integral part of the Greek sacrifices; *Sacrifice*, 99–100.

40. Nock, "The Cult of Heroes," 151.

41. Athenaeus describes some of them as "dinner-chasing sophist." Ath. *Deipn.* 1.4.

42. Similar practice is seen in Judaism, like the discussion of the Torah at table, e.g., Sir 9:15–16; Philo *Contempl.* 75–78; *m. Abot.* 3.3. A study of the symposium motif in Luke is found in D. E. Smith, "Table Fellowship," 613–38; Smith and Taussig, *Many Tables*, 29.

43. See Plut. *Quaest. conv.* 717B; Lucian *Symp.* 5.

These fellowship meals were held in public halls or club buildings. Private fellowship meals followed by symposia were also a common feature. Usually they were held on occasions such as weddings or memorials and within the family, or could be extended to friends' circles by invitation.[44]

Fellowship Meals Customs and Practices

In Greco-Roman society it was usually the evening communal meals which were considered more important and were established as a formal social institution. The host or patron usually provided the meals for all. There was also a practice in which the meal was financed by equal contribution from all the members. This type of fellowship meal was known as the *eranos* (ἔρανος) and has been recorded since the time of Homer and into the 2nd century.[45] An average member of the community participated in the symposium once or twice per month, while for some it was a daily affair.[46] In order to understand more clearly the function and significance of the meal practices, we need to analyze how the meals were organized and held, and the customs associated with them. While the focus is on the formal evening meals or banquets, since most of the literary data deals with them, nonetheless, it does not exclude the informal meals and their roles in the communities.[47]

An outline of the procedure and order of a fellowship meal can be constructed based on the literary and other forms of evidence we have.[48] Firstly, the invitation to fellowship meals followed certain motifs, such as honoring a patron or the gods, as it is evident in Plato and others.[49] Oral

---

44. Lucian *Symp.* 8.

45. Cf. Hom. *Od.* 1.226–227; see also Aelius Aristides *Sarapis*, 54.20–28; Aristophanes *Ach.* 1085–1149; Lucian *Lex.* 6, 9, 13; Xen. *Mem.* 3.14.1.

46. Lucian *Par.* 15. Cf. Aune, "Septem Sapientium Convivium," 74.

47. For a study on the meal customs among the Greeks see Becker and Göll, *Charikles*, 89–108, 310–55. Fisher's article "Greek Associations," 2.1167–1197. For Roman customs, see especially Balsdon, *Life and Leisure*, 19–54; Fisher, "Roman Associations," 2.1199–1225.

48. Cf. Smith, *From Symposium*, 27–28; also see Klinghardt, "Typology Meal."

49. For the general motif, see Plato *Symp.* 174A and Xen. *Symp.* 3–4. See also the references to invitations in Sir 13:9 and in the Parable of the Great Banquet, Matt 22:1–10=Luke 14:16–24. Cf. Smith, "Historical Jesus at Table," 468; Smith and Taussig, *Many Tables*, 23–24.

Fellowship Meals: Practices in the Ancient World

or written invitation could be served by the host or by a slave *vocator*.[50] The meal would usually begin with washing of the hands/feet by servants/slaves, which may be for hygienic or ritual purposes. Plato thus writes: "So the attendant washed him and made him ready for reclining."[51] The attendants or slaves would again bring water for washing their hands after they had reclined.[52]

The guests were then positioned at the table by the host or owner of the house according to their rank or status;[53] this was an important feature of the Greco-Roman meal customs as lack of definite seating arrangements were considered offensive and could contribute to disorder.[54]

In Homer's time the common posture at the table was sitting, but gradually for relaxation and ease they took to reclining on couches leaning on their left arm while they were eating.[55] Then reclining became the standard posture adopted at the table and was a central feature of the meals.[56] Scholars assume that this custom originated in Greece around eighth to sixth century BC and that it was borrowed from the Assyrian culture.[57] Smith postulates that when this custom was adopted by the Greeks: "they also adopted the trappings, or customs and 'social codes' that went with

---

50. D'Arms, "Slaves at Roman Convivia," 172. Though uninvited guests motivated by various reasons were often part of these gatherings (Plut. *Quaest. conv* 709A-E). Plutarch mentions them as "shadows" Plut. *Quaest. conv* 707A, and as "parasites" by Lucian *Par.* 15.

51. Plato, *Symp.* 175A.

52. "Water is poured over our hands; the tables are spread; we sup and, after ablution, we now offer libations to the gods." Aristophanes *Vesp.* 1216. Cf. also Ath. *Deipn.* 11.462c-d.

53. Plut. *Quaest. conv.* 615D, 619B; Lucian *Symp.* 9.

54. Plut. *Quaest. conv.* 615C-D.

55. Ath. *Deipn.* 1.11–12; 8.363–64; 9.428b. Cf. Stein, "Symposia Literature," 17.

56. H. Blümmer stresses that even at ordinary Greek meals, people regularly reclined, *Home Life*, 203.

57. Jean-Marie Dentzer postulates that the custom originated in Greece around the sixth century BC. "Aux origins," 215–58; *Le motif du banquet*, referred from Smith, "Meals and Morality," 321. Fisher is of the view that the practice of reclining on couches came from the Near East (*ca.* 750 BC). The earliest example of reclining at banquet can be seen in the iconography of Assurbanipal of Nineveh dating from the third quarter of the seventh century BC. The motif appears on Greek reliefs later in the sixth century BC: "Reclining figures at banquets appear first on Corinthians vases about 600 BC, then regularly on Attic vases, paintings and reliefs, and at around the same time in the work of the lyric poets, first perhaps in the lines of the Spartan poet Alcman." Fisher, "Greek Associations," 2.1170–71.

it."[58] It was connected with luxury, wealth, and power. So when this custom was also adopted by the Romans and the Jews, it was simply not a matter of changing posture, but they also incorporated the social conventions and values associated with the posture.

Since it was associated with luxury and status, it functioned to maintain stratification in the community. It was distinguished from sitting which symbolized a lesser status. Thus reclining was prescribed only for free citizens in the Greco-Roman practice; apart from them, others like women, children, and slaves, were not expected to recline, but rather sit. To recline was one of the signs of manhood. Thus Aristotle states that young men were not allowed to watch performances of comedy or iambic verses until: "they reach the age at which they are permitted to participate in the reclining [at symposia] and getting drunk, by which time their education will have made them completely immune at the harm of such things."[59] In certain cultures, in order to recline, a male child had to undergo an initiation rite, which also indicates his coming of age. For example, Athenaeus alludes to that sort of practice:

> In Macedonia it was not customary for anyone to recline at dinner unless he had speared a wild boar without using a hunting net. Until then they must eat sitting. Cassander, therefore, at the age of thirty-five continued to sit at meals with his father, being unable to accomplish the feat, though he was brave and a good hunter.[60]

Among the Greeks the formal banquet was called the *deipnon* (δεῖπνον) or *symposion* (συμπόσιον) which was basically the term for the first and the second table. The term *cena/comissatio* or *convivium* was given to the Roman meal.[61] Then there was the Greco-Roman *eranos* meal or the "pot luck dinner" in which the cost was shared among the participants.[62] The *eranos*

---

58. Smith, *From Symposium*, 18–19.

59. Aristotle *Pol.* 1336b 20–24.

60. Ath. *Deipn.* 1.18a.

61. Cicero points out that the Latin term *convivium* means literally "co-living," in contrast to the Greek terms *symposium*, "co-drinking," which may indicate their ultimate concern for social harmony (*Fam.* 9.24). For a comparison of Greek and Roman order of the Meal see Smith, *From Symposium*, 37 and Coutsoumpos, *Paul and the Lord's Supper*, 44–46.

62. Regarding the cost for the banquet, there were two types. "Those for which the cost was divided among the participants and those to which the guests were freely invited (PW, 4:1201–2). Family symposia and invitational symposia belong to the latter group, while the religious meals of various clubs or associations belong to the former group. Cf.

Fellowship Meals: Practices in the Ancient World

practice can be traced back to Homer's days. The visitors either contributed with money or food in baskets.[63] For the family symposia the costs were usually covered by the family host.

The Greco-Roman meal usually consisted of two courses, the main course: δεῖπνον/*cena*, followed by the symposium or ποτός (*potos*), the "drinking party" which consisted of drinking and entertainment of different kinds. This part of the banquet was set aside for serious drinking.[64] Athenaeus elucidates this:

> For now the floor and all men's hands are clean,
> And all the cups, and since the feasters' brows
> Are wreathed with garlands, while the slaves around
> Bring fragrant perfume in well-suited dishes;
> And in the middle stands the joyful bowl,
> And wine's at hand, which never deserts the guests . . .[65]

During the Roman period, wine was often drunk during the meal as well as during the symposium.[66] But generally the division between courses as described above continued. This is confirmed in Plutarch's reference to (μετὰ δεῖπνον).[67] Sometimes a third course followed the δεῖπνον which consisted of appetizers to aid the drinking.[68]

After the first course was over the beginning of the second was marked by the removal of the tables and the bringing in of the wine bowl for mixing the wine.[69] The banquet meal was usually extravagant and elaborate, as this was also an occasion where the host would exhibit their wealth and

---

Ath. *Deipn.* 8.362." Aune, "Septem Sapientium Convivium," 71–72.

63. Hom. *Od.* 1.226–27. Also Xen. *Mem.* 3.14.1. The popularity and significance of the *eranos* meal among the Greeks and Romans is seen in Plut. *Sept. sap. conv.* 150 D; Ath. *Deipn.* 362E.

64. Becker and Göll, *Charikles*, 333–47.

65. Xenophanes of Colophon quoted in Ath. *Deipn.* 11.462c–d.

66. Smith, *From Symposium*, 31.

67. Plut. *Quaest. conv.* 612 E–F.

68. It was also called the "second tables" or the "dessert" course (*tragēmata* or the *secunda mensa* for the Romans), which would consist of various fruits, salty nuts, and spicy dishes. The purpose was to provoke thirst and for greater enjoyment of the drinking. E.g., Ath. *Deipn.* 3.109 DE, 4.129, 14.640 B–F, 641 D–E, 642 A–F, 643 A–D; Gellius, *Noct. att.* 13.11.6–7. Cf. Smith, *From Symposium*, 30; Smith & Taussig, *Many Tables*, 3.

69. The proportion of water to wine varied, but common mixtures were five parts water to two parts wine or three parts water to one part wine. Ath. *Deipn.* 10.426d; cf. Smith and Taussig, *Many Tables*, 26.

status.⁷⁰ As a result gluttony and intoxication were also characteristic of these meals.⁷¹

The beginning of the drinking session was marked by religious solemnity. Prayer or a libation also accompanied the meal at the beginning and to mark the end of a course. At the beginning of the symposium offering of a libation to the gods or singing of a hymn took place.⁷² During these times the house gods and the geniuses of the host and the emperor were invoked and sacrifices were also made.⁷³

Plato depicts a meal in like manner: "After this, it seems, when Socrates had taken his place or 'reclined' and had dined with the rest, they made libation and sang a chant to the god and so forth, as custom bids, till they betook them to drinking."⁷⁴ In this case a libation is made to the gods before the start of the second part. There is also indication of a chant or song accompanying the libation.⁷⁵ This ceremony probably was done to mark the transition between the two courses. In some cases there were two libations offered to the gods before the drinking party started, as Athenaeus writes:

> And on this account, the Greeks invoke the good Deity at the cup of unmixed wine, which is served round to them at dinner, paying honor to the Deity who invented wine; and that was Bacchus. But when the first cup of mixed wine is handed round after dinner, they then invoke Jupiter the Savior, thinking him the cause of this mixture of wine which is so unattended with pain, as being the author of rain.⁷⁶
>
> Amphictyon, the king of the Athenians, having learnt from Dionysus the art of mixing wine, . . . he made a law to bring an unmixed wine after meals only just enough to taste, as a token of the

---

70. Macrobius *Saturnalia* 13.3.12, gives a proper description of the range of dishes served at the fellowship meals. Cf. Aune, "Septem Sapientium Convivium," 71–72; Smith, *From Symposium*, 31–38.

71. Lucian *Par.* 5; Ath. *Deipn.* 5.178; 12.527. Cf. Matt 11: 16–19; Luke 7: 31–35.

72. Plato *Symp.* 176A; Xen. *Symp.* 2.1.

73. Horace *Carm.* 4.5.31–32, Servius, *Aeneid* 1.730, Petron. *Sat.* 60, Dio Cassius *Hist. Rom.* 51.19.7, *Acta Fratrum Arvalium*, ed. W. Henzen, 15, 42–43. Cf. Lampe, "Corinthian Eucharistic Dinner Party," 3.

74. Plato *Symp.*176A; also see Xen. *Symp.* 2.1; Martial *Epig.* 11.31.4–7; Ath. *Deipn.* 2.58c; Plut. *Quaest. conv.* 713 A; 615 B; 734A.

75. Cf. Smith, *From Symposium*, 30.

76. Philonides the physician quoted in Ath. *Deipn.* 15.675b-c. Thus Fisher observes that: "Clearly, at least at the start, the communal drinking continues to be felt as a sacred act of communion." "Greek Associations," 2.1173.

power of the Good Deity. But the rest of the wine was put on the table ready mixed, in whatever quantity any one chose. And then he enjoined the guests to invoke in addition the name of Zeus the Savior, for the sake of instructing and reminding the drinkers that by drinking in that fashion they would be preserved from injury.[77]

There were instances where even more libations were offered. The first cup from each of these bowls would then be dedicated to different deities: "the first to the Olympians, the second to the Heroes, and the third to Zeus Savior."[78] The practice of offering prayers and sacrifices of food before or during the meal indicates the close association of the fellowship meal with their belief in the deity/deities. It was a natural thing for the participants to acknowledge the gift of food to the gods, such that they were seen as the host of every meal. This would be particularly more strongly felt when the meals were observed in a religious setting, and when the participants took part of the food from the sacrificial altar.

The presence of the flute girls was considered requisite for the proceedings.[79] Crowns were distributed during these rites as tokens of freedom from god.[80] Probably they went to quite an extent to make the banquet as dramatic and ritualistic as possible. But this was with an intended purpose as the social and religious elements were never divorced from it.

There was also a practice where a presiding officer or *symposiarch* (συμποσίαρχον) was selected from among the participants before the symposium, who would then set the rules for the drinking party to follow. This was done so that there would be some sort of decorum and order.[81] The number of participants differed depending on the place. In the Greek *deipnon*/symposium usually thirty-six or more guest participated in the event.

---

77. Philochorus quoted in Ath. *Deipn.* 2.38c–d.

78. Pindar. *Isthm.* 6.10; also cf. Gulick, *Life of the Ancient Greeks*, 148, and Blümmer, *The Home Life*, 212–13.

D. Aune comments that "while the basic structure of the symposion remained the same through the time of Plutarch, the specific deities invoked and honored exhibits wide variety in the sources. Dionysos, however, was customarily honored at symposia because of intimate association with wine, intoxication and ecstasy" "Septem Sapientium Convivium," 71. Cf. Otto, *Dionysus: Myth and Cult*, 143–44.

79. Lucian *Symp.* 46; Ath. *Deipn.* 4.129, 13I, 150; 8.349; Plut. *Sept. sap. conv.* 150D.

80. Ath. *Deipn.* 3.101; 9.409; Plut. *Quaest. conv.* 615B; *Sept. sap. conv.* 150D.

81. Plutarch includes a talk entitled "What Sort of Man the Symposiarch Must Be," *Quaest. conv.* 620–622b.

In the Roman *convivium* six, nine, or twelve guests took part in the meal.[82] Usually three guests would be assigned to a couch with three couches arranged around low tables.

At banquets organized by the rulers or rich patrons, regular hand-outs known as the *sportula* or *apophoreton* were offered.[83] These gifts, which consisted of food and money, were distributed according to the status of the participants.

The symposium following the banquet included entertainment and a number of activities which would go well into the night. Most of the Greco-Roman writers depict a lot of activities during the entertainment hour. For instance we see in Xenophon's description about a symposium: "when the tables had been removed and the guests had poured a libation and sung a hymn, there entered a man from Syracuse, to give them an evening's merriment."[84] There is mention of different types of entertainment, like the flute girls, party games, gambling, dramas or performances by actors, mimes, acrobats, jugglers, strippers, clowns, or jesters, dances, recitations of moral poems, and talks and debates over a wide range of different topics ranging from political, religious, moral, abusive, to erotic.[85] A good example of this kind can be seen in a famous description of an orgiastic Roman banquet in the section on the banquet of Trimalchio in Petronius' *Satyricon*.[86] Vase paintings of symposia from this period also depict this sort of environment. The presence of the harp/flute girls was necessitated for the singing of the libations and hymns;[87] and usually they remained throughout the symposium.[88]

Physical contests were also popular, they include plays, enactments of mythological stories, dancing, balancing exploits and games. A well-known

---

82. Aune, "Septem Sapientium Convivium," 71. Plutarch also writes that couches were shared, and some rich people built large dining-rooms that had the capacity to hold thirty couches or probably even more. Plut. *Quaest. conv.* 5.5

83. E.g., Suetonius *Vesp.* 19; Petron. *Sat.* 56.

84. Xen. *Symp.* 2.1, also 3.1; 9.3–7; Cf. Pliny the younger *Ep.* 1.15; Sir 32:3–6.

85. Lucian *Dial. Meretr.* 15; Ath. *Deipn.* 2.39, 479; 4.134; Plut. *Vit. pud.* 531B; *Quaest. conv* 622C; Lucian *Par.* 51; cf. Aune "Septem Sapientium Convivium," 74; Fisher, "Greek Associations," 2.1174; "Roman Associations," 2.1208.

86. Petron. *Sat.* 26–78.

87. Lucian *D Meretr.* I, 3, 6, 12, 15. In the fourth century BC the price for hiring flute girls was regulated (two drachmas maximum), probably to keep the price of a reasonable symposium within the reach of the citizens. Cf. Fisher, "Greek Associations," 1181–82.

88. Cf. Becker and Göll, *Charikle*, 241-50, 344; Blümner, *Home Life*, 171, 216.

Fellowship Meals: Practices in the Ancient World

game called κότταβος (*kottabos*), which probably originated from Sicily was popular among the revelers. It involved flicking dregs of wine from one's cup or spitting at a target in the room.[89]

Furthermore, sexual liaisons and promiscuities were very common.[90] Xenophon gives a description of a symposium of Socrates in which a dance was performed enacting the erotic encounter of Dionysus and Ariadne on their wedding night which aroused the people to such extent that: ". . . those who were unwedded swore that they would take to themselves wives, and those who were already married mounted horse and rode off to their wives that they might enjoy them."[91] Sexual relations between adult men and pubescent or adolescent boys were also common at these meals.[92] But Romans tended to disapprove of homosexual relationships as they saw it as "typically Greek and decadent."[93] Along with erotic paintings on walls, wine bowls, cups, and other objects as visual stimuli, certain things like the dimming of the lights were carried out to facilitate these behaviors.[94] Most often the flute girls were prostitutes and this would explain the orgies that happen during these meals.[95] Apart from this, women, as a rule, were not allowed to be part of the symposia except in family symposia.[96]

Drinking and merriment were very much the central focus of this part of the banquet. Thus it often resulted in intoxication,[97] leading further to violence and fights.[98] At the end of the symposia people also went on

---

89. Ath. *Deipn.* 427d; 666d-668e; Fisher, "Greek Associations," 2.1174.

90. Cf. Lucian *Symp.* 46; Ath. *Deipn.* 4. Cf. Gowers, *Loaded Table*, 101, 200n319.

91. Xen. *Symp.* 9.2-7.

92. Xen. *Mem.* 2.6.28; Xen. *Symp.* 8.

93. Fisher, "Roman Associations," 2.1209.

94. Plut. *Quaest. conv* 761D.

95. "Greek vase paintings, particularly on drinking cups and wine bowls, attest to the ubiquity of flute girls at symposia as well as to their talents as prostitutes." Aune, "Septem Sapientium Convivium," 71-72.

96. Plut. *Quaest. conv.* 612F. Though, among the Romans there was more extensive participation of respectable women. Fisher, "Roman Associations," 1199-1200. See Aune, "Septem Sapientium Convivium," 71-72 for a detailed discussion on the presence and role of women in the symposia.

97. Lucian *Symp.* I7; Ath. *Deipn.* 2.36.

98. Plato *Leg.* 2.671A, 3; cf. 1.640A, 1; Lucian *Symp.*; Plut. *Quaest. conv.* 716F; *Alex.* 38; 52.8-9. Philo, *Flacc.* 136. Cicero includes accounts of the debaucheries and problems associated with the meals and also his disapproval; *Cat.* 2.33-34; *Att.* 1.16; *Phil.* 2; *Cael.* 35. The situation is also reflected in the many satires from Greco-Roman writers, e.g., Petron. *Sat.* 28-78.

drunken processions to a new party, or to serenade lovers. This often led to gate-crashing, which was a potential source of disorder.[99] This practice called the κόμος (*komos*) is often depicted on painted pottery and art. These drunken antics often ended up in fights leading to social and political problems. Due to such social disorders becoming a common occurrence, symposia were restricted or forbidden from time to time, as in the case of Sparta and Crete.[100]

The second part of the banquet became quite popular and was observed more enthusiastically, so that the term symposium became to be associated with the whole banquet as such.[101] This became an important social custom in the Greco-Roman world, and the form remained basically the same from Homer to the end of antiquity.[102]

Moral and Social Response

Based on the scenarios described above, there is a tendency among scholars to visualize all Greco-Roman fellowship meals, as ending in debauchery and drunkenness but this was not always the case. There were moralists and thinkers among others who rejected this form of meal practices. They advocated a more sober and mannered symposia in which likeminded people could participate. Instead of other merriments and entertainments they opted for more elevated conversation, moderate drinking, engaging in topics deemed appropriate and helpful to the society. Limits were set and appeals were made in this regard for others to follow. In Plato's *Symposium* we see a clear example of this kind:

> Since it has been resolved, then, said Eryximachus, that we are to drink only so much as each desires, with no constraint on any, I next propose that the flute-girl who came in just now be dismissed:

---

99. Polybius records that Antiochus Epiphanes frequently disrupted parties by his gate crashing. 26.1.4; also cf. Plato *Symp.* 223B

100. Thus Pittakos, the Mytilenaean ruler imposed double penalties on people causing drunken assaults and problems of this kind. Cf. Aristotle *Pol.* 1274b 17–18, 1311b 23–24. Becker and Göll, *Charikles*, 334.

101. Paul, "Symposia and Deipna," 158.

102. Cf. Becker and Göll, *Charikles,* 333–47, which describes the symposium in the fifth and fourth centuries BC with copious references to primary sources. Aune, "Septem Sapientium Convivium," 70–71.

Fellowship Meals: Practices in the Ancient World

let her pipe to herself or, if she likes, to the women-folk within, but let us seek our entertainment today in conversation.[103]

Plutarch who suggested that a flute girl should not be present at the symposium expresses the same.[104] Cicero advises that the topic of reading or discussion ranging from politics to art should be agreeable, edifying, and enjoyable, while avoiding backbiting and boasting. He also mentions etiquette concerning the preparations, participants, time, and place of meeting for the meals.[105] Horace in his works *Odes*, *Satires* and the *Epistles* also deliberates on the dangers of excessive luxury and promotes moderate drinking and pleasures in general. His writings also dwell on the quality of the food, the social relationships of the participants, entertainments during the symposium, and the moral value of the symposium. For this reason the symposiarch was also chosen before the beginning of the party so that there would be some sense of order and control over the proceedings.[106] Likewise appeals were made by different writers to maintain decorum and friendship which were supposed to be the component of an ideal meal. Also seen in Plutarch is his assertion that the gods would be offended by disorderly and unruly behavior at the symposia and so to abstain from them.[107] Rather he implores them to behave and to discourse at table taking part in the conversation in a civilized manner, which was also appropriate and in keeping with the ideal banquet. Thus the main emphasis of his writings in *Quaestiones Convivales* (Table-Talk) is on meal customs and etiquette.

There were moral oppositions from many of the Greco-Roman thinkers against the lavish expenditures spent for the symposia.[108] Even among the poorer citizens, as Cicero mentions in *For Murena*, was a preference to see the rich spend their wealth on public buildings rather than on

---

103. Plato *Symp.* 176E. No set rules were laid down for the conversation. Plutarch describes that even Plato "did not prepare himself for the contest like a wrestler, that he may take the faster hold of his adversary. . . . Questions should be easy, the problems known, the interrogations plain and familiar, not intricate and dark, so that they may neither vex the unlearned nor frighten them from the disquisition. . . . The discourse should be like our wine, common to all, of which everyone may equally partake." *Quaest. conv.* 614 C. Cf. Stein, "Symposia Literature," 19.

104. Plut. *Quaest. conv.* 616A.

105. Cicero *Off.* 1.134–35.

106. Plutarch strongly advocated this idea of reinstating the office of the symposiarch to maintain order and decorum at the parties. *Quaest. conv* 620A-622B.

107. Plut. *Quaest. conv.* 615A.

108. Cato the Elder in Plutarch's *Parallel Lives*, "Cato the Elder," 16.

these forms of private luxury and patronage.[109] Another example is from Athenaeus, describing the philosophical dinner he states vividly:

> Heaven forbid!—that they should indulge in intemperance when they came together, but that they might carry out with decency and refinement the practices which accord with the idea of the symposium.[110]

This was the kind of symposium that the writers were advocating through their works. In general the symposium described in their literary works, the idealized meal that the writers wished for, were to be set as models/examples to be followed.[111] Consequently, there seemed to be a desired effect, as the philosophical talks were more held not only by the philosophical schools but other groups as well during the drinking party in lieu of other entertainment.[112]

The state also tried to impose laws to curb the excesses at the meals.[113] Augustus is reported to have restricted lavish dinner parties and wedding feasts and enforced laws against forms of moral decadence associated with it. Augustus also tried to set an example in how a proper *convivium* should be conducted without being extravagant.[114] Tiberius had banquets that were frugal and tried to restrict lavish expenditures.[115] Thus there were different forms of fellowship meal practices within the same community

---

109. "The Roman people disapproves of private luxury, but admires public magnificence." *Mur.* 36.76.

110. Ath. *Deipn.* 5.186a. He mentions that the decent and ideal symposia conducted by the philosophical associations was established on the original model of Plato's Academy, Ath. *Deipn.* 183c-186b.

111. Smith "Meals and Morality," 320.

112. Plut. *Quaest. conv.* 612E-F; 7.7; also Plato *Symp.* 176E; Xen. *Symp.* 3.2-3; Ath. *Deipn.* 5.185a. Smith postulates that following this model, Jews and Christians developed their meal tradition "in which discourse on the law or the biblical tradition was designated as the appropriate topic for table fellowship gatherings." *From Symposium*, 281.

113. Attempts were made to prevent disorderly conduct during the fellowship meals. These are attested by various regulations for *collegia*. ILS 7212, pag. II.25-Lanuvium; SIG3 1109.73ff—Iobacchi.

114. Reported by Suetonius in *Lives of the Twelve Caesars*, "Augustus" 73–82; Suetonius and Cassius Dio in his *Roman History* following on the theme of "bad" emperors, also give critical accounts of those emperors who conducted lavish banquets and conducted improperly. E.g., Gaius (Caligula), Domitian, Claudius and Nero. Cf. Fisher, "Roman Associations," 2.1211.

115. Though he had doubts on whether sumptuary legislation could be popular or effective. Tac. *Ann.* 3–54.

accommodating the different social needs and demands. The general depiction of the Greco-Roman meals as ending in excesses was not entirely true and this view needs to be taken into consideration in the interpretation of the fellowship meals in Corinth.

FELLOWSHIP MEALS IN THE JEWISH CONTEXT

Having seen the fellowship meal practices in the Greco-Roman world, we will now survey the meal traditions in the different communities in Jewish society focussing on those features that will contribute to the interpretation of the Lord's Supper.

The importance of fellowship meals in the Jewish society can be deduced from the number of meal practices associated with both social and religious events. Jeremias captures it well when he defined the meal practices in Judaism as:

> to invite a man to a meal was an honor. It was an offer of peace, trust, brotherhood, and forgiveness; in short, sharing a table meant sharing life. . . . In Judaism in particular, table-fellowship means fellowship before God, for the eating of a piece of broken bread by everyone who shares in the meal brings out the fact that they all have a share in the blessing which the master of the house had spoken over the unbroken bread.[116]

Jewish literature on fellowship meals advocates the idea that it was not only the formal fellowship meals that were considered important, but among the Jews even the ordinary meals were seen as significant. This is inferred from the use of benedictions or thanksgiving for the meals in the beginning and at the end.[117] This is evident in some of the ancient literature like the *Sibylline Oracles*, which states that "Jews sometimes contrasted their blessed daily meals with pagan sacrifices."[118] Also the prayer in *Didache* 9.3–4 which was based upon a Jewish prayer tradition reiterates that everyday food was "a heavenly gift conferring life and wisdom."[119] The practice of benediction was probably based on the concept that it will imbue the particles of food

---

116. Jeremias, *New Testament Theology*, 1.115.

117. Burchard comments that: "For one thing, benedictions were to be used whenever a man consumed anything larger than an olive, and if the occasion was a meal, some benedictions were to be repeated during its course." "Importance," 113.

118. *Sib. Or.* 4:24–30.

119. See the discussion in Chesnutt, *From Death to Life*, 133.

and drink with the spirit of life which in turn will permeate the person who partakes of the meal.[120] This understanding is also expressed in the words of R. Simeon: "But if three have eaten at one table and have spoken over it words of the Law, it is as if they had eaten from the table of God, for it is written, And he said unto me, this is the table that is before the Lord."[121] Jeremias also highlights this fact that even the "ordinary" daily Jewish meals where a blessing is pronounced were considered as solemn occasions.[122]

The significant role of fellowship meals is further inferred from the food laws and other purity regulations enacted in the OT to preserve the sanctity of the fellowship meals.

Fellowship Meals in the OT

Fellowship meals and the food motif appear prominently in the OT. This study will try to highlight some of the important passages where meal practices play a significant role in Israel's history.[123] The fellowship meal ideology in the OT was also based on the basic principle of hospitality in the ancient world, which was considered as a moral duty and mark of righteousness. As P. King observes "the two basic obligations of hospitality are to feed and to protect the guest or stranger."[124] This implies that sharing a meal even with strangers, puts the host under an obligation to protect the guest from danger.[125]

---

120. Cf. Burchard, "Importance of Joseph and Aseneth," 117.

121. *M. Abot* 3:3; Ezek 41:22.

122. J. Jeremias, "The Last Supper," 91–92. See also the brief comments by J. Jeremias, on the solemnity of meal in "This is My Body," 196–203, esp. 196–97; and more recently Feeley-Harnik, *Lord's Table,* 94: "every Jewish home, every Jewish table, possessed the sanctity of the priest, the temple, the altar."

123. For a survey of meal and meal customs in the OT, see G. Schramm, "Meal Customs (Jewish)," in *ABD* 4.648–650; Jenks, "Eating and Drinking," in *ABD* 2,250–254. For listings of food mentioned in the Bible see Juengst, *Breaking bread*. On hospitality in the OT, see Douglas, *Implicit Meanings,* 249–75; King, "Commensality," in *Hesed Ve-*Emet, 53–62. For a study of meal practices in the OT in a sequential order see Steer, "Eating Bread;" and Blomberg, *Contagious Holiness*. For a review on literature on OT meals see Blomberg, *Contagious Holiness,* 32–33.

124. Philip King, "Commensality in the Biblical World," 53. A number of examples can be seen, where provision of accommodation, food and water, care for the visitors' animals, and protection from harm are provided in Gen 18:4; 19:2; 24:23–25, 32; 26:30; 31:54; 43:16–24; Josh 2:1–6; Judg 19, 21–22; 2 Kgs 6:22–23.

125. Gen 19:1–11; Judg 19:21–22.

Fellowship Meals: Practices in the Ancient World

As in many ancient cultures, in the OT fellowship meals functioned in varied ways in different contexts. From cultic and sacrificial environments where specialized meals accompanied animal sacrifices to social events, fellowship meals played an important role. They were synonymous with fellowship in all aspects of life.[126] More importantly, they occur in the key events in the salvation history of Israel. They were an integral part of the ratification of covenants, celebration of victories, anointing of kings, and other state ceremonies and family celebrations.[127] The occurrences of fellowship meals in the OT in connection with important events further indicate that they underscore and carry an additional significant message.[128]

Likewise fellowship meals marked the significant moments in the lives of the patriarchs, kings, and prophets. For example, in 1 Sam 13:1-15; 14:1-46; 15:1-33; 20:1-42; 28:3-25 the repeated meal scenes serve to highlight the tragedy of Saul's decline. David's failings are also set in the context of meal-scenes; his adultery and the plotting of the murder of Uriah (2 Sam 11:1-17), death in his family (2 Sam 12:1-25), the rape of Tamar (2 Sam 13:1-22), murder of Amnon (2 Sam 13:23-29), and Absalom's rebellion (2 Sam 15:1-12).[129] After Elijah hands over the prophetic mantle to Elisha, he responded by providing a feast for the people (1 Kgs 19:19-21). Job's restoration by Yahweh is also represented by two food events (Job 42:7-9, 11).

---

126. E.g., Gen 14:18-20; 26:26-31; 29:22, 27-28; 31:44-46, 51-54; Josh 9:3-15; Judg 9:26-28; 2 Sam 3:20; 9:7, 10-11; Prov 15:17; 17:1. Cf. Feeley-Harnik, *Lord's Table*, 85-86.

127. Examples where fellowship meals occur include visits from strangers (Gen 18:2-8; 19:1-3); religious feasts and sacrifices (Exod 18:12; 34:15; 1 Kgs 1:9); royal coronations (1 Chr 12:38-40; 29:22. 1 Kgs 1:39-41); anniversaries (Exod 12:14; Esth 9:22); celebration upon the beginning or finishing of a great work (Gen 29:22; Judg 14:10; Prov 9:1-5; 2 Sam 6:19; Judg 16:23); victory celebrations (Gen 14:18-19); harvest times; sheep shearing (2 Sam 13:23-27); family events such as marriage, birthday, mourning (Gen 29:22, 40:20; Judg 14:10-17; Jer 16:5-9; Ezek 24:16-17) and even weaning (Gen 21:8); Abraham honors the weaning of Isaac with a great feast. The meal expresses Abraham's joy and gratitude for Yahweh's covenant faithfulness. Cf. Steer, "Eating Bread," 38.

128. So Blomberg: "Eating and drinking in Genesis are thus never ordinary matters. That is not to say that Abraham and his descendants did not normally eat ordinary meals. But the ones chosen for inclusion in this book all convey additional meaning, usually in the establishment of harmony or peace where there has been estrangement, or in celebrating important gifts of God to his people . . ." Blomberg, *Contagious Holiness*, 36.

129. See also 1 Sam 1:1-18; 7:2-14; 9-10; 16:1-13; 2 Sam 3:1-21; 6:1-19. Cf. Steer, "Eating Bread," 55-56.

Exclusion and Judgment in Fellowship Meals

Food is the commonest form of gift, given to relatives (Gen 32:3–21), acquaintances (Gen 43:1–11), Kings,[130] and prophets[131] continuing with the theme that sharing food creates bonding.[132]

Kinship and Fellowship Meals

Fellowship meals formed an important part in creating and maintaining friendship and loyalties among individuals, families, and tribes. In many instances relationships were formalized by sharing and eating together, as it symbolically creates bonding. Robertson Smith understands it "as confirming or even as constituting kinship in a very real sense."[133] Thus covenants, treaties, and settlements between people were frequently expressed and solemnized with a meal. Numerous examples to this effect are mentioned in the OT, for instance, the story of Isaac who requested a meal of his favorite food from his son Esau in order to recognize him formally as his first-born and bestow his paternal blessing upon him (Gen 27). Jacob by trickery established himself as the first-born. The blessing could not be revoked, because the meal was eaten (Gen 27:33). Fellowship meals used for reconciliation and settlement can be seen in the story of Isaac and Abimelech where they affirmed the peace covenant between them (Gen 26:30–31); and between Jacob and Laban (Gen 31:54).[134] Because of the ability of fellowship meals to create and foster relationships, the meal is also the first step toward the ultimate reconciliation between Joseph and his brothers (Gen 43:24–34).[135] The story of Adonijah's attempt to succeed King David at the expense of Solomon, also reveals how he tried to influence support and foster alliances by inviting people to dine with him.[136] The failure in his bid is also depicted in the abrupt end to a meal (1 Kgs 1:49). In another story diplomatic relationship is achieved when Elisha instructs the king of Israel to provide food and water for a raiding group of Arameans. After the

---

130. 1 Chr 12:38–40; 2 Sam 16:1; 17:27–29.

131. 1 Sam 9:6–7; 1 Kgs 14:1–3; Amos 7:12; Mic 3:5.

132. Food motif is also used to portray the prosperity of the kings (1 Kgs 4:7–23).

133. Smith, *Religion of the Semites*, 274.

134. Hamilton explains that in the process the individual who is the host admits (or re-admits) the other into their "family" circle. Hamilton, *Genesis*, 207.

135. In Gen 43:34 Joseph expressed his special affection on Benjamin through the portion of food given to him.

136. I Kgs 1:9, 19, 25, 41, 49.

great feast, the Arameans return home and "stopped raiding Israel's territory" (2 Kgs 6:23). This makes those who betray others with whom they have shared food the worst kind of traitors.[137]

On the other hand, refusal to accept an invitation to a meal or eat together would mean severance of a relationship. When Jeroboam invited "a man of God out of Judah" but was refused, it signified God's disapproval of him (1 Kgs 13:1, 7–10).[138] In a conflict situation, eating with a group or party demonstrated a change of allegiance or loyalty to that person or party. The animosity between Abimelech and the lords of Shechem is vividly expressed when the latter "went into the temple of their god, ate and drank, and ridiculed Abimelech" (Judg 9:27).[139] In summary we can see the power of the fellowship meals to create or destroy relationships. Acceptance or rejection to eat together had corresponding effects in both the social and religious spheres. In this way fellowship meals were closely linked with the judgment theme in the OT.

Food Motifs in the OT

The food motif also plays a prominent part in the OT belief system, which is a further indication of the importance of the fellowship meal institution. It demonstrates the close relationship between material and spiritual/religious realities. As commented above, the food motif in the OT signifies a bigger theological meaning that underlies its usage.[140] From the beginning of Genesis food is mentioned as part of the plan of creation. And God is depicted as the host as well as the source of all provisions (Gen 1:29). God's provision of food to his people shows his favor and bestowal. The covenant with Noah also is associated with the gift of food as well as restrictions with it (Gen 9:3, 4).[141] This food motif is then tied up with the covenant between Israel and God. To symbolize God's place among the Israelites, bread was

---

137. Ps 41:9; Obad 1:7.

138. Cf. Also 1 Sam 20:34; Esth 1:9–22. On the motif of refusing to eat and drink in the Old Testament, see Sharon, "When Fathers Refuse," 135–148.

139. Also see 1 Kgs 13:11–32.

140. As Steer states: "Food imagery is part of a nexus of liberative, transformative motifs." Steer, "Eating Bread," 84.

141. This prohibition, as with the earlier one with Adam, maintains the distinction between God and human beings. They reflect the fellowship meal ideology where stratification can be achieved by the manner food was shared. Cf. Steer, "Eating Bread," 46.

placed on the altar (Exod 25:30). Likewise as a reminder of the covenant with Israel, twelve loaves were to be placed at the altar (Lev 24:8).

The promise of food was a central part of the covenant God made with Israel.[142] God's relationship with Israel throughout the history is linked with the food motif. The repeated complaints by the people regarding the provision of food had disastrous results.[143] The breakdown in the relationship is also summed up in the account of an idolatrous and immoral meal with Moabite women (Num 25:1–3).

The promised land of Canaan is also portrayed as "a land flowing with milk and honey" that portrayed the prosperity and abundance of God's blessing for Israel (Exod 3:8). This is indicative of God as the host for Israel. This motif is continued with the concept of redemption where it is presented as a heavenly banquet where God will be the host (Isa 25:6–8).[144] God's word and wisdom is also embodied and symbolized by food in the Wisdom Literature. In Proverbs, Wisdom and Folly are embodied in a contest of meals (Prov 9:1–18).[145] In the Song of Songs, eating and drinking is also symbolic of marriage and relationship.[146] By linking food motifs with the blessings of God, as well as the approval and relationship between God and Israel, fellowship meals in the OT become an integral part of the judgment motif.

Fellowship Meal and Covenant

Like in other ancient cultures fellowship meals in the OT also expressed an intimate relationship between Israel and God. G. Feeley-Harnik remarks that "food was one of the most important languages in which Jews expressed relations among human beings and between human beings and

---

142. Lev 26:3–5; Deut 8:7–10; Eccl 2:24–25; 9:7; 10:19; Prov 15:17; 17:1.

143. Num 11:4–6; 20:2–13; 21:4–5.

144. God as the host is a common theme in the Psalms (23:5; 78:15–31; 136:26; 36:8; 104:14–15, 21, 27–28; 145:15–16; 147:9). God's universal offer of salvation is also depicted through meal imagery (Ps 22:26–29; 36:8–9). The minor prophets provide glimpses of the future hope in which the fortunes and prosperity of God's people are restored by depicting it as an age of plentiful harvest and with abundant foodstuffs (Joel 3:18; Amos 9:13b; Hos 2:22; Zech 8:19; 9:17). Cf. Blomberg, *Contagious Holiness*, 50–51.

145. On the theme of meal fellowship in Proverbs see Blomberg, *Contagious Holiness*, 52.

146. There are at least fifty-four references to food imagery in the Songs of Songs that reveal the relational dimension of food. Cf. Steer, "Eating Bread," 74.

Fellowship Meals: Practices in the Ancient World

God."[147] Many of the people's encounters with God happen in the context of a fellowship meal. Therefore, Oesterly argued that every covenant was symbolized by a meal, and even when there is no reference to a meal in the text, it is "simply because the feast is taken for granted; it was the necessary sealing of the covenant which constituted the union between the two parties."[148] In the Exodus account the covenant between God and Israel was confirmed by a fellowship meal between Moses and the elders before God (Exod 24:9–12). Such ceremonies are described as "eating before God" or "in the presence of the Lord."[149] W. R. Smith elaborates the concept behind such practices; he states that when sacred food is shared together, as "the same substance enters into their flesh and blood," it establishes some sacred unity of life between the participants, and "a living bond of union between the worshippers and their god."[150] By entering into a covenant ratified through fellowship meals both parties were now entitled to maintain and fulfil their obligations to the covenant. Pedersen even argued that the word for "covenant" (*berīth*) is derived from the verb "to eat" (*bārā*).[151]

The covenant was to be commemorated annually by "all the congregation of Israel" (Exod 12:47). This celebration was not only restricted to the past deliverance but was linked with the future salvation of Israel. In this way fellowship meals were a prominent aspect of their worship life and were closely connected with sacrifices. W.R.Smith rightly states that: "Everywhere we find that a sacrifice ordinarily involves a feast, and that a feast cannot be provided without a sacrifice."[152] He also asserts that: "Throughout the Semitic field, the fundamental idea of sacrifice is not that of a sacred tribute, but of communion between the god and his worshippers by joint participation in the living flesh and blood of a sacred victim."[153]

Important events in the history of Israel were therefore marked by celebration in the form of fellowship meals. The entry into the promised land

---

147. Feeley-Harnik, *Lord's Table*, 151.

148. Oesterly, *Sacrifices in Ancient Israel*, 169; cf. Steer who adds that Oesterly's argument from silence "seems reasonable;" "Eating Bread," 38–39.

149. Exod 18:12; Deut 12:12, 17–18; 14:26; 16:11, 15; Lev 3:1–16; 23:40. In these contexts "God himself was assumed to participate symbolically by receiving the choice portions of fat, which were burned on the altar. . ." *IDB*, 2:261. Also see Feely-Harnik, *Lord's Table*, 87–88.

150. Smith, *Religion of the Semites*, 313.

151. Pedersen, *Israel*, 2:306n1.

152. Smith, *Religion of the Semites*, 237.

153. Ibid., 345.

was marked by a Passover celebration (Josh 5:10–12) and thereafter the renewal of the covenant at Mount Ebal was marked by a sacrificial meal (Josh 8:30–35). Twenty years later, the covenant was renewed again at Shechem and once again a fellowship meal takes central place (Josh 24:1–28).[154]

During Solomon's reign the dedication of the Temple was marked by a national celebration which coincided with the feast of Tabernacles, signifying a renewal of the covenant with God.[155] Again, in Ezra the reconstruction of the Temple was followed by a great sacrifice of dedication and by the observance of the Passover and the Feast of Unleavened Bread (Ezra 6:6–22). The sequence of meal events signified the renewal of the covenant and celebrated God's restoration of the Temple worship.[156]

By tying the fellowship meals with a very important aspect of Jewish faith, participating in fellowship meals in a cultic context became very much to be understood in terms of judgment. Hence they were linked with being part of the chosen community, the future deliverance and blessings of the nation. This link between covenant and fellowship meals is further realized in the celebration of the festivals.

Fellowship Meals, Festivities and Celebrations

We notice that in the OT, fellowship meals were an important part of the festivals instituted to commemorate significant events in Israel's history. The main component of the festivals, the fellowship meal was a powerful means of remembering God's covenantal faithfulness, as well as reaffirming their loyalty to God.[157] Along with the Passover, which we will be dealing with separately, the important festivals mentioned are the Unleavened Bread, which was a communal agricultural feast. It was a prelude to the Feast of Weeks, which came at the end of harvest time.[158] The Feast of Weeks also known as the Harvest Feast or the Day of First Fruits commemorated the

---

154. Steer rightly stresses that in the face of the threat of syncretism "the meal signifies the peoples' renewed commitment to Yahweh, as well as their corporate identity." Steer, "Eating Bread," 53–54.

155. 1 Kgs 8:62–66; cf. 2 Chr 7:1–10.

156. Since salt is one of the important ingredients, a particular intimate covenant came to be known as "covenant of salt," and it signified the strong and permanent character of the relationship between God and his people. Exod 30:35; Ezek 43:24; Num 18:19; 2 Chr 13:5; Lev 2:13. See more on this in "Salt," *NIDNTT*, 3.444–45.

157. Cf. Steer, "Eating Bread," 88–89.

158. Exod 23:14–25; Deut 16:1–17; Num 9:1–14.

covenant at Sinai.[159] Then the third annual feast that commemorated God's sustenance during the journey to the Promised Land was the Succoth, also known as the Feast of Tabernacles, Booths, or Tents, the Feast of Ingathering, the Feast of the Lord, or simply the Feast (Lev 23:42–43). Other festivals mentioned are the Feast of Trumpets, also called Rosh Hashanah, which marked the beginning of the civil New Year; and Purim, celebrating the deliverance of the Jewish people from their enemies in the time of Esther.[160] In all these festivities food sacrifices were followed by fellowship meals in the families and community. These sacrifices and fellowship meals signified the renewal of the covenant with God. It was a reminder that they were still in covenantal relationship.[161] But just as fellowship meals confirmed and strengthened the relationship between God and Israel, likewise they also reveal the deterioration between them.

The Passover Meal

The study of the Passover meal is of significance as it has been considered as the closest link to the Lord's Supper tradition. In the OT the Passover meal was considered the most important annual celebration, especially after the destruction of the Temple. It was a family event, later on, during Josiah's reform, with emphasis on Jerusalem as the preferred place of celebration, the Passover became a great national celebration (2 Kgs 23:21–23).

In the Mishnah we see a basic form of the Passover meal structure.[162] The rules of conduct at the meal are made clear from the beginning:

> . . . no man may eat until it becomes dark. And even the poorest in Israel must not eat unless he reclines down to table, and they must not give them less than four cups of wine to drink, even if it is from the [Paupers'] Dish.[163]

---

159. "Because this feast fell in the third month, the Feast of Weeks came to commemorate the covenant at Sinai, which occurred in the third month after leaving Egypt." Steer, "Eating Bread," 78.

160. Another annual feast that was observed later was the Hanukkah or the Feast of Dedication, which commemorated the re-dedication of the Temple by the Maccabees in the second century BC.

161. See "Feasts," in Ryken, *Dictionary of Biblical LiteratureI*, 279.

162. *m. Pes.*10:1–9. Danby, *Mishnah*.

163. *m. Pes.*10:1.

It was partaken by all reclining on the table, which was a standard practice of that time;[164] though it was more of a rule for the Passover meal.[165] Instone-Brewer reports about: an anonymous exegesis inferred from Exod 13:18, that reclining started as soon as they left Egypt, because it says:

> "And God turned the people to the way of the wilderness" (Num.R. 1.2), the verb "to turn" (sabad בְּבָס) means "to recline" in the *hiphil*. They reclined on couches arranged typically in a "U" formation, possibly with another set in a 'T' formation if they were too many guests. The poor who did not own couches could construct them from blankets on boxes or even on floor-mats (Philo, *Contempl.* 69).[166]

This interpretation would reiterate the explanation given in *b. Pes.* 10.8a, which says that reclining to be practised even by the poorest, was to demonstrate "freedom," that they were no longer slaves. Reclining was a common practice in the Greco-Roman world but the implication differed from one another. For the Jewish community it was more of a theological statement, indicating "liberation from the bondage." In like manner, social equality was demanded at the Passover meal, that even the poorest should have access to the meals.

Prayers/benedictions which were very much integral to the fellowship meals were said over the wine cups during the Passover.[167] Discourse as part of the meal was an important event at the Passover meal. *m. Pes.* 10.4 states: "They mix the second cup for him and here the son asks his father. . . . Why is this night different from all other nights?" And he begins with the words "A wandering Aramean was my father;"[168] this allows the father to explain the whole history behind the meal recalling the exodus event. The meal becomes an important conveyor of tradition and history and by bridging time and space gave the people identity and a sense of belonging to their history. Some scholars are of the view that the Passover meal

---

164. Thus the term "reclining" often became synonymous with "dining." Noy, "Sixth Hour" in *Meals in a Social Context*, 138.

165. See *m. Pes.* 9:5.

166. Instone-Brewer, "Tractate Pesachim," 60. But the influence of the Greco-Roman customs in this regard is generally accepted. Dembitz, "Seder," in *The Jewish Encyclopedia*), 11.144: "Why do all of us 'lean around'? In allusion to the Roman custom at banquets—which became current among the Jews. The father or master of the house then answers: 'we were slaves to Pharaoh in Egypt and the Lord delivered us thence.'"

167. *m. Pes.*10:2, 7.

168. Deut 26:5.

Fellowship Meals: Practices in the Ancient World

has been influenced by the Greco-Roman symposia tradition. They see similarity between the "table-talk" of the symposia and the discourse at the Passover meal, as well as the posture and format of the meal. Based on the similarities, some consider that the Passover meal tradition was modeled on the Greco-Roman tradition.[169]

This was followed by singing of the *Hallel* (Ps 113–118) and a benediction of redemption (*m. Pes.* 10.6).[170] The procedure was very similar to the basic fellowship meals procedure observed in the Greco-Roman world.[171] Since the members of the whole household had to partake in the Passover, there was no restriction for women at the meals unlike in some of the Greco-Roman meals. Women though present, had no major part in the Seder liturgy, since the Mishnah even talks of the paschal lamb being prepared by the men of the household.[172]

---

169. The main proponent of this theory is Stein, who argues that while the purpose is to commemorate the redemption from Egypt, the Greco-Roman influence lies in "more than words and habits." "The Haggadah thus borrowed with extraordinary discrimination the external pattern of sympotic literature but remained single-minded in the pursuit of its sole aim, the religio-historical celebration of the Exodus from Egypt." Stein, "Influence of Symposia Literature," 33. Smith also claims that the literary form of the haggadah is related to the literary form of the symposium. *From Symposium*, 150.

For a comparison of the Jewish Passover liturgy to Greco-Roman meal customs, also see Bahr, "The Seder of Passover," 181–202; reprinted in Fischel, *Essays in Greco-Roman and Related Talmudic Literature*, 473–94; Bokser, *Origins of the Seder*, 62–66. Though there are similarities between the Jewish and Greco-Roman traditions, Bokser is cautious about Stein's conclusion and argues that the symposia did not provide the impetus for the development of the Passover seder. Rather the similarity reflects the general characteristics of dinner in antiquity. But he also admits that the "rabbinic circles may have drawn upon banquet practices to enrich what they were doing." He understands the development in terms of "transference" where an institution is replaced or substituted by another.

170. Stein writes: "Affinities between Kiddush and Hallel on the one side and prayers and songs as a constituent part of a Greek symposium on the other are of a general nature"; "The Influence of Symposia Literature," 26.

171. Smith suggests that the division of the meal is consistent, of course, with the symposium tradition. *From Symposium*, 147–49.

172. *b. Pes.* 8:1; Only one Baraitha reckons with the possibility of women partaking in the table talk: "The wise son asks his father (about the laws of Passover), and if he is not wise, the wife asks her husband," *b. Pes.* 116a. Joshua ben Levi suggested that women should be provided the four cups as they were part of the Exodus event (*b. Pes.* 108b). The issue of reclining for women was also contested. *Pes.* 108b states that it was not necessary for a woman to recline at her husband's side, except for a lady of high standing, but *y. Pes.* 37b allows reclining for all without any social distinction. Cf. Stein, "Influence of Symposia Literature," 31.

Four cups of wine were drunk at the Passover meal. *m. Pes.* 10.7 talks about the third and fourth cups:

> After they have mixed the third cup he says the Benediction over the meal. [Over] a fourth [cup] he completes the *Hallel* and says after it the Benediction over song. If he is minded to drink [more] between these cups he may drink; only between the third and the fourth cups he may not drink.

The blessing over the third cup, identified as the "Cup of Blessing,"[173] normally marked the end of any Jewish formal meal (i.e., on every Sabbath and festival day). But in the Passover meal, a "fourth" cup of wine, followed by the second half of the *Hallel*[174] and a blessing song signaled the end of the meal. Tosefta explains the use of wine at the meal: "It is a religious duty for a man to bring joy to his children and dependants on the [Passover] festival. And how does he give them joy? With wine, since it says [in Ps 104:15]: wine to gladden the heart of man."[175] This understanding was incorporated at the Passover meal, but with certain restriction. It was considered that drinking during a meal did not produce drunkenness, in contrast to drinking after a meal, as is expressed in *y. Pes.*10.8: "wine after the meal caused drunkenness; that which is in the midst of the meal does not cause drunkenness." Further Tosefta 10.1 cites and glosses Mishnah 10.1 and specifies the nature, amount, and potency of the drink: ". . . R. Yehudah says, and as long as it has the taste and appearance of wine." Based on this concept, they could drink additional cups of wine before the "third cup," but they had to conclude with the "fourth cup" after the meal, and after which it was prohibited. This application of the "fourth cup" soon became a part of the rite as *m. Pes.*1.1 expresses: "they give [a poor person] not less than four cups of wine, even if he [must be] supported by charity."[176]

This restriction in the Mishnah to one cup of wine after the "third cup" was meant to maintain its solemn occasion and to prevent the meal from degenerating into an ordinary meeting, which usually ended in drunkenness and debauchery. This is made clear in the following verse: "After the Passover meal they should not disperse to join in revelry . . ."[177] Here

---

173. See *m. Ber.* 6:5 and *m. Ber.* 7:5b.

174. The second half of the *Hallel* starts at Ps 114 or Ps 115 and ends at Ps. 118. Cf. *m. Pes.* 10:6.

175. *t. Pes.* 10:4; Tosefta included games to keep children awake; *t. Pes.* 10:9b.

176. Cf. Instone-Brewer, "Tractate *Pesachim*," 73.

177. *m. Pes.* 10:8. See Instone-Brewer for more discussion on the interpretation of this tradition, "Tractate *Pesachim*," 73, 77.

Fellowship Meals: Practices in the Ancient World

we see the structure of the meal evolving as a response or reaction to the popular culture and tradition of that time. The usual fellowship meal would conclude with the symposium, which consisted of different forms of entertainment and drinking. But here it was modified to suit the context and appeal was made to avoid the "revelry." By doing so, the peculiar identity of the community was preserved. In fact this kind of restriction was required as some of the people were carried away by the Greco-Roman influences. This is evident in Philo who describes the popular culture and complained that some of the Jews were imitating the Roman style of banqueting. He explains in detail the elaborate couches used for reclining and the array of cups and goblets used for drinking and the presence of the flute-girls and entertainers, indicating the moral abuse and corruption.

> And perhaps some people may be inclined to approve of the arrangement of such entertainments which at present prevails everywhere, from an admiration of, and a desire of imitating, the luxury and extravagance of the Italians which both Greeks and barbarians emulate, making all their preparation with a view to show rather than to real enjoyment, (49) for they use couches called triclinia and sofas all round the table made of tortoiseshell, and ivory, and other costly materials, most of which are inlaid with precious stones; silver thread; and others brocaded in flowers of every kind of hue and colour imaginable to allure the sight, and a vast array of drinking cups arrayed according to each separate description; for there are bowls, and vases, and beakers, and goblets, and all kinds of other vessels wrought with the most exquisite skill, their clean cups and others finished with the most elaborate refinement of skilful and ingenious men; (50) and well-shaped slaves of the most exquisite beauty, ministering, as if they had come not more for the purpose of serving the guests than of delighting the eyes of the spectators by their mere appearance. . . . the last tables brought in are reserved for the drinking bouts and the after-dinners as they call them.[178]

The Passover further shows the centrality of meals in Judaism, it became an important celebration in the lives of the people, owing to its connection to the motif of deliverance and restoration. In keeping with the times, and based on the popular culture of that time they must have adopted certain features and included those practices appropriate to their needs. According to *b. Ber.* 33a the addition of wine to the Passover celebration was instituted

---

178. Philo, *Contempl.* 48–50 = 54.

in the time of the "Great Assembly" (*Anshei Keneset Ha-Gedolah*), whose period extended from Ezra to the beginning of the Tannaitic era.[179] So throughout the centuries the Passover celebration has also evolved in the way it was celebrated. Many of the similarities between the Passover and the Greco-Roman meal practices would indicate that the rabbis used the popular meal traditions in order to make themselves relevant.[180] In doing so, they were also in danger of being overtaken by the current climate. Thus a scheme was put in place to check some of the inappropriate practice so as not to compromise the community's social and religious beliefs and values. Here we observe a community trying to enhance its identity, by conforming to a certain extent to the Greco-Roman way of life.

Intertestamental Period

A significant amount of literature on fellowship meals from the intertestamental period further attests to their importance in the socio-religious life of the people. Many of the meal motifs in the OT recur in the literature from this period. Food motifs play the same pivotal role to express the relationship with God.[181] The nation is reminded of the events out of Egypt where God provided them with food (2 Esd 1:17–23). The future salvation and coming of the new age are described as an age of plenty with abundance of food.[182] There is a lot emphasis on sacrifices, festivities, and feasting as a form of celebration.[183] The Additions to Esther and Daniel further develop some of the meal motifs found in the OT books. Ben Sira includes a number of texts on the theme of feasting that are similar to Proverbs.[184] The different authors also stress the fellowship meal as a boundary

---

179. Erwin R. Goodenough was of the view that the use of wine in Jewish ceremonies was due to the contact with the mysteries especially that of Dionysus. *Jewish Symbols*, 126–28. For the significance of wine in Jewish tradition, see M. Smith, "On the Wine God," 815–29.

180. See Bokser, *Origins of the Seder*, 65–66.

181. For example, the expectation that God will feed his people again with the new manna. Wis 16:20; 4 *Ezra* 1:19; 2 *Bar.* 29:8.

182. 4 *Ezra* 8:52–54; 2 *Bar.* 29:5; *1 En.* 62.14); Cf. Charles, ed., *Apocrypha and Pseudepigrapha*, 2.497–98.

183. 1 Esd 1:122; 4:63; 5:51–55; 7:10–15; 8:85; 9:50–55; Jdt 16:20.

184. These include dangers of eating with the wicked 9:9, the powerful (13:8–13), and the stingy (14:10); also warning against feasting lavishly (18:32), against overeating (37:29–31). Cf. also Sir 29:22.

Fellowship Meals: Practices in the Ancient World

marker.[185] In contrast to the canonical Esther (2:8), in Additions to Esther, Esther avoids the king's food: "And that thine handmaid hath not eaten at Aman's table, and that I have not greatly esteemed the king's feast, nor drunk the wine of the drink offerings."[186] The refusal to partake in others' fellowship meal stands as a testament to their faith and identity in the midst of adverse trials.[187]

They also exhibit a lot of similarity in terms of practice and format with the Greco-Roman practices. Ben Sira, which comes from about 200 to 180 BC, contains many of the fellowship meal traditions especially rules of etiquette which were intended as a sort of instruction for the community.[188] The meal motif and tradition reflected in Ben Sira shows a lot of similarity with the contemporary Greco-Roman writers.[189] The verse in 12:12, "Do not put [your enemy] next to you, or he may overthrow you and take your place. Do not let him sit at your right hand, or else he may try to take your own seat," implies that the seating arrangement was done according to ranking at the table. Normally in the Greco-Roman context the host would take the first place with the most honored guest sitting at his right, followed by others relative to their status.[190] So the instruction is that if an opponent is present, care should be taken that the honored place is out of bounds for him.[191]

The "symposiarch" who had a prominent role in the organising and ordering of the Greco-Roman meals also became part of the meal practices in Jewish fellowship meals. In Ben Sira 32:1–2 the responsibility of the "symposiarch" is stated:

185. Cf. Tob 1:6–12; 4:17; Jdt 10:5, 10–13; cf. 12:5–9; 3 *Macc.* 3:2–5; *Let. Aris.* 144–153; *Jub.* 6:35b; 22:16.

186. Add Esth 14:17.

187. 1 Macc 1:62–63; 2 Macc. 6:18—7:42; 4 *Macc.* 5–18; For the points in this paragraph see Blomberg, *Contagious Holiness*, 66–73.

188. Martin Hengel and others see the influence of the Greco-Roman meal customs in his writings. *Judaism and Hellenism*, 2.150. Also Smith, *From Symposium*, 135. The reflection of the Greco-Roman meal conventions in the book might be a result of Ben Sira 39:4, where the author states that he received part of his education by travelling foreign lands.

189. Smith observes that Ben Sira was well versed in Greek symposium literature like, that of Plato, Xenophon, and others and therefore his meal ethics were derived from the Greek tradition. Probably his school was modelled after the Greek philosophical schools. *From Symposium*, 142–44.

190. Plato *Symp.* 175C, 222E; Becker and Göll, *Charikles*, 318.

191. Smith, *From Symposium*, 136.

> If they make you master of the feast . . . be among them as one of their number. Take care of them first and then sit down; when you have fulfilled all your duties, take your place, so that you may be merry along with them and receive a wreath for your excellent leadership.

It consisted of regulating the sitting arrangement, to the distribution of wine and overseeing proper conduct at the symposium. There are instructions for proper conduct during the meals throughout the book.[192] Many of the meal ethics taught here, from avoidance of excessive drinking[193] to showing concern for others,[194] are similar with much of the Greco-Roman literature on meals.

Ben Sira, likewise mentions entertainment in the form of music as part of the fellowship meal which corresponds well with the musical entertainment which was an integral part of the Greco-Roman meals.[195] This probably occurred in the second part of the meal—the symposium where drinking accompanied the entertainment.[196] Along with this, table discourse was very much present during the course of the meal. He writes:

> Speak, you who are older, for it is your right, but with accurate knowledge, and do not interrupt the music. Where there is entertainment, do not pour out talk; do not display your cleverness at the wrong time.[197]

The elaborate description of how a proper conversation should be conducted at the meal correlates with the Greco-Roman symposium as advocated by the moralists.[198] Based on these similarities, Smith concludes that the form of the meal described in Ben Sira, indicates a relation to Greco-Roman meal traditions.[199]

The pseudepigraphic *Letter of Aristeas*[200] depicts similar meal practices; the story reports about the Palestinian envoys in Alexandria who have

---

192. Sir 9:15–16; 18:37; 19:1–3; 29:21–23; 31:12–30; 32:1–2, 11; 37:27–31; 41:19.

193. Sir 19:1–3; 31:25–30

194. Sir 31:15–17; 41:19.

195. Sir 32:3–6, 40:20–21; Plato *Symp.* 176E.

196. Sir 32:5, 6: ". . . is a company singing when wine is served. . . .is string music with delicious wine."

197. Sir 32:3–4.

198. Cf. Sir 9:15–16; 13:8–13, 21–23; 32:7–9; 33:4–6; 34:9–12; 37:16–26; 39:8.

199. Smith, *From Symposium*, 144. Contra Blomberg, *Contagious Holiness*, 67.

200. About 100 BC.

Fellowship Meals: Practices in the Ancient World

come to translate the Hebrew Bible into Greek take part in a "party" given in their honor by the king. Everyone participated in the meal by reclining. It is then followed by prayers over the food and table talk with discussion on the art of good and just government.[201]

Writers from the intertestamental period show that fellowship meals were an important part of the Jewish belief and hope. In the midst of their dispersion and turmoil, the call to preserve their identity through the fellowship meals provide hope of restoration to the people. It was a reminder that God will again judge the people and restore them. The meal ethics further shows that judgment was an inherent theme in the observance of the meals, directing the people to maintain the integrity of their fellowship meals as they were linked with God's future promises.

Literature from the intertestamental period does exhibit a lot of affinity to the Greco-Roman practices. The hellenization of the Mediterranean world during the intervening period between the Testaments suggests that there were influences in terms of culture and practices on the Jewish society. The similarities with the Greco-Roman practices also indicate that the fellowship meals had parallel functions in the Jewish society.

We shall further study some of the Jewish communities from the intertestamental period where fellowship meals appear prominently and which have often been linked with the Lord's Supper tradition.

Discipline and Judgment in Qumran

Another community where the fellowship meal seemed to play a pivotal role in the functioning of the community is the Qumran community.[202] A statement found in the Rule of the Community describes the events that took place at a meal and affirms the view that fellowship meals occupied a central place in the community life:

> They shall eat in common and bless in common and deliberate in common. Wherever there are ten men of the Council of the Community there shall not lack a priest among them. And they shall all sit before him according to their rank and shall be asked their

---

201. Stein argues that the literature shows heavy dependence on the Greco-Roman sympotic literary pattern. "Influence of Symposia Literature," 20.

202. The Qumran community is considered as an offshoot of the Essenes and there is now a strong consensus that the Essenes described by Josephus are identical with the community at Qumran. Cf. Vanderkam, *Dead Sea Scrolls*, 71–98.

> counsel in all things in that order. And when the table has been prepared for eating, and the new wine for drinking, the priest shall be the first to stretch out his hand to bless the first-fruits of the bread and new wine.[203]

For the Qumran community participation in the communal meal was a badge of their membership. Josephus writes: "Before he may touch the common food, he is made to swear tremendous oaths."[204] Only full-fledged members of the community who were in good standing could participate in the meals as these texts shows:

> And when he approaches the council of the community he shall not touch the Purity [*taharah*] of the Many until they have examined him about his spirit and actions, until a full year has been completed by him.[205]

> Let him not touch the Drink [*mashqeh*] of the Many until he has completed a second year amongst the men of the Community.[206]

Here the reference to "Purity" and "Drink" probably refers to the food and wine at the fellowship table as the community gave much importance and significance to the fellowship meals. 1QS 5:13 also states: "let him not enter the water so as to touch the Purity of the men of holiness." Rabin understands that the reference to "water" and "purity" in the texts refer to a ritual bath which was necessary in order to touch "the purity." This means that "the purity" was "ritually pure food."[207] Lieberman and Rabin think that this "purity" was similar to the rabbinic *tohorot* which refers to ritually clean articles, especially food.[208] Newton, further suggested that "the

---

203. 1 QS 6:2–6. Similar description is also given by Josephus *J.W.* 2.129–328. "After the purification, they assemble in a special room which none of the uninitiated is permitted to enter; pure now themselves, they repair to the refectory, as to some sacred shrine. When they have seated themselves in silence, the baker serves the loaves in order. . .Before the meal, the priest gives the blessing, and it is unlawful to partake before the prayer. The meal ended, he offers a further prayer; thus at the beginning and at the close they do homage to God as the bountiful giver of life." *J.W.* 2.131. Likewise Josephus indicates the sitting arrangement when he describes that they were served "in order" *J. W.* 2.130.

204. Jos. *J. W.* 2.139.

205. 1QS 6:16, 17.

206. 1QS 6:20, 2. Also in 1QS 5:13: "let him not enter the water so as to touch the Purity of the men of holiness."

207. Rabin, *Qumran Studies*, 7, 8. Cf. Baumgarten, "Sacrifice and Worship," 148.

208. Lieberman, "Discipline," 203. Rabin, *Qumran Studies*, 8. Also supported by

Fellowship Meals: Practices in the Ancient World

purity and the drink" refers to: "all the pure things that belonged to the community and which were involved in its expiatory life as a substitute for the Temple in Jerusalem. Like the Jerusalem Temple, all objects and participants were required to be in a state of purity so as to enable the divine presence to dwell in their midst."[209]

The reason behind this belief was, as Newton points out, that the Qumran community "saw itself as a priestly community in its own right" and "as a replacement of the defiled Temple of Jerusalem and as a dwelling place for God."[210] The Temple had become worthless, as the priests had become polluted resulting in the departure of God's presence.[211] The Qumran community now had become the dwelling place of God.[212] Thus the motif of the "messianic banquet" was strongly emphasized in the community in their effort to affirm their theological stand.

This is vividly expressed in some of the texts where the community is equated with the "holy house for Israel and a foundation of the holy of holies for Aaron" and "a dwelling of the holy of holies for Aaron . . .and a house of perfection and truth for Israel."[213] Some have suggested, based on this text that the community compared itself to the interior of the Temple, the Holy Place, and the Holy of Holies where utmost purity was to be maintained.[214] For this reason the main emphasis of the community was to fulfil the requirements demanded by the biblical laws pertaining to temple purity, so as to maintain and preserve the community to be habitable for the divine presence.[215]

Fellowship meals became the means to give expression and realisation to their conviction that God was present in the community. This understanding was based on the Temple as the special dwelling place of God, and

---

Ringgren, *The Faith of Qumran*, 218; Vermes, *Dead Sea Scrolls*, 79; Burrows, *Dead Sea Scrolls*, 377.

209. Newton, *Concept of Purity*, 26. He goes on to say that "Purity" also refers to "knowledge of the purity rules peculiar to the sect which, in particular at Qumran, are connected with the use and consumption of food." 24.

210. Ibid., 14; also see Vermes, *Dead Sea Scrolls: Qumran in Perspective*, 81.

211. Cf. CD 5:6, 7; 20:22; 1QS 5:19, 20.

212. This idea is reinforced in the Scrolls by the association of the community with the angels and the Spirit of God; 1QS 11:7-9; 1QH 3:21, 22; 6:13: 1QM 12:1ff. 4QFl 1:4; 1QM 7:6; 4QMa; 4QDb Cf Newton, *Concept of Purity*, 49.

213. 1QS 8:5, 6.

214. Wernberg-Moller, *Manual of Discipline*, 124; Newton, *Concept of Purity*, 14–15.

215. Cf. Exod 28:43; 30:17–31; 40:31–2; 1 Kgs 8:10–13.

this notion became part of the community's belief. Though the community had distanced itself from the Temple, the purity laws associated with the Temple were strictly followed as they saw themselves as the replacement to the Temple and the inheritors of what was to come. In order to maintain that status now in their community they endeavor to maintain the purity of the place (Lev 21:17–23).[216] This entailed not only the priest, but the whole community following the rules with regard to purity. Therefore washing and other rituals were now practised in accordance with priestly purity and all would take a ritual bath before and after each cultic action.[217] So meals were eaten in "purity" by the members, as formerly only the priest did at the Temple in Jerusalem, in order to keep up with their own designation as the "Holy Ones." This was also done so that the community was in "constant preparedness for the re-establishment of the Temple under their auspices at the end of the present age."[218]

The high purity maintained at the fellowship meals and the close association of the fellowship meals with their salvific worldview suggest that the community at Qumran considered their meals as sacred. In fact they were considered as equivalent to the sacrifices at the Temple and so the participants at the meals were to be in a high state of purity. For this reason, their food was prepared only by the priests.[219] Kuhn interprets Josephus. *Ant.* 18.1–5: " . . . being excluded from the Common Court of the Temple they offer sacrifices by themselves" to support the view that the meals were considered a substitute for the Temple sacrifices.[220] Based on this feature, Kuhn concluded that the fellowship meals also "took on a new meaning, mediating salvation from God."[221] Based on the view that the meals were

216. 1 QS 3:4, 9; 1QS 5:13. Cf. Newton, *Concept of Purity*, 32; Ringgren, *Faith of Qumran*, 220. Neusner suggests that even before the destruction of the Temple, some groups met regularly to enjoy fellowship and eat their meals in strict levitical purity and so the same could have been the case with the Qumran community (cf. Lev. 22:6). "The Fellowship," 127.

217. On the sacramental nature of these practices see Kuhn, "Lord's Supper," 68. Also Flusser, "Dead Sea Sect," 229.

218. Newton, *Concept of Purity*, 33.

219. In lieu of the Temple sacrifices, daily baths and sacral meals became the main activities of the community. Though they did not have access to meat offered for sacrifices, they still continued to follow the regulations prescribed for the meals of the priests in the Temple. Kuhn, "Lord's Supper," 68.

220. Ibid.

221. Ibid., 68–70. Also the requirement for ten men at a fellowship table, according to Kuhn "points to the cultic character of the meal." 1QS 6:1–6.

Fellowship Meals: Practices in the Ancient World

sacramental in nature, some see a direct connection between the Qumran meals and the Lord's Supper.[222]

They also believed that the Messiah who would save them was present with them during the fellowship meals. For instance in the Rule of the Congregation (1QSa) we see a clear picture of the community's understanding of the meal in relation to the Messiah. In 2:11–22:

> This shall be the assembly of the men of renown called to the meeting of the Council of the community when the Messiah shall summon them. He shall come at the head of the whole congregation of Israel with all the sons of Aaron the Priests, to the assembly, the men of renown; and they shall sit in the order of dignity . . . And they shall gather for the common table, to eat and to drink new wine, when the common table shall be set for eating and the new wine poured for drinking, Thereafter, the Messiah of Israel shall extend his hand over the bread, and all the Congregation of the Community shall utter a blessing, each man in the order of his dignity. It is according to this statute that they shall proceed at every meal at which at least ten men are gathered together.[223]

As is typical of this motif, the Messiah is present in the fellowship meal and participates actively with the people. Frank Moore Cross, among others, thinks that the Qumran community celebrated its common meals as a "liturgical anticipation of the Messianic banquet."[224] Cross asserts that in the meantime the lay head and the priestly head of the community stood in the stead of the Messiahs of Aaron and Israel. This implies that the recurring meal of the sect was somehow construed as a "foretaste" of the eschatological banquet.[225] Though there are questions regarding how this was seen as

---

222. Kuhn, "Lord's Supper." Cf. also Pryke, "Sacraments," 543, 552. On the other hand, Newton and others argue that the meals were non-sacramental in nature. Newton, *Concept of Purity*, 33. van der Ploeg, "Meals of the Essenes," 171. See Schiffman, *Reclaiming the Dead Sea Scrolls*, 333–38, who also disputes the idea that the Essene meal was a sacred meal. Though there are disagreements on the nature of the meals, we see that there was a close association between the fellowship meals and salvation. So, we can surmise that it was not the meals that brought about salvation but salvation was so closely identified with the fellowship meal that it became identified with salvation itself. Thus participating in fellowship meals implied that a member was worthy to be a recipient of that gift.

223. Cf. 1QSa 2:17–22.

224. Cross, *Ancient Library*, 77.

225. Ibid., 88; K. Kuhn also expresses a similar idea; "The Lord's Supper," 71. But J. F. Priest sees it as an eschatological meal in the future "Messiah and the Meal," 97–98.

Exclusion and Judgment in Fellowship Meals

actualized in the present by the community, it can be seen as an eschatological expectation being acted out symbolically in faith in the present using the fellowship meals.[226] The fellowship meals thus became effective and powerful symbols of expressing and living out the community's aspiration.

This understanding made the fellowship meals closely connect with their identity.[227] Therefore they also functioned as boundary markers. In the Qumran community, there were strict requirements before one could take part in the communal meal. 1 QSa 2:3-10 puts emphasis on exclusion of all impurity, including physical blemish:

> No man smitten with any human uncleanness shall *enter* the assembly of God.... No man smitten in his flesh, or *paralysed in his feet or hands, or lame, or blind,* or deaf, or dumb, or smitten in his flesh with a visible *blemish* . . . for the angels of holiness are [with] their congregation] . . . let him not *enter* among [the congregation], for he is smitten.[228]

The Scrolls also include a number of ethical rules to be followed at the meals.[229] When a novice was accepted into membership of the community after a rigorous initiation process, one of the main benefits was his access to the community fellowship meal (1QS 1:11, 12), which was a sign of belonging fully to the community and a participation in its future promises. The whole process took a period of more than two years.[230] The process of purification involved ablutions, repentance, instructions and study of the Torah.[231]

In like manner the members were disciplined or punished for breaking a code of the community by prohibiting them to partake in the fellowship meals.[232] The duration of the expulsion depended on the nature of the

---

226. Some are of the view that they considered themselves already to be living in the dawn of the new age, Schiffman, "Communal Meals," 45-56.

227. Cf. Bilde, "Common Meal," 162, 163.

228. Cf. 1QM 7:4-6; 4QCD; 11QTemple 45:12-14.

229. For example, 1QS 4:10: "No man shall interrupt the speech of the others before his brother has finished speaking, Nor shall he speak of his rank."

230. Cf. Newton, *Concept of Purity*, 25.

231. 1QS 3:1; 5:13, 14; 6:22.

232. The Scrolls mention a number of acts which were considered violation of the community laws causing impurity, they include speaking against the priest; for lying (CD 22:3); disrespectful behavior towards a fellow member, especially one of higher rank (1QS 6.25-7); for unjustly and deliberately insulting one's companion (1QS 7:4, 5; cf. Lev 6:1-5); for speaking evil of another member. (1Qs 7:15, 16; cf. Lev 19:16).

offense and could vary from ten days to two years.²³³ In serious cases, like transgressions committed intentionally, slandering the community, sins which were blasphemous in nature, the law breakers were permanently expelled from the community as these sins were considered to bring higher level of impurity and repercussion.²³⁴ The reason is that when a member breaks the rule of the community he becomes unclean and might pollute the rest, so he has to be separated from the "Purity of the Many."²³⁵ Similarly the exclusion includes exclusion from the "drink of the Many" and "new wine" of the community.²³⁶ Since liquids were considered as prime conveyors of impurity and as being susceptible to impurity,²³⁷ the outcast member was prevented from sharing in them. This was done so that the presence of God in the community would not be affected. All these processes were similar to the Temple system where the priest who offended was removed from the sanctuary until he was cleansed of the sins.

An expelled member becomes an outsider and has to undergo and fulfil all the requirements just like a new novice before he can return and participate in the fellowship meals. During the period of his expulsion he has to live on the periphery of the life of the community. He must first repent from his wickedness and have his deeds purified before he can be made clean by a bath; finally his case has to be judged and accepted by the community, and then only was he allowed to join in the fellowship.²³⁸

The Qumran community exhibits an example where fellowship meals were used extensively to define their social boundaries and segregate themselves from others. It was an effective tool in implementing their belief system and maintaining their distinct identity. It worked effectively for the

233. 1QS 6:24–25; 7:15–16, 18–20.

234. 1QS 7:3, 5, 16, 18; 8:21–24. Cf. Newton thinks the time duration of the expulsion was in lieu of sin offerings offered at the Temple by offenders. He also observes that the Qumran sect: "made little or no distinction between ceremonial and moral transgression; both caused the individual to become impure and in turn to pollute the community. Nor was any distinction made between inner and outer purity; the whole of man was made impure by sin. (1QS 3:8, 9). *Concept of Purity*, 46, 48–49.

235. The term "Purity of the Many" frequently appears in the scrolls. The term "Many" probably referred to the community and more specifically to the members in the community (1QS 5:13, 8:17). Cf. Wernberg-Moller, *Manual of Discipline*, 101; Newton, *Concept of Purity*, 23.

236. 1QS 6:5, 1QSa 2:17–18.

237. This concept is seen in Lev. 11:38 and in Rabbinic tradition. Rabin, *Qumran Studies*, 9

238. Cf. 1QS 5:13–14; 6:22; 1QS 7:18–20; 8:16–17.

community due to the strong association of the meals with their religious beliefs. Their belief in the presence of God in the community reinforced their commitment to the practices and thus they were very much preoccupied with the maintenance of purity in the community.

Some have argued that there were Greco-Roman influences on their practices. Smith assumes that the washing or ablutions are similar to the practices in other Greco-Roman fellowship meals. The role of the priest during the meal, by pronouncing the blessings on the food and drink[239] was similar to the role of the symposiarch in Greco-Roman meals. Also noticed at the meals described, was the order of ranking maintained at the meals.[240] This is reminiscent of the general practice at fellowship meals in the Greco-Roman world. The priest who presided over the meal was probably the highest in rank and thus entitled to give the blessings over the meal.[241] Since the community lived in great high veneration of the Torah, there was a constant study and meditation by the members, and this was carried out during the meal sessions. This practice appears to be quite similar to the symposium in Greco-Roman fellowship meals.[242] But these external similarities cannot prove beyond a certain limit the extent of the Greco-Roman influences on this community, as the meanings and theology associated with the meals were completely different to that of the Greco-Roman traditions. There is also no indication that the group ate their meal reclining, which was one of the hallmarks of the Greco-Roman meal.[243] In that sense, we can assume that their meal practices were a development and reaction to the current practices which were seen as a total contradiction of their religious tenets.

To enforce their religious system and their interpretation of the Torah, the fellowship meal of all the activities, became an indispensable tool for the community. It became more than a symbolic representation of a reality but a tangible expression of their aspirations, beliefs, and identity. In that sense the distinction between symbolic representation and reality diminishes, as revealed in some of their texts.

239. Cf. 1QSa 2:11–12.

240. 1QS 6:1–4.

241. There were other rules concerning ones behavior towards other members of the community 1 QS 5:7; 5: 24—6:1; 6:8–13. "These rules represented the same kinds of concerns as were found in Greco-Roman clubs;" Smith, *From Symposium*, 155.

242. Smith envisages again that the study and discussion of the Torah during the meal is similar to the Symposium tradition. *From Symposium*, 154.

243. Cf. Schiffman, *Eschatological Community*, 56.

Fellowship Meals: Practices in the Ancient World

In their quest for spiritual holiness and to prepare themselves as the remnant of God's people, they avoided contact with the world, including other Jewish communities.[244] It is no surprise then that the Greco-Roman influence is minimal on this community. However these characteristics of the fellowship meal in a sense were not unique to the Qumran Community alone; similar features can be observed in other communities and cultures but it differed in terms of meanings, values, and intensity.

Therapeutae, Fellowship Meal and Identity

Philo's description of the Therapeutae and their activities which he differentiates from the Essenes, throws light on another community and their emphasis on communal meals.[245] Philo compares the practices of this community with the Greco-Roman fellowship meals as recorded by Plato and Xenophon. He writes:

> Among the banquets held in Greece there are two celebrated and highly notable examples, namely those in which Socrates was also present . . . which was thought worthy of being commemorated by men who were imbued with the true spirit of philosophy both in their dispositions and in their discourses, Plato and Xenophon, for they recorded them as events worthy to be had in perpetual recollection, looking upon it that future generations would take them as models for a well managed arrangement of future banquets.[246]

The description by Philo shows that the Greco-Roman meal traditions were well known among the different Jewish communities. The elaborate description of the meals and the symposium that followed the meals indicate that the meal tradition of the philosophers became popular in certain circles, unlike many of the fellowship meals that ended in debauchery and drunkenness.[247] The Therapeutae community observed the meals in similar fashion to that of other groups, but also distinct in their own ways. Like

---

244. For a comparison between Jesus' meal practices and the Qumran meal see, Dunn, "Jesus, Table-Fellowship, and Qumran," 263–65. The similarity is seen in the eschatological out-look of the meals. The dissimilarity lies in the way purity and exclusivism was observed and maintained during the meals.

245. For further description on this community, see Schürer, *History of the Jewish People*, 2.591–97.

246. Philo *Contempl.* 57.

247. Ibid., 58–59.

the Qumran community, the meals were held in "purity," wearing white garments.²⁴⁸ Ranking at the table was practised:

> ... and after having offered prayers the elders sit down to meat still observing the order in which they were previously arranged, for they looked on those as elders who are advanced in years and very ancient . . .²⁴⁹

Women also participate in the feast but they sat apart from the men, on the left. At the same time the community emphasized freedom and equality among the members. This is seen in the description that slaves were not employed for serving, for it was described as:

> contrary to nature, for nature has created all men free but the injustice and covetousness of some men who prefer inequality, that cause of all evil, having subdued some, has given to the more powerful authority over those who are weaker.²⁵⁰

Ranking and social equality were both maintained at the meals. Philo records that they reclined for all their meals; and it was probably a compulsory practice.²⁵¹ But many contrasting features are also noticed in their practice. Keeping in line with their religious inclination luxurious and rich items were shunned. So though they reclined, which was generally associated with status and luxury, their custom was devoid of such comfort. Thus they had rugs of coarsest materials and cheap mats in place of luxurious items.²⁵² They had simple and plain food, cold water instead of wine, "and hot water for old men who are accustomed to a luxurious life."²⁵³ Surely they used the fellowship meals to express their identity, based on their beliefs and likewise define their community boundaries.

Symposium was an integral part of their meal and likewise it was based on their religious conviction as expressed here: "they pray to God that the entertainment may be acceptable and welcome and pleasing."²⁵⁴ Everything was influenced by the same principle to attain "the perfection

---

248. Ibid., 66.

249. Ibid., 67.

250. Ibid.. 70; cf. 71.

251. Ibid., 69.

252. Ibid.: "they practice a liberal, gentlemanlike kind of frugality, hating the allurements of pleasure with all their might."

253. Ibid., 73.

254. Ibid., 66.

Fellowship Meals: Practices in the Ancient World

of virtue."[255] Therefore instead of entertainment of sorts, during this time there was exposition of the sacred scriptures/law by the elders, followed by interpretation and instruction, and by singing hymns of thanksgiving, in honor of God.[256] An appeal was made in this regard by Philo that the meal practices of the Therapeutae were a better option than the popular meal cultures. Philo saw their meal practices in keeping with the divine ordering. He extols their prayers, the chastity of their women who sat apart, and the meal activities which were conducted in simplicity and solemnity, and where everyone was treated equal. So he writes:

> But since the entertainments of the greatest celebrity are full of such trifling and folly, bearing conviction in themselves, if anyone should think fit not to regard vague opinion and the character which has been commonly handed down concerning them as feasts which have gone off with the most eminent success, I will oppose to them the entertainments of those people who have devoted their whole life and themselves to the knowledge and contemplation of the affairs of nature in accordance with the most sacred admonitions and precepts of the prophet Moses.[257]

The close association of the fellowship meals with the community in all matters attest to the fact that they considered the fellowship meals as an integral part of their social and religious identity and expression. We can notice that fellowship meals were used as a form of discipline for the whole community in order to attain or reach perfection for the future blessings and also to reinforce their belief as the chosen community.

Fellowship meals were used and interpreted to suit the needs of the community. In the case of the Therapeutae, their fellowship meal tradition seemed to have developed as a reaction to the cultures around. The meal descriptions in Philo might be an idealisation to some extent but show the intention of the writer/community to have an idealized society, which they believed could be achieved, beginning from the meal practices to using them as a tool for societal transformation.

---

255. Ibid., 72

256. Ibid., 74.

257. Ibid., 64; Smith postulates that Philo's description is "an idealization based on his desire to picture them as an ideal Jewish philosophical school." *From Symposium*, 159.

Exclusion and Judgment in Fellowship Meals

Law, Fellowship Meal and the Pharisees

The different groups in Judaism observed their own meals practices mainly for maintaining their identities in line with their belief systems. This is also noticed prominently among the Pharisees who dominated the scene after the destruction of the Temple. Neusner estimates that a remarkable 67 percent of the rabbinic traditions about the Pharisees before AD 70 deal directly or indirectly with meal practices.[258] The Pharisees whose prime concern was faithfulness to the law and its purity regulations made their pharisaic fellowship meal function chiefly as a boundary marker.[259] Morton Smith suggests that the development of the importance of the fellowship meal was due to the Deuteronomic tradition that prohibited sacrifice outside Jerusalem, so that non-sacrificial worship was developed in different forms which manifested prominently in meal practices; later on it became the norm and basis for the formation of the sects. Thus he concludes: "It is no accident that the essential act of communion in all these groups is participation in common meals."[260]

The importance of fellowship meals in the Pharisaic circle is stated in *bt. Ber.* 55a: "R. Johanan and R. Eleazar both explain that as long as the Temple stood, the altar atoned for Israel, but now a man's table atones for him."[261] The text implies that the fellowship meals were considered to be cultic in nature and this is also noticed in the number of ritual purity laws observed at the tables.[262] There is a debate as to how far this was carried on. Neusner on one hand suggests that:

> They [Pharisees] therefore held one must eat his secular food, that is, ordinary, everyday meals, in a state of purity *as if one were a Temple priest*. The Pharisees thus arrogated to themselves—and to all Jews equally—the status of the temple priests and did the things which priests must do on account of the status. The table of every

---

258. Neusner, *From Politics to Piety*, 86; see further Neusner, *Rabbinic Traditions*, 3.303–4.

259. Neusner, *Idea of Purity*, 64–71.

260. M. Smith, "Dead Sea Sect," 352.

261. Epstein, *Babylonian Talmud*, 354. This probably refers to the Friday traditional meal of the Sabbath which was held in private homes and was considered to be atoning in nature.

262. Cf. Mark 7:1–15.

Fellowship Meals: Practices in the Ancient World

Jew in his home was seen to be like the table of the Lord in the Jerusalem Temple.[263]

This was based on their literal understanding of Exod 19:6: "you shall be to me a kingdom of priests and a holy nation." Therefore for everyone who observed the Levitical laws of purity the fellowship table possessed the sanctity and character of the altar of the Temple.[264] For Neusner "the observance of the laws extended to the meals, thus all meals were special."[265] This along with the observance of the laws of ritual purity outside the Temple characterized the Pharisees.[266] This is opposed by E. P. Sanders; who makes the point that the Pharisees were not as rigid as they are believed to be, and there was interaction with the Gentiles even at the table.[267] However, there is a stronger inclination to believe that the Pharisees had applied the purity laws in a stricter way to maintain their identity and their devotion to the Torah.[268] This meant that the rules applied even to ordinary food. The gospel account reflects that reality when the Pharisees questioned Jesus and his disciples for eating with unwashed hands, foods which were definitely ordinary, and when they were neither priests.[269]

The Mishnah also talks about different associations (*Havuroth*) that were formed for the purpose of observing fellowship meals on religious occasions.[270] Morton Smith defines the associations as: ". . . groups whose members observe the same interpretation of the purity rules and therefore can have table fellowship with each other."[271] In the *Havuroth* only those who were already pious Jews were qualified to become *Haverim* or "companions."[272] They were characterized by their meticulous observance

---

263. Neusner, *Idea of Purity*, 65.

264. Neusner, *Politics to Piety*, 83.

265. Neusner, "Two Pictures," 537.

266. Ibid., 532.

267. Sanders, "Jewish Association," 178.

268. Cf. Harrington, *Impurity System*, 267–81. Also Dunn, "Jesus, Table-Fellowship, and Qumran," 260: "Table-fellowship was at the heart of many Pharisees' self identity; for them Sirach's counsel, 'Let *righteous* men be your table companions,' would be a basic rule of life."

269. Mark 7; Luke 11:38; Matt 23:25. Cf. Harrington, *Impurity System*, 53.

270. Association meetings that are found in *m. Erub* 6:6 and *m. Pes.*10:8 can be reliably dated before 70 AD, see Instone-Brewer and Harland, "Jewish Associations", 9.

271. Smith, "Dead Sea Sect," 352.

272. See more on the requirement to enter the havuroth; most had to do with the observance of food laws and table fellowship (*m. Dem.* 2:2–3, *t. Dem.* 2:2–3:15, *y. Dem.*

of purity laws as opposed to the lax observance of the 'ammei ha-'arets or "people of the land." J. Bowker, more accurately describes the *Havuroth* as "a movement within a movement, a kind of extreme deduction, drawn from the basic Hakamic vision (that holiness should be possible for all men), which emphasized the progress possible in attaining the further degrees of holiness by its careful rules and ranks."[273] The purpose for having the *Havuroth* was to promote the observance of the laws of tithing and to observe the *halakoth* in regard to the eating of food in a state of purity.[274] Since food was considered susceptible to defilement, so fellowship meals were exclusive to the members of the association only.

The association membership was determined by three things: eating together, avoiding interaction with other associations during the meal, and registering for the meal beforehand. Each member of the association had to physically attend and join in the meal, and the criterion of their attendance was that they should eat at least a mouthful of food.[275] Since the Passover meal had to be eaten within the house, the associations mentioned here were meeting to partake in some form of fellowship meals.[276] J. Jeremias suggested that the *Havurah* meals were not cultic meals but ordinary meals.[277] J. Neusner also draws attention to this effect:

> Nowhere in the rabbinic traditions about the Pharisees do we find a reference to ritual gatherings of the Pharisaic party, as a whole or in small groups, for table-fellowship . . . in the rabbinic traditions no sectarian ritual meal is ever mentioned . . . we find no stories of

22d-23a and *b. Bek.* 30b-31A). Cf. Neusner, "Fellowship," 129-36; Chesnutt, *From Death to Life*, 200-201.

273. Bowker, *Jesus and the Pharisees*, 35; Chesnutt, *From Death to Life*, 199-200.

274. *t. Dem.* 2:11-14; *m. Dem.* 2:2-3, *y. Dem.* 22d-23a cf. *b. Bek.* 30b-31a contain rules for the Novitiate. Chesnutt, *From Death to Life*, 199-201.

275. *m. Pes.* 8:7 specify it as "an olive's bulk"; cf. Instone-Brewer and Harland, "Jewish Associations," 7.

276. A suggestion is that: "They may have met to eat a fellowship meal, or peace offering which had to be consumed within two days (Lev 7:16). It could be offered and cooked on the day before the Sabbath then eaten by the association group on the Sabbath when everyone had free time to attend. In this case there would be no need for other household members to attend, though presumably they could if they wished. It could therefore be an all-male meal, as was common for other association meals in the Greco-Roman world." Instone-Brewer and Harland, "Jewish Associations," 11.

277. For example, J. Jeremias has shown that *b. Ros Has.* 29a-b and *b. Ber.* 46a, in which some had found evidence for cultic meals, are actually concerned with blessing said over the bread at ordinary daily meals. *Eucharistic Words*, 30n1.

Fellowship Meals: Practices in the Ancient World

> how the *haverim* gathered to eat.... The editorial and redactional framework is silent about table fellowship. The narrative materials say nothing on the matter.[278]

Though the halakoth contains rules pertaining to ritual meals no such meal is ever depicted.[279] Neusner's explanation is that there were no ritual meals as such among Pharisaic groups, but their everyday meals were solemn occasions:

> These facts point to one conclusion: the Pharisaic groups did not conduct their table-fellowship meals as rituals. The table-fellowship laws pertained not to group life, but to ordinary, daily life lived quite apart from heightened, ritual occasions. The rules applied to the home, not merely to the cultic center, be it synagogue, Temple, or sectarian rite house (if such existed). While the early Christians gathered for ritual-meals and made of these ritual meals the high point of their group-life, the Pharisees apparently did not.[280]

The Pharisaic groups thus centered their focus on the ordinary, everyday meals and the various rules had to be observed daily, for every meal.[281] All the evidences point to the fact that meals occupied an important place in their community.

Food items at the fellowship meals were used as boundary markers for the associations in the community. For instance:

> Five associations who sabbathed in one dining hall: The School of Shammai says: [they need] a community marker ('*eruv*) for each association. But the School of Hillel says: [they only need] one community marker for all of them. And they agree that in the situation where some of the groups are in [different] rooms or attics, then they need a community marker for each association.[282]

The '*eruv* or "community marker" which is discussed in detail in this section of the Mishnah relates to a portion of food. The different schools debated, if many associations come together in a public place whether they need one community marker or one for each. *m. Erub.* 7:10–11 indicate it

---

278. Neusner, "Two Pictures," 534–35.

279. But through inference from these rules, some suggest that there was ritual gathering of some sort, E.g., Oppenheimer, "*am Ha-aretz*," 136.

280. Neusner, "Two Pictures," 535.

281. Cf. Ibid., 535–36; see also Neusner, *From Politics to Piety*, 86–90.

282. *m. Erub.* 6:6.

usually was a loaf which the participants contribute together to pay for it and which is shared during the evening meal of the Sabbath. By partaking in the "community marker" they become officially bonded to a particular association formed for the occasion.[283]

The reason for having a "community marker" was to fulfil the requirement of the law in case there were a number of associations in a dining-hall, by helping to form a boundary to separate the groups for religious and practical reasons.[284] Also the unity designated by the "community marker" enabled the households of an association to perform certain tasks during the Sabbath. By extending the area by virtue of their association with different households, the families could carry out certain activities allowed by the Law, which would not have been otherwise possible.[285]

Among the Pharisees, fellowship meals were linked with their interpretation and observance of the Law in every detail. Since their observance of the Law was related with the concept of reward and punishment from God, fellowship meals also became an important part of their lives. As the community members met together fellowship meals played an important role in the functioning of the group, meeting the needs of the community at different levels of their socio-cultural and religious life. It defined the community's identity and gave expression to their religious beliefs. Since eating and assimilation of ideology were considered synonymous; to eat or partake in others' meals implied a person's participation in the whole system, therefore maintaining self-identity was also attained by abstaining from fellowship meals belonging to others. This is a continuous theme in the literature in Judaism.

---

283. "A 'community marker' is a portion of food which becomes a legally valid way of linking together a group of people as if they were one household." Instone-Brewer and Harland, "Jewish Associations," 12.

284. Ibid. They suggest that the purpose was to fulfil the requirement that the members participating in a meal had to recline, facing each other but not the members of another association. In case this is unavoidable due to presence of many groups in a hall, then the "community marker" acted in a symbolic way of creating that boundary separating the different groups and also by bringing unity within that group through the participation in that single loaf. They conclude: "each group would be then defined by this symbol of their unity rather than by their physical separation during the meal"

285. Ibid., 9.

Fellowship Meals: Practices in the Ancient World

Exclusion, Inclusion in Joseph & Aseneth

The Jewish-Hellenistic legend of Joseph and Aseneth which depicts the importance of meal practices in Judaism is another significant literature which has been seen as having a close affinity to the Lord's Supper tradition.[286] The expression "to eat the blessed bread of life and to drink the blessed cup of immortality" has led some to see this as an allusion to the Lord's Supper.[287] There are numerous references to meal practices and food motifs in the text[288] which has been a matter of debate with some suggesting Christian interpolation.[289] Kuhn and others see the reference to "oil" in the text as formulaic references to some sort of cult meal similar to the Essenes.[290] On that basis, the meal is seen as mediating immortality.[291] On the other hand, some scholars have argued that the meals described in Joseph and Aseneth are not cultic meals but ordinary meals. Jeremias sees the reference to the anointing of the guest before the meal, the bread, cup, and ointment as referring to ordinary Jewish meal rather than a special sacramental rite. But he sees solemnity attached even to the "ordinary" meals where a blessing was pronounced.[292] Burchard also thinks that the meal terminology is a reference to the daily Jewish meal, which itself had a solemn religious character.[293] Since the daily meals were accorded the same importance in the

---

286. Regarding the date: "Most scholars would agree nowadays that *JosAs* was written in Greek in the Egyptian Diaspora no later than Hadrian (117–138) or more probably Trajan (98–117), and not earlier than 100 BC." Burchard, "Importance of Joseph and Aseneth," 104.

287. Kilpatrick sees similarity in Joseph and Aseneth and the Lord's Supper, and suggested the significance of *Joseph and Aseneth* for the understanding of the Last Supper. Both the meals are sacramental and exhibit a common pattern, he thinks that the cultic meal in Joseph and Aseneth was related to the Lord's Supper, though not as its model. Kilpatrick, "Last Supper," 6.

288. *Jos. Asen.* 8:5, 9; 15:5; 16:16; 19:5; 21:21.

289. But this is now rejected by most; see Kuhn, "Lord's Supper," 75; Kilpatrick, "Last Supper," 6.

290. Kuhn, "Lord's Supper," 75. Oil was used for a wide range of purposes, from dietary, medicinal to religious functions, it was also used as an important symbol in many of the Jewish writings; Chesnutt, *From Death to Life*, 134.

291. Kuhn, "Lord's Supper," 76.

292. Jeremias, "Last Supper," 91–92.

293. "For one thing, benedictions were to be used whenever a man consumed anything larger than an olive, and if the occasion was a meal, some benedictions were to be repeated during its course . . . This goes well with the idea that the threesome 'bread, cup, and ointment' reflects the traditional triad 'bread, wine, oil' as used for the basic means

53

other Jewish sects, the meals described in Joseph and Aseneth were probably the daily meals. Chesnutt observed that the meal terminology here bears a close similarity with the non-ritual character of the Pharisaic fellowship meal, which was used as an antithesis to the heathen meals defiled by idolatry. In both instances the meals were considered highly and they functioned to define the identity of the community.[294] Thus the consensus in that the reference to food, drink, and oil (8:5–7) in Joseph and Aseneth is a reference to ordinary fellowship meals which embody the complete way of being in the Jewish society, in contrast to Gentile existence. But Kuhn's observation that the meals were sacramental is valid to a certain extent as one can see the qualifying genitives—life, immortality, incorruption that follows the description of the meals.

The reason for using the meal terminologies was that, as Chesnutt rightly shows:

> the effort to maintain a distinctively Jewish way of life in precisely those areas in which susceptibility to Gentile impurity was considered to be the greatest, namely, food, drink, and oil contaminated by association with idolatry. So representative of Jewish identity in a Gentile environment is the peculiarly Jewish use of these three items that the entire life *more judaico* comes to be expressed in a triad or dyad so formulaic that it has been assumed—probably mistakenly and certainly too readily—to be a liturgical formula referring to a special ritual meal.[295]

The importance of fellowship meals associated with the observance of purity laws seemed to be behind the use of meal terminology in Joseph and Aseneth.[296] The strong salvific language used here suggests that there was a strong belief that by partaking in the Jewish way of life embodied in the fellowship meals, one could attain "life" and "immortality" in contrast to the Gentile practices which would lead to death. The meal also refers to prose-

---

of human subsistence which in turn goes back to similar triads summarizing the produce of the land." Burchard, "Importance of Joseph and Aseneth," 113.

294. Chesnutt, *From Death to Life*, 178–79 He further asserts that: "the context wherein these concerns were operative seems to have been ordinary meals and, more generally, routine daily conduct, rather than communal gatherings for ritual meals. Thus there is even greater reason for comparing the 'meal formula' in *Joseph and Aseneth* with the table fellowship tradition in Pharisaic circles than with other traditions where communal meals of a *ritual* or *sacramental* character appear."

295. Ibid., 135.

296. Ibid., 133.

Fellowship Meals: Practices in the Ancient World

lytism, and in a way similar to the membership in the Qumran community where it was confirmed with the participation in a meal. The meal stands as a designation of Aseneth's renunciation of idolatry and her conversion to the God of Israel. Some scholars see similarities to the mysteries in the text.[297] H. C. Kee likewise observes that Aseneth's participation in a meal to be part of the Jewish way of life is modelled after the Isaic initiation.[298] The similarities with the other Jewish groups as well as other cultures indicates the author's use of common meal motifs, at the same time shows his own unique interpretation of those traditions. Here Aseneth's partaking in the food implies her new identity. The implication is that, by eating the bread, drinking the cup, and being anointed with the ointment, she participated in life, immortality, and incorruption. Unlike the Qumran community she gains immediate access to the benefits the meal represented.[299]

The meals in Joseph and Aseneth show the significant role they played in the theology of Gentile conversion. The references to meal practices show how they functioned as a boundary marker and gives identity to the participant and an expression and realisation of one's faith. Thus partaking in a meal was identified with a person taking over a complete new way of life in itself. The use of meal terminology in the story shows how meals were used in conveying the history and faith of the people. The meals represent not only the way of life and culture but the principles and values that lie behind those practices. Thus the need to maintain the fellowship meals as the vehicle of communicating God's gifts to the people requires that they separate themselves from the defilements of the Gentile world characterized by idolatry.[300] Joseph and Aseneth show how the ideal Jew can preserve

---

297. M. Philonenko, in particular, developed the notion that the bread, cup and ointment in Joseph and Aseneth represented a sacramental meal comparable to those of the cults of Attis, Cybele, Mithra and Isis; by providing the same promise of immortality offered in those cultic meals, the author of Joseph and Aseneth hoped to attract his readers, to the Jewish mystery cult. *Joseph et Aséneth*, 63–64; E. W. Smith, supports Philonenko's view that the bread-cup-ointment formula is part of the evidence for an initiation liturgy in *Joseph and Aseneth* comparable to that of the mystery religions and is designed to show that conversion to Judaism confers the benefits offered by the mysteries. "*Joseph and Asenath*, 23–26, 32. See Chesnutt's critique: "Even if Philonenko and Smith are right that JA represents Judaism as conferring the *benefits* of the mysteries, it would not necessarily be by means of a *sacred meal* that Judaism confers those benefits." *From Death to Life*, 251.

298. Kee, "Socio-Cultural Setting," 399, 403.

299. Chesnutt, *From Death to Life*, 188.

300. *Jos. Asen.* 7:1; see also 8:7.

his or her identity through the meal practices, and thereby become part of God's family.

Eschatological Judgement and the Messianic Banquet

The importance of fellowship meals in Judaism is further enhanced and attested by the meal motif associated with the future hope and judgment. The joys of the end-time are symbolized as a great and bountiful banquet. It is symbolized as a time when God gathers the entire community in a great banqueting hall to celebrate in a lavish eschatological banquet. This motif is further heightened with the presence of the Messiah at the meal, celebrating together with the people God's final victory and judgment. Even in other religious cults and associations, the motif of 'sacred food' and the presence of gods in the fellowship meals is a concurrent theme, but in Jewish literature this occurs more prominently.[301] This meal tradition is the basis of the meal stories in the Jesus tradition and also that of the early church.

A whole range of fellowship meals dealing with the end-time or afterlife can be put under the purview of this term, and not only those which have a reference to the Messiah.[302] In the OT there are a number of passages that refers to this meal motif.[303] Blenkinsopp argues that the motif of the eschatological banquet appears first in Isa 25:6. The image is part of the ceremony of the accession of Yahweh to the throne on Mount Zion and in Jerusalem.[304] Similar traits are also found in other traditions, e.g., the *Enuma Elish* (3.129–38) and the Ugaritic Baal texts (SIN 35–59) also speak of banquets following the victory and ascension to the throne of Marduk and Baal respectively.

This motif is further enhanced in the Wisdom and Apocalyptic literature, where food symbolising wisdom and other divine qualities is offered to the righteous at the end time.[305] In *Odes Sol.* 6:8–18, it is the "living water

---

301. Even among the Greeks and Romans the festive banquet was used to symbolise a joyous afterlife; e.g., Plato *Resp.* 2.363.c-d. Lattimore, *Themes in Greek and Latin Epitaphs*, 52. This is also seen in Greek funerary reliefs whereby the deceased is pictured reclining at a banquet. Cf. Smith, "Messianic Banquet," 66.

302. Smith, *From Symposium*, 166; see more on the origin of the motif from mythological stories of the ancient Near East, in which the gods wage a battle and the victory is celebrated with a great banquet; 166–169.

303. Mic 5:2–4; Zech 9:17; and Ezek 34:23–24; Isa 25:6; 65:13–14.

304. Blenkinsopp, *Isaiah 1–39*, 357.

305. *1 En.* 24:4–25:7; *T. Levi* 18:11; *4 Ezra* 1:19; 8:52; Wis 16:20; Ps 78:25; Rev 2:7;

Fellowship Meals: Practices in the Ancient World

of eternity" that snatches the soul from death.[306] Likewise the manna "bread from heaven" in the Exodus account is associated with divine food that confers wisdom and eternal life.[307] Also mentioned in Joseph and Aseneth is the "bread of life" and the "cup of immortality" and a honeycomb which is identified as the food of the angels that provides immortality to all who eat of it, echoing a similar theme.[308] In Judaism, food symbols related to the idea of immortality or eternal life to be bestowed at the end time, run throughout the extant literatures as a prominent theme.[309]

The eschatological banquet motif continues to appear in the pseudepigraphical literature. *1 Enoch* and *2 Enoch* depict that the "elect" are the ones who will eat with "Son of Man forever and ever."[310]

From ancient times, victories at war and deliverance have been celebrated with feasting, so also, the motif of the "messianic banquet" associates with it as the main theme the fight and victory over the malevolent forces.[311] The main features of the messianic meal include celebration in the presence of the Messiah of victory over primordial enemies with an abundance of food and wine, and eternal joy. This is followed by the gathering of the nations and judgment which takes place in the form of reversal of fortunes for the participants.[312] This motif is also seen in another form—the wedding banquet, along with victory celebration this also incorporates the commemoration of kinship and bonding of the people with divine entities, which is symbolized in a sacred marriage.[313] This motif is used frequently

---

22:2, 14, 19.

306. Cp. *Odes Sol.* 11:7–8, 30:1–7.

307. Exod 16:1—17:7; Num 11:7–9; 20:2–13; see the interpretation of this tradition by Philo *Leg.* 2:86; 3.166–170; cf. 1 Cor 10:1–13.

308. *Jos. Asen.* 16:14; the "bread of life" is also identified with manna. See Burchard, "Joseph and Aseneth," 114, 116.

309. For more on Food Symbolism in Judaic Tradition, see Feeley-Harnik, *Lord's Table*, 71–73; Goodenough, *Jewish Symbols*, 12.94–131; Jeremias, *Eucharistic Words*, 233–240.

310. *1 En.* 62:13–14; *2 En.* 42:5; The Messianic banquet is also present in *3 En.* 48:10; similarly in *2 Bar* 29:4–8; cf. *4 Ezra* 6:52; *1 En.* 60:24 and *Baba Bathra* 74b (Babylonian Talmud).

311. Cf. 1 Chr 12:38–40 reflects this tradition. Also Isa 25:6–8; Smith, "Messianic Banquet," 64–65.

312. E.g., *1 En* 62:12–14; *2 En* 42:5; *3 En* 48A.9–10; Isa 25:2–8; Joel 2:24–26, 3:18; *2 Bar.* 29:1–4; cp. The "unfailing table" of *4 Ezra* 9:19; Smith, *From Symposium*, 169; Blomberg, *Contagious Holiness*, 77.

313. Smith, "Messianic Banquet," 68. On the connection of the wedding banquet

in both the OT and NT to describe the relationship between God and the people.[314] In many instances it is connected with the apocalyptic banquet tradition.[315]

Questions have been raised as to whether these meals were actually practised or whether they are just mythological presentation of a narrative world. Based on the data, the general consensus is that the eschatological or messianic banquet was more of a mythological and literary presentation of the aspiration and climax of the end-time scenario.[316] However, in some circles like the Qumran community there were meal practices where there were literal expressions of this motif. We have noted that some of the leaders took a symbolic role of the Messiah at the meal.[317] All these texts are a product of a social context reflecting the values of the times, so to put all the depiction of the fellowship meal, as a literary depiction seems far-fetched. Cross's suggestion that the text should be seen as a "liturgical anticipation" of the Messiah and their meals as a "foretaste" of the eschatological banquet is tenable.[318] So given their theological stand and belief, their meals were considered messianic in nature, as it was held in honor of the Messiah with a belief that he was present and experienced by the members existentially. The association of fellowship meals to past and future events implied that they have the ability to transcend time and history. Thus they were related with the commemoration of historical events to the celebration of future events. They brought a sense of belonging to people at the events through their participation in the meals. Therefore, in all probability these meals were observed with anticipation of the future hope and perhaps to a certain extent were seen as a proleptic event. It was a participation in a yet to-be fulfilled eschatological expectation of the end time events.

---

with the mythological motif of the victory banquet, see Collins, *Combat Myth*, 223–24. On the theme of "sacred marriage" in ancient Near Eastern myth and ritual, see esp. Pope, *Song of Songs*, 374–75, 504–10.

314. Hos 2:1–23; Isa 54:4–8; Ezek 16:7–8; John 3:39; 2 Cor 11:2; Eph 5:23–32.

315. Isa 54:5—55:5; Matt 9:15//Mark 2:19–20//Luke 5:34–35; Matt 22:1–14; 25:1–13; Luke 14:7–11; John 1:1–11; 3:29; *Gos. Thom.* 104; Rev 19:7–9; 21:2, 9; 22:17; Smith, "Messianic Banquet," 68.

316. Cf. Smith argues that the messianic banquet is a literary narrative rather than historical, "Messianic Banquet," 69; "Table fellowship," 158.

317. Cf. Cross, *Ancient Library of Qumran*, 88.

318. Cross, *Ancient Library of Qumran*, 90; also Kuhn, "Lord's Supper," 65–93.

Fellowship Meals: Practices in the Ancient World

Black's statement, "every meal in Judaism was in a sense a religious meal"[319] is not far-fetched looking at the meal practices in Judaism, and the way the people interpreted food as one of the most important forms in which God's promise and word was embodied.[320] They epitomized the entrance into God's realm of blessedness. Partaking in meals symbolized participation and belonging to God's covenant. Thus fellowship meals can be considered as an integral expression and embodiment of their way of life, a norm for their religious faith and socio-political entity.

CONCLUSION

The meal practices in the Greco-Roman world, especially seen in the different clubs and associations, show the important role fellowship meals played in the communities and how they directed their daily interaction with one another and with the surroundings as well. They provided the means to the people for social and religious interaction and to maintain their own identities. Though there are different names given to the meals practices, they were held basically for companionship and association, thus they can all be categorized as "fellowship meals."

Though most of the data on meal practices in the Greco-Roman context have focussed on fellowship meals in the form of the symposia which developed into a formal institution, we should not overlook the importance of the ordinary Greco-Roman meals as well. First all the meal descriptions in the literature cannot be categorized as symposia on the basis of some features, because some of the features like reclining were widely practiced in different settings as well. Secondly, the importance of food and meal traditions was not limited to a particular form of observance like the symposia but its universal appeal and application transcended all forms and permeated all cultures.

The survey of the Jewish literature reveals that fellowship meals played a pivotal role in the functioning of the community as in the other communities in the Greco-Roman world. The remarks of Rabbi Yochanan and Rabbi Eleazar who said, "a man's table makes atonement for him" is a clear example of it.[321] It clearly indicates the central role of the fellowship meals

---

319. Black, *Scrolls and Christian Origins*, 115.
320. Feeley-Harnik, *Lord's Table*, 91.
321. *b. Ber.* 55a.

Exclusion and Judgment in Fellowship Meals

in the socio-religious life of the people.[322] Just as they celebrated God's faithfulness in the past through their meal practices, in like manner the future hope and restoration was expressed and celebrated through the fellowship meals. We have observed that the different groups in Judaism used the fellowship meals to express their identity and belief system. Thus we see similarities as well as different practices among the groups. From a cultic perspective to an eschatological one, their practices varied.

The dietary laws were based on the Law and reflected their belief system of being a "called out" community. There was a high evaluation of fellowship meals and a strong concern to maintain purity during the meals to consummate and maintain this identity. We notice that fellowship meals and judgment motif were closely connected, and the concept of judgment was integrated into the fellowship meal traditions. Moreover the imagery of fellowship meals was used to express and develop their theology. We can see this in the messianic banquet and other motifs, which were important metaphors in defining the whole belief system in Judaism. Here we see the merging of theological motifs with the fellowship meal tradition to enhance its appeal and wider usage, making it more meaningful and contextual. The anticipation of the end time and the expectation of the fulfilment of future hope were brought closer as the communities participated in the fellowship meals.

Meals in general became the ground of social and religious distinction between Jews and non-Jews, and helped them to maintain their identity. At the same time, there are many similarities between the Jewish practices especially in the intertestamental period to that of the Greco-Roman customs. There can be no doubt that the Greco-Roman practices have made their mark in Judaism. For example, during this period, in Jewish society reclining had become the standard posture at both social and religious events. But the meanings associated with these practices differed according to their own cultural and religious interpretation. Status, which was strongly associated with the Greco-Roman meals, was not the same at the Jewish meals, though ranking was practised to a certain extent. Likewise, washing before eating, had evolved into a religious ritual in Judaism.[323] However, the reception of the Greco-Roman customs was mixed. For instance, Philo also reflects on the Greco-Roman meal practices and goes on

---

322. See Bruce Chilton who advocates the view that the temple sacrificial system was replaced by the fellowship meals which acted as a surrogate system; *Feast of Meanings*.

323. *m. Hag.* 2:5. Cf. John 2:1–2; Mark 7:3; Luke 7:44–46.

to denounce the symposia as immoral and vulgar.[324] Some groups like the Qumran community and Therapeutae developed their meals as a counter reaction to their culture, thus we see negligible impact on their community. But this was just part of the whole picture as some of the meal practices advocated by the moralists and philosophers were also emulated by the different groups in Judaism. Nonetheless the similarities as well as the dissimilarities in meal practices reveal how meal traditions developed to define the cultural and religious identity of the different communities.

---

324. Philo points out the negative influences of the Greco-Roman associations and their practices at the tables: "There are vast number of parties in the city whose association (*thiasoi*) is founded in no one good principle, but who are united by wine, and drunkenness, and revelry, and the offspring of those indulgencies, insolence; and their meetings are called synods (*synodoi*) and couches (*klinai*) by the natives." *Flacc.* 136.

CHAPTER 2

Fellowship Meals
Their Roles and Functions in the Ancient World

INTRODUCTION

WE HAVE SEEN IN the earlier chapter that fellowship meals appear prominently in both the Greco-Roman and Jewish traditions. In this chapter we will look at the specific roles and functions of fellowship meals in the different cultures of the ancient world that made them indispensable for the functioning of societies. Then we will consider how a judgment motif is associated with the fellowship meal traditions. In the process we will also compare the different traditions and see how they can contribute to the study of the Lord's Supper in Corinth.

COMMUNAL BONDING

One of the salient features of fellowship meals is their ability to create bonding among the participants. This communal aspect of the meal is observed wherever people gathered for fellowship meals. Thus one chief aim of meal cultures in the ancient world was to form new affiliations and further strengthen this communal bonding among the participants. To be invited or to join together for a meal denotes that a person was accepted and was an integral part of the group.

Fellowship Meals: Their Roles and Functions in the Ancient World

In the Greco-Roman context, Plutarch refers to this as "the friend-making character of the table" in his works.[1] Implying that, one function of the fellowship meal was its cohesive character as it brought about κοινωνία (koinonia) and the strengthening of social ties or kinship.[2] The very act of coming together to eat and the sharing of food at a table were symbolic of the bonding that was being created among the participants.[3] Thus, Plutarch reproved certain behavior that might upset the whole process: "But where each guest has his own private portion, companionship perishes."[4] The reason is that when individual portions/shares are distributed it "kills sociability and makes many dinners and many diners with nobody anybody's dinner-companion..."[5] Thus no one is a "fellow-diner" (σύνδειπνος) with "anyone," i.e., when equitable and proper sharing is not followed the whole purpose of the fellowship meal is defeated.

Keeping this concern in mind the number of participants was usually ideal and according to the size of the banquet room so that it would not hinder proper conversation and bonding among the participants.[6] Plutarch again writes on this matter:

> If both space and the provisions are ample, we must still avoid great number, because they in themselves interfere with sociability and conversation. It is worse to take away the pleasure of conversation at table than to run out of wine.... People who bring together too many guests to one place do prevent general conversation; they allow only a few to enjoy each other's society, for the guests separate into groups of two or three in order to meet and converse, completely unconscious of those whose place on the couches is remote and not looking their way because they are separated from them by showy dining rooms... that hold thirty couches or more. Such magnificence makes for un-sociable and unfriendly banquets where the manager of a fair is needed more than a toastmaster.[7]

---

1. Plut. *Quaest. conv.* 614 A–B; *Cat. Maj.* 25.4.

2. Cf. Plut. *Quaest. conv.* 660A–B; 643B–E.

3. Cf. Diogenes Laertius 8.35, where the "friends" in Pythagoreanism had as the symbol of their unity the sharing of "one bread." "Not to break bread; for once friends used to meet over one loaf, as the barbarians do even to this day; and you should not divide bread which brings them together."

4. Plut. *Quaest. conv.* 644C.

5. Ibid.,. 643A.

6. Cf. Ibid. 5.5; 678E–F.

7. Ibid., 679B–C.

Anything that would hinder bonding and development of friendship at the table was to be avoided. With this in mind the seating arrangement usually consisted of three couches laid out in a "C" shape so that everyone could see each other.[8] The name of a dining hall *triclinium* was derived from this practice of having three couches τρίκλινον. Plutarch again suggested that along with the sharing of wine from the same cup, even the topic for discussion should be properly chosen so that everyone present will be able to participate in it, and thus further enhance the amiability of the fellowship meal.[9] The main activities of the clubs and associations were also centered on fellowship meals, as they were effective means of bringing cohesion among the members.

Meals eaten in funerary banquets in honor of dead family members indicate the notion of continuing the communal bonding even in the afterlife. The Greeks believed that the deceased was not only present at the funerary banquet held at the deceased's house after the funeral but he/she was actually hosting it.[10] This expression shows how fellowship meals were a strong symbol for the belief system in the Greco-Roman world. We have already noted this character in the Jewish communities that the fellowship meal was a principal way of developing and nurturing personal and social relations.

Communion with the Gods

Fellowship meals were an integral part of religious practices. In fact they occupied a central place in the worship of most of the religious groups in the ancient world. Basically they were extensions and part of the worship and sacrifices in the temples, and food sacrificed to the gods was part of the meals.[11] They were considered to create bonding among members and with

---

8. This can be seen in an archaeological excavation of a *triclinium* at Ostia. Instone-Brewer and Harland, "Jewish Associations," 10.

9. "Indeed, just as the wine must be common to all, so too the conversation must be one in which all will share." Plut. *Quaest. conv.* 614D–E.

10. Artemidorus *Onir.* 5.82.7.

11. Rowley mentions similar examples in the OT, Deut 14:22–26 and other references where such sacrificial meals before God were enjoyed. This common practice was also found among the Canaanites (Judg 9:27), Babylonians (Dan 5:1–4), and Egyptians, including their several rituals (Exod. 32:6). Rowley, *Worship in Ancient Israel*, 125–26.

the gods/goddesses; this is especially the case in meals that were considered as sacramental.[12]

In the fellowship meals where sacrifices were part of it, the gods were thought to be present as guest or host in the meals held in their honor.[13] So bonding happened in two levels, by eating the food from the altar a solemn bond of union was formed firstly among themselves, and then secondly with the deities. Through the sacrificial banquets people believed that a connection was made with the deity; the offering of the sacrificial food at the altar and the burnt offering symbolized the consumption of the food by the god. This type of offering was called the τραπεζώματα (*trapezomata.*)[14] In this type of fellowship meal there was a belief that the food that had come in contact with the altar was affected by the "spirit of divinity" and it became sacred food. This idea is seen in the legend that describes the origin of the Bouphonia at Athens. Farnell suggests that people taking part in such meals "might be conscious of a real sacramental communion" with the deity.[15] Nock comments that Romans perhaps had a deeper understanding of this sacred rite.[16] The communion between the participants and the gods was thought to be achieved by partaking in the same flesh of the offered animal and thus created a bond between them.[17] The significance of these sacrificial meals was due to the belief that the participants ate of the god's table in his presence or because of their partaking of the food set before the god, at the altar or before an image or statue. A good example is seen in Aristides's hymn to Serapis (26–28):

> What Homer said of all the gods, that they may be turned and appeased, is confirmed most strikingly by Sarapis: so many turns does he turn for the well being of those who at any times need him. Wherefore men have the true partnership in sacrifices with this god alone above all others: they invite him to their hearths and set

---

12. The term sacramental is used here in a broader sense referring to the meal events where the gods were believed to be present and were involved in the fellowship meals. For the kind of fellowship or bonding that was achieved see the discussion in Angus, *Mystery Religions*, 131–33.

13. Homer terms a sacrifice a "meal of the gods" (*Od.* III 336; see *Od.* VII 201–3 where the gods could be seen dining with the Phaeacians. Cf. Ovid *Fast.* IV 743ff.; for more examples see Nock, "The Cult of Heroes," 153–54.

14. Gill, "Trapezomata," 117–18.

15. Farnell, "Sacrificial Communion," 312–13.

16. Nock, "Cult of the Heroes," 153–54. Cf. Tac. *Ann.* 13.17.

17. Nock, "Cult of the Heroes," 148–49.

> him in the chair as guest and entertainer (*hestiator*): so that where some make up one party and some another, Sarapis alone makes up all parties and is lord of the feast for those who at any time come together under his auspices. . . . He is at the same time participant in libations and the receiver of libations . . . there is a similar partnership—as of equals in honor with an equal in honor,—of men with him in other matters: so merchants and sea captains do not just give him tithes, but they share with him equally as a fellow merchant and partner in all their undertakings.[18]

The characteristic feature of the sacrificial meal was the strong association with the gods who acted as the host of these meals and were supposed to be present with the participants.[19] For example, the Oxyrhynchus Papyri reveals the invitation sent by the gods to the inhabitants of the town: "The exegetes requests (sic) you to dine in the (temple of) Demeter today, which is the 9th, beginning at the 7th hour (1 p.m.)"[20] A comparable invitation to dine "at the table of Lord Serapis" is found in at least three other papyri—Oxyrhynchus Papyri 110, 523, 1484.[21] This is also seen from stone inscriptions of the cult banquets of Zeus at Panamara in the region of Caria in Asia Minor; in this inscription the god invites various cities of the region to attend his festive celebration:

> Since the god invites all the people to the feast and provides a table shared in common and offering equal privilege to those who come from whatever place they may come . . . I [priest] invite you [the Rhodians] to the (house of the) god to share in the festivity which he [the god] provides.[22]

It further states "because there exists between our cities a kinship to one another and a commonality of sacred rites."[23] Thus through this kind of association social and political ties were also forged and the meals functioned

---

18. Cited from Nock, ibid. 150.

19. Cf. M. H. Jameson who states: "in a larger sense the gods were the hosts in their sanctuary and the meal came from the animals given to the gods," "Sacrifice and Ritual: Greece," 972. More examples of gods depicted as hosts and guest at the table are presented in Nock, "Cult of Heroes," 152, 154–55; Angus, *Mystery Religions*, 128.

20. Oxyrhynchus Papyrus 1485 in Grenfell, *Oxyrhynchus Papyri* XII, 243–44.

21. Grenfell *Oxyrhynchus Papyri* I, 177; III, 260; XII, 244; XIV, 180. Also see Youtie, "Kline of Sarapis," 13–14.

22. Hatzfeld, "Inscriptions de Panamara," 74; translation from Smith, *From Symposium*, 81.

23. Hatzfeld, "Inscriptions de Panamara," 73–74.

Fellowship Meals: Their Roles and Functions in the Ancient World

to further define and strengthen these relationships between individuals and communities. A general view is seen in the writings of Xenophon: "The goddess provided for the worshippers barley, bread, wine, and dried fruit, and a portion of the sacrificial victims from the sacred land and a portion of the animals captured in the hunt."[24] This explains why these meals are referred to as the "table of the god" with the priest acting as the representative of the god.[25]

In other cases the gods were guests at the banquet.[26] This is seen in the sacrificial meal θεοξένια (*theoxenia*), which literally means "hosting the gods." In these meals the presence of the god was probably represented by his cult image and by assigning a place and food at the table.[27] In the *Iovis Epulum* the worshippers participated in serving the god at the banquet.[28] All these data indicate the important role the cultic meals played in the mystery religions and cults.[29] The meals were connecting links between the deities and the worshippers and a platform to express their devotion and experience the divine reality.

In the mystery religions, initiates underwent secret ceremonies to attain membership into the cult and it was believed that through these ceremonies they became recipients of "salvation." Here also the essential element of the mystery was a fellowship meal which was considered as sacred in nature.[30] By participating in the meal the initiate got a new status and identity and the sacred meal acted to enhance the bond between the initiate with the deities, in whose fate the partaker receives a share.[31] A

24. Xen. *Anab.* 5.3.7–13.

25. Xen. *Symp*, IX

26. Aristides comments that at the banquet table, the god was at once host and guest, *Aristides* 45.27.

27. Youtie, "Kline of Sarapis" 13–14. Cf. Smith, *From Symposium*, 78.

28. Angus, *Mystery Religions*, 128; Also see Nock, "Cult of Heroes," 152–53. He states that: "A god could be host or guest. He is guest in various rituals of Theoxenia and Theodaisia, as again in ordinary sacrifice to which he was invited; the dead also were invited to meals."

29. "The frequent observance of sacred meals maintained the communion among the *mystics* of Cybele, Mithras, or the Baals." Cumont, *Oriental Religions*, 41.

30. Cf. *Metam.* 11.24 Apuleius himself calls it a sacred or religious dinner by which Lucius' initiation was "duly consummated."

31. Apuleius *Metam.* 11.21–24, the initiation takes place by partaking in a sacred meal. There is a preparatory abstinence from "unhallowed and unlawful foods" and after the initiate undergoes a number of different procedures like purification and ablution, finally the initiation is consummated on the third day by participating in a celebratory meal.

good example of this kind can be seen in the cult of Serapis. The union was achieved through the means of the fellowship meals and thus the meals came to be denoted as "couch of Serapis."[32]

This sacramental feature associated with the fellowship meals was common to many of the religious groups. One of the popular cults in the Greco-Roman world, the Eleusinian mysteries, held their annual festival which consisted of rites and a festive meal that were considered sacramental in nature.[33] The cult of Dionysus and the Mithraic mysteries which were widespread in the ancient world also show that there were feastings which involved being intoxicated and the partaking in the raw flesh of a bull slaughtered for the purpose in which the god was thought to be incarnated.[34] By drinking and feasting on the flesh they were seen as "incorporating the god and his power within."[35] This was a sacred meal in which the worshippers by consuming the flesh sought to become one with the god.[36] Only those initiates who had attained certain requirements were admitted to the meal.[37]

The description of the cult meals in the form of liturgy and hymn in the Mystery Cult of Isis and Serapis by Lucius[38] and by Aelius Aristides[39] along with the Oxyrhynchus Papyri that talk about meal invitation of these cults involving Serapis, indicate that the meals were regarded as sacramental. Bultmann argues further that the idea of communion brought about by the sacramental meal was not unique to the mystery religions alone; but it was wide spread in primitive and classic cults.[40]

Though the issue of sacramentality of these cult meals is still debated, it is clear that they played significant religious as well as social roles in the community. One can agree with Horsley who concludes that: "although it

---

32. Aristides *Sarapis*, 26–28.

33. Mylonas, *Eleusis and the Eleusinian Mysteries*, 224–26.

34. Euripides *Bacch.* 64–168.

35 See Cumont, *Mysteries of Mithra*, 115–60; Vermaseren, *Mithras*, 103; Ferguson, *Backgrounds of Early Christianity*, 243.

36. Koester, *History, Culture, and Religion*, 181.

37. Cumont, *Mysteries of Mithra*, 158.

38. Apul. *Metam.* 11.

39. Aristides, *Aristides*.

40. Bultmann, *Theology*, 1.148–49.

Fellowship Meals: Their Roles and Functions in the Ancient World

was a matter of some disagreement earlier in the century, there is now a clear consensus that these banquets had a fundamental religious character."[41]

In the Jewish context we have noted that they played an important part in cementing their relationship with God, among themselves and with the other nations. Thus bonding through covenants, treaties, friendships and settlements between people were frequently formalized and celebrated through fellowship meals.[42] Likewise they were the mainstay in the religious expression of the people.[43]

Therefore, meal practices had an important role in the functioning of the community as it created community ties and further strengthened their bonds. Some have raised reservation in regard to the extent of creating new communal bonding during the meals, but there are evidences suggesting that communal bonding can take place even among strangers, as seen in some of the tribal communities in the Near East.[44] In the NT also the narratives show that fellowship meals were an integral part of Jesus' ministry and of the newfound community in reaching out to people in the periphery. The fellowship meal in the form of the Lord's Supper emphasized the social bonding in the community and we can conclude that it was a means of incorporating new members into the community. Thus, the fellowship meal was an indispensable institution in the ancient world to foster and maintain community ties and their relation with the deities. This feature of the fellowship meal practices formed one of the bases of their association with the judgment motif in ancient cultures.

SOCIAL DIVISION AND STATUS

The stratification of society based on social, economic, and political status was a driving force in Greco-Roman society. One principal way of achieving this was through the practice of fellowship meals, which were used to create and maintain social divisions and status. In ancient cultures, to dine

---

41. Horsley, *New Documents*, 6.
42. Gen 26:30–31; 27:33; 31:54.
43. Exod 24:9–12; 1 Kgs 8:62–66.
44. Smith is of this view: "however, that while meals were effective and widely used for celebrating community solidarity, they were not capable of creating a community *in themselves*. Rather communal bonds of some sort would need already to exist before a group would gather for a meal. The meal may help to enhance those bonds but it would not create bonds that do not exist originally." "Historical Jesus at the Table," 470.

at the table of the kings and emperors represented the highest honor and status.⁴⁵ This feature was practised even at the fellowship meals in many of the clubs and societies. In the Greco-Roman society the symposium was initially dominated and controlled by the aristocratic class, and it was a means of displaying one's wealth.⁴⁶ Thus it was also called an "aristocratic banquet" or "reclining banquet" to describe this same custom.⁴⁷ Maintaining the status and position of patrons at the fellowship meal was seen as a necessity to maintain the social system and to keep control over society.⁴⁸

Originally the banquet seems to have been an exclusive affair reserved for men only (who were free citizens), as women, children, and slaves were excluded from it.⁴⁹ In late antiquity, women were allowed to take part in the pagan Roman banquets and slaves were also included on special occasions.⁵⁰ Even when they were present the women were seated separately from the men or in the lowest couch.⁵¹ This was also the case with the youth

---

45. See Fisher, "Roman Associations," 1214–1215 for Roman emperors and their banquets. We can see a number of examples of this kind even in the OT. 2 Sam 9; 1 Kgs 2:7; 2 Kgs 25:27–30; and Jer 52:31–34.

46. Ath. *Deipn* 128–30d.

47. Schmitt-Pantel, "Sacrificial meal," 15. This was no surprise as organizing a banquet involved a lot of expenditure and usually slaves would be involved.

48. For example, as was the case in Greek society, aristocracy over the city. Schmit-Pantelt, "Sacrificial Meal," 15. Suetonius, *The Deified Augustus* 2.74: reports how Augustus paid strict attention to rank and status at a dinner party as it contributed to the stability of the state by reminding all persons that they should know their place and be content with it. D'Arms, "Roman Convivium," 308–20.

49. In family occasions women were part of the table fellowship (Plut. *Quaest. conv.* 612F) or else the other reason for their presence would be for entertainment at the symposium and usually they turn up to be prostitutes (PW, 4:1203). Though an incident is mentioned by Plutarch where Melissa and Eumetis attended the symposium, but they remained silent through out and leave well before its conclusion (*Sept. sap. conv.* 150D–155E). Likewise there is no mention of women involved at the table talk in the symposium of Plato, Xenophon, and others.

Aune also observed that women holding positions in religious societies would in fact be part of the cult symposia (e.g., Poseidippos as summarized in Ath. *Deipn*. 9.377). He concludes that "the inclusion of women in some cultic activities constituted a considerable innovation;" Aune, "Septem Sapientium," 71–72.

See K. E. Corley who suggests that by the first century CE the scenario was changing in the Greco-Roman society. Women from wealthy families are seen to be reclining at the meals indicating a shift in the status of women. So ". . .the inclusion of women in Christian meals would have been noteworthy but not unique." *Private Women*, 24–79.

50. Cf. Lucian *Sat*. 13. Fisher, "Roman Associations," 2.1201.

51. E.g., Lucian *Symp*. 8; Ath. *Deipn*. 14.644d. In the Homeric accounts, Queens like

Fellowship Meals: Their Roles and Functions in the Ancient World

Autolycus who was seated next to his father who reclined, even though the banquet was given in his honor.[52] Even at a later time when reclining was more inclusive and included women in its fold, there was still a debate and stigma attached to sitting at the table.[53] For example, Lucian writes about a certain man who states that it is "womanish and weak" to sit at a table, when he was invited to sit rather than recline as there was no more room on the couches when he came late.[54]

Status was also associated with the type of fellowship meals organized by the various clubs and associations. Some trade guilds were formed by members having lowly profession, and people attending fellowship meals organized by such groups were frowned upon. This is noticeable in a comment made by Plutarch:

> ... if ignorance and lack of culture keep company with wine, not even that famous golden lamp of Athena could make the party refined and orderly... The outcome of undisciplined chatter and frivolity, when it reaches the extreme of intemperance, is violence and drunken behaviour—an outcome wholly inconsistent with culture and refinement.[55]

Fellowship meals were organized by the patrons and in return they expected the participants to reciprocate through honoring or acknowledging the status of the patrons, which also included meals. For example, an inscription from Delos reveals that an association of merchants, shippers, and warehousemen on Delos called the Berytian Poseidoniastai, honored their benefactor, a Roman banker named Marcus Minatos son of Sextus, who provided funds for their welfare and banquets.[56]

Arete among the Phaeacians, Helen at Sparta and Penelope at Ithacan were present during the symposia, but they do not seem to participate fully in the eating and drinking (*Od.* 1.225–226; 9.5–10). In the beginning women probably had to sit but by the late republic, they were able to recline in equality (Cicero *Fam.* (9.26). Fisher, "Roman Associations," 1201. Cf. Stein, "Symposia Literature," 31–32.

52. "Autolycus took a seat by his father's side; the others, of course, reclined." Xen. *Symp.* 1.8.

53. Jesus is also depicted as reclining in most of his meals. Cf. Jeremias, *Eucharistic Words*, 48–49.

54. Lucian *Symp.* 13.

55. Plut. *Quaest. conv.* 716D–E.

56. *IDelos* 1520 (153/2 BC); more examples are seen in *IDelos* 1521 and other inscriptions. Cf. Ascough, "Forms of Commensality," 19–21.

Exclusion and Judgment in Fellowship Meals

Invitations to fellowship meals would also denote a person's importance or rise in society; at the same time refusal of an invitation would mean the host's inferior social status.[57] The disparities based on class were displayed during the meals, as guests had to be entertained and served by the servants/slaves of the host.[58] Social ranking was seen prominently at the arrangement of assigned places for reclining at the table where people would be seated according to their social status. Plato describes the position and status at the table which were assigned by the owner of the house.[59] There were also instances where two or more of the same status would share the same couch.[60] In general the seating arrangement at the table was done clockwise from the highest to the lowest position.[61] There were also the "lesser" guests—often known as "shadows" (*umbrae*)—"hangers-on" of important guests, or "those used as reserves if the more distinguished guests failed to turn up."[62]

It was considered offensive to deprive someone of his accustomed honor at the table. Therefore, guests had to be seated at the table according to their relative position in society.[63] The theme "each man according to his worth" seemed to have been followed at the tables.[64] So certain places at the table were considered to be most honored, and others would be arranged accordingly, though the location varied from the practice of one people group to another.[65] These honored places at the table seemed to be taken seriously. Plutarch talks about an occasion where many guests had assembled and had reclined in places they wished. A guest (probably a per-

---

57. Cicero showed his disregard when asked to dinner by a municipal gentleman of whom he has never heard (*Fam.* 7.9; 7.16).

58. Plato *Symp.* 175A, 213B.

59. Ibid., 177D-E.

60. It is indicated both in the literature and in vase paintings of Greek banquets. Smith and Taussig, *Many Tables*, 24-25.

61. Smith and Taussig, *Many Tables*, 24.

62. Fisher, "Roman Associations," 2.1205-6.

63. Lucian *Symp.* 9.

64. E.g., "Timon will say that one ought not to rob the other guests of the honour due to position by granting the position of honour to one of them . . . . for the man who turns an individual's prerogative property is committing a theft, and the recognition due to virtue, kinship, public service, and such things he is giving to the foot-race and to speed. Though he thinks that he avoids being offensive to his guests, he draws it down all the more upon himself to be so, for he offends each one of them by depriving him of his accustomed honour." Plut. *Quaest. conv.* 617C.

65. Cf. Smith, *From Symposium*, 10.

Fellowship Meals: Their Roles and Functions in the Ancient World

son of high order) came and refused to enter saying "he saw no place left worthy of him."[66] He also indicates that for the Romans there was also a place for guest of honor, which was the highest position and was designated to be that of the "consul." The name would suggest that its position was associated with political power and reputation.[67] All this data reflects a consciousness for social status and division in society in relation to the custom of reclining. Lucius Apuleius even comments that the ability to drink while reclining was what distinguished man from animals.[68]

Plutarch continues to give a description of how different people hold different places in honor:

> the Persians the most central place, occupied by the king; the Greeks the first place; the Romans the last place on the middle couch, called the consul's place; and some of the Greeks who dwell around the Pontus . . . contrariwise the first place of the middle couch.[69]

Status at the meals was a potent issue and there were discussions on whether they needed to follow the conventional custom of assigning places or do away with the ranking.[70] Perhaps this issue is addressed in the Mishnah, when it indicates that even the poor are to "recline" at the meal.[71]

In some instances the host would divide the guests into two groups. While the first group which consists of his closest friends and those with higher standing in the society were invited into the *triclinium*, the rest would then be accommodated outside at the *atrium* where treatment was less than equal.[72] Fellowship meals thus were a good indicator of a person's status in society.

Ranking at the meal thus became the norm for most of the Greco-Roman meals and it was considered a sign of "good order" that should characterize a banquet.[73] Plutarch comments that failure to do so would

---

66. Plut. *Quaest. conv.* 615D.

67. See the discussion in Plutarch's *Quaest. conv.* 619B: "Why the place at banquets called the consul's acquired honour."

68. Apuleius *Metam.* bk. 10.

69. Plut. *Quaest. conv.* 619B.

70. Cf. ibid., 615–17.

71. *m. Pes.* 10:1.

72. Cf. Murphy-O'Connor, *St. Paul's Corinth*, 158–59.

73. Smith and Taussig, *Many Tables*, 33.

lead to "disorderliness."[74] Along with the honored position, a person of high status could also be entertained with a better quality or quantity of food he was given.[75] So guests with higher status would receive better quality and quantity of food, likewise lesser quantity and quality for people of lower status indicating their position. This was a usual practice in the *collegia* where officers were assigned larger quantities of food than other ordinary members.[76] Pliny for instance writes about his experience at a banquet with disfavor:

> ... I happened to be dining with a man-though no particular friend of his-whose elegant economy, as he called it, seemed to me a sort of stingy extravagance. The best dishes were set in front of himself and a select few, and cheap scraps of food before the rest of the company. He had even put the wine into tiny little flasks, divided into three categories, not with the idea of giving his guests the opportunity of choosing, but to make it impossible for them to refuse what they were given. One lot was intended for himself and for us, another for his lesser friends (all of his friends are graded) and the third for his own freedmen. My neighbour at table noticed this and asked me if I approved. I said I did not. "So what do you do?" he asked. "I serve the same to everyone, for when I invite guests it is for a meal, not to make class distinctions; I have brought them as equals to the same table, so I give them the same treatment in everything." "Even the freedmen?" "Of course, for then they are my fellow-diners, not freedmen." "That must cost you a lot." "On the contrary." "How is that?" "Because my freedmen do not drink the sort of wine I do, but I drink theirs."[77]

Timon the brother of Plutarch vents his displeasure against such abuses as "the rich lording it over the poor."[78] This practice of serving different types of food to different guests according to their social status at the fellowship meals was another custom that reinforced the social distinction in the society. This practice was widespread in the clubs and guilds.[79] Usually

74. Plut. *Quaest. conv.* 615E.
75. Cf. Lucian *Sat.* 17; Mart. *Epig.* 60; Juvenal *Sat.* 5.156–70.
76. Meeks, *First Urban Christians*, 68.
77. Pliny the younger *Ep.* 2.6. Also Mart. *Epig.* 3.60; 1.20; 4.85; 6.11; 10.49; Juvenal complains of such a practice during a banquet where the rich were served with better wine and food and where the poor were mistreated. Juvenal *Sat.* 3.81, 152–56; 5.152–55.
78. Plut. *Quaest. conv.* 1.2.
79. For example, hierarchy was very much a part of the Iobacchoi association. Cf. Crossan, "Who and What Controls your Banquet?" 304–5.

Fellowship Meals: Their Roles and Functions in the Ancient World

the symposiarch or the host would be expected to assign the place to the participants and also to oversee the distribution of food and drinks to these special guests.[80] Many of the satirists also write about how guests from a lower social class were humiliated during meals through insults and nasty games, reinforcing the ranking system.[81]

Feasts given in honor of gods or in celebration of victories and other occasions also fuelled the system. On these occasions the rich would give lavish banquets for the community as an indicator of their wealth and power. Fellowship meals thus were an expression of the social division in the community on the basis of socio-economic criteria, and they provided a means to maintain the patron-client system of the ancient society.

In the Jewish context, ranking at these meals can be noticed among the sectarian groups like the Essenes and the Therapeutae, though not on the same level as the Greco-Roman practices.[82] Among the other groups like the Pharisees, stratification was on the basis of the purity laws within the group, as well as in relation to outsiders.[83] Thus in Judaism the practices were different to that of the Greco-Roman culture. The stratifications were rather based on the interpretation of the Law applied to the fellowship meals.

Fellowship meals thus functioned as a means of creating social rankings and status as well as maintaining that classification or division of status. This is so because the fellowship meal was an important social institution, and for many of the groups the fellowship meal was the chief and sometimes the only common activity for them. This is evident in many writings, including the Gospels, where fellowship meals provided a platform to display and assert a person's social status and ranking and for enforcing those rankings and other cultural norms in the society.[84] Thus, it was a prestige

---

80. Plut. *Quaest. conv.* 615C-D.

81. Mart. *Epig.*; Juvenal *Sat.*; Petron. *Sat.* 59; Lucian in *De mercede conductis* (*Salaried Posts in Great Houses*) reports that Greek philosophers and rhetoricians were humiliated by their Roman employers and hosts during banquets. For an explanation on honor and shame, patronage and reciprocity, that prevailed in the Greco-Roman world of the first century see, deSilva, *Honor, Patronage, Kinship and Purity*, 23-42.

82. Philo, *Contempl.* 67.

83. In the Qumran community the placement of individuals at the communal meal was specified according to their rank in the community, *Rule of the Congregation* [1QSa] 2:11-22.

84. Cf. Luke 14:1-24.

issue for many to get their proper place at the fellowship meals in recognition of one's social status in the society.

There was lot of symbolism and meaning associated with the practice of fellowship meals. They were in fact a reflection of societal norms and values. Therefore the participation in the meals conveyed a deeper reality and this insight should assist us in interpreting the meal practices in Corinth.

SOCIAL IDENTITY

In ancient cultures fellowship meals were one of the principal ways of marking the differences among social groups. Since meals represented societal values and norms, they were used as boundary markers between various groups, and therefore they became a means of defining a community. Thus even the symposium in the Greco-Roman context was 'a social institution' whereby through association people asserted their own identity.[85] Fellowship meals had manifold functions in society out of which bestowing shared social identity to the participants was one of the most important.

Partaking at a table defined the person in relation to the group and also his place in the larger society. In the Greco-Roman world, fellowship meals developed into a more formal institution and functioned in similar manner among the various clubs and religious associations. Fisher asserts that:

> . . . most, if not all, of these groups defined themselves, at least in part, in cult terms, reinforcing their identities through shared sacrifices to particular deities; and third, such gatherings regularly involved shared feasting on the sacrificed meats and shared drinking of wine.[86]

Meals defined the group by functioning as the arena in setting prescribed norms according to their belief system. This is seen in the various laws of etiquette and other procedures set for the meals. The Guild of Zeus Hypsistos[87] is a good example of how the fellowship meal functioned to define a

---

85. Schmitt-Pantel, "Sacrificial meal and *Symposion*," 15.

86. Fisher, "Greek Associations," 2.1168.

87. The Guild of Zeus Hypsistos was an Egyptian form of organization that shared the characteristics of both Greek and Egyptian religious associations. Its statutes are preserved in a papyrus copy that dates from the latter Ptolemaic period, or circa 69 to 58 BC. Roberts et al., "Gild of Zeus Hypsistos," 59; Pausanias 2.2.8 tells of three images of Zeus at Corinth: one without epithet, one of him as Chthonios, one of him as Hypsistos.

Fellowship Meals: Their Roles and Functions in the Ancient World

group's identity and activity. They described themselves as "the association (*synod*) of Zeus Hypsistos." Though the term *synod* (σύνοδος) was especially used in Egypt as a generic term for religious and other types of associations, it was also used to describe associations in relation to a private dinner or an annual dinner established by a bequest.[88] The term was also used by Philo, to refer to the dining clubs in Alexandria: they "are called synods and couches by the natives."[89]

The statutes of the Guild of Zeus Hypsistos contain statements that define the groups in relation to the fellowship meals:

> May it be well. The law which those of the association of Zeus the highest made in common, that it should be authoritative ... he should make for all the contributors one banquet a month in the sanctuary of Zeus, at which they should in a common room pouring libations, pray, and perform the other customary rites on behalf of the god and lord, the king.[90]

These associations or groups were frequently coupled with the name of the god worshipped by the group and in whose honor the meals were eaten.[91] In these fellowship meals the procedures were also in keeping with their political and religious ideology.[92] Hence the libations were directed to the patron deity and the civic rulers in whose honor the meals were celebrated. They were made to conform to their political aspiration and their religiosity. In this manner the meals facilitated and preserved their political and religious identity, providing them with a tangible content and meaning to their belief system.

The partaking in the fellowship table of the cults and religious associations was synonymous with identifying with its beliefs and likewise similar to acquiring one's identity in relation to the group. The different customs practised at the table, like ranking, and distribution of food also reinforced their individual identity and distinction even within the same group. In some cults, through the eating of sacred food, the believers were thought to be fusing themselves with the deity to create a new deified identity.[93]

---

88. Roberts et al., "Gild of Zeus Hypsistos," 72; Smith, *From Symposium*, 107.
89. Philo, *Flacc.* 136. Cf. Smith, *From Symposium*, 107.
90. Quoted from Roberts et al., "Gild of Zeus Hypsistos," 41–42.
91. Roberts et al., "Gild of Zeus Hypsistos," 72–73.
92. Smith, *From Symposium*, 108.
93. E.g., the eating of a raw flesh in the cult of Dionysus was considered as partaking in the nature of the deity by which the person gets a new identity.

Exclusion and Judgment in Fellowship Meals

One of the principal ways in which the Jews in general maintained their identity was through the various food laws associated with purity and holiness (Deut 13–14), so that they would become "a people holy to the Lord your God . . . out of all the peoples on earth" (Deut 14:2).[94] The dietary laws defined the way the people could interact with others and within their own group. Thus they played the role of a boundary marker, and functioned to define and reinforce the identity of the people in the midst of diverse practices. As Feeley-Harnik explains: "their observance hallows the individual and sets him and the group to which he belongs apart from others."[95]

So mixing with Gentiles in a fellowship meal was seen as an abomination in some circles.[96] This has to do with the understanding that eating was synonymous with one's beliefs and values. Food and drink were thought to be especially prone to cultic contamination in primitive religions, and since meat from sacrifices, offerings and prayers to the pagan deities were the normal practice of the meal customs, the Jews were restricted from freely mingling with the Gentiles. The prophets thus made a connection between food and idolatry and warned time after time against eating with the Gentiles (Ezek 33:25; Hos 9:3).[97] Daniel's story and his refusal to eat the king's food portray the general attitude and beliefs related with the food laws (Dan 1:8). Eating the king's food was in effect accepting the culture and norms of a foreign ruler.[98] By abstaining from the court's food Daniel and his friends maintained their identity and expressed their fidelity to God.[99]

Many of the communities and religious groups in the Jewish society also had meals as a main point of reference for identification. This is prominently seen among the Essenes at Qumran, the Therapeutae, the Pharisaic

---

94. Tacitus in his report on the Jews, includes the observation that "in dining and in sleeping, they keep themselves strictly apart . . ." *Hist.* 5.4–5.

95. Feely-Harnik, *The Lord's Table*, 7.

96. Eating with Gentiles was considered polluting, for they ate "unclean" food that was furthermore likely to have been offered to idols. They ate "swine's flesh and broth of abominable things is in their vessels" (Isa 65:4; see also 66:3, 17). See explanations on the dietary laws in Blomberg, *Contagious Holiness*, 39.

97. But even other nations had their own dietary laws. In Gen 43:32, the Egyptians would not eat with the Hebrews for it was considered as an abomination to the Egyptians.

98. Since, "By eastern standards to share a meal was to commit oneself to friendship; it was of covenant significance." Baldwin, *Daniel*, 83.

99. See more on the issue of dietary laws in Daniel in Blomberg, *Contagious Holiness*, 62.

groups and reflected in most of the literatures, e.g., the story of Joseph and Aseneth. Thus there was an elaborate process of purification for a member in order to partake of the "common food."[100] This was because participation in the fellowship meals was regarded as a confirmation of one's membership in the community and the acceptance of its tenets. Thus in a way it was akin to having one's identity through participation in the meals.

In this context, there are arguments regarding the level of interaction between the Jews and Gentiles. We understand that stricter rules were followed among the sectarian groups, but in the Greco-Roman context, the common people would have interaction with others even in terms of dining together.[101] The *Letter of Aristeas* illustrates that if an appropriate menu was provided, then Jews could dine at a Gentile's table.[102] Josephus also describes how the Jews in Antioch mingled with the Gentiles in the period prior to the Jewish revolt: "they grew in numbers . . . and were constantly attracting to their religious ceremonies multitudes of the Greeks, and these they had in some measure incorporated with themselves."[103]

Thus fellowship meals became an integral part of defining and maintaining the identity of the individual and the community by creating and defining boundaries between various groups in the society. In fact they were so synonymous with the identity of the community itself that breaking the rules or social codes associated with them was equivalent to violating the community itself.[104] So even for the new Christian community fellowship meals became a means of defining and expressing the beliefs and values of the community. They served as a boundary marker for the new community.

---

100. Josephus, *J.W.* 2, 138–39.

101. For the interaction between Jews and others in terms of fellowship meals see Hein, *Eucharist and Excommunication*, 8–10; Blomberg, *Contagious Holiness*, 95; Dunn, *Jesus, Paul and the* Law, 142–48. Dunn discusses in detail the provisions in Judaism whereby they could mingle with the Gentiles. He argues that ". . . If such views were consistently and rigorously applied, no devout Jew could even have considered participating in table fellowship with a Gentile. But that is by no means the whole story. For there were Gentiles towards whom even the rabbis could maintain a very positive and welcoming attitude—Gentile converts to Judaism and Gentiles who showed themselves sympathetic to the religion of the Jews." 143.

102. *Let. Aris.* 182. *m. Ber.* 7:1; *m. Abod. Zar.* 5:5, and *b. Abod. Zar.* 8a-b, contains discussion of the conditions on which Jews might accept invitations to and participate in Gentile banquets. Cf. also Acts 15 where provision is made for Jews and Gentiles to intermingle in the same community.

103. *J. W.* 7.3.3 § 45.

104. Cf. Smith, *From Symposium*, 109.

Exclusion and Judgment in Fellowship Meals

Likewise, Paul builds on that tradition, rectifying some aspects, as the new community was formed on the basis of new laws and requirements. Laws and practices which were part of the fellowship meal tradition but did not conform to the new teachings were done away with; and new laws were added to conform to the teachings of the Risen Lord (Acts 15).

MORALITY AND ETHICS

We have already noted in chapter 1 the attempts to reform some of the features of the meal practices that were deemed detrimental to the society. Here we will discuss further how morality and ethical concerns were an integral part of the meal traditions. By forming and fostering relationships among participants, fellowship meals also involved further commitment and reciprocity. Communal bonding and social ethics were part of the same scheme in the fellowship meals. As the meal created community by bringing in cohesion among the participants, it was further designed to lead to ethical responsibility and obligation. Thus it was also a tradition that once a person was invited to a meal, he should also return the favor, ensuring that there was a reciprocal exchange of hospitality between them.[105] Among ancient Greek cultic associations there was a tradition where honored members were granted the right to carry away portions of a sacrifice.[106] Based on this tradition in the Greco-Roman context, apart from organizing the meals, host and patrons also gave gifts to the guest at dinner according to their status. The term *apophoreton* (*sportula* among the Romans) was used to denote this practice.[107] Though it was partly a demonstration of patronage and hierarchy, at the same time it denoted social dependency and obligation. The early church in Acts 6 exhibits a similar practice.[108]

Plutarch, in one of the discussions, talks about the reason for the custom of the ancient Romans, not to leave a table empty. He quotes Eustrophus:

---

105. In ancient cultures, reciprocity was a norm; cf. Exod 2:20; D'Arms, "Control, Companionship, and Clientela," 331–34; mentioned in Finger, *Of Widows and Meals*, 173.

106. See *SIG* 1025.46; 1026.4.

107. Suetonius *Vesp.* 19; *Dom.* 7; Petron. *Sat.* 56.

108. *Acts of Peter* (19–29) and Hippolytus also mention this practice among Christians. Cf. White, "Regulating Fellowship," 183–85.

Fellowship Meals: Their Roles and Functions in the Ancient World

> ... So too the kings of Persia (they say) not only always send portion to their friends and officers and body guards, but even see that the slaves' dinner, and the dogs' dinner, are served on their table, in so far as this is feasible, considering all who serve them sharers in table and hearth. For by passing out food even the most sullen of wild beasts can be tamed.[109]

We also see a political motif here, nonetheless the social obligations at the fellowship meals were to be extended to the less fortunate in society. Fellowship meal practices thus were also a program of economic redistribution whereby people belonging to the lower economic class benefitted.[110]

Plutarch also includes a rationale behind such practices. He cites Lucius who recalled hearing from his grandmother that the table is sacred and that nothing sacred should be empty:

> that the table is in fact copied from the earth. For besides nourishing us, it is both round and stable, and by some it is properly given the name of "hearth." Just as we expect the earth always to have and produce something useful for us, so we do not think a table should be seen, when it is abandoned, bare and carrying no load of luck.[111]

This indeed indicates the table was considered as a sacred arena where one's conduct was important, as it might lead to further implications. Fellowship meals were symbolic of a deeper reality.

There are evidences that the different associations or trade guilds went beyond just sharing meals. Members provided one another with loans, with or without interest, with the meals fostering that kind of relationship for transaction and sharing of goods.[112] In Homer the term *eranos* frequently refers not only to a pot-luck dinner but to a practice where interest-free loans or donations are given to people in difficulties. In a further development it

---

109. Plut. *Quaest. conv.* 703E.

110. Also see Hippolochus's description of Caranus's feast, where a lot of wealth was distributed among the guests, Ath. *Deipn.* 128; cf. Ath. *Deipn.* 194c–195f; 196a–203d; 210c on Ptolemy II and other kings who conducted feasts for their citizens. Thus Fisher comments: "... it is nonetheless true that ordinary citizens were heavily dependent on the largesse both of the ruler (monarch or protector) and of the wealthiest citizens." Fisher, "Greek Associations," 2.1191–92; cf. "Roman Associations," 2.1215.

111. Plut. *Quaest. conv.* 703B.

112. Ascough, "Forms of Commensality," 22–23. Also see Blomberg, who maintain that social concerns were limited within one's own social group; *Contagious Holiness*, 64.

Exclusion and Judgment in Fellowship Meals

referred to money collected by the acquaintances of a slave to buy his or her freedom, which would be repaid later.[113]

In Judaism while the dietary laws reinforced the people's identity and acted as a kind of barrier to outside influences, at the same time social and ethical concerns were integrated into the fellowship meals and juxtaposed alongside the attempt to maintain their exclusive ethnic and religious identity. Thus there were laws to incorporate the marginalized, the poor, and the outsiders into the community.[114] This is also seen in the Passover celebration. In *m. Pes.*10:1 "the pauper bowl/dish" was the collection for the itinerant poor, which was different from the *basket* collection for the poor in the community.[115] This is perhaps why Josephus mentions the presence of a large number of beggars during Passover in Jerusalem.[116] Normally, non-family members of a Passover association had to pay their share for the expenditure of the sacrifice;[117] so this fund was to enable the poor to pay their contribution to partake in the Passover.[118] In Sirach, the Jewish sage devoted an extensive section to meal etiquette under the rubric, "Judge your neighbour's feelings by your own and in every matter be thoughtful."[119] He writes about one's conduct at the table and proper behavior towards others.

Social ethics were also part of the meal etiquette. Smith and Taussig assert that under the "symposium laws" etiquette was included as an important ethical category,[120] such that a person's manners and behavior at the table should serve for the common good of the members. Hence, there were rules and regulations governing behavior at fellowship meals. For example, the above concerns are included in the statutes of the Guild of Zeus Hypsistos:

---

113. Cf. Fisher, "Greek Associations," 2.1188.

114. E.g., Lev 23:22; In Num 9:1–14 provision is made to include those who were unable to participate in the first Passover celebration because of ceremonial impurity, and circumcised resident aliens share in the covenant meal of the people. Cf. Josh 8:33, 35.

115. Re. *m. Pea* 8:7.

116. Jos. *J.W.* 2.10.

117. *m. Pes.* 7:3

118. Cf. Instone-Brewer, "Tractate *Pesachim*," 60–61; he adds "No doubt most householders would have happily welcomed a poor person without charge, but they probably wanted to pay so that they felt they had a real portion in the sacrifice, just as people wanted to pay the Temple Tax in order to share in the Temple sacrifices (*m. Sheq.* 3:3)"

119. Sir 31:15–31.

120. Smith and Taussig, *Many Tables*, 31–32.

Fellowship Meals: Their Roles and Functions in the Ancient World

and they shall be present at all command occasions to be prescribed for them and at meetings and assemblies and outings. It shall not be permissible for any one of them to . . . or to make factions or to leave the brotherhood of the president for another, or for men to enter into one another's pedigrees at the banquet or to abuse one another at the banquet or to chatter or to indict or accuse another or to resign for the course of the year or again to bring the drinkings to nought or . . . to hinder the (leader?)[121]

Here the members were required to be present for all the occasions and participate for the full year that the statutes cover. It was considered illegal to join other groups during this period. They were prohibited to cause schisms, accuse or abuse members within the group. More importantly they were not to do anything that could be detrimental to the group or cause dissolution of the convivial occasion. The rules covered numerous aspects of their social-religious life, from proper conduct and behavior within the club, to sincere worship.

Similar rules are seen in the statutes of the College of Diana and Antinous,[122] an Italian funerary society of the second century CE, and in the association of devotees of Dionysus/Bakchos who called themselves *Iobakchoi*—the Athenian society of the second century CE.[123] In these associations the banquet was the main activity, the rules were in regard to one's behavior and conduct at the table, so that the monthly banquet could be celebrated with proper decorum. They provided extensive and significant information about the religious clubs and showed how fellowship meals were an important means for expressing themselves and their identity, and in the process became synonymous with their identity itself. By describing the rules of conduct they defined their identity as distinct or separate from other groups. These meal ethics are good evidence of how fellowship meals defined one's behavior and relationship with others in the community. Again, though these rules were meant for the meal context, nonetheless

---

121. Text and translation from Roberts et al., "Gild of Zeus Hypsistos," 41–42.

122. The rule states: ". . . If any member desires to make any complaint or bring up any business, he is to bring it up at a business meeting, so that we may banquet in peace and good cheer on festive days" (lines 2.23–24 Statutes of the College of Diana and Antinous: Translation from Lewis and Reinhold, *Roman Civilization*, 2.273–75).

123. See Smith, "Meals and Morality," 324. Though the inscription of this all-male *Iobakchoi* association dates to the second century C.E the association was formed much earlier, with their own meeting hall west of the Acropolis, near the Aereopagus; Crossan, "Who and What Controls your Banquet?" 304.

there was scope for pursuing them further outside the meal settings, as the following discussion indicates.

Social obligation was a topic that was being frequently discussed by the Greco-Roman writers during the fellowship meals. The occasion of a fellowship meal thus became a setting for philosophical discourses for many of the philosophical schools and other associations.[124] They provided a platform for many of the moralists and thinkers to voice their social concern and their call for ethical responsibility towards others. These discussions on social ethics during the symposium following the main course became so popular in the Greco-Roman society that they developed into a literary form of their own.[125] This tradition can be traced to Plato's *Symposium*, who spoke of "symposium laws," which became a standard for others to imitate.[126] Plato's *Symposium* describes a meal at which Socrates was present. During the symposium, the philosophical discussion centered on the ethical concept of ἔρως or "love."[127] Other topics delving into social concerns and obligations for fellow members were discussed, and Plato advocates that this should be the preferred subject for discussion at the fellowship meals. This became a familiar theme in later works of this genre; and was held in high esteem in some circles. Plutarch exhibits a good example of this type when he describes his writing as following the symposium tradition of the famous philosophers: "the most famous of the philosophers . . . Plato, Xenophon, Aristotle, Speusippus, Epicurus, Prytanis, Hieronymous, and Dio of the Academy, who all considered the recording of conversations held at table a task worth some effort."[128] They were to be emulated, as they were examples for proper conversation at fellowship meals.[129] Plutarch further describes topics of discussion that were suitable for the symposium:

---

124. A description is given by Aulus Gellius which describes regular dinner meeting at the home of the philosopher Calvisius Taurus: "At the entertainments which it was the custom of us young men to hold at Athens at the beginning of each week, as soon as we had finished eating and an instructive and pleasant conversation had began . . . (*Noctes Atticae* 15.2. 3)." Smith, "Meals and Morality," 321.

125. Cf. Smith, "Meals and Morality," 321–22. Stein, "Influence of Symposia Literature," 13–44; reprinted in Fischel, *Essays*, 198–229.

126. These laws were to safeguard all symposia from disintegrating and to promote "friendship" rather than enmity. *Leg*, 2.671C–672A. Smith, "Meals and Morality," 321–23.

127. Cf. Plato *Symp*. 177E.

128. Plut. *Quaest. conv.* 612D.

129. Ibid., 613.

Fellowship Meals: Their Roles and Functions in the Ancient World

> Some are supplied by history; others it is possible to take from current events; some contain many lessons bearing on philosophy, many on piety; some induce an emulous enthusiasm for courageous and great-hearted deeds, and some for charitable and humane deeds. If one makes unobtrusive use of them to entertain and instruct his companion as they drink, not the least of the evils of intemperance will be taken away.[130]

The reason for choosing such topics, as he suggests, was that they were appropriate and instructive. Moreover, they should be profitable and for the "primary good" of all. Just as they shared out of the same meal, so also the discussion should be communal in nature where everyone could participate in it.[131] Plutarch also underscored "the friend-making character of the table," which was an ethical category in Greek philosophy.[132] According to Plutarch, it is not only about sharing food and wine but engaging with one another in conversation and fun that should ultimately lead to "friendship."[133] Thus behavior and discussion at a meal were to be guided by this principle, as his writings reveal.

The common practice of presenting more and better food to special guests in the Greco-Roman context meant that the wealthier had more for themselves, which also implies that they showed less consideration for the welfare of the poor. This practice was condemned by many of the conscientious people of the time. Thus Juvenal and others gave a critical evaluation of this custom and spoke out against this sign of inequality.[134] Plutarch strongly emphasized that there should be equality and fair treatment among the guests.[135] Failure to do this causes "injustice and strife."[136] Thus he also supported the idea of reinstating the office of symposiarch to maintain order and propriety at the table so that no one was affected.[137] By inference the Moralists were speaking out against the social injustices of society which also manifested at fellowship meals.

---

130. Ibid., 614A-B.
131. Cf. Plut. *Quaest. conv.* 614D-E.
132. Plut. *Quaest. conv.* 612D; Smith, "Meals and Morality," 322–23.
133. Plut. *Quaest. conv.* 660B.
134. Juvenal, *Sat.* 5.152-55, and Mart. *Epig.* 3.60; 4.85; Pliny the Younger *Ep.* 2.6.
135. Plut. *Quaest. conv.* 642C.
136. Ibid., 644C.
137. Ibid., 620A–622B.

Exclusion and Judgment in Fellowship Meals

The connection between the ethical aspect and fellowship meals is found in other Greco-Roman literature, especially in the form of satire.[138] In these works the writers were critical of the system in society where injustices were being done. These works use motifs associated with the meal practices and appeal to all for ethical and moral responsibility towards others in society.[139]

The very notion of sharing at a table also brought an awareness of one's obligation towards another in the community. Unlike today's context, there appears to be an intricate connection between fellowship meals and morality and ethics. Social ethics were never divorced from the fellowship meals as these two went hand in hand in order to make the system feasible. Furthermore the fellowship meal settings were the primary or main activity for many of the groups. Hence, we see the inner dynamics of a meal setting and the various ethical or religious teachings of ancient cultures co-existing together.

The social-ethical concerns connected with the fellowship meals were a reflection of the corporate dimension that was characteristic of the ancient world. An individual act was considered as the expression of the whole community, and this applied even to the fellowship meals where actions had to be understood in the context of the wider community. Therefore, even when it comes to dining they had to act according to the laws set or else there were wider repercussions for the individual and the whole community. Thus various food laws and purity laws were enacted and maintained in the communities. This is especially relevant to the Corinthian context and Paul who saw the community as the embodiment of the Body of Christ, which was to be reflected even at fellowship meals. In similar terms we will see that Paul's admonishment and advice to the Corinthians are closely linked with the fellowship meal traditions.

---

138. On Greek and Roman satire see especially Ramage et al., *Roman Satirists*; Duff, *Roman Satire*.

139. See Smith, "Meals and Morality," 323: "Here the banquet functions as a symbol for the pretensions of cultured living, and thus serves an ethical function, for by ridiculing the society there represented, satire implicitly refers to a standard of conduct that should be present. Thus the banquet carries a symbolic force in itself, functioning as a kind of paradigm for comments on social ethics."

Fellowship Meals: Their Roles and Functions in the Ancient World

Egalitarianism

Since social division and status were a big concern in the meal practices, attempts were also made to reform that practice. Hence it appears as a prominent subject in the work of many Greco-Roman writers who advocated equality at the meals. Just as food was shared from a common table creating communal bonding, they also appealed that all the participants were to be considered equals at the table. This was often promoted as a standard procedure of the meal etiquette.

This theme of egalitarianism is found as early as Homer, where "equal banquets" are said to characterize the dining habits of the heroes,[140] and down the centuries in the writing of the Greco-Roman moralist and philosophers.[141] The pledge of equality at fellowship meals was offered to the worshippers of Zeus Panamoros.[142] The fellowship meal of the cult at Panamara, which was to be characterized by "equality" (ἰσότιμος), probably indicates the need for breaking down social barriers based on class and status, which were often the case in other meal contexts. In this case, since worshippers came from different cities, there was also the issue of ethnicity and political affiliations. This might have exacerbated the issue of equality as some groups got special preferences and privileges based on their place of origin. The objective was to ensure that all participants took part in the festivity with a certain degree of equality for the festive period. And probably this "equality" was achieved by the abolition of special assigned places at the table and by doing away with the entertaining of special guests with "different quality or quantity of food."[143]

In *Saturnalia*, the theme of equality is stressed in the dialogue between the god Kronos, the father of Zeus and Lucian. Kronos, also known as Saturnus, gives laws to govern conduct at the Saturnalia, Kronos's own festival. This was one of the most popular Roman festivals in which slaves

---

140. Hom. *Il.* 1.468, 602; 2.431; 1.554; 1.707; 7.357.

141. Cf. Smith and Taussig, *Many Tables*, 33–34.

142. "Since the god invites all men to the feast and provides a table shared in common and offering equal privilege to those who come from whatever place they may come..." Inscription printed in *Bulletin de correspondence hellenique* 51 (1927) 73–74; mentioned in Smith, *From Symposium*, 82. Since ranking was practised at the meals, question has been raised on what is meant by the term "equal"? It is still inconclusive; "but that some sense of equality was a strong part of the 'social code' of meals is nevertheless apparent." Smith and Taussig, *Many Tables*, 33–34.

143. Cf. Smith, *From Symposium*, 82–83.

were permitted to take the place of their master, including at the banquets. In these banquet laws, the god (i.e., Kronos) instructs the people: "Let every man be treated equal, slave and freeman, poor and rich."[144] The law basically dwells on the theme of equality and freedom for which the festival was celebrated and known. Accordingly Kronos continues:

> Each man shall take the couch where he happens to be. Rank, family, or wealth shall have little influence on privilege. All shall drink the same wine, and neither stomach trouble or headache shall give the rich man an excuse for being the only one to drink the better quality. All shall have their meat on equal terms. The waiters shall not show favour to anyone. . . . Neither are large portions to be placed before one, tiny ones before another, not a ham for one and a pig's jaw for another—all must be treated equally.[145]

An important aspect of this instruction is its association with judgment. The instruction comes with the implication that if they are not followed judgment will follow.[146] Kronos further demands:

> Every rich man shall inscribe these laws on a slab of bronze and keep it in the centre of his hall, and read them. And it must be realized that as long as this slab shall last neither famine nor plague nor fire nor any other harm shall come to their house. May it never be taken down! For if it is, Heaven avert what is in store for them![147]

This stark warning is given to the people, that the banquet rules on equal treatment would be observed during the fellowship meals. These laws indicate the attempt by moralists of those days to advocate equality at the banquets, with religious sanctions for wider acceptance as authoritative instructions. This motif appears in the works of many more writers. Xenophon recounts how Socrates taught people how to treat everyone equally at the meals, such that some of the rich participants were ashamed for not sharing with others.[148] Plutarch also dwells strongly on this motif of equality in his *Table-Talk*. He repeatedly emphasized equality among the guests.[149] In one instance he refers to a banquet where everyone agreed to

144. Lucian *Sat.* 13.
145. Ibid., 17. Also cf. Stein, "Influence of Symposia Literature," 29.
146. Lucian *Sat.* 10; also 12.
147. Ibid., 18.
148. Xen. *Mem.* 3.14.1.
149. Plut. *Quaest. conv.* 613F.

Fellowship Meals: Their Roles and Functions in the Ancient World

give up their assigned places at the table based on ranking;[150] arguing that the real essence of the fellowship meal is to instil equality and friendship and has nothing to do with "disorderliness" which has been associated with an abolition of ranking at the table by some.[151] Hence he also promotes a tradition regarding Lycurgus, who instituted common meals in order that "there may be for all an equal portion of food and drink and so that . . . the rich man may have no advantage at all over the poor man."[152] He further writes:

> If in other matters we are to preserve equality among men, why not begin with this first and accustom them to take their places with each other without vanity and ostentation, because they understand as soon as they enter the door that the dinner is a democratic affair and has no outstanding place like an acropolis where the rich man is to recline and lord it over meaner folk?[153]

This is instructive of the fact that the participants should put aside their scheme of societal status and ranking when they come to the fellowship meals. Athenaeus also speaks about a similar situation at fellowship meals, where equality was exhibited when both slaves and masters gathered for the same symposium.[154] Whether this was achieved realistically or not is not clear but this strongly suggests that Plutarch and other moralists were trying to advocate a new egalitarian social order using the backdrop of fellowship meal practices.

This concept of equality at fellowship meals is also exhibited in the Passover liturgy, which demands that there should be equal treatment given to the poor at the Passover table: "And even the poorest Israelite should not eat until he reclines at his table. And they should provide him with no fewer than four cups of wine, and even if the funds come from public charity."[155]

---

150. "And indeed, if the continuous toasts and the serving of food, and the conversation and discourse as well, shall be in strict conformity with the order of the guests' seating, our party will become in all respects a completely viceregal affair instead of a friendly gathering." Cf. *Quaest. conv.* 616C–F; 615E.

151. Plut. *Quaest. conv.* 615E.

152. Plut. *Mor.* 226E.

153. Plut. *Quaest. conv.* 616E–F.

154. "The Arcadians entertain at their celebrations masters and slaves, setting one table before them all; they freely serve food for all to share, and mix the same bowl for all." quoting Theopompus, ca. 410–370 BC; Ath. *Deipn.* 4.31; 149.

155. *m. Pes.* 10:1.

On the other hand, this notion of "equality" seemed to be in constant contrast and in tension with the issue of social stratification at the fellowship meals. Smith clarifies these seemingly contrasting features of the meal practices: "some individuals might be considered more 'equal' than others. Equality would not be understood as it is today, but rather would operate along with concepts of social status."[156] This is well reflected in Philo, who states that at the table of the Therapeutae equality was the rule of the day, and inequality was considered as the cause of all evil. At the table there were no slaves as it was considered "absolutely and wholly contrary to nature, for nature has created all men free" and women also shared in this feast. Yet women reclined apart from the men in a separate section of the room, moreover there were special places reserved for the elders at the table.[157] Thus they communicated both the values of equality as well as stratification and in the process created tension in certain cases as the boundaries were not well defined.

The fellowship meal traditions indicate their ability to accommodate the needs of the community in various ways. They may appear to be contradictory sometimes as they accommodate different cultural customs and values, nonetheless it shows the important role it played in the community. The advocacy of certain societal values and norms through these fellowship meals shows the potential it had to achieve the desired goals. Thus many of the writers used fellowship meal motifs to appeal for an egalitarian-based ideal society. Paul's appeal to the Corinthians should also be understood in the light of this environment.

SOCIAL POLITICS

Fellowship meals and politics were closely connected in the ancient world. Kings and rulers organized them to display their power and strength, to woo their subjects, and to forge alliances and treaties.[158] We have already seen ample examples in the OT revealing how fellowship meals were used for various purposes that were political in nature. They played an important

---

156. Smith, *From Symposium*, 11.

157. Philo, *Contempl.* 67–72, "and having offered up these prayers the elders sit down to meat, still observing the order in which they were previously arranged . . ." (67).

158. Hom. *Il.* 9.68ff.; *Od.* 4.5ff.; Ath. *Deipn.* 194c–195f; 614e–615a; Alexander was well known for conducting symposia both on campaign and in his palaces. Cf. Fisher, "Greek Associations," 2.1189–90.

Fellowship Meals: Their Roles and Functions in the Ancient World

part in bringing about reconciliation and settlements between people and nations.[159] They were part of the ploy to influence and win support and alliances.[160] Consequently, refusal to attend a feast denoted a change of alliance or loyalty.[161]

In the Greco-Roman context, symposium was also an important political institution. Meals were usually organized or paid for by the wealthy or the aristocrats, hence they undoubtedly tried to take advantage of the system for their own social or political gains.[162] As mentioned earlier, it was "a kind of organ of social control, exercised by the aristocracy on the city."[163] An example is seen from Aristophanes, who portrays symposia as the characteristic of the upper class and the top political "establishment." So Philocleon is taught the complete sympotic behavior, as a person to gain importance in society needed to know how to conduct himself in a symposium.[164] They were important in maintaining the socio-political system as they were used by the rulers and elites to cement their relationship with their subjects. Since fellowship meals involved reciprocal hospitality, it was also an important means to maintain contacts and friendship among the ruling class. Furthermore, the emperors and rulers gave lavish banquets to gain favor from the people and also to set an ideal image of themselves.[165]

In the Greco-Roman world the formation of clubs and associations contributed to their collective identity as a social group, leisure activities and more importantly for social security. We have noted that the meal

---

159. Gen 26:30–31, 54; 43:24–34; 2 Kgs 6:23.

160. 1 Kgs 1:9, 19, 25, 41, 49.

161. E.g., Judg 9:27; 1 Sam 20:34.

162. The same can be said of the hero-cults, where the patron or the patron's family would provide the resources for the banquets involving sacrifices and festivals, in order to remember and honor the cult figures, in the process maintaining their status and influence over the members. E.g., the cult of the *augustales* helped the emperor to consolidate his position as the chief source of loyalty, devotion, and patronage.

163. Schmitt-Pantel, "Sacrificial Meal and Symposion,"15. The importance of meal institution for a society is well reflected in Plato's *Laws* and Aristotle's *Politics*. Their analysis on the Spartan and Cretan social customs and institutions, among others, particularly the issues of common meals for the citizens, formed the basis for their general discussion of law and morality. Cf. Fisher, "Greek Associations," 2.1177, 1181.

164. Aristophanes *Vesp.* 1122–23; also see Cicero, *Att.* 13.52, how he entertained Caesar and his entourage with a banquet, demonstrating he "knew how to live."

165. E.g., Alexander and his successors regularly organized banquets to maintain close ties with their companions and allies and to consolidate their reign. Cf. Fisher, "Greek Associations," 2.1190.

Exclusion and Judgment in Fellowship Meals

practices were an important cohesive factor among the members, and this in turn was used effectively in advancing their policies. It is then not surprising that many of these associations were actively involved in the politics of that time for their own advantage. Candidates running for public posts thus had to win over the leaders of these groups and associations. Hence, Cicero's brother Quintus advises Cicero as a candidate for the consulship:

> Next, take into account the whole city, all the private groups [collegia], country districts, and neighborhoods. If you can win over the leading men in these to your friendship, you will through them easily gain the crowd.[166]

Formation of such groups also called ἑταιρεία (*hetaireiai*) was part of the political changes in Greece as members were frequently involved in political and other legal activities promoting each other.[167] People who had political ambitions therefore were very much involved with these groups.[168]

Therefore from the time of the archaic Greece, the state rulers were often wary of the dangers of these groups that could cause dissent and political disorder. For example the Bacchanalia groups in 186 BC were seen as a serious threat to social order by the state. Among the many allegations against the groups, the serious one was that the cults were demanding greater loyalty and commitment to themselves rather than the state. Seeing the threat to the social and political order, the groups were brutally suppressed and laws were passed limiting the formation and liberty of such associations. Again, in 64 BC a senatorial law was passed suppressing all collegia "not held to be in the public interest." These restrictions were loosened and imposed from time to time by the different rulers.[169] Aristophanes thus comments that a man was suspected of tyrannical ambitions if he bought

---

166. *On Canvassing for the Consulship* 30; cited from Lewis and Reinhold, *Roman Civilization*, 1.396. Thus, in 55 BC the consul Crassus passed a law specifically aimed at associations involved in electioneering through unfair means.

167. Aristotle *Pol.* 1311b.23f. For more examples on the political association with the symposium in Greek societies see Fisher, "Greek Associations," 2.1176–77, 1185.

168. Plato *Theaet.* 173d: "and the strivings of political clubs (*hetaireiai*) after public offices."

169. See, Suetonius *Jul.* 42; *Aug.* 32; Pliny the Younger, *Ep.*10.34, 35, 93, 94. Cf. In regard to the Jews see, Josephus, *Ant.* 14.10.8; Dio C. *Hist. Rom.* 60.6.6; Suetonius, *Claud.* 25.4. Fisher, "Roman Associations," 2.1200, 1204, 1210.

Fellowship Meals: Their Roles and Functions in the Ancient World

expensive fish in the market.[170] This suspicion against the groups and associations forms the background to the persecution of the early church.[171]

The formation of the different social and religious associations during the Hellenistic period increased manifold, but in many cases they needed approval from the senate or the emperor as a precautionary measure.[172] These groups and associations became a significant feature of the social and political life in the Greco-Roman society and the fellowships meals were an integral part of their meetings.[173] Thus fellowship meals formed an essential part of the socio-religious and political system and made direct impact on the politics of the ancient world. This connection between the fellowship meals and political ideologies in the ancient world will be important as we discuss the issue of division at the Lord's Supper in Corinth.

THE SACRED AND SECULAR DIMENSIONS

Another important question can be raised in regard to whether a dichotomy existed between sacred and secular meals in ancient times, since studies on the Lord's Supper tend to focus on the religious meals as its antecedent, and even the Lord's Supper is placed in the category of "sacred or religious meal." This idea is based on the foundational premises of the sociology of religion that sees the sacred and the profane as two separate realms of human existence. This division between the sacred and secular as two different realms can be misleading, since in ancient culture and practices, both were interwoven and interrelated because social and religious life were very much integrated.

This first indication of an association between the sacred and secular characteristic, is that prayer, libation, and even sacrifices were part of fellowship meals of both types. Therefore Plato speaks about the libations and a chant to the god before the start of a symposium of a secular nature.[174]

---

170. *Vesp.* 488–89.

171. Cf. Tertullian *Apology* 38.

172. In about AD 7 Augustus enacted a law that every *collegium* must be sanctioned by the emperor or the senate, with consideration given to charitable and religious associations and those who showed loyalty to the emperor and state. Cf. Suetonius *Aug.* 32.1; *ILS* 2.1.4966.

173. Hence the comment: "Greeks could see the dining room as a microcosm of the political world." Slater, "Peace, the Symposium and the Poet," 206.

174. Plato *Symp.* 176a.

Similarly Plutarch describes how the participants sing praises to Bacchus, and ascribe praises to the power of god at philosophical banquets.[175] In Plutarch's *De Musica*, the paean is recited at the end of the banquet and sacrifices are offered to Zeus, the other gods, and the muses. These libations, invocations, and sacrifices offered to the gods and heroes before the start of the symposium in social gatherings and non-cultic banquets[176] clearly attest to both the secular and religious elements present in these practices.

So describing the meal practices in antiquity, Athenaeus summed up in the following words: "Every gathering among the ancients to celebrate a Symposium acknowledged the god as the cause for it, and made use of chaplets appropriate to the gods as well as hymns and songs."[177] He also quotes Xenophon's description of a symposium in the *Anabasis* vi: 1, 5: "After they had poured libations and sang the paean, the Thracians rose up to begin the programme dancing in armour to a flute accompaniment."[178] Vulgar dances sometimes went together with hymns to Aphrodite and Dionysus.[179] Thus in analyzing Athenaeus's book, David E. Aune concludes:

> In both tradition and practice, the symposion was regarded as a social expression of Greek religion (Ath. *Deipn.* 5.192), and so was begun with offerings of food-portions to appropriate divinities (Ath. *Deipn.* 5.179) and concluded with libations and the singing of hymns to appropriate divinities (Ath. *Deipn.* 5.149). Frequently meat from sacrificial animals appears to have been preferred for the δεῖπνον proper (Ath. *Deipn.* 4.140, 173; n. 459; 12.534).[180]

Even in the clubs, associations and occupational groups, which were secular in nature, cultic functions were an integral part of their meetings making it difficult to distinguish them from the cultic or religious associations.[181] Cole explains the rationale behind the practice: "No body of Romans would

---

175. Plut. *Quaest. conv.* 615B.

176. In fact this was a common occurrence, e.g., Horace *Carm.* 4.5.31–32, Servius *Aeneid* 1.730, Petron. *Sat.* 60, Dio C. *Hist. Rom.* 51.19.7.

177. Ath. *Deipn.* 5:192b.

178. Ath. *Deipn.* 1:15e.

179. Ath. *Deipn.* 15:631d. Cf. Stein, "Symposia Literature," 26; who concludes that: "there was thus no strict demarcation line between the sacred and the profane in this type of literature and in the pattern of life it tried to depict."

180. Aune, "Septem Sapientum Convivium," 71.

181. Fisher, "Roman Associations," 2.1209; Also Schmitt-Pantel, "Sacrificial meal and Symposium," 24.

Fellowship Meals: Their Roles and Functions in the Ancient World

have thought of forming any kind of organization without procuring the sanction and protection of the gods."[182]

S. R. F. Price argues likewise, that these feasts were not only social events but religious as well. In the imperial cults sacrifices seem to have given way to feasts, but nonetheless the feast had religious significance.[183] Even though sometimes the religious expressions were not explicit, they were implicit in the meal practices. This is the case in most of the meals in a Greco-Roman context.

Cultic meals, sacrifices, and religious feasts also demonstrate that the secular dimension was never far removed. Crossan clearly explains the reason why the two were inseparable:

> There was no clear separation between those vertical and horizontal dimensions, since the patronal system permeated animal sacrifices, priestly offices, and civic meals as much as any other aspect of ancient life. Public sacrifices did not so much distinguish between immortal gods and mortal humans as announce and reinforce the hierarchy from the gods down along a scale of human participants and spectators.[184]

In the statute of the Guild of Zeus Hypsistos and the Isis cult the religious rite also served to meet the social and political concerns by giving self-identity to the group.[185] Even in the case of sacrificial meals, which were clearly intended to be religious, it was just a matter of the religious component of the meal being enhanced by its association with the sacrifice. They were in fact indistinguishable from the other social meals as similar form and pattern were followed in both types of association.[186]

---

182. Cole, *Love-Feasts,* 29–30.

183. He comments: "it is in fact possible to show that as early as Homer the name of the deity need not be expressed and that emphasis could be place on the banquet . . . but this emphasis on feasts in that context is perfectly compatible with the idea that sacrifices formed a system in which the relationship with the god remained important and was stressed at certain stages . . . Sacrifice, rather than being moribund, was integrated into the life of the city." Price, *Rituals and Power,* 229–30.

184. Crossan, "Who and What Controls your Banquet?" 297–98; for examples of cultic associations with social and financial interests see Ascough, "Forms of Commensality," 22–23.

185. Cf. Roberts et al., "Gild of Zeus Hypsistos," 41–42; Smith, *From Symposium,* 80, 108.

186. Smith, *From Symposium,* 67, 85.

Exclusion and Judgment in Fellowship Meals

In the mystery religions the sacrificial meals were not confined to the temples alone. They were also conducted in private homes.[187] This is seen in the meals of Serapis, which were held in the temple of Serapis, or in other temples and in private homes as well.[188] Moreover, secular meals also were held in the temple precincts. A good example can be seen in the invitations sent out for meals that is found in the Oxyrhynchus Papyri:

> Dioscoros invites you to dine at the wedding of her son on the 14th of Mesore in the temple of Sabazius from the ninth hour, Farewell.[189]

> Diogenes invites you to dinner for the first birthday of his daughter in the Serapeum tomorrow which is Pachon 26 from the eight hour onwards.[190]

What is significant about this invitation is that these secular meals were held in the temple, showing the blending of the secular and religious spheres.[191] So both secular and religious meals were held in different settings, suggesting that these two features were intertwined. Furthermore, it indicates that the nature of fellowship meals cannot be considered from the place it was held.

Likewise when it comes to the practices and behaviors of the participants during the meals, many try to judge them according to modern categories. So their entertainments and revelries associated with the meals look vulgar and demeaning and in complete contrast to modern reckoning of the term "proper" or "solemn."[192] This is a result of not fully grasping the concept of "sacred" and religious expression in the ancient world. In sects like Gnosticism, their aim was to negate and break the bondage of the world and the body, through their indulgence in "worldly pleasures." Another example can be cited in the practice of temple prostitution or similar events during the course of the meal celebration, which was considered sacred and redeeming. Thus we need to identify with their worldview in order to understand their social and religious concepts and expressions which constitute an important component of the meal.

187. For archaeological evidences see Crossan, "Who and What," 315–16.
188. Roberts et al., "Gild of Zeus Hypsistos," 78.
189. *P.Oxy* 2678.
190. *P.Oxy* 2791.
191. Smith and Taussig, *Many Tables*, 23–24.
192. Cf. Smith, *From Symposium*, 79.

Fellowship Meals: Their Roles and Functions in the Ancient World

The study shows that any distinction of the meal as sacred or secular seems to be non-existent.[193] The line that separates the sacred and the secular meals is blurred and in many a case it is absent, though in some meals there might be a greater emphasis on the religious aspect and in others on the secular aspect. The same can be said about blessings associated with meal imagery in the OT, whether they are material or spiritual, literal or metaphorical.[194] Hence we need to take into account fellowship meals in a non-dichotomous manner to have a comprehensive understanding of the social settings of the ancient world.

This is of significant importance in explaining the situation that arose in the church at Corinth. As even in the Corinthian context the fellowship meals seem to be a combination of both secular and sacred categories. This will also give us a broader dimension in our analysis of the meal traditions in relation to the Lord's Supper, instead of confining our study to sacred and religious meals only.

JUDGMENT MOTIFS AND FELLOWSHIP MEALS

We have seen that fellowship meals were an integral part of the social and religious expressions. We will now look into the meal traditions and study the extent to which judgment both as a religious and social category existed.

Divine Judgment

First, we have stated that fellowship meals were part of the religious system, and were the main means of access to the gods and of experiencing the divine realm. The deities were considered to be part of the fellowship acting both as a host and guest.[195] This meant that fellowship meals were seen as

---

193. Price: "Modern scholars wrongly tend to divide what was a single Greek semantic field into two, and to distinguish between religious and secular aspects . . ." *Rituals and Power*, 229.

194. Thus Childs comments: "In the past, commentators have debated at length whether the blessings . . . are of a material or a spiritual nature. But surely to formulate these two dimensions in a dichotomy is a false way to state the question. Much like the book of Deuteronomy, which describes the joy of Israel's inheritance as eating and drinking before the Lord in sheer delight (8:7–10; 12:15), so also for second Isaiah the material and spiritual gifts for Israel are closely fused and cannot be torn apart." Childs, *Isaiah*, 434.

195. Numerous examples in this regard in the Greco-Roman context have been

Exclusion and Judgment in Fellowship Meals

the means to achieve bonding and relationship with the deities. In many of the Hellenistic cults, especially the mystery religions, the notion prevailed that participation in the cultic sacrificial meals created a unity or a κοινωνία between the deity and the participants in the fellowship meal.[196] In some instances, through the consumption of the food the participants experienced and partook in the nature of the deity.[197] Therefore, to be part of the fellowship meals was a privilege and a sign of approval and acceptance by the deities. This correlates with the concept of judgment: to be part of such meals meant that they were judged and accepted by the gods to be part of the community. This correlation is further reinforced with the fellowship meals asserting the social and religious identity of the participants. Consequently, in the various cults and religious associations, meals became an integral part of the initiation or membership into the group.

Since gods were thought to be actively present at the meals, rules and regulation concerning one's behavior were enacted so as not to offend the gods. Offenses were often ritual or cultic in nature. Homer mentions transgressions, such as arrogance in the face of the gods,[198] and the neglect of sacrifices.[199] Since meals were the means of fellowshipping with the gods, breaking the rules and regulation amounted to contempt for the gods. Athenaeus mentions how Cinesias and his friends were punished for breaking the rules by having a feast on a day when they were not supposed to have one:

> And accordingly, each of those men perished, as it was reasonable to expect that such men should . . . as an example to all other men, that they may see that the immortal Gods do not postpone the punishment due to men who behave insolently towards their Deity, so as to reserve it for their children; but that they destroy the men themselves in a miserable manner, inflicting on them greater and more terrible calamities and diseases . . .[200]

---

pointed out. E.g., The gods could be seen dining with the Phaeacians. Hom. *Od.* 7.201-204; Serapis as host at meals in his honor. Aristides *Orations* 45.27. Cf. Klauck, "Presence in the Lord's Supper, 69–70; Nock, "Cult of Heroes," 153–54. Likewise in Judaism where Yahweh was host of the meals. E.g., Philo *Spec.* 1.221; 1QS28a 2:11–22.

196. E.g., Demosthenes, *Orationes* XVIII, 280; Plato *Symp.* 118b; Euripides *El.* 637; Plut. *Quaest. conv.* II. 10, 1. Cf. Klauck, *Herrenmahl und Hellenistischer kult*, 40–165.

197. Cf. Porphyry *Abst.* 2, 10; 2, 29; Paus. *Descr.* I, 24, 4; I, 28, 10.

198. Hom. *Il.* 24.606.

199. Hom. *Il.* 5.177–78; 9.533–38; cf. also Livy 22.9.7.

200. Ath. *Deipn* 552.

Fellowship Meals: Their Roles and Functions in the Ancient World

Livy reports about sickness and death that followed when a festival was not duly performed.[201] An imperial inscription from Pisidia also describes a scene about the god Zeus Trosos who was offended with the servants of Meidon for eating un-sacrificed meat. The god struck Meidon dumb for three months until he received an instruction in a dream to record the incident for future.[202] This reflects a general belief in Greco-Roman world that diseases were the result of attack by the gods or *daimones* (δαίμονες).[203] Homer in his *Odyssey* remarks that disease is the result of attack by an "evil [or base] daimon."[204] In another instance, Hesiod denotes that diseases are personified evils set loose by Pandora that wander the earth and attack humans:

> But the rest, countless plagues, wander amongst men; for earth is full of evils and the sea is full. Of themselves diseases come upon men continually by day and by night, bringing mischief to mortals silently; for wise Zeus took away speech from them. So is there no way to escape the will of Zeus.[205]

Celsus, writing around the first half of the first century AD, notes that long ago diseases were attributed to the anger of the gods.[206] This idea was

---

201. Livy 41.16.1–2; 41.16.9 then reports about blessings and success for having done properly the religious ceremonies and festivals.

202. Herrmann and Polatkan, *Das Testament des Epikrates*, 58–62. Cited from White and Yarbrough, *Social World*, 294.

203. Martin shows extensive evidences in this regard, beginning from pre-Socratic Greek texts. He writes: "The belief that disease was due to divine displeasure or attack was thus quite common in pre-Hippocratic Greece and continued in classical Greek literature and thought." An example can be seen in the account of the purifying of Athens from the plague by Epimenides, (Diogenes Laertius *Lives* 1.110.) He also cites Kudlein: "For Homer as well as the culture represented by him, internal diseases are usually caused by supernatural beings" (Kudlein, "Early Greek Primitive Medicine," 305–36; 312). Martin, *Corinthian Body*, 153–54n59, 62.

204. κακὸς δαίμων, Hom. *Od.* 10.64; 5.396.

205. Hesiod *Op.* 100–105. The concept of the divine origin of disease is also found in the works of Euripides, Aeschylus, Sophocles, and Aristophanes. Cf. Martin, *Corinthian Body*, 154.

206. Though he disagreed with this view, nonetheless it shows the popular understanding of the time. Celsus *On Medicine*, Prooemium 4. Martin also comments that: "The popularity of the idea was one reason why the Hippocratic author of the *The Sacred Disease* had to work so hard to refute—or at least modify—it . . . In arguing against this belief, he does not so much refute it outright and attribute the disease to other, 'natural' sources, as argue that all diseases are divine in the sense that all disease is part of nature, which is imbued with divinity (or divinities). Diseases are all part of natural processes,

Exclusion and Judgment in Fellowship Meals

also prevalent among other cultures. For example an inscription from the Near East states that:

> With expiations and sacrifices I prayed to the Lord (Phrygian deity) that he might save my body, and he restored my body. For this reason I dissuaded any from eating the sacred unsacrificed flesh of goats, since otherwise you will detect my chastisements.[207]

Similar notions about disease and sickness were also prevalent among the Jews.[208] In Judaism sickness was a form of bondage to the powers of evil and sin and sickness were intimately associated.[209] Even in apocalyptic circles, the common belief was that "God could call upon demons or natural powers to inflict bodily illnesses, paralysis, fever, or even death."[210] This belief in divine judgment in the form of physical infirmities was associated with the fellowship meal practices.

To avoid this form of judgment, Plutarch categorically appealed that one's behavior even at the table talk should be proper and regulated so that everyone is benefited. If not, the good fellowship was thereby destroyed and "Dionysus is outraged."[211] One's behavior during the meals was important as a person's action might provoke the gods and make them angry. On that basis Plutarch emphasizes that there should be equality and fair treatment among the guests.[212] In *Saturnalia* the god Kronos warns the people for breaking the rules at meals. An important aspect of this instruction is its association with judgment. The instruction comes with the implication that if the rules are not followed judgment will follow. "I am well assured that they will abide by the laws, or else they will at once be liable to the severe

---

which include divine processes. It is therefore correct *in one sense* to ascribe disease to divinities but wrong to think simplistically that a person's body is 'defiled by a god.' (*Sacred Disease* 4; see also §§1 and 21)" Martin, *Corinthian Body*, 154n63.

207. Cited from Oepke, "νόσος," *TDNT* IV:1093–94.

208. "Many Jews of the Hellenistic period, though certainly not all, held similar views: *Jubilees* 10, 17, says that good angels taught Moses medicine in order to protect human beings from the diseases of demons." Martin, *Corinthian Body*, 153–54n62.

209. Job 2:6; Luke 13:10–17; Mark 2:1–12; John 9:1–2.

210. Roetzel, *Judgment in the Community*, 117. Cf. Wis. 2:24; Heb 2:14; Schürer, *History*, 3.198, 243. Weiss, *Der erste Korintherbrief*, 131.

211. Plut. *Quaest. conv.* 615A: καὶ καθύβρισται ὁ Διόνυσος.

212. E.g., Plut. *Quaest. conv.* 642C.

Fellowship Meals: Their Roles and Functions in the Ancient World

penalties appointed for disobedience."[213] Disobedience to these banquet laws was considered as disobedience to the god himself:

> Whoever acts otherwise, let him know that it is not I, the lawgiver, whom he slights, but he does injury to Kronos himself, who has appointed me lawgiver of his festival.[214]

This stark warning was given to the people, so that the rules would be observed during the fellowship meals.

We find similar concepts were prevalent in Judaism. In Leviticus, the dietary laws given to the priests had the implicit warning that the presence of God would depart from the sanctuary if the laws were violated.[215] This belief was closely tied up with the idea that there was protection from diseases inside the community of the faithful.[216] So judgment was very much part of the fellowship meal traditions in the Jewish context. This is clearly elucidated in the fellowship meal tradition of the Qumran community.

Since participating in a meal also meant accepting the beliefs and ideology of the religious associations or groups, breaking the rules or joining other meals was considered to be apostasy. In order to maintain the purity and integrity of the fellowship meal practices, different groups had their own rules and regulations to keep away ritual and cultic pollutions, and to prevent offending the gods. In Judaism, keeping or breaking the dietary laws became an integral part of judgment, because breaking them denoted compromising their beliefs.[217] In the prophets, Israel's decadence and religious hypocrisy is portrayed in the meals they conducted.[218] The nation's sins are exposed in their meal practices as meals denote more than the consumption of food.[219] Thus the communities were preoccupied in maintaining the laws and regulations associated with the meal practices, as we have seen with the Pharisees and other groups.

Furthermore, in the ancient world it was a popular belief that the gods were the protectors and preservers of the earth. From Poseidon and Zeus, we see many other gods who were hailed as savior and protector of the

---

213. Lucian *Sat.* 10; also 12.
214. Ibid., 10.
215. Lev 7:19; 11:40; 17:15; 22:3–4; also see Harrington, *Impurity System*, 51–52.
216. See Exod 15:26; Deut 7:12–15; 28:58–69; *Jub* 10:1–13.
217. Cf. Ezek 4:9–17.
218. Amos 2:6–8; 5:21–24; 6:4–7.
219. Isa 1:11–17; 5:11–12, 22–23; 28:7–8.

cities and citizens.²²⁰ They were attributed to victories, and protection from enemies and calamities.²²¹ Hence during the fellowship meals, through prayers and sacrifices the gods were invoked for protection upon the people. Xenophon mentions one such example: "There-upon they made offerings to the gods who avert evil and to those who grant safety . . ."²²² Another inscription says that:

> In the annual feasts of Zeus in Magnesia they pray for the protection of the city, country, citizens, wives, children and other residents, for peace, for wealth, for the growth of the grain and other fruits and cattle.²²³

In similar manner, gods were the source of blessings or punishment for humans. This divine judgment was expected in the present time through sickness, pestilence, and other natural calamities. The ancient Greeks and Romans therefore attributed all misfortunes to the wrath of the deities.²²⁴ Disastrous events in political and historical life were also related to the gods.²²⁵

The connection between judgment and meal imagery is a common occurrence in the OT. There are rhetorical expressions where meals are used in both a positive and negative sense.²²⁶ The judgment of God brings to an end the supply of food and celebratory feasts.²²⁷ The prophets constantly wrote on the theme of judgment using food imagery to depict the nation's apostasy and the impending judgment that follows.²²⁸ In Jeremiah

---

220. *Homeric Hymn to Apollo,* 22.5: "Hail, Poseidon, Holder of the Earth, dark-haired lord! O blessed one, be kindly in heart and help those who voyage in ships!" Zeus as protector: Pindar *Ol.* 5.17; Aeschylus *Suppl.* 26–27. *SIG3* III, 985, 60–62.

221. The freeing of the Greeks before the battle of Cunaxa was due to Zeus, Xen. *Anab.* 1.8.16. The saving of the Delphi from the Gauls was due to Zeus and the Pythian Apollo, *SIG3* I, 408, 6–7. Isis and Serapis are frequently called deliverers; Artemidorus *Onir.* 2, 39 (p. 145); Apul. *Metam.* 11.21.

222. Xen. *Hell.* 3.3.4.

223. *SIG3* II, 589, 26–31.

224. Hom. *Il.* 1.9–10, 43–44; 9.530–38; Hom. *Od.*10.64; 5.396; Plato *Phaedr.* 244 d-e; Cl. Al. *Strom.* VI, 3, 31, 1; Plut. *Sera.* 12.161; Livy 2.36.5; 9.29.11; Tac. *Ann.* 14.22; Hesiod *Op.* 100–105

225. Livy 9.9. 3; also Tac. *Ann.* 16.16; Cic. *Nat. d.* III, 38 (91): "the divine anger brought about the destruction of Corinth and Carthage."

226. Cf. Gen 3:14, 17.

227. Isa 3:17; 7:21–22; 9:19–20; 24:7–11; 32:10; 65:13.

228. Ezek 4:12–13; 24:1–14; 39:17–20; Mic 6:14–15; Hab 2:15–16, 3:17; Joel 1:15–20.

Fellowship Meals: Their Roles and Functions in the Ancient World

God's judgment includes a failed harvest and famine.[229] In Amos, the fellowship meal becomes the occasion upon which God's judgement was to be manifested (Amos 8:10). Similar expression is found in Hosea, where God's judgment upon Israel's apostasy is expressed through negative meal imagery.[230]

Conversely, divine blessings are also expressed using meal or food imagery. Usually they are in the form of plentiful harvest and food products. Wine is depicted prominently in Greek literature as the god Dionysus' blessing on humanity.[231] Euripides also mentions that:

> The god, the son of Zeus, delights in banquets, and loves peace, giver of riches, goddess who nourishes youths. To the blessed and to the less fortunate, he gives an equal pleasure from wine that banishes grief.[232]

In fact, even fellowship meals were considered as an expression of divine judgment. As Pausanias describes:

> For the men of those days, because of their righteousness and piety, were guests of the gods, eating at the same board; the good were openly honored by the gods, and sinners were openly visited with their wrath.[233]

Clearly, not only was judgment associated with the fellowship meals, but fellowship meals were also considered as a form of judgment in the Greco-Roman traditions.

In Judaism such motifs appear prominently where food becomes a source of blessing. They share the common idea that eating and drinking especially in a cultic context meant appropriating divine blessings.[234] Wisdom and Apocalyptic literature meal imagery expresses the giving and receiving of divine blessings to the righteous.[235] The psalmist pictures God's protection and care for him using the image of a meal (Ps 23:5). Furthermore, God's restorative judgment upon Israel is expressed in terms of meal

---

229. Jer 8:13; see also 14:3–6, 13–16; 24:10; 29:17–18; 32:2; 34:17; 44:12–14.

230. Hos 2:9, 12; 4:8–16; 5:7, 12; 7:4–14; 8:7–13; 9:2–16.

231. Henrichs, "Changing Dionysiac Identities," 3.140–43, 159–60.

232. Euripides, *Bacch.* 417–20.

233. Paus. *Descr.* 8.2. 4.

234. Exod 24.9–11; Cf. Wainwright, *Eucharist and Eschatology*, 22–23.

235. Ps 78:25; Prov 9:1–6; Song 5:1; Sir 6:19; 15:3; 24:19–21; *1 En.* 24:4—25:7; T.Levi 18:11; *4 Ezra* 1:19; 8:52; Wis 16:20; Cf. Wainwright, *Eucharist and Eschatology*, 23–24.

imagery, food productivity, and security. The righteous are blessed by the provision of food, characterized by both quality and quantity. The future restoration is also depicted in the form of a bountiful harvest and a time of plenty.[236] Zephaniah equates God's judgment to a sacrificial meal and a joyous festival for which the invited guests are consecrated.[237]

Since gods were the author of both wrath and blessings, humans had to appease them in different ways in order to placate them from their wrath and to gain favors, fortunes and blessings. One principal way of achieving this was through sacrifices and expiations where fellowship meals were an integral part. From Homer onwards this idea was quite prominent; thus the main function of the cults was to appease the gods.[238] The Greco-Roman writers constantly discussed how to reconcile and make peace with the gods. Xenophon writes in this regard:

> Nay, be not down-hearted, Euthydemus; for you know that to the inquiry, "How am I to please the gods?" the Delphic god replies, "Follow the custom of the state;" and everywhere, I suppose, it is the custom that men propitiate the gods with sacrifices according to their power. How then can a man honour the gods more excellently and more devoutly than by doing as they themselves ordain?[239]

These sacrifices "fostered the divine-human relations and preserved what the Romans called the *pax deorum*, the peace with the gods."[240] In Judaism, fellowship meals involving sacrifices were very much part of the cult, and they served as means of worship as well as atonement.[241] In this way judgment motifs were closely related with fellowship meal practices as they embodied a bigger reality.

Disciplinary actions in the form of expulsion or exclusion from the meals were practised on offending members. Since fellowship meals were the main activities in the communities, it was an effective means of

---

236. Isa 33:15, 16; see also 23:18; 30:23; Amos 9:13–15; Jer 31:5, 12–14. Cf. also Hos 13:5–6; 14:7; Joel 2:24–27; Mic 4:3–4; 7:14.

237. Zeph 1:7; 3:17–18.

238. Hom. *Il.* 9.219; Plato *Leg.* 10.910a discusses laws concerning these practices in public and private places. Cf. also *Phaedr.* 244 d-e.

239. Xen. *Mem.* 4.3.16.

240. See Crossan, who also notes that meals commonly followed the sacrifices. "Who and What," 297–98.

241. Lev 4:3–4; 5:14–15; 6:24–25.

Fellowship Meals: Their Roles and Functions in the Ancient World

punishment. It meant that the punished member was effectively cut-off from the activities of the community. We have noted that this was rigorously practised in sects like the Qumran community. We can infer that the different religious cults and associations followed this form of judgment since fellowship meals functioned as boundary markers, as a form of membership, and were considered as the main connecting links between the deities and the worshippers.[242] This was a form of judgment that has a number of social as well as religious implications. First, it was a form of social discipline and ostracism, as a person's transgression might affect the whole community. As Plato expresses:

> For all these reasons their action should be governed by the law now stated; and a further reason is this—to prevent impious men from acting fraudulently in regard to these matters also, by setting up shrines and altars in private houses, thinking to propitiate the gods privily by sacrifices and vows, and thus increasing infinitely their own iniquity, whereby they make both themselves and those better men who allow them guilty in the eyes of the gods, so that the whole state reaps the consequences of their impiety in some degree—and deserves to reap them.[243]

Secondly, it was a religious disciplining as well; to be a cast-out member implied that the person was no longer under the favor or protection of the gods. This belief was tied up with the fellowship meal practices, since participating in these meals implied that they were part of the community under the protection and care of the gods.

Fellowship meals were also closely related with the after-life notion among the ancients. Among the Greeks and Romans the festive banquet was used to symbolize a joyous afterlife.[244] This is also seen in Greek funerary reliefs where the deceased is pictured reclining at a banquet.[245] Their

---

242. See the discussion on pp. 37–45 for the Qumran community and pp. 64–69 for the Greco-Roman context.

243. Plato *Leg.* 10.910a–b.

244. E.g., Plato *Resp.* 2.363c–d. "For they conduct them to the house of Hades in their tale and arrange a symposium of the saints, where, reclined on couches crowned with wreaths, they entertain the time henceforth with wine, as if the fairest meed of virtue were an everlasting drink."

245. In the Totenmahl reliefs the deceased hero is depicted as reclining on the foremost couch. These iconographies from Athens and other parts of Asia-Minor originated ca. 600 BC. For more iconographies and funerary reliefs see, Avramidou, *Codrus Painter*, 43–46.

aspiration of immortality is often expressed in terms of meals with the gods. This was based on the belief that certain food contained inherent life qualities or a means of mediating supernatural gifts. In Greek literature the food and drink of the gods was identified as ambrosia and nectar, which conferred immortality on people.[246] Lucian in *Dialogue of the Gods* tells about Ganymede, who when he tastes ambrosia is "no longer human but immortal"; he drinks immortality in the nectar.[247] In Joseph and Aseneth, a honeycomb represents the food that provides immortality.[248]

In this manner, in some circles to partake in fellowship meals symbolized a foretaste of the future or the after-life state. Thus the term "the table of the gods" referring to this kind of fellowship meal was often used among the ancients.[249] They were also signs of self-identification with divine blessings. For example, by participating in the mysteries the initiates participate in the salvation or victory of the gods.[250] In the Eleusinian mysteries, the members have better preferences in the underworld:

> Happy is he among men upon earth who has seen these mysteries; but he who is uninitiate and who has no part in them, never has lot of like good things once he is dead, down in the darkness and gloom.[251]

One of the main functions of the funerary association was to guide the deceased for the after-life. At the end of the banquet, "the period of uncertainty regarding the deceased's soul ceased, and Hades accepted him."[252] Many of the collegia thus functioned as funerary clubs with the funeral ceremonies involving fellowship meals.[253] There was an inherent eschatological expectation and realization present in these meal traditions.

We have seen that this motif occurs prominently in Judaism, especially in the form of the Messianic or eschatological meal. God's judgment is depicted in the form of meal imagery; the future salvation is shown as a

---

246. Hom. *Od.* 5.1; *Il.* 5.335-42; 19.38-39.

247. Lucian *Dial. d.* 4.3 and 5.

248. *Jos. Asen.* 16:14; also "living water of eternity" in *Odes Sol.* 6:8-18; 11:7-8, 30:1-7. Cf. Gen 2:9.

249. Xen. *Symp* IX, Aristides, *Hymn to Serapis* 26-8; *P.Oxy*, 110, 523, 1484.

250. Cf. Apul. *Metam.* 11:21.

251. *Homeric Hymn to Demeter/Ceres*, 482-83.

252. Avramidou, *The Codrus Painter*, 46.

253. Different inscriptions on the collegia show that about a fifth of them had concern for the proper burial of their members. Fisher, "Roman Associations," 1222-23.

Fellowship Meals: Their Roles and Functions in the Ancient World

feast in the presence of the Lord.[254] Conversely, those who are judged are precluded from the feast.[255] Fellowship meal traditions became part of the Jewish eschatological and apocalyptic traditions to express God's judgment on the people. The Qumran community specially held strongly to this belief that their meals were part of the eschatological meal. Judgment therefore became very much an integral part of the fellowship meal celebration. Those who participated in the meals implied that they became part of the "elected" ones. The story of Judith depicts a scene where fellowship meals became the deciding factor and the difference between life and death. She kills Holofernes, the Assyrian commander, to prevent the people from violating the dietary laws and thereby avoid God's judgment.[256]

Human Judgment

At the social level, since fellowship meals permeated all aspects of social life and they represented the societal norms and values, people could be judged by their dining habits in terms of their social life and identity. Thus the people with whom one eats, the place, the manner and occasion became all the more important to gain social recognition and approval. This kind of social verdict associated with fellowship meals based on socio-cultural or even ideological bases was very common in the Greco-Roman context. In the different associations and cults, the meals became the means of inclusion of members into the community as well as the means of exclusion.

This form of judgment in the community was because of the connection between fellowship meals and social and religious identity. Participation in a fellowship meal was a sign of acceptance or membership into a social group, starting from the family unit, to the larger social clubs and associations, to nations. Acceptance or rejection of people was denoted by the acceptance or rejection of food offered. Thus they functioned as boundary markers where the participants were under the obligation to follow the rules and regulations of the community. As Mary Douglas has maintained, meals represented all the ordered system of society, hence challenging the

---

254. Isa 49:9–19; 48:21; 55:5; Ezek 34:13–31; Zech 9:17.

255. Isa 65:13, 25; cf. Ezek 39:17–20. J. N. Oswalt summarizes the concept: "to be blessed is to have enough to eat and drink, to have reason to rejoice and exult out of a glad heart . . . To be cursed is to suffer hunger and thirst, to be ashamed and in despair with a broken spirit." *Isaiah*, 2.650.

256. Jdt 10:5, 10–13; 11:11–15; 12:5–9. Cf. Jones, *Apocrypha*, 58–59.

social values associated with the meals was considered a threat to society.[257] To participate in fellowship meals meant that a person had to undergo different levels of social scrutiny. Though strict regimented rules and systems applied to fewer societies, at a general level it was applicable to all groups; whom one can invite or dine with, was a pertinent question for all.

We have noted that social values, boundaries, statuses. and hierarchies were reinforced through the meal institution. Thus ranking during the meals was an important part of the culture. People were judged according to their own socio-economic and cultural bases to be assigned places at the table. This again had further repercussions within the society, as a person's place at the fellowship meal was closely related to one's status and position in the community.

Plutarch writing about this practice even uses forensic terminology. Presenting an argument of Timon he writes:

> more inept is the man who, instead of playing host, makes himself a juryman (δικιαστήν) and a judge over people who do not call upon him to decide an issue and are not on trial (κρινομένων) as to who is better than who, or worse; for they have not entered a contest (ἀγῶνα), but have come for dinner.[258]

In the Jewish context, this sort of practice was mostly confined to the different groups and sects, who defined themselves and others in relation to the Law. Thus purity laws and regulations became important criteria for the different groups to judge and decide whether one was acceptable or not to be part of the fellowship meal and ultimately part of the community. Hence, the meal traditions of the Qumran community, the Therapeutae, the Pharisees, Joseph and Aseneth, reveal that one of the main objectives of the meal practices was related to the inclusion or exclusion of members into the community.

Lastly, fellowship meals were also used as means of judgment. Both reward and punishment could be enacted through the meal institution. Thus people were rewarded or honored through meals, or punished by excluding them from meals. This sort of judgment had fatal consequences in ancient agrarian society. Josephus in his report about the Essenes states that:

> But for those that are caught in any heinous sins, they cast them out of their society; and he who is thus separated from them does

---

257. Douglas, "Deciphering a Meal," 80.
258. Plut. *Quaest. conv.* 616C.

often die after a miserable manner; for as he is bound by the oath he hath taken, and by the customs he hath been engaged in, he is not at liberty to partake of that food that he meets with elsewhere, but is forced to eat grass, and to famish his body with hunger, till he perish . . .[259]

It was a system where social and political justice could be enacted. Since fellowship meals functioned to maintain social order and stability, actions were taken against those who went against the prescribed rules.

Fellowship meals were used as a medium of relationship with the gods and with one another. So the judgment motifs were inherently present in the meal practices and involved different aspects of personal, social and divine judgment. These different categories of judgment were all interrelated. There was an innate understanding that judgment and participation in the fellowship meals went hand in hand. Just as fellowship meals were a microcosmic reflection of their societies, they also were macrocosmic reflection of a greater reality, as these connections with divine judgment showed. By participating in them people were involved in a reality that had much bigger implications.

GRECO-ROMAN INFLUENCES AND JUDEO-CHRISTIAN MEAL PRACTICES

The survey of fellowship meals in the ancient world has revealed their indisputable importance in societies. But questions have been raised as to whether fellowship meal practices in the different cultures came from a common tradition with similar meanings, or reveal variant traditions with divergent meanings.

D. E. Smith and M. Klinghardt, who have done a comparative study on Jewish and Greco-Roman meals focusing on the formal banquet, have stressed the similarities between them, and uphold the view that there existed a basic form of a common banquet tradition in all the cultures and it was adapted to various settings. Smith especially postulates that during the period of about 300 BC to AD 300, the Greco-Roman banquet tradition became the standard practice for all throughout the Mediterranean world and influenced other practices including Jewish meal practices.[260] The common

---

259. *J.W.* 2.143.

260. Smith, *Symposium*, 14–15; Klinghardt, *Gemeinschaftsmahl und Mahlgemeinschaft*; Klinghardt, "Typology of the Community Meal."

Exclusion and Judgment in Fellowship Meals

custom of reclining is seen as an indicator of this common tradition.[261] On the other hand there are scholars who have questioned this view, as there are also a number of dissimilarities that exist between the traditions.[262] Though the significance of fellowship meals was common to all the different cultures, there is no concrete evidence to show that they all evolved from a single tradition. Even reclining which had become a trademark of the Greek-Roman practices, had been adopted by the Greeks from the Assyrians around 750 BC. There were also differences between the Greek and Roman practices. Unlike the Greeks, in Roman circles it was more acceptable to invite wives to the fellowship meals. We have noted that even within Greco-Roman meal practices, there were different forms. Hence, it is not proper to categorize all meal practices under the same classification. Many were characterized by prurient activities, primarily drunkenness combined with hedonism. But that was not the case for all. Moralists and philosophers like Plato developed their own versions which were also followed widely.

In all probability these meal traditions existed independently carrying their own social codes and meanings.[263] This is evident in the different meanings and connotations they had in different communities.[264] In the process of the development, meal traditions have evolved, adopting and adapting from one another. But meal practices and food in general had a universal appeal and importance which are manifested in their roles and functions that was applicable to all traditions. At the same time, these commonalities do not mean that they were attributed the same standard in all cultures, since what may be acceptable and decent in one culture may be of different value and meaning in another culture. Hence the meaning of meal practices including the food items differed from culture to culture. So similarities in the meal traditions do not mean dependency. Similarly the practice of reclining had different connotations; for Jews it had a religious

---

261. Smith further stresses that as the meals took similar forms they also shared similar meanings and interpretations. *From Symposium*, 2, 14.

262. See Burkert, "Oriental Symposia," 8, points to a number of contrasts between the Greco-Roman and Jewish practices. Cf. Blomberg, *Contagious Holiness*, 94–96; Feeley-Harnik, *Lord's Table*, 71–106.

263. Mary Douglas postulated that food in itself constitutes a code which carries different social messages; Douglas, "Deciphering a Meal," 61.

264. For instance, meanings associated with different food differ from culture to culture. This is seen in the number of discussions on food items in the symposia literature. Plutarch for instance includes a discussion that centers round the question why the Jews abstain from pork, because they worship the pig, or because they have an antipathy against it; *Quaest. conv.* 4.5. Cf. Stein, "Influence of Symposia Literature," 18–19.

Fellowship Meals: Their Roles and Functions in the Ancient World

meaning and for others a social meaning. The fellowship meals were associated with defining and maintaining social identities, but the criteria differed from culture to culture. For the Jews the criteria were different based on their own food and purity laws, moreover even within Judaism they differed from one sect to another. This analysis will be important in interpreting the fellowship meal practices in any particular socio-cultural context, including the Lord's Supper in Corinth.

Furthermore, analysis of the meal practices shows that from the time of Homer onwards, and well beyond the Hellenistic period, the Greek symposium had a dominating influence on other practices.[265] The style and procedure of this form of the fellowship meal became quite popular that many of the communities incorporated this feature into their practices.[266]

The influences from foreign practices on Jewish meal traditions have been noted as early as the eighth century BC.[267] Later on the Greco-Roman meal pattern and style was assimilated in some of the Jewish practices, including the Passover.[268] The literatures from the Intertestamental period and other rabbinic works do exhibit a lot of affinity with the Greco-Roman practices. The level of assimilation is indicated by the meal etiquette and warnings in the literature of this era, particularly in Sirach.[269] Shimoff explains that: "the rabbinic ideal of life was threatened by Hellenization, their response to this challenge was to adapt the Hellenistic banquet by excising the most offensive excesses."[270] Again, though it is apparent that some form of modification has taken place in the Passover and other meals; apart from the procedure and structural influences of the Greco-Roman meal traditions, one cannot be sure to what extent their ideology and beliefs were also influenced. Shimoff has emphasized that among the Pharisees, the rabbis accepted the banquet tradition as long as it was modified and it did not infringe upon their religious system, which meant rejection of idolatry and

---

265. Burkert, "Oriental Symposia," 7.

266. For the influence of Greek tradition of the symposium see, Fisher, "Roman Associations," 2.1189, 1200–1203, 1224.

267. Amos 6:4–7; cf. also Isa 5:11–12, 22–23; 22:13; See Blomberg, *Contagious Holiness*, 56–57.

268. Smith reiterates that from the period of the Second temple to the early rabbinic period the Greco-Roman banquet tradition influenced Jewish practices, exhibiting these similarities. *From Symposium*, 134.

269. Sir 31:12–42; also see Smith, *From Symposium*, 135–45.

270. Shimoff, "Banquets," 452; cf. also Stein, "Influence of Symposia Literature," 20.

Exclusion and Judgment in Fellowship Meals

illicit sexual activity.²⁷¹ But this might not be applicable to all the groups, as for other groups that were more liberal in their outlook, even ideological assimilation was part of the progress, hence the people were warned time and again of idolatry associated with the fellowship meals.

The review of the Jewish literatures also indicates that the influence of the Greco-Roman meal tradition in Jewish culture was not as uniform as some have suggested. Moreover, different groups within Judaism responded differently. In general the level of assimilation depended on a group's interpretation of the Torah. Thus in groups like the Qumran and Therapeutae communities the level of influence seemed to be minimal, but the impact of Hellenization can be seen in the way communities reacted and developed their own meal traditions against the prevailing practices.

The analysis of the meal practices in Corinth should also be treated in a similar fashion. In this wider context the early church also developed their own fellowship meal tradition making changes and modifications to suit their belief system as the new community advanced. Hence, the fellowship meals in Corinth should not be seen as purely Greco-Roman in nature, but as a meal tradition that has evolved and developed following the cross-cultural conventions of that time. In the process both Greco-Roman and Jewish expression of meal traditions were incorporated into the meal tradition of the Christian community. This is elucidated when Paul relates it with the Passover theology as well as with the Greco-Roman meal ideology.

CONCLUSION

The multiple functions of fellowship meals show the important roles they played in communities. In the ancient agrarian era where food supply and procurement would have been no easy task, the values and functions associated with food were even more significant and definitive. Their universal practice and appeal is evident from the many traditions preserved in the extant ancient literatures. The importance of meals led ancient writers to delve into the theme of the meal motif which became a literary genre in itself. The works especially of Plato and Xenophon became influential and exerted their influences in the Greco-Roman world. Since they were very much associated with all aspects of life, people were often characterized by the meals they observed.²⁷² Hence, the proverbial saying was coined that:

271. Shimoff, "Banquets," 447, 449.

272. Thus, Emperors were characterized by the banquets they held; see Fisher,

Fellowship Meals: Their Roles and Functions in the Ancient World

"from one's eating habits one could determine a person's morality, piety, sociability, efforts for war or peace, parentage and friendships."[273]

The fellowship meal was an important socio-religious institution in the ancient world. The different groups, clubs, and associations centered their activities on the fellowship table. The meals made tangible an expression of the values and beliefs of the people. The fellowship meal in its different manifestations had significant roles in community life in maintaining social, cultural, and religious traditions and thereby asserting their identity. The different types of meals surveyed indicate that they contain 'codes' and so provide us with a social perspective into their life-situation. At the same time interpretation of the meals differed from one another on the basis of their societal values and norms. Hence, the meal etiquette seen in the ancient literatures were more than table manners but reveal a rich tradition and values of their social and religious world. The analysis of the meal traditions in the literatures shows that though the meanings associated with them may differ from one culture to another they had definite functions in the ancient societies. For the study of the Lord's Supper, all these points need to be assimilated. Instead of concentrating on individual types of meals we need to study the meal practices in this wider socio-cultural context, as there is a common underlying principle in all the meal traditions that can contribute to our interpretation of the Lord's Supper.

Sacred and secular aspects were merged in the fellowship table and were at times indistinguishable. It was just a matter of which feature was emphasized more at the table. It was this connection of the fellowship meals with the religious sphere that gave them a spiritual impetus and function. Moreover, the association of the meals with past history and with future expectations indicates that they were considered as events which transcended time and space dimensions. Hence they were an integral part of their religious expressions and practices.

We have noted that judgment was an integral part of the fellowship meal traditions. In fact this can be considered as one of the most important features of the fellowship meal practices that made it a very important institution in the ancient world. This association with judgment also made them effective tools for challenging and changing the social, political, and cultural ethos and system. Based on these findings we will study the Lord's Supper in Corinth and Paul's response to the Corinthian situation.

"Roman Associations," 2.1211–12. Cf. Matt 9:10–11.

273. Blomberg, *Contagious Holiness*, 91.

CHAPTER 3

Fellowship Meals in Corinth
The Abuse at the Lord's Supper

INTRODUCTION

THE PASSAGE ON THE Lord's Supper that Paul presents in chapter 11 is an important account that has wider implications for the church. For centuries it has contributed to and influenced the understanding and interpretation of the Lord's Supper and continues to do so. Numerous studies have been done on the many issues related to the Lord's Supper in Corinth and especially in regards to Paul's interpretation. Much depends on the interpretation of the Corinthian situation for deriving a proper understanding of the theology of the Lord's Supper. But there is no general consensus on the subject matter and it remains an elusive issue and a point of contention. In recent times scholars such as Theissen have tried to explain the issue at Corinth from a sociological perspective and have succeeded to a certain extent.[1] But there are questions about the approach, as to whether the issue at Corinth was simply a sociological issue alone. Moreover the whole issue of social status which has been emphasized in these studies is found to be more complicated and a multi-dimensional phenomenon.[2]

---

1. Theissen, *Social Setting*, 69–120, 145–74. See also Lampe, "Corinthian Eucharistic Dinner party," 1–15; Horrell, *Social Ethos*, 64–72.

2. See the argument in this regard by Meeks, *First Urban Christians*, 53–70. He

Fellowship Meals in Corinth: The Abuse at the Lord's Supper

This study is an attempt to look at the whole issue of the Lord's Supper in Corinth, analysing the social, cultural, and religious factors that have contributed to the problem. The study specifically looks at the issue at Corinth in comparison with the traditions and significance of fellowship meals in the ancient world. The function and importance of fellowship meals in the ancient world have already been noted, which also gains prominence in the ministry of Jesus and in the early church. In the light of that, we now analyze the fellowship meal at Corinth and see how the traditions and the setting have influenced them and Paul's response to the situation.

THE CHRISTIAN COMMUNITY IN CORINTH

The church at Corinth was strategically located because the city of Corinth was an important center for trade and commerce in the ancient world.[3] The city had risen as a strong economic and military power due to its strategic location at the southwestern extremity of the isthmus that connects the mainland of Greece with the Peloponnese. This enabled Corinth to exert immense political and commercial influence in the ancient world.[4] It also became a center of great intellectual and academic activity, with numbers of halls for rhetoric and philosophical schools, which drew "travelling professors and lecturers."[5]

---

takes into account this aspect in his sociological analysis of the Corinthian society: "For example, one might discover that, in a given society, the following variables affect how an individual is ranked: power (defined as 'the capacity for achieving goals in social systems'), occupational prestige, income or wealth, education and knowledge, religious and ritual purity, family and ethnic-group position, and local-community status (evaluation within some subgroup, independent of the larger society but perhaps interacting with it.) ... The generalized status of a person is a composite of his or her ranks in all the relevant dimensions." 54.

3. The wealth of Corinth is referred to as early as Homer; *Il.* 2.569, 570; cf. 13.664; Strabo *Geogr.* 8.6.20; 8.377; An indicator of its economic upturn was the resumption by Corinth of the Isthmian games, sometime between 7 BC and AD 3. After the destruction of old Corinth these games were continued in Sicyon. Another factor that contributed to the Corinthian wealth, was banking. Plutarch (*Mor.* 831a) names Corinth as a banking center along with Patrae, and Athens. Moreover it was famous for its production from artisans. Cf. Theissen, *Social Setting*, 100–101.

4. For an overview of Corinth and its history see Strabo *Geogr.* 8.361, 381; Paus. *Descr.* 21.2; Dio C. *Hist. Rom.* 43.50; Murphy-O'Connor, *St. Paul's Corinth*, 151–52; Bornkamm, *Paul*, 68; Conzelmann, *First Epistle*, 11–12; Thiselton, *First Epistle*, 1–17; Meeks, *First Urban Christians*, 47

5. Goudge, *First Epistle*, xv–xvii.

Being a commercial port city, the socio-religious context of Roman Corinth was diverse. Under the Roman rule, the city was introduced not only to their laws but also their culture and religions. The influence of Greek religion, philosophy, and arts at Corinth remained strong; at the same time the mystery cults of Egypt and Asia and Judaism also made their mark.[6] Greco-Roman writers have recorded many of these religious traditions found in Corinth. Pausanias mentions at least twenty-six shrines and temples devoted to the many gods and goddesses.[7] One of the main religious activities of these groups was the participation in cultic fellowship meals (cf. 1 Cor 8–10). Archaeological sites in the city show couches and tables cut into the rock used by the followers of Dionysus and Asclepius for cultic meals.[8]

It was a place where different people, cultures, and religions blended; its rich diversity was also exhibited in the form of art and architectural structures as archaeological excavations have confirmed.[9] New Corinth was thus a cosmopolitan city and its population comprized of Romans, Greeks, Orientals, and Jews. The society was classified into different classes based on status, wealth, and power.[10]

These distinctions in terms of social rank and status played an important role in society, and they were displayed and reinforced, especially

---

6. E.g., The sanctuaries of Poseidon, Artemis, Asclepius and Isis in Paus. *Descr.* 2.2.3. The evidence of Jews in Corinth is shown by an inscription: "[Syn]agogue of the Hebr[ews]." The date of this inscription cannot be narrowly determined, but it gives sufficient confirmation to Acts 18:4. Philo also mentions a Jewish colony sent to Corinth (*Gaius* 281). Cf. Barrett, *New Testament Background*, 50; Deissmann, *Light from the Ancient Near East*, 13.

7. Paus. *Descr.* 2; Apul. *Metam.* 11; cf. Murphy-O'Connor, *St. Paul's Corinth*, 78–80; Fee, *First Epistle*, 3.

8. So also at the sanctuary of Demeter and Core; Stambaugh and Balch, *New Testament in its Social Environment*, 158–59; Coutsoumpos, *Paul and the Lord's Supper*, 64–65.

9. Cf. Theissen, *Social Setting*, 100.

10. For a description of the social order and stratification in the Roman Empire and of Corinth, see Horrell, *Social Ethos*, 64–72. He comments that: "Within this established order was a social hierarchy in which rank and position were strongly defined and displayed. Wealth, legal standing, and family origin were all important . . . From the perspective of those near the top of the pyramid, manual and wage-labour were degrading, and slaves were despised. The poor, it seems, were held in contempt, basically because they were poor," 72. For the Corinthian context also see Savage, *Power Through Weakness*, 19–53; Morris, *First Epistle*, 17–19; Talbert, *Reading Corinthians*, xvi–xviii; Witherington, *Conflict and Community*, 5–19, 24–28; Chow, *Patronage and Power*, 38–82.

Fellowship Meals in Corinth: The Abuse at the Lord's Supper

through the fellowship meals or banquets. Corinth, being a Roman colony, was no different from others.[11]

The pivotal role that Corinth played in the ancient world also made the early church focus its mission there; as such it became an important base for Paul.[12] As people from different social customs and religious cultures became part of the Christian community in Corinth, they undoubtedly brought with them their own worldviews, practices, and attitudes about gods, rites, and principles, creating problems in the church. This is well elucidated in Paul's first letter to the Corinthians as he deals with the manifold problems, the abuse at the Lord's Supper being one of them.

These problems developed after Paul left the city, sometime around AD 51–52 and the letter was written approximately three years later. The first letter to the Corinthians was Paul's response to their letter (1 Cor 7:1), possibly brought by Stephanas, Fortunatus, and Achaicus (1 Cor 16:17), and possibly the report heard from Chloe's people.[13]

The church at Corinth, the first functioning congregation in Achaea, was clearly the outcome of the work and mission of Paul. Paul came to Corinth on his second missionary journey, after a not too successful visit to Athens.[14] The evidence for this is based on the account in Acts 18:1–17. The events and persons described here can be compared with external evidences to come to a possible dating. The reference to the edict of Claudius, according to Orosius, a fifth-century historian, happened in AD 49.[15] The mention of Gallio as the proconsul of Achaia during this time is probably dated to AD 50–51.[16] Basing on these dates, Paul's arrival in Corinth is likely to have happened towards the spring of AD 50, and his departure as the fall of AD 51. Then the approximate date of 1 Corinthians written

11. MacMullen, *Roman Social Relations*, 111, 116.

12. "It is likely, however that Paul came to the city, not primarily because of the challenge presented by its particular wickedness, but because its importance in international commerce made it strategic for his program to evangelize the Gentile world." Orr and Walter, *1 Corinthians*, 119.

13. 1 Cor 1:11; cf. 1 Cor 5:1; 11:18.

14. Paul's 18 months stay at Corinth probably happened between AD 49 and AD 52. Barrett, *First Epistle*, 5; Fee, *First Epistle*, 4, 5.

15. Orosius, *History*, VII.6.15.

16. Barrett, *New Testament Background*, 48–49; Deissmann had calculated that Lucius Junius Annaeus Gallio, a brother of Seneca, the famous philosopher and a tutor of Nero, came to office on July 1, AD 51. Cf. Craig and Short, "First Epistle to the Corinthians," 4; Murphy-O'Connor, *St. Paul's Corinth*, 149, who suggest AD 51–52, as the year of Gallio's office.

in Ephesus (1 Cor 16:8) would be about AD 56, taking into consideration his stay for a year and a half in Ephesus and his trip to Syria.[17] The epistle also gives the evidence that other missionaries, some of them very different from Paul had been in work in Corinth, Apollos and Peter with very great probability (cf. Apollos: Acts 18:24–28; 19:1; 1 Cor 1:12; 3:4–9; Peter: 1 Cor 1:12; 3:22; 9:5; 15:5), and if not Peter himself some of his disciples, though we cannot be certain about the level of their influence in the church.

What was the social setting of the Corinthian congregation? This question comes to the forefront, as it is an important key in understanding the complex issues at Corinth.[18] By establishing the social reality and position of the Corinthian Christians we can ascertain to a certain extent the reasons for the dispute at the Lord's Supper and the response issued.

As with the city of Corinth itself, the sociological makeup of the church in Corinth also seemed to be diverse.[19] The church in a way reflected the makeup of the city. It certainly consisted of both Jews and Gentiles (1 Cor 12:13); based on 1 Cor 12:2, Horrell suggests that the Gentiles were probably more in number than the Jews, "some of whom may previously have been 'God fearers.'"[20]

What was the social status of the Christian community? The earlier view of many scholars was that they belonged to the lower class. On the basis of literary analysis, Deissmann concluded that Christianity was a movement within the lower class.[21] Celsus, a polemical Greek writer described Christians as follows:

> Their injunctions are like this: "Let no one educated, no one wise, no one sensible draw near. For these abilities are thought by us to be evils. But for anyone ignorant, anyone stupid, anyone uneducated, anyone who is a child, let him come boldly." By the fact that they themselves admit that these people are worthy of their God,

---

17. Orr & Walter, *First Corinthians*, 120.

18. See Holmberg, *Sociology*; Coutsoumpos, *Paul and the Lord's Supper*, 58–59; on the debates regarding the principles and methodology of a sociological approach to the NT.

19. Cf. Acts 18:1–8; 1 Cor 1:10–17; 16:15–17; Rom 16:23.

20. Horrell, *Social Ethos*, 91; cf. Fee in support of this view suggests that chaps 6:1–20; 8:1—10:22; 12:2; 15:1–58 indicate they were chiefly Gentiles. Thus, the picture that emerges is one of a predominantly Gentile community; *First Epistle*, 4.

21. He compared the language of the New Testament with the vulgar Koine of the non-literary papyri of the ancient world and came to the conclusion that they belong to the lower class. Deissmann, *New Testament*, 105–6.

they show that they want and are able to convince only the foolish, dishonorable, and stupid, and only slaves, women, and little children.[22]

Ernst Troeltsch considers that the social standing of the early Christians have been fairly low. Most of them belonged to the urban areas but from the lowest class of society. Part of these groups would have been artisans, house slaves, freedmen, and free workers, but not belonging to any real social class.[23] This is also based on Paul's reference in his letter to the Corinthians that few of them were wise, influential or of noble birth.[24] For long, the consensus was that Christianity was a movement among the lower class, and that its appeal among these groups depended not only on ideological factors but social as well.[25]

However, there is a stronger consensus emerging among scholars that the social situation of the Christian community was more diverse. This begins with E. A. Judge, who questioned the common notion that Christians came from the lower class.[26] He stressed that although originally Christians came from the Aramaic community in Palestine, they flourished and their writing spread among Jewish and Gentile believers living under the influence of the urban Greco-Roman Society and institutions.[27] This meant that the community also consisted of people from the higher Roman ranking system. Here he differentiated separate times and settings of early Christianity. Thus the movement around Jesus in its rural setting was not the same as Jewish Christianity in Jerusalem, not to mention, decades later, the Christians in Syria, Corinth or Rome.

Judge's view about the socially-mixed character of the early church has received much support from scholars, such as Martin Hengel, who writes:

> What Pliny the Younger, as governor of Bithynia in Asia Minor, wrote to the emperor Trajan, also applied to the communities founded during the mission of the apostle to the Gentile: "many . . . of every class . . . are endangered now and will be endangered in the future (by the new 'superstition': *multi enim . . . omnis ordinis . . . vocantur in periculum et vocabuntur*). That is, there were

22. Origen, *Contra Celsum*, 158.
23. Troeltsch, *Social Teaching*, 22–25.
24. 1 Cor 1:26–28.
25. Gager, *Kingdom and Community*, 96.
26. Judge, *Social Pattern*, 52.
27. Ibid., 52–54.

members of Christian communities in all strata of the populace, from slaves and freedmen to the local aristocracy, the decurions, and in some circumstances even to the local nobility of the Senate . . ." The majority of early Christians will have belonged to the "middle class" of antiquity from which the "godfearers" of the Jewish mission were recruited (cf. Acts 13:43, 50; 16:14; 17:4, 17; 18:7).[28]

Hengel stressed the point that as Christianity made inroads, frequently new members that joined the church were of the "upper class." According to Eusebius, in the time of Commodus (180–192), "Large numbers even of those at Rome, highly distinguished for wealth and birth, were advancing towards their own salvation with all their households and kindred."[29] Acts gives a picture where the new converts include those coming from wealthy or high social backgrounds.[30] For instance Paul and his colleagues came from a high social class of Hellenistic Judaism. Likewise many of the Gentiles in high positions, including senators, joined the church along with their entire households; so also the slaves and poor people (Acts 11:14–18; 16:15). Meeks concurs with the "emerging consensus" that "a Pauline congregation generally reflected a fair cross-section of urban society."[31]

Malherbe has questioned Deissmann's presupposition about the relation between social rank and literary culture. Malherbe warns about reading too much into the literary character of early Christian literature as a community product or reflecting the actual circumstances of the Christian community and proposed that the literature of the New Testament indicates that Deissmann's evaluation of the social status is too low.[32] Likewise, Holmberg has also contended that the association between the literary level of a document and the social level of its author (not to speak of its readers) is not straightforward.[33] Holmberg further argues that the negative commendation given by a critic like Celsus that Christians belonged

---

28. Hengel, *Property and Riches*, 36–39.

29. Eusebius *Hist. eccl.* 5, 21, 1; Hengel, *Property and Riches*, 64–65.

30. Acts mention a number of prominent people who became Christians, the list includes Joanna the wife of Chusa, who was the financial administrator of Herod Antipas; the centurion Cornelius; the Athenian assessor, Dionysius; Menahem, the friend of Herod Antipas; Sergius Paulus, governor of Cyprus. Cf. Coutsoumpos, *Paul and the Lord's Supper*, 61.

31. Meeks, *First Urban Christians*, 73.

32. See Malherbe, *Social Aspects*, 13.

33. Holmberg, *Sociology*, 55.

Fellowship Meals in Corinth: The Abuse at the Lord's Supper

to the lower and uneducated section of society should not be accepted at its face value. It was part of his anti-Christian propaganda directed towards the higher class segment of the society attracted to Christianity. He wanted to remind them that this new religion attracted only the insignificant and lowly people and excluded the "upper-class."[34]

The majority of scholars now strongly refute the view based on 1 Cor 1:26-28 that the Christian community belonged to the lower class. According to them this cannot be the basis to conclude that the social constituency of Christians come from a lower stratum of society.[35] Rather this description is to be taken as a rhetorical debate at the beginning of the epistle and should be understood with the other sociological categories that Paul uses.[36] First Corinthians 1:26 should rather be considered as suggesting that though many of them come from humble backgrounds, it also indicates that some of them were from better and higher positions.[37] For instance the congregation included Gaius, the city treasurer of Corinth whose wealth and house were sufficient to provide hospitality for Paul and the whole church.[38] All these indicate that as Christianity progressed into the non-Jewish environment, it also attracted educated and socially higher placed converts.[39] So it was not only a religious movement of the lower classes as has been assumed. F. V. Filson summarized it well:

> Once we recall that Gaius...Erastus...Crispus...and Stephanas all lived at Corinth, we realize that the words "not many mighty" in 1 Corinthians 1:26 must not be taken to mean "none." The apostolic church was more nearly a cross section of society than we have sometimes thought. The fact that the poor predominated must not obscure this truth; the poor have always outnumbered the wealthy.[40]

---

34. Ibid., 41-42.
35. Cf. Coutsoumpos, *Paul and the Lord's Supper*, 59.
36. Theissen, *Social Setting*, 70, 71.
37. Cf. 1 Cor 4:8-13; Origen *Cels.* 3.48; Filson, "Significance," 111; Judge, *Social Pattern*, 59; Theissen, *Social Setting*, 72-73; Schrage, *Der erste Brief*, 1.208-210; Horrell, *Social Ethos*, 95.
38. Kee, *Christian Origins*, 97.
39. Holmberg, *Sociology*, 29.
40. Filson, "Significance," 111. Likewise, Gager asserts that the early Christians did not actually exist at the absolute bottom level of the social class, nor did they come exclusively from the aristocratic group or the middle classes. Gager, *Kingdom and Community*, 106-8.

Exclusion and Judgment in Fellowship Meals

In Paul's description of the social makeup of the Corinthian congregation, in 1 Cor 1:26–29; 4:10, three categories of people are mentioned: those who are wise, those who are powerful, and those of noble birth.[41] Apparently it shows that the church included all classes of people, rich and poor, slaves and freedmen. Judging by the names and their apparent social position most of the people named by Paul probably belonged to the upper class, and it appears that they were a minority within the congregation. Since Paul would name, in all probability, the most active and important members of the congregation, we assume they had a leading role in the community and exerted much influence in the decision making of the church.[42] Some of the people named in the letter were probably merchants, such as Aquila and Priscilla. The majority of the Corinthians mentioned by Paul probably were wealthy and enjoyed high social status, such that they could invest their time and money in travel, which in those days was expensive.[43] Paul, likewise, simply assumes that the Corinthian community could manage to bring its own collection to Jerusalem (1 Cor 16:3). At the same time there were people who belonged to the lower social-economic status, for example, Chloe's people who were "probably slaves or dependent workers" (1 Cor 1:11).[44] It is observed that those of the lower strata scarcely appear as individuals in the Corinthian correspondence.[45]

The situation likewise reflects a mixed urban community which was a diversified community. As we will notice, there is no indication that the conflict is between people of the same social status who were meeting in a

41. The "powerful" can refer to those with political power; it can also refer to those who are wealthy. Since in Greco-Roman society, "money is continually given by the powerful to their dependents, and this transfer of cash downwards in the social scale is the main instrument by which the status of the powerful is asserted." Judge, "Social Identity," 211.

42. Cf. Theissen, *Social Setting*, 70–73; Holmberg, *Sociology*, 45–47. Edwards comments that the "leisure, administrative skills, education, and affluence" of wealthy Christians, "gave them enormous advantages for becoming the local, indigenous leaders in the congregations that Paul founded"; Edwards, "Sociology," 438.

43. Of seventeen persons (or circles of people) named by Paul, nine were engaged in travel: Aquila, Priscilla, Stephanas, Erastus, Sosthenes, Crispus, Phoebe, Gaius, Titius Justus. Of these nine, Sosthenes (1 Cor 1:1; Acts 18:17) possibly was not a Corinthian. Theissen, *Social Setting*, 91–95.

44. There is also a possibility that Achaicus, Fortunatus, and Tertius belonged to the lower class, (1 Cor 16:17; Rom 16:22), and the social standing of Jason, Lucius, and Sosipater remains unclear. Cf. Theissen, *Social Setting*, 93, 95, 115n53. Also see Horrell, *Social Ethos*, 96–98; H.-J. Klauck, *1 Korintherbrief*, 10.

45. Cf. Theissen, *Social Setting*, 102.

Fellowship Meals in Corinth: The Abuse at the Lord's Supper

sort of association common in the Greco-Roman world formed to support people with the same trade/profession. As Christianity spread rapidly in the Greco-Roman world, the believers came from all the segments of the society, reflecting the diversity of the Greco-Roman world and its social class systems. Kyrtatas rightly comments:

> The early Christian communities, it is now accepted, had complex social structures, drawing members of both sexes from all ages and social classes (as Pliny had noticed in the early second century). In the large cities of the Roman empire, such as Rome and Alexandria, there seem to have been many more of the educated and of the upper classes than was once thought.[46]

Thus the Christian congregation in Corinth encompassed various groups and classes, many cultures, ethnic and social identities and thus various interests, customs, assumptions, and stratification.[47] The church in Corinth portrays how Christianity made inroads into the urban environment, and in the process its outlook also changed, from a reform movement inside Palestinian Judaism to a Hellenistic movement based in the urban cities of the Greco-Roman world.[48] Some were wealthy having considerable influence, while some were slaves and household servants or manual workers.[49] Certainly, this phenomenon led to constant differences among themselves and contributed to the problem at the Lord's Supper.

---

46. Kyrtatas, *Social Structure*, 185.

47. Some are still cautious because the evidences provided by both the older consensus and the new consensus to prove that the early Christians were poor, middle-class, or high-class are inadequate to portray a full description of the social level of the first Christians. But the common view that early Christianity was a proletarian movement has been rejected over the view that the early church was socially more diverse. Moreover it has been emphasized in both these perspectives that each Christian congregation has to be studied in its contemporary society setting, as the message and literature of the NT is closely related with the reality and context of the social world of the early church. Cf. Meeks, *First Urban Christians*, 72–73; Coutsoumpos, *Paul and the Lord's Supper*, 63.

48. Stambaugh and Balch, *New Testament*, 52–55.

49. Cf. Witherington, *Conflict and Community*, 22–23; He also asserts that the believers in Corinth were better off than some of the other churches in Macedonia, since Paul talks about the Corinthians having a surplus of assets (2 Cor 8:1, 2, 14).

FELLOWSHIP MEALS IN THE EARLY CHURCH

The New Testament gives ample examples to show that fellowship meal practices were a characteristic feature of the life of Jesus. Many agree with the view that Jesus offered the kingdom to the outcasts and sinners by means of the fellowship meals.[50] His actions symbolized the new kind of relationship he offered and a realization of the Kingdom of God. Through the fellowship meals he invited his disciples to celebrate the joy of the present experience and anticipated its consummation in the future. In general many scholars have noted the importance and significance of fellowship meals in the ministry and teaching of Jesus.[51] In fact the importance of fellowship meals in the ministry of Jesus put him in direct confrontation with the religious leaders and the Temple authorities that ultimately led to the Cross.[52]

Evidence also shows the Lord's Supper as it was instituted and practised in the early church was an elaborate fellowship meal. It was not a separate ritual meal instituted in isolation but was part of the whole schema of the ministry of Jesus in which fellowship meals played an important part.[53] The early church likewise continued with this practice regularly, which was nonetheless a common practice of that time.[54] Unlike an annual Passover

---

50. The idea figures prominently, with some variation and elaboration, in the recent studies of Breech, *Silence of Jesus* 22–64; Borg, *Conflict, Holiness and Politics*, 78–121; Borg, *Jesus*, 101–102, 131–33; Crossan, *Historical Jesus*, 260–64, 332–53; Chilton, *Temple of Jesus* 137–54.

51. For instance, Bartchy, "Table Fellowship," 796–800; Bartchy, "Historical Jesus," 175–83; Neyrey *Social World*, 361–87; Koenig, *New Testament Hospitality*; Smith, "Historical Jesus," 466–86; Blomberg, *Contagious Holiness*, 78–80; Chilton, *Feast of Meanings*; Heil, *Meal Scenes*; Perrin, *Rediscovering*.

Others who emphasize on the theme of Jesus' table fellowship with the outcast as part of the historical Jesus data are Bornkamm, *Jesus of Nazareth*, 80–81; Jeremias, *Parables*, 227; Jeremias, *New Testament Theology*, 115–16; Vermes, *Jesus the Jew*, 224; M. Smith, *Jesus the Magician*, 122–23, 152; Hengel, *Charismatic Leader*, 67.

52. See the arguments in Chilton, *Temple of Jesus*, 154–55.

53. E. Lohmeyer in particular has suggested that it is against the full background of meal-parables and meal-activity in the ministry of Jesus that the Lord's Supper is to be seen; "Vom urchristlichen Abendmahl," 168–227, 273–312 and TRu 10 (1938): 81–99; and "Das Abendmahl in der Urgemeinde," 217–52; Wainwright gives a convincing argument on the similarities both in form and meaning between the Lord's Supper and the meals of Jesus' ministry, *Eucharist and Eschatology*, 42–52.

54. Pliny's letter to Trajan mentions that Christians gathered "to partake of food-but food of an ordinary and innocent kind"; He defined them as a "political association" on the basis of their gatherings for communal meals, like other Greek and Roman clubs.

Fellowship Meals in Corinth: The Abuse at the Lord's Supper

meeting their regular fellowship meals included the remembrance of the Lord's death and resurrection where the main meal was followed by the Eucharistic remembrance.[55]

As we have noted earlier, even among the early Christians the fellowship meals functioned to create and define their identity as a new community, by acting as a boundary marker.[56] In fact some of the earliest controversies in the early church were due to issues about community identity and solidarity enacted in their communal meals.[57] The very act of coming together and sharing a meal was a powerful symbol for social bonding in the ancient world. So the early church prescribed certain food, to ensure commensality at the table and thus to effect shared identity as Christians.[58] In this manner the fellowship meal became a "catalyst" by creating social bonding and a sense of belonging, as Gentiles became part of the church.

FELLOWSHIP MEALS IN CORINTH

The Christian community at Corinth, like any other group or association in the ancient world, also met together for fellowship meals.[59] We can deduce from Paul's letters that fellowship meals were a regular part of their

---

Pliny the Younger *Ep.*10.96.

55. Cf. *Did.* 10:1: "after you are filled."

56. Schottroff notes that immediately after the death of Jesus, the Lord's Supper "was already the action that created the identity of the groups that were coming into being, and hence also the locus of belief in the resurrection." Schottroff, "Holiness and Justice," 51.

57. Cf. Gal. 2:11–14 talks about a controversy of interpretation of communal meals between the parties of James and of Peter. Since fellowship meals served as a strong focus for the identity of the church, they had to tackle the question of inclusion of others. See the discussion in Kreider, *Communion Shapes Character* 35–36; White, "Regulating Fellowship," 179; Also Rom 14:1—15:13 and 1 Cor 5:11 where Paul even tells them not to eat with those who were involved in immoral activities.

58. Acts 15:20, 29; 21:25. Unlike the Jewish dietary laws or the boundary markers of circumcision, these food laws were not intended to separate or divide the community, but they were to ensure an inclusive community through common fellowship meals. The meal provided the occasion and ideology for the inclusion of Gentiles into the community. Neyrey, "Ceremonies in Luke-Acts," 382; Smith, *From Symposium to Eucharist*, 185.

59. In many aspects the early Christian groups functioned similarly to their contemporary associations and clubs. See the comparison between the Christian groups and Roman clubs, guilds, and associations in Meeks, *First Urban Christians*, 78–79.

worship (11:18, 11:33); and played a significant role in this community; as such that he had to deal firmly with the issues about food offered to idols and abuse at the fellowship meals which otherwise could be detrimental to the community. The fellowship meal certainly had the role of a community marker for the church in Corinth. Paul asserts this aspect of the fellowship meal in 1 Cor 10:17 when he uses the bread as the symbol of unity.[60]

Fellowship meals were held at private homes which served as the house churches.[61] A likely scenario was that wealthy members of the church invited the rest to their private homes which was the focal meeting point for the congregation. The householders who hosted the church for its meeting functioned as patrons of the church.[62] Naturally the patrons would also extend the cultural practice of hospitality, which was usually centered around sharing food with one's guest.[63] This would mean that both the communal meal and worship took place at the same place. Nonetheless this was customary in Greco-Roman circles for other social events and entertainment to continue after the fellowship meals. Thus the church at Corinth would have the communal worship during the symposium.[64] This form of practice found popularity through the Greco-Roman practice of

---

60. Instone-Brewer and Philip observe that the bread would have reminded the Jews in the congregation of the bread which was used as a boundary marker for the community and was symbolically eaten at a communal meal on the evening of Sabbath. "Jewish Association," 9.

61. Since Christianity was not a recognized religion in the first century AD, there would have been no public meeting place, such as the Jewish Synagogue. Hence the only facilities available would have been the private homes. Murphy-O'Connor, *St. Paul's Corinth*, 153–54. Meeks, *First Urban Christians*, 75.

62. Cf. Rom 16:5. On the sociological significance and function of house churches in Paul and early Christianity, see especially Filson, "Significance," 105–6; Theissen, "Social Stratification," 83–91; Malherbe, *Social* Aspects, 60–112; Banks, *Paul's Idea of Community*, 26–36; Branick, *House Church*.

63. For a study of hospitality in the NT see Koenig, *New Testament Hospitality*, 1–12.

64. To adjourn the fellowship meal and change the location for worship would have been considered quite "inhospitable" in their setting. Moreover, the absence of an official place for worship for the early Christians meant that the dining place was the most appropriate location.

Smith further suggests that the discussion in 1 Cor 12–14 takes place at table after supper. It bears a marked similarity to the form taken by the activities at a symposium. 1 Cor 14:26 is a reminiscent of the philosophical banquets attended by Aulus Gellius where each guest brought a topic for discussion at the symposium (Gell. *Noct. att.* 7.13.1–4); *From Symposium*, 79, 201–2.

the formal fellowship meal which consisted of the *deipnon* and symposium, which by this time had become a standard procedure.

As it was the case in many of the ancient fellowship meals, the meal events at Corinth were both a social and a religious occasion.[65] Fee comments in this regard that, in general, cultic meals were linked with several social festivities. During seasons of festivity or at important times, like marriage, good fortune, and especially at death, families or friends were invited to temples or shrines to participate in fellowship meals and worshipping idols.[66] This would explain how the Lord's Supper was also part of the fellowship meal at Corinth. This would have been a normal practice for many of the new converts coming from pagan background.

The reference to the fellowship meal in 1 Corinthians 11 describes an occasion where the community gathered together to celebrate and have fellowship. The letter provides some idea about the structure of the meal and what happened during the course of the meal, and the situation that created the conflict (1 Cor 11:17–22). As Paul states there were divisions during the meals, with some members going ahead with the meal, and some being humiliated and left hungry. As we have noticed in the background study of fellowship meals, the disorder at Corinth was fairly similar to some of the Greco-Roman meal traditions.[67]

Analysis of the Corinthian Situation

In order to explain the dispute at Corinth, scholars have tried to compare the fellowship meal reported in Corinthians with different fellowship meals prevalent during that time. Peter Lampe thinks that the meal was based on the Greco-Roman *eranos* meal tradition, where everyone brought their contribution to the occasion.[68] In chapter 11, the phrase "one's own meal,"

---

65. See the earlier discussion on fellowship meals in chapter 3, where we have concluded that both social and religious meanings were associated with the observances. Thus, offering of food, prayers, libations, and the singing of hymns were common practices even in meals of a secular nature. For example, Plutarch and others mentioned that during philosophical feasts in the context of birthdays and wedding ceremonies, food was offered to the gods, and the priest, but the majority of food was prepared for eating as a social event or a festive meal before the god. Plut. *Quaest. conv.* 717B; Lucian *Symp* 5.

66. Fee, "εἰδωλόθυτα Once Again," 184.

67. Aune, "Septem Sapientium," 75–78; Theissen, *Social Setting*, 160–62, Lampe, "Das korinthische Herrenmahl," 198–202; Horrell, *Social Ethos*, 105n249.

68. Lampe gives a detailed comparison between the Corinthian fellowship meal and

which Paul uses to refer to the abuse would mean that those who brought food for the community table ate it themselves instead of sharing it. He suggests that the richer Corinthians understood their eating early after the analogy of a dinner at "first tables" and were not concerned about the late comers who had no time or money to prepare sufficient food baskets for themselves.[69] Then the richer Corinthians seem to have interpreted the beginning of the sacramental eucharistic meal by analogy to the beginning of the pagan second tables. Paul's practical advice was to show that an *eranos* only becomes a truly communal meal once the foods brought by the participants are shared.[70]

He considers that not only the dinner parties could be organized as an *eranos* but also the cultic meals, like that of the sacrificial meal of the Sarapis cult.[71] He indicates that the Lord's Supper mentioned by Paul in 1 Cor 11:20–21 and 10:14–22, in all probability had the same characteristics as that of the Greeks but to a different god.[72] But his explanation does not answer Paul's description of some people going "hungry," if everyone brought their share of food to the meeting, nor does it make full sense of Paul's advice that they should eat at home.

G. Theissen's argument had gained a lot of attention. He argued that the basic tensions in these fellowship meals are best explained along sociological lines.[73] Based on Paul's comments which seem to indicate that the primary issue at the fellowship meals appears to be a social tension within

---

a Greco-Roman *eranos* meal. Lampe, "Corinthian Eucharistic Dinner Party," 1–15. Also see Coutsoumpos who stresses that the church at Corinth has been influenced by the Greco-Roman meal *eranos*. Its model and ideology lay behind the development of the Christian *eranos* meal at Corinth; *Paul and the Lord's Supper*, 132.

69. Plutarch describes a similar situation where guests would bring their own food and probably eat at their own convenience and time. Hence he comments that "where each guest has his own private portion, fellowship perishes." *Quaest. conv.* 644C.

70. Lampe, "Eucharist," 38–39.

71. Ibid., 39. Cf. Aelius Aristides *Sarapis* 54.20–28.

72. He sees similarity between the sacramental meal in Corinth and the second table of a pagan meal. It began with religious acclamations and sacrificial rites, for example, a libation for the emperor (Horace *Carmina* 4.5.31–32; Petron. *Sat.* 60; Dio C. *Hist. Rom.* 51.19.7); this was replaced by the Christian breaking and blessing of the bread. It then ended with a toast to the good spirit of the house and with the mixing of the first jug of wine; similarly, the eucharistic meal ended with the eucharistic cup. Singing and libation which accompanied the mixing of the first jug was replaced by the blessing of the eucharistic cup. Lampe, "Eucharist," 40.

73. Cf. Theissen, *Social Setting*, 96–97.

Fellowship Meals in Corinth: The Abuse at the Lord's Supper

the congregation, Theissen reconstructs the social conditions underlying the disturbances in Corinth and analyzes Paul's "social intention" in his interpretation of the Lord's Supper. Theissen relates the situation in Corinth to the practices in the *collegia* where some were assigned larger quantities of food than other members. He points out that unlike the church in Corinth most clubs and guilds were more socially homogeneous and therefore conflicting expectations might have arisen in the latter.[74] He also relates it with the Greco-Roman custom where the patron makes the banquet an occasion to display his social status. We have noted that this was done by provision of different quantities of food and of varying quality to the invitees according to their social status. The result would be that some would end up in humiliation.[75] This was a common practice and it was done to maintain social stratification in the society.

Theissen's contention is that there was division primarily between the rich and the poor.[76] This internal social stratification was the reason for the division and problems in Corinth and this was manifested specially in the Lord's Supper. The wealthier members acted as the host of the gathering and probably provided the food for all. In doing so they provided both greater quantity and better quality of food and drink to their social equals than to participants of lower status. As a result there was conflict between "different standards of behaviour," between "status-specific expectations and the norms of a community of love."[77]

He sees 11:22 as an indication to this reality, "those who have nothing" as opposed to those who are getting too much to eat and drink. Problems also started when the wealthy, who would have more spare time in the evening began to eat ahead (11:21), before the poorer members, who presumably were still at work, can arrive. The timing of their meals also distinguished the rich from the poor.[78] This would also ensure that the rich

---

74. Theissen, "Soziale Integration," 190–91.

75. Pliny the Younger *Ep.* 2.6. Also Mart. *Epig.* 3.60; 1.20; 4.85; 6.11; 10.49; Juvenal *Sat.* 3.81, 152–56; 5.152–55.

76. A majority of scholars emphasize on the socio economic disparity as the cause of this tension. Cf. Konradt, *Gericht und Gemeinde*, 404, fn., 1083; Marshall, *Last Supper*, 109; Lampe, "Das korinthische Herrenmahl," 192; Klauck, *Herrenmahl*, 293; Barrett, *First Epistle*, 261; D. Garland, *1 Corinthians*, 533–34, 542–44; Fee, *First Epistle*, 531–45; Engberg-Pedersen, "Proclaiming the Lord's Death," 598.

77. Theissen, *Social Setting*, 162–63.

78. Barton adds that by these means the rich were trying to extend their influence in the church. Through their behavior they were trying to enforce their status and their

got better quality and quantities of food.[79] Paul's words "one's own meal" (11:21) would also mean that they were eating their own contribution to the communal meal. Probably they were doing this prior to the utterance of the Eucharistic words (11:23–26), at which point the individual contributions would become the "Lord's Supper" (11:20) and would then be community property.[80] Presumably the wealthy people were claiming their rights over better food at the meal, just as the positions of honor at the table were considered to be theirs.[81] Passakos adds that some of these wealthier Christians wanted to retain the earlier social barriers as masters and slaves. They did not want to forfeit their social advantages when they associated with believers of lower social and economic status.[82] All these actions would be normally acceptable according to the Greco-Roman meal customs.

In the process the rich and wealthy also appear to have been bringing food in huge quantities and were indulging themselves in gluttony and drunkenness, while the poor came with less or no food and ended up hungry. With their ostentatious display of wealth and class they were creating social stratification through their actions. Self-indulgence, gluttony, and drunkenness for which Paul condemns them (vv. 20–21) could have compounded the strife.

Theissen's description of the fellowship meal in Corinth fits well with the Greco-Roman situation and his explanation of "status-specific expectations" of a sharply stratified society as the root of the conflict is reasonable. However, Theissen's view, although appealing, has been questioned on many fronts. First, if those stratifications were the reason for the conflict, Paul does not correct the inequities; in 11:33–34, he simply advises them to eat at their homes.[83] Theissen's reconstruction of social class and status needs to be critically studied as social status need not be equivalent to social

---

dominance over others by imposing shame (1 Cor. 11:22). Barton, "Paul's Sense of Place," 237.

79. Theissen, *Social Setting*, 151–53.

80. Theissen also suggests that the rich people did not see the need to share the food that they brought with the poorer people because of the understanding that Paul's instruction on the Lord's Supper stated only bread and wine as part of the Eucharist meal. *Social Setting*, 153–62.

81. Ibid., 145–74.

82. Passakos, "Eucharist in First Corinthians," 198.

83. Smith, "Meals and Morality," 327–28.

class.[84] Meeks has questioned the criteria by which Theissen has analyzed the social setting of the Corinthians. He raises the question:

> Is social status best understood as a single dimension or as the resultant of several different dimensions? Because Theissen has assumed a single dimension, or an average of several dimensions, he concludes that high status entails a high degree of integration, an assumption which other evidence seems to contradict.[85]

Meeks contends that earlier it was measured on a single scale but social status is a multidimensional phenomenon. Moreover several other considerations are involved.[86] Social status was also associated with the Greco-Roman clubs and associations, whereby members were provided with alternative means to status, which otherwise would not have been available because of their social class.[87]

The historical comparison made by Theissen is true to a certain extent but it does not represent the full historical reality. While social division was an issue at the meals, there were also other factors involved with the fellowship meals. We have noted that in the ancient cultures, social stratification was not merely based on socio-economic reasons, but political, religious, cultural and ideological factors were also at play. Thus meals were very much associated with the politics and ideologies of the different groups and communities in maintaining their own identities.

Then who are these "have-nots" in 1 Cor 11:22? Do they not refer to the poor in the community who are being humiliated by the rich, by giving preference to their friends or others belonging to the upper class? Smith postulates that the reference to the issue of status and social class in ancient literature should not be taken in literal terms. In Greco-Roman literature

---

84. See the comments by John G. Gager in a review of works by Robert M. Grant, Abraham J. Malherbe, and Gerd Theissen, Gager, "Review," 180; and on class and status in general, see MacMullen, *Roman Social Relations*, 88–120.

85. Meeks, *First Urban Christians*, 70.

86. "For example, one might discover that, in a given society, the following variables affect how an individual is ranked: power . . . , occupational prestige, income or wealth, education and knowledge, religious and ritual purity, family and ethnic-group position, and local-community status . . . The generalized status of a person is a composite of his or her ranks in all the relevant dimensions." Meeks, *First Urban Christians*, 54.

87. For instance in the club membership of the College of Diana and Antinous, slaves and other individuals were included, to whom civic status was not available. MacMullen, *Roman Social Relations*, 76–77.

the conflict between rich and poor at meal appears as a literary *topos*.[88] Smith continues to assert that though the meal customs did provide social distinction among the guests according to their status, "these levels of status could all be within the same basic economic and cultural level, and often were."[89] So Paul's reference to the "have-nots" is not an issue between the rich and the poor but a literary *topos*, discussing the issue of status which involved other factors deemed more important than economic factor.[90] Stephen M. Pogoloff adds that the reference to humiliation and shame of the poor is rather puzzling, "since honor and shame are normally much more a concern for the upper class."[91] Therefore the division at the Lord's Supper was not simply a social issue but other factors were involved.

Smith's view is based on the view that the fellowship meal at Corinth was modelled on the Greco-Roman banquet, specifically that of a philosophical meal where the meal was followed by the symposium that included discussion of topics that were related to their school of thought.[92] He goes on to suggest that in 11:23–25 the consecration of bread is similar to the bread ritual that marked the beginning of the *deipnon* proper. Likewise the blessing of the cup reflects the wine ceremony that customarily ended the *deipnon* and began the symposium in Greco-Roman formal meals. All these suggest that the Greco-Roman practices have been adapted and reinterpreted according to the self-identity of the Christian community.[93] There is also a logical relationship between the activities of chapter 11 and

---

88. E.g., *Quaest. conv.* 616F. Plutarch's brother Timon spoke against the rich lording it over the poor. It is not a contrast between social classes, but between extravagant wealth and "the simple life." Cf. Smith, "Meals and Morality," 328.

89. He further suggests that though the Corinthian community contained slaves (1 Cor 7:21–22), such a classification of status need not indicate poverty, Smith, "Meals and Morality," 328. Cf. Bartchy, *First Century Slavery*, 40–44.

90. Smith, "Meals and Morality," 328. He states that the issue rather involved the issue of unity and status in regard to spiritual gifts (chapters 12–14). Also Smith "Table fellowship," 139.

91. Pogoloff, *Logos and Sophia*, 254. He also considers it as a literary *topos* which deals with a social issue of people who suffered at the hands of the rich. But they are "not actually poor, but upper class persons who were not as rich as their host."

92. He asserts that the Greco-Roman banquet ideology was adapted for use in Jewish and Christian communities (see Acts 20:7); Smith and Taussig, *Many Tables*, 27–28. He equates the meal at Antioch and Corinth (Gal 2:11–12 and 1 Cor 11:20) as representing the same basic meal tradition, namely the Greco-Roman banquet; likewise the meal practices at other Pauline churches including Galatia and Rome (Rom 14:1—15:13); Smith, *From Symposium*, 174–77.

93. Smith, "Meals and Morality," 325.

Fellowship Meals in Corinth: The Abuse at the Lord's Supper

chapters 12–14. Both describe events taking place at the same assembly.[94] Thus the description of Christian worship in chapters 12–14 is in line with the symposium format following the banquets of clubs and associations.[95] Paul then drew from the meal tradition to give his interpretation to the Lord's Supper tradition. So the form of the Greco-Roman banquet can explain many of the problems in Corinth that Paul writes about.

While Smith gives an interesting take on the issue at Corinth it does raise some concerns. Smith's main drawback is his emphasis that everything was influenced by the Greco-Roman banquet tradition. The evidence indicates otherwise; as we have discussed, the fellowship meals which were quite prevalent in the Mediterranean world had different cultural meanings and ideologies associated with them in the different communities. The similarities do not amount to interdependence, neither does the adaptation of the format or structure mean that values and ideologies were also borrowed per se. Moreover some of the values were common traits present in all cultures. Since the Greco-Roman culture became prominent in the beginning of the early Christian centuries, it became influential, and was adapted to reinforce values and ideas already present in the fellowship meals. But not everything was accepted; the reaction was also in the opposite direction. This reaction is clearly seen in the works of many of the ancient writers, so also in Paul. Therefore, Smith's analysis of the situation at Corinth also needs to be taken with reservation.

We have already observed that the church at Corinth consisted of people from different socio-economic backgrounds, and they do not exhibit that kind of homogenous community. Moreover, the influence of the Greco-Roman meal traditions on the NT text also needs to be viewed cautiously. While the depiction of fellowship meals in the literature highlights the use of meal themes and motifs, not all description of meals in literature are necessarily literary creations.[96] Themes or motifs in literary works should rather be considered as reflections of the historical or so-

---

94. Cf. 11:20: "when you come together for a meeting . . ." and 14:23: "if then the whole church comes together for a meeting . . ." Also, Bornkamm, "On the Understanding of Worship," 176n2; Aune, "Septem Sapientium," 78; For the unity of chapters 10–14 see Smith, "Meals and Morality," 326.

95. Smith, "Meals and Morality," 325–26.

96. See Smith's analysis of Luke's gospel as a literary work according to the symposium tradition. He also claims that the stories about Jesus' meal fellowship are literary idealization in Smith, "Table Fellowship as a Literary Motif," 613–38. For a useful critique on Smith's view and approach see Blomberg, *Contagious Holiness*, 20–22.

133

cial realities, or else they will have less value and serve no purpose for the readers. The meal motifs assumed their importance as a literary theme because of their significance in society. This is further elucidated by the extant meal practices in different communities to this present time. So the meal descriptions are not simply literary idealisation but reflect the values of the social world, and a lot can be deciphered from these writings. This is proved true when Paul gives the church at Corinth practical options to deal with their problems. So the reference to the 'have-nots' is not simply a literary *topos*, but Paul is dealing here with real life issues and in this case stratification in the community.

Since the previous attempts to explain the Lord's Supper in Corinth based on particular meal practices do not fully explain the situation we need to consider an alternate approach. In chapters 1 and 2 we have already shown the importance of fellowship meals in the ancient world and we have seen that fellowship meal practices in Corinth has incorporated traditions from both Greco-Roman and Jewish contexts, and since the main issue here in Corinth is basically regarding fellowship meal practices our analysis of the situation should be based on pan-cultural fellowship meal traditions as a whole.

We have seen that fellowship meals were used in the Greco-Roman societies by the various groups to promote themselves and also by the individuals to gain positions in the community. This involved honor and shame, with some being assigned rank and status at the table, with better food provisions, while some were left feeling humiliated. This was a normal practice in the ancient world where fellowship meals were used to achieve many purposes: status, rank, honor, position, and identity.

The scene in Corinth also reveals that kind of situation. Since we have noted that it was not purely based on socio-economic reasons, the most probable conclusion is that the different groups were involved in a power struggle within the community based on ideological or sectarian ideas. In the process they were using the fellowship meals to gain influence from the groups, and at the same time exert their dominance over the other opposing groups. As was the case with many of the associations, the patron was honored for providing the banquet for the group. The host or the patron in the church probably expected the group that he favored to return the favor to him by supporting his cause or give control over the group. Then Paul's use of the word "have-nots" probably refers to the group in the community who were at a disadvantage including wealthy people who were

Fellowship Meals in Corinth: The Abuse at the Lord's Supper

being relegated with the others by the patron. This then is not a social class but rhetorical expression on the part of Paul.[97] So the groups consisted of people belonging to different social classes which would reflect the patronage system in Roman society.[98] Moreover, since discretion lies on the host or patron to invite and choose people for the meals and the ranking, we assume that the groups on each side consisted of mixed people from different social backgrounds.[99] The reference to the "hungry" then is a temporal reference to the people who are now being mistreated by the patron/s and their supporters in their struggle for dominance. They now ended up hungry because the patron assigned them a lesser amount of food.

Nonetheless, socio-economic factors have an important role here, as only the rich patrons will be able to host the community for the weekly fellowship meals and worship. Hence, the conflict was a multi-tiered conflict, involving a number of factors.

The situation at Corinth during this period complicated the issue in the church. Suetonius refers to several famines and shortages of food during the reign of Claudius (AD 41–54). Josephus also alludes to the increase of prices during this period.[100] B. W. Winter points out that the food crises in Corinth during the period of the early days of the church would have compounded the issue.[101]

Also the selection and division of the guests to be seated either at the *triclinium* or the *atrium* or *peristyle* depending on their status might have

---

97. We assume that the struggles were between people/leaders who were better off in the community, and so both parties would want to gather as much support from all the members. If it was simply between the rich and the poor then the dynamics will not work. For Paul's letter as a rhetoric see Collins, *First Corinthians*, 18–19, 429–30.

98. The Roman society was "based on patronage, not class stratification. . .Thus society resembled a mass of little pyramids of influence, each headed by a major family— or one giant pyramid headed by an autocrat-not the three-decker sandwich of upper, middle, and lower classes familiar to us from industrial society. . ." Carney, *Shape of the Past*, 63. Cited from Crossan, "Who and What Controls your Banquet?" 292. Also see Finger, *Of Widows*, 171.

99. Ascough "Forms of Commensality," 37.

100. Suetonius *Claud.* 18.2; cf. Tac. *Ann.* 12.43; Dio C. *Hist. Rom.* 40.11; Josephus *Ant.* 3.320–21. Cf. also Acts 11:29–30.

101. The eastern half of the empire was having a significant food crisis, caused in part by a famine in Egypt in the mid and late forties. Winter, "Secular and Christian Responses," 100; Garnsey, *Non-Slave Labour*, 44–45 adds that during food shortage the slave had more security because of his place in the household. The freedman artisans and workers were more insecure because they were exposed to a steep rise in the price of grain.

worsened the problem at Corinth. Murphy-O'Connor also stresses that those who arrived late would find themselves outside the *triclinium*.[102] So this also became a place for discrimination and aggravated the division.[103] All these factors contributed to the social tension in the community.

Identity of the Groups

The reference to "divisions"[104] (σχίσματα, 11:18) which also appears in 1:10 and 12:25 and "factions" (αἱρέσεις, 11:19) makes it evident that the church had tensions and divisions, which is a primary concern for Paul.[105] But who were these groups that were involved in the dispute? Paul does not mention them by name in this particular chapter. Different groups have been postulated. Schmithals suggested that the main group were Gnostics who were opposing the sacrament. They were trying to besmirch the Lord's Supper and turn it into a "profane feast."[106] So Paul was rebuking the Gnostics for the destruction of the community and the cultic element as well. There is no sufficient evidence in this regard; these are only conjectures.[107] Bar-

---

102. He assesses that the main dining room could accommodate twelve people. Murphy-O'Connor, *St. Paul's Corinth*, 158–59. Hays suggests nine guests in this dining area. R. Hays, *First Corinthians*, 418–19. Also see Murphy-O'Connor for archaeological descriptions of Greco-Roman dwellings; *St. Paul's Corinth*, 178–85. Murphy-O'Connor estimates that the atrium without its decorative pieces, could hold up to fifty , or else it could be between thirty to forty, *Keys to First Corinthians*, 183. Hays suggests between thirty to forty people, *First Corinthians*, 196. Thiselton suggests between twenty to thirty people, *First Epistle*, 861.

103. So also Collins, *First Corinthians*, 418–19; Thiselton, *First Epistle*, 859.

104. Though some scholars like Munck have argued that there was no "party" in the church at all, Munck, *Paul and the Salvation of Mankind*, 167, there is a major consensus on the existence of "parties" in the church: Barrett, *Essays on Paul*, 4–6; Theissen, *Social Setting*, 54; Conzelmann, *1 Corinthians*, 34; Fee, *First Epistle*, 47. For a discussion on the identity of the groups in the letter see Hurd, *Origin of 1 Corinthians*, 96–107; Barrett, "Sectarian Diversity at Corinth," 95; Winter, *Philo and Paul*, 183–84; Chow, *Patronage*, 102–107; Clarke, *Secular and Christian Leadership*, 95; Carter, "Big Men in Corinth," 58–59.

105. M. M. Mitchell, rightly observes 1:10 as the "thesis statement" for the whole letter, *Paul and the Rhetoric of Reconciliation* 1, 138–57.

106. Schmithals, *Gnosticism in Corinth*, 225; Also Meeks, *Moral World*, 68–70, 133; Collins, *First Corinthians*, 17.

107. "The problem was caused neither by the Corinthians' theological confusion about sacramental facets of the Lord's Supper nor by a conflict over Eucharistic theology." Garland, *1 Corinthians*, 533.

Fellowship Meals in Corinth: The Abuse at the Lord's Supper

rett suggests the possibility that some Jewish Christians may have insisted on kosher food and thereby separated themselves from the Gentile believers.[108] This scenario seems unlikely as the text implies that the whole congregation still came together for the fellowship meals. Barrett also suggests that some of the Corinthians were "behaving as if the age to come were already consummated."[109] It meant that they were considering themselves as superior, above others and in deep communion with the divine that they did not consider other participants at the fellowship meals.[110] Some consider that some of the members, influenced by their exalted Christology and pneumatology considered themselves "satiated" (4:8), and with their new view of individual freedom considered the Lord's Supper as having a magical effect.[111] So the idea that by partaking of the Lord's Supper they became immune from sin and exempt from judgment also played a part in their behavior at the meeting.[112] Thus to refute this kind of idea Paul compares the church with Israel of Old (cf. 1 Cor 10:1–13), though they were fed with manna, when they were unfaithful, they came under divine judgment; so also at the Lord's Supper. It does not immunize them from sin and divine judgment. Other possible groups are also indicated in the letter: A freedom party (5:2); ascetics (chap. 7), pneumatics (chap. 12), and skeptics (15:12–19).[113] The different groups suggested above are not surprising since Alexandrian Judaism, Jewish Christianity, and Hellenism, all seem to have made some impact at Corinth.[114] However, there is no clear indication that the above-mentioned groups existed as a "group" or "faction" unlike the other factions which Paul has already identified in chapter 1. Nonetheless the above discussions support the view that theological and ideological

---

108. Barrett, *First Epistle*, 261.

109. Ibid., 109. Fee talks about it in terms of "spiritualised eschatology" *First Epistle*, 12; "Their outlook was that of having arrived (see 4:8)—not in an eschatological sense but in a 'spiritual' sense." *First Epistle*, 339; Also Thiselton, "Realised Eschatology," 523; Horrell, *Social Ethos*, 120–23.

110. See also Passakos "Eucharist in 1 Corinthians," 199.

111. The idea that the Corinthians thought that the Lord's Supper worked in an automatic or quasi-magical manner, and partaking of the supper automatically exempted them from judgment is widely recognized. See Barrett, *First Epistle*, 220, 223; Käsemann, "Pauline Doctrine," 126; Fee, *First Epistle*, 443.

112. Cf. Conzelmann, *1 Corinthians*, 194.

113. See Barrett who proposes more potential parties in the letter, "Sectarian Diversity," 287–95.

114. Barrett, *Essays on Paul*, 3.

factors were involved at the abuse during the fellowship meal.[115] Hence the behavior of the Corinthians was not only socially motivated but there were also religious and theological dimensions to the division and the conflict. This is not surprising as the sacred and secular dimension were an integral part of the fellowship meals.[116]

Since Paul has already named the groups in chapter 1 where the community was divided on the basis of the allegiance to the different leaders, the most probable explanation is that the earlier dissension found its way even into the fellowship meal in chapter 11.[117] Paul further writes in 3:3 about the jealousy and strife in the community which he connects with the leaders of the groups.[118] Similarly in 3:12 he forbids boasting in men with a reference to the groups.[119] Since fellowship meals were used in different cultures for political and social gains it is probable that these are the groups who are also the main protagonist in this Lord's Supper episode. So now at the Lord's Supper the various leaders were struggling for position of influence in the church, as the main underlying issues as we have observed here are of position and status.[120] Accordingly the divided loyalties among the members led to divisions in the community and contributed to this tension at the meal.

---

115. This would also include the issue of food offered to idols (chaps 8–10). Since the Lord's Supper was part of the fellowship meal where the food (meat) of such origin was included in the menu; it implies that the issue at the table involved many factors apart from socio-economic factors.

116. Horrell rightly observes that: "Sociological and theological perspectives should not be viewed as mutually exclusive alternatives, although their forms of analysis and priorities are very different." *Social Ethos*, 119.

117. Most accept the presence of groups in chapter 11 but they see it as an issue between the rich and the poor. So they consider that the division in chapter 11 is different from the splits in 1:10 or 3:1–4. So, Fee, who indicates that the issue in chapter 11 is a result of a sociological factor, unlike the division in chapter 1:10–12 where it was caused due to their allegiances to their leaders or to "wisdom;" Fee, *First Epistle*, 537. So also Barrett, "Sectarian Diversity," 293; Fitzmyer, *I Corinthians*, 433; Chow, *Patronage*, 102–7; Hays, *First Corinthians*, 198.

118. Winter sees the charge of envy and strife as evidence of sophist opponents since their debates were marked by quarrelling and a love for supremacy. So these were groups with affiliation to their favorite teachers, *Philo and Paul*, 203–4.

119. Cf. Carter, "Big Men in Corinth," 54.

120. Some commentators do relate the present problem to the same factions as in 1:10; e.g., Lietzmann and Kümmel *An die Korinther I, II*, 55; Lindemann, *Der erste Korintherbrie*, 250. Fitzmyer, *I Corinthians*, 433; Witherington, *Conflict and Community*, 248. But again they see the division here as between the rich and poor like the rest.

Fellowship Meals in Corinth: The Abuse at the Lord's Supper

Since fellowship meals functioned as boundary markers, there is a strong possibility that in Corinth, some of the members were using the fellowship meals to reinforce their identity as belonging to a different faction or group.[121] The fellowship meal being the main meeting point and activity for the Christian community, this would have been the occasion for them to exercise and promote their views.

Just as the social make-up of the community was diverse, the issue at the supper seems to be complex. The problem seems to be a product of not only sociological factors but a multifaceted issue, involving social, economic, cultural, religious, and theological motives, requiring a combined approach to the whole issue at hand.[122]

In short the problem had arisen mainly due to the clash of ideology and culture.[123] It was a clash between the teaching and ethics of the new community and the prevalent culture and customs. Inevitably the new members in the community have imported the prevalent practices which contradict the core values of the Gospel. The situation is understandable, as different people groups gather with their own social, cultural, and religious backgrounds, influencing their attitudes and behavior in the community.

PAUL'S RESPONSE TO THE CORINTHIAN SITUATION

Paul then proceeds to correct their attitude and action during the meeting. Apparently Paul had already anticipated this concern in his previous reference to the meal in 10:17. As it has been reported to him, Paul knew the nature of the abuse; therefore he tries to change the totally unacceptable behavior of the Corinthians, to that which is in keeping with the true nature of the gospel message. Paul's response to the situation indicates that he

---

121. Though there were divisions in the church, but since the Corinthians still met together as one group, and sought Paul's advice, the inference is that the church did not break up, but their relationship was strained and it was "no longer a unified and harmonious community." See, Barrett, *First Epistle*, 261; Chow, *Patronage*, 88, 94.

122. Horrell comes close to this interpretation. He avers that: ". . . the 'theological' interpretation of the Corinthian church's problems (viz., the 'theology' of wisdom, power, and knowledge) and the 'sociological' interpretation (viz., a socially stratified congregation in which the behaviour of the socially prominent members is causing particular concern) may be brought together rather than separated as alternatives once it is recognised that Paul's 'theological' opponents are a particular group within the congregation comprising at least some of these higher status individuals." *Social Ethos*, 123. Also Malberbe, *Social Aspects*, 84.

123. Cf. Murphy-O'Connor, *Paul: A Critical Life*, 273.

considered their practice as having some serious flaws. The letter indicates that the abuse took place when the main meal course took place and not during the time when the bread and wine were shared to remember the Lord.

Paul's most serious charge is that it is not the "Lord's Supper" (11:20).[124] It shows that he considers the whole of the fellowship meal as the "Lord's Supper" and not only the ceremony where the bread and wine were shared.[125] The text shows the meal practices in Corinth can be measured against the prevalent meal practices and ideology of the ancient world. Like any other fellowship meal, the secular and the sacred seems to be entwined even in this case. Paul's intention in quoting the Last Supper tradition to instruct them clearly shows that he considered the Lord's Supper an integral part of a complete fellowship meal.

Likewise with Jesus, the institution happened in the context of a communal meal where the whole event of the passion was foretold. By using this term Paul's intention is to bring out the real significance of the meal: that it pertains to the Lord.[126] But through their actions the term "Lord's Supper" has become a misnomer as they have made the Lord's Supper into their own private meals violating the very nature and sanctity of the meal the name stands for.[127] Christ has created this new and inclusive com-

---

124. Some contest that the term recalls Hellenistic mystery cults at which the cult-god is thought to be present. The terminology is similar to the Sarapis cult, where the meal is termed "the couch of the Lord Sarapis"; Aelius Aristides, *Sarapis* 54:13–15. See Weiss, *Earliest Christianity*, 2.640-41; Maccoby, "Paul and the Eucharist," 267; Fee comments that the term reflects the cultic meals, which Paul now transfers to the Christian meal in contrast to the pagan table; *First Epistle*, 539n42.

125. Also Custer, "When is Communion Communion?" 404.

126. According to Fee, the term denotes "in honor of the Lord," *First Epistle*, 539–40; Thiselton suggests that it is "a term which denotes the *focus* of thanksgiving, salvation, and sharing." *First Epistle*, 864.

127 What does Paul mean by stating that it is no longer the Lord's Supper? Does the believer's action affect the efficacy of the Lord's Supper? Calvin underscores this point when he says:"the efficacy of the sacraments does not depend upon the worthiness of men, and that the promises of God are not in the least impaired or destroyed by the badness of men . . . the body of Christ is offered to bad men just as much as to good. . .For, in the Supper God does not cheat the wicked by a mere representation of the body of His Son, but really does hold it out to them; and the bread is not an empty sign for them, but a pledge of His faithfulness. Their rejecting it does not damage or alter the nature of the sacrament in any way whatever." Calvin, *Commentary*, 252. Käsemann expresses the same: "We do not by our own lack of reverence, render his gift ineffective, nor turn the presence of Christ into absence. We cannot paralyse God's eschatological action; salvation despised becomes judgment . . ." Käsemann, *Essays on New Testament Themes*, 125.

Fellowship Meals in Corinth: The Abuse at the Lord's Supper

munity consisting of both Jews and Gentiles which Paul has time again advocated.[128] The Lord's Supper enables them to have this realization in the present; when this does not happen then it is no longer the "Lord's Supper." Paul's concern here is to divert the attention from their selfish acts to the Lord himself. The Lord's Supper cannot be eaten in an atmosphere of mistrust and inequality just as it was not possible for them to participate in the table of the Lord and the table of the demons (10:21).[129]

Paul rebukes them for their individualism as "each one" (11:21) went ahead with his or her own meal as it defeats the whole purpose of "coming together" (11:20) and the unity it was supposed to create.[130] The picture that emerges here is two sided. On one hand it can be understood in a temporal sense that some of them were going ahead in eating their meals in private.[131] At the same time it can also be seen as a practice where some of them were eating without sharing with others.[132]

Both these interpretations seem possible in this context, in the sense that though it is a communal meal, some went ahead with their meals and even when they were eating together it became a private affair for there

---

In short the abuse at the Lord's Supper meant that it no longer functioned as originally intended. It still remains the Lord's Supper, but its purpose is changed.

128. Cf. Gal 2:11; Rom 15:7.

129. Bruce, *1 and 2 Corinthians*, 110.

130. The term does not refer to every member, but its emphatic position highlights the individualistic behavior of some of the members. So this is "in contrast to Paul's emphasis that they are eating *together as the church*." Fee, *First Epistle*, 541.

131. This correlates well with 11:33, where he advises them to wait for one another; then the main problem is that some were simply starting to eat before the others arrived. Theissen, "Social Integration," 151–53.

132. A more common meaning of προλαμβάνειν when its object is food is simply "to eat." So it can mean that the fellowship meal was conducted in such a way that it was made of individual meals rather than a communal meal. Bornkamm, "Lord's supper and Church in Paul," in Bornkamm, *Early Christian Experience*, 126; Conzelmann, *1 Corinthians*, 194–95, 202–3. Cf. Burton, *Syntax of the Moods and Tenses*, 50–51 who remarks that the aorist infinitive "to eat" in 11:21 does not indicate action antecedent to the principal verb. So "the grammatical considerations would suggest that we translate the aorist articular infinitive as indicating the time during which the activity of the main verb took place." See also the discussion in Plut. *Quaest. conv.* 643F-644A, 644D. So Garland comments that the phrase "each one goes ahead" vs. 21 does not imply a private meal eaten before hand but refers to something that takes place in the presence of all—"during the meal." Garland, *1 Corinthians*, 541. Also Witherington, *Conflict and Community*, 249; who suggests that when the wealthy were served first with better portions, "then the poor in the atrium get what is left over." To bring out the force of the verb, it is also translated as—"to devour"; Hallbäck, "Sacred Meal," 170.

Exclusion and Judgment in Fellowship Meals

was no fellowship. When each one went ahead with his own meal without sharing, it ended in gluttony and drunkenness, which was not in keeping with the character and nature of the meeting. The description given here indicates that the Corinthians were following the conventions of that time where people would usually get drunk during the symposium. In any case, Paul stands to prevent them bringing in any distinctions to the common meal of believers, where Christ had made them all one, signified by their all eating of the one loaf (10:17).

He then raises a series of rhetorical questions to the Corinthians to reconsider their actions.[133] "Do you not have houses to eat and drink in?" Here Paul seems to be drawing on a double contrast: they should not assimilate times when they entertain guests for meals with when they invite fellow believers for the Lord's Supper. Secondly the homes being used as a sacred space for the church fellowship meeting was not to be confused with other social and domestic use of the place.[134] Some commentators conclude that Paul wanted only bread and wine to be served at the eucharistic meal and did not want the Corinthians to have a fellowship meal between the breaking of the bread and the blessing of the Cup.[135] But this interpretation does not fit in with Paul's further instruction to wait for one another to eat together in 11:33. Moreover Paul would be contradicting himself and humiliating the "have-nots," if his advice was for the wealthier Christians to eat at home and share only the bread and wine with the "hungry ones."[136]

Paul rebukes them again, that when they promote their personal interest at the fellowship meals they were despising the "church of God" and more importantly the gospel itself.[137] Their actions have transformed a solemn occasion into an occasion of humiliation and abuse. Their selfish action against their own brethren went against the very notion of what Christ did for them and the communal meal that signified the benefits they

---

133. Cf. 1 Cor 11:22. His rhetorical questions are intended to reduce the "sated" to a position of humiliation as they have done to the poor. Fee, *First Epistle*, 543.

134. Barton, "Paul's Sense of Place," 225–46; He further comments, Paul seeks to reorder "social relations in the church by restricting the intrusion of household-based power." 239; cf. Witherington, *Conflict and Community*, 242.

135. E.g., Theissen, "Social Integration," 145–46; Klauck, *Herrenmahl*, 294, 371.

136. Lampe, "Eucharist," 41–42.

137. The genitive shows that "the church is more than simply a human society in institution; it belongs to *God*. To show contempt for *the church, which is God's*, is to despise what God has made his own, and on which God has set his love, and therefore given it status and honor in his own eyes." Thiselton, *First Epistle*, 864.

Fellowship Meals in Corinth: The Abuse at the Lord's Supper

were having.[138] In their behavior those who were abusing the "have-nots" (11:22) were sinning against Christ. This connection can be seen in the body analogy that Paul uses in v. 27.[139]

From the outset Paul has been a staunch advocate for equality and concern for others at the table. The core values of his motives seem to have derived from Jesus himself whose ministry was marked by fellowship meals, and who finally instituted the commemorative supper.[140] Jesus' action marked a new beginning, freed humanity from the present age including divisions of any kind. It is now at the table that they were in communion and identification with the Lord (10:16). In like manner they had to exhibit the kingdom ethics based on love at the table as a starting point, as it was a preview of the coming kingdom.

To remind them of this significance, Paul now quotes the Last Supper tradition (11:23-26), which nonetheless has been expanded by him.[141] He uses the tradition to remind them of the significance of the fellowship meal. The words and acts of Jesus at the Last Supper should be taken as the basis for a solution to the problem and a model for a correct and proper fellowship meal.

Paul's Interpretation of the Lord's Supper Tradition

The Lord's Supper tradition that Paul cites in 1 Cor 11:23-26 is considered by most scholars as representing the earliest account in the New Testament.[142] It gives us a description of the structure and procedure of the

---

138. Similarly, Thiselton maintains that Paul's concern was that "the love for the other, the outsider, the 'weak,' which characterized the death of Christ, was thrust aside." *First Epistle*, 850.

139. Thus Hays writes: "The problem is not desecration of the sacred elements but rather offense against Christ himself... The thought is similar to the idea expressed in 1 Cor 8:12," i.e., sinning against a fellow believer is sinning against Christ; *First Corinthians*, 201.

140. The practice of fellowship in the early church was an attempt by the church to imitate his life. "This is where the continuity between Jesus and early Christianity is to be found." Breech, "Jesus and his Table Companions," 59.

141. Most commentators believe that the words "on the night when he was betrayed" (11:23), the command for "remembrance" (11:24, 25), and "For as often as you eat this bread and drink this cup, you proclaim the Lord's death until he comes" (11:26) are to be taken as Paul's expansions. E.g., Jeremias, *Eucharistic Words*, 106-7; Marshall, *Last Supper*, 51.

142. Contra Jeremias who considers Mark's account as the earliest based on its

Lord's Supper which was an integral part of the fellowship meal. As we have already noted, the procedure at Corinth is very much similar to the format of a Greco-Roman fellowship meal.[143] This does not necessarily mean that the Lord's Supper was based on it but it indicates that the practice was influenced by the prevalent culture of that time.

There is a general consensus that there are two main Lord's Supper traditions in the NT, that of Luke and Paul on the one hand, and that of Mark and Matthew on the other.[144] Paul's account is similar to Luke's, but differs from the one represented by Mark and Matthew. According to the history of the tradition, it is believed that Matthew's account is a further development of Mark. Both traditions are rooted in the same history; however there are differences in the cup saying and the appearance of the "remembrance" motif in Paul/Luke. Again when Luke's version differs from Paul in the cup saying it has similarities to that of Mark/Matthew. So it has been argued that Luke represents an independent tradition, or a mixture containing features derived from the Marcan as well as the Pauline account.[145] Most likely, they

---

linguistic characteristic. But he also admits that there are many idioms in these verses which are foreign to Paul, indicating that the verses are pre-Pauline. *Eucharistic Words*, 104, 118–19. Higgins also argued that Mark's Gospel, which was written later, has many Aramaic expressions and could be considered an older text than Paul's version. Higgins, *The Lord's Supper*, 24; Davies, *Paul and Rabbinic Judaism*, 249.

But the view that Paul's account is more primitive than that in the Gospels has commanded more support. Behm, "klaw," in *TDNT*, 3.730–2; Marxsen, *Lord's Supper*, 4–8; Schweizer, *Lord's Supper*, 10–17; Jones, *Christ's Eucharistic Presence*, 10. Maccoby along with Lietzmann goes to the extent that Paul was the originator of the eucharist, and that the eucharist itself is not a Jewish, but an essentially Hellenistic rite, showing principal affinities not with the Jewish *qiddush*, but with the ritual meal of the mystery religions. Maccoby, *Paul and Hellenism*, 91; Lietzmann, *Mass and Lord's Supper*, 172–74. Contra Johannes Weiss states that the tradition of the Lord's Supper is not an innovation of Paul, but older than Paul which was already in use, *Earliest Christianity*, 642–46. Schottroff comments "this account by Paul brings us closer to the life of the historical Jesus than almost any other traditions in the New Testament . . . Paul's version offers a very old snapshot of the oral tradition of the first generation of Jesus' followers." "Holiness and Justice," 51.

143. Smith, "Meals and Morality," 325.

144. For a comprehensive discussion of the Lord's Supper traditions see: Palmer, *Sacraments and Worship*, 38–215; Cullmann and Leenhardt, *Essays on the Lord's Supper*; Delorme et al., *Eucharist in the New Testament*; Küng, *Sacraments*, 43–112; Clements et al., *Eucharistic Theology*; Marxsen, *Lord's Supper*.

145. For a summary discussion on the issues regarding the origin and relationship between Paul's account and the Synoptic Gospel see Schweizer, *Lord's Supper*, 10–17; Marshall, *Last Supper*, 39–40; W. Marxsen, *Lord's Supper*, 5. Fee, *First Epistle*, 555: implies that Luke follows an independent tradition and that 22:19–20, reflects the unmodified

Fellowship Meals in Corinth: The Abuse at the Lord's Supper

represent adaptations of a common tradition, adapted according to their theological application. For instance the repeated remembrance motif with the addition of v. 26, which is Paul's own interpretation of the institutional words, indicates where Paul's concerns lie.

This citation of the tradition along with the allusions to his teachings in 7:10 and 9:14, give an indication that the Corinthians were familiar with the Jesus traditions, which they had failed to observe (11:2, 17, 22). So Paul now reminds them of the importance and meaning of the Lord's Supper which should govern their actions too. This is the point of the γάρ with which the verse begins.

From the outset Paul appeals to the authority of the tradition by referring to its divine origin that he has received it "from the Lord" (11:23).[146] The verbs "received" (παρέλαβον) and "passed on" or "handed on" (παρέδωκα) are seen as technical terms which correspond to the Hebrew *qibbel* and *masar*, which connote the transmission of religious instruction in Jewish circles.[147] It appears that the main reason why Paul uses the technical terms is to emphasize the authority of this dominical tradition, which ultimately comes from the Lord.[148] At the same time the basic agreement with the gospel accounts indicates that Paul's claim of dominical continuity is proved valid.

There is a debate regarding how Paul received this tradition from the Lord. Was Paul trying to imply that the Lord communicated immediately to him the truth in question, in the Damascus road experience, or in a special divine revelation without any kind of mediation?[149] Or the Lord him-

---

version of the Pauline text.

146. Some claim that the tradition of the Lord's Supper does not originate from Jesus himself; but this claim does not hold much weight. E.g., Meier, "Eucharist," 335–51; Crossan, *Historical Jesus*, 360–67.

147. Moule, *Worship*, 24. The analogy of the words with Jewish tradition has been questioned by Barrett, since the vocabulary is found in ancient Greek usage long before this was in any way influenced by Jewish usage. Barrett, *First Epistle*, 264–266; Conzelmann also comments that they are technical terms in both Greek and Jewish world in the preservation of traditions. But in the case of Paul he transmits the tradition "independent of human authority." *1 Corinthians*, 195–96. Jeremias argues that this is a notion of an old, established tradition that Paul was reminding the Corinthians of, seen in 1 Cor 15:3. Paul here uses the same technical terms παραδιδόναι and παραλαμβάνειν; *Eucharistic Words*, 101.

148. Also Horsley, *1 Corinthians*, 160; Schrage, *Der erste Brief*, 3.29–31.

149. In Gal 1:12 a similar claim is made here about his encounter with the risen Lord. H. Maccoby refutes Jeremias's view that the verbs used by Paul indicate that the

self was the origin of the tradition and in due course the tradition reached Paul, who thus had it *from the Lord* not immediately but by unbroken transmission.¹⁵⁰ Fee and others suggest that it is most probable that when Paul says "I received it from the Lord," "he probably does not mean that Jesus gave these words to him personally and directly; rather, what he himself 'received' had indeed come 'from the Lord,' but in the sense that Jesus himself is the ultimate source of the tradition."¹⁵¹ O. Cullmann has come

---

account is derived from the tradition of the church, not from a personal vision. He points out the verb לבק in the Rabbinic literature (*m. Abot*: "Moses received (לבק) the Torah from Sinai.") refers to the transmission of tradition, but also mentions the first step in that process, the receiving of the tradition from God himself. So he argues that when Paul said "I received (παρέλαβον) from the Lord," he considered himself as the starting a process of tradition, not from other human beings, but rather from the exalted Lord himself. "Paul and the Eucharist," NTS 37 (1991) 247-48; Lietzmann proposed that Paul received the revelation from the Lord and is the originator of a type of the Lord's Supper with its emphasis on the death of Jesus, which is different from the Jerusalem type. *Mass and Lord's Supper*, 208.

150. Hunter argues for this view: If a special direct revelation had been in Paul's mind, he would have used the preposition παρά, not ἀπό as in Gal 1:12; 1 Thess 2:12; 4:1; 2 Thess 3:6, where he employs παραλαμβάνειν with the preposition παρά. In each case it signifies a direct receipt; ἀπό here therefore indicates the ultimate source. "From the Lord" is simply another way of saying what he said before, "Not I, but the Lord" (1 Cor 7:10). Paul emphasizes that the ultimate authority for what he quotes is the Lord himself. 1 Cor 11:23-25 is, therefore, like 1 Cor 15:3-4, a piece of *paradosis* mediated to Paul by the pre-Pauline church. In short, this was a liturgical form of words used in administering the Lord's Supper in some pre-Pauline church. Cf. Hunter, *Paul and his Predecessors*, 19-20. See Maccoby, "Paul and the Eucharist," 247-267, who comments that the argument regarding the use of the preposition is inconclusive. The argument seems to be theological rather than strictly grammatical.

Higgins believes that Paul considered himself to be receiving and handing down the tradition, unmodified by the church, which ultimately goes back to Jesus. He mentions many scholars such as M. Goguel, J. Weiss, A. Schweitzer, M. Dibelius, F. L. Cirlot, E. Gaugler, Théo Preiss, R. Bultmann and J. Héring who support this view; Higgins, *Lord's Supper*, 26. A similar view is also expressed by Marshall, *Last Supper*, 11, 112; and Wolff, *Paulus an die Korinther*, 263; Hofius, "Lord's Supper," 75-115; Talbert, *Reading Corinthians*, 76.

151. Fee, *First Epistle*, 548; Marshall also observes that Paul was talking about an existing formal tradition and thus was using Rabbinic terminology in handing over that tradition. Marshall, *Last Supper*, 32.

If this is the case, obviously Paul heard it before he came to Corinth, and he must originally have heard it in some existing Christian church. There are only three real possibilities, Antioch, Damascus and Jerusalem. Antioch was the church from which Paul set out on his missionary work and Damascus was the church with which he had his first Christian contacts after his conversion. Bornkamm and others support the view that Paul received the tradition when he was in Antioch, before he began his mission. He also

Fellowship Meals in Corinth: The Abuse at the Lord's Supper

up with another view in this regard. He states that "the Lord" takes the place of "tradition." In 11:23, Paul's statement: "I received (by tradition) from the Lord" implies that the Lord is not only the historical Jesus as the chronological origin of the tradition, but the glorified Lord who is behind the communication of the tradition, who works in it.[152] A possible compromise solution is that Paul immediately received the factual tradition by human means, but received the interpretation of it directly from the Lord.[153] This view seems to be more probable in this context; where Paul quotes the tradition and then interprets them drawing its insight and authority from the Lord.[154] By referring to the divine origin Paul's intention is to show that the fellowship meal practice in the church neither originates in nor is based on human conventions and values but comes from a higher authority.

Paul then links this tradition to the Last Supper of Jesus by the words "on the night he was betrayed."[155] Likewise the Lord's Supper was based

---

mentions scholars G. Kittel, A. Schlatter, J. Jeremias, R. Bultmann, E. Käsemann, and W. G. Kümmel who support this view; Bornkamm, *Early Christian Experience*, 130.

Hunter supports the view that Paul first heard the words in Damascus after his conversion. It was in Damascus that the converted Paul was received into the Christian community. Since he received baptism there, it is altogether likely that there too he first came to know the sacramental table-fellowship of the Christian church; Hunter, *Paul*, 20; also Héring, *First Epistle*, 100–101.

Marshall thinks that since Christians from Jerusalem took their knowledge of Christianity from Jerusalem and founded both these two churches, and since Paul visited Jerusalem within three years of his conversion (Gal 1:18) it is therefore extremely likely that Paul's knowledge of how the Lord's Supper should be celebrated goes back to the practice of the church in Jerusalem. Marshall, *Last Supper*, 32. So the general view is that though Paul must have heard it from Christians in the Diaspora, ultimately the source originated from Jerusalem. Also Conzelmann, *1 Corinthians*, 196.

152. Cullmann, "Kyrios as Designation," 189.

153. Barrett, *First Epistle*, 265. Lietzmann indicates that Paul received in a vision by special revelation the real meaning of the Eucharist as a commemoration of the death of Christ. The substance of the revelation was the command to "do this in remembrance of me." Lietzmann, *Mass and Lord's Supper*, 208–9. Lohmeyer disagrees with Lietzmann's view; he suggests that the command "do this in remembrance of me" forms the crux of the new emphasis on the essence of the Lord's Supper which Paul received as part of the tradition. But he considers the language of the account as un-Pauline as the phrase "remembrance" (ἀνάμνησις), is not used by Paul in any other place. Lohmeyer, "Vom Urchristlichen Abendmahl," 168–227.

154. 1 Cor 10:15–16 gives an indication that the Lord's Supper tradition was already known to the Corinthians. So it seems clear that Paul did not receive the Lord's Supper tradition by direct revelation as Maccoby and others claim. Cf. Coutsoumpos, *Paul and the Lord's Supper*, 118.

155. The specific time reference places the event in the realm of a historical time and

on the Last Supper that Jesus ate with his own disciples. Fee reasonably argues the announcement of the betrayal at the Last Supper was a reminder to the early Christians about the passion and the crucifixion of Jesus by Rome, which was nonetheless handed over to them by one of their own—"a poignant reminder indeed at the Table where they experienced anew forgiveness and life."[156]

The Antecedent of the Lord's Supper

This issue whether the Last Supper was a Passover meal or not has been a subject of debate for centuries. The reference to the time of the Last Supper in Paul gives no indication that it was a Passover meal. The Synoptic Gospels indicate that the Last Supper took place on Thursday evening, which was the 15th of Nisan. John's Gospel reports that Jesus was crucified on the afternoon of Nisan 14th, therefore, the meal that he had shared with the disciples the night before could not have been a Passover celebration.[157]

The discrepancies have led some scholars to explore other prototypical meals. The main concern to reconstruct an original historical event behind the meal has to do with the interpretation and theology of the Lord's Supper. Depending on whether its affinity or source of origin was to the Passover meal or some other meal, that factor would determine in interpreting the tradition. The Passover theory has been postulated by J. Jeremias and others.[158] Other theories that have been put forward include the sabbath *kiddūsh* theory, which suggests that Jesus and his disciples formed a religious guild or *haburah*, like the so called *haburoth* which are said to have held weekly meals on Friday afternoons, concluding with the *kiddūsh* of the

---

not a myth. Wolff, *Paulus an die Korinther*, 264; A. Lindemann, *Der erste Korintherbrief*, 253.

156. Fee, *First Epistle*, 549n26. Hays on the other hand sees here the work of God in the whole process. He insists that this theme eclipses the proposed allusion to betrayal by Judas and provides "the background against which 1 Cor 11:23 must be understood." Hays, *First Corinthians*, 198.

157. Higgins, *Lord's Supper*, 14.

158. Jeremias shows 14 features of the Last Supper as corresponding to the Passover meal; *Eucharistic Words*, 62–88; Cullmann and Leenhardt, *Essays on the Lord's Supper*, 39–43; Higgins, *Lord's Supper*, 56–57; Marshall, *Last Supper*, 57–75; Wolff, *Der erste Brief*, 228–29; Schrage, *Der erste Brief*, 2:436–37; Bornkamm, *Early Christian Experience*, 140–43; Fee, *First Epistle*, 549; Thiselton, *First Epistle*, 869.

Sabbath.¹⁵⁹ Another view is the Passover *kiddūsh* theory, in which the meal is considered to be a combined commemoration of the Sabbath and the Passover *kiddūsh*.¹⁶⁰ Scholars have also suggested another form of sacred meal, the *todah*, which was based on the Old Testament (Lev 7:12–15).¹⁶¹ It was a thank offering for deliverance from sickness or other threats. They see the *todah* as the pattern of the Lord's Supper where the salvific death of Jesus is remembered, with thanksgiving.¹⁶² Other theories include sectarian meal like that of the Qumran community, and Hellenistic meal like that of Joseph and Aseneth.¹⁶³

Annie Jaubert has tried to harmonize the discrepancies found in John and the Synoptic Gospel by suggesting that Jesus was following a solar calendar mentioned at Qumran and in the book of Jubilees rather than the official lunar calendar of Jerusalem.¹⁶⁴ According to her theory, in this calendar, the Passover always fell on a Tuesday, so Jesus was arrested on Tuesday evening and put to death on Friday.¹⁶⁵ In a similar manner P. Billerbeck explains that both John and the Synoptics are right, because in the year of the crucifixion, the Pharisees and the Sadducees disagreed about the date of the new moon, and so their calendars differed by a day. Jesus and his disciples followed the Pharisaic calendar and ate eating the Passover a day earlier than the Sadducees. The Synoptics follow the Pharisaic calendar and

---

159. E.g., Lietzmann, *Mass and Lord's Supper*, 170–71, suggested that it "corresponds exactly in its ritual to one of the Jewish meals, invested with religious solemnity, which might be held by a company of friends, הרובה whenever they felt the need." Similarly, Otto, *Kingdom of God*, 278, assigned the Last Supper to the category of "the religious festive meal, a "cheber" or a "cheburah" with sacramental character and with ritualistic peculiarities." Dix, *Shape of the Liturgy*, 50–51, likewise argued that "the type to which it conforms is the formal supper of a *Haburah*."

160. Brilioth, *Eucharistic Faith*, 10; Box, "Jewish Antecedents," 357–69; Clark, *Approach*, 44–46.

161. This was the view of Xavier Léon-Dufour, *Sharing of the Eucharistic Bread*.

162. See Jeremias who rejects the *kiddūsh* and other theories, *Eucharistic Words*, 27–31; cf. Kodell, *Eucharist in the New Testament*, 48–49.

163. K. G. Kuhn indicates that it is similar to that of an Essene cultic meal; "The Lord's Supper," 78. Cf. Black, *Scrolls and Christian Origins*, 115. Marshall, *Last Supper*, 26–27, notes the similarity with the Jewish story of Joseph and Aseneth.

164. Jaubert, *Date of the Last Supper*, 95–101.

165. But the NT does not indicate that there was a two-day gap between Jesus' arrest and crucifixion; moreover her primary evidence the Syriac Didascalia of Salamis comes from the third century. Cf. Kodell, *Eucharist in the New Testament*, 54.

John the Sadducaic.¹⁶⁶ J. Pickl suggests that it was normal for Galileans to do the Passover sacrifice on the 13th while those in Judea on the 14th. Due to insufficient time and the number of participants, the Temple priests let some of the people bring the Passover sacrifice a day earlier.¹⁶⁷ None of the theories can satisfactorily give explanation or are conclusive; as there are no concrete records in the Gospels, these theories remain hypothetical.¹⁶⁸

Among all the theories, the Passover theory is the strongest contender, but serious objections have been raised by many against it.¹⁶⁹ This view accords with the stated aim of the authorities, to have done with Jesus prior to the feast.¹⁷⁰ Accordingly many scholars suggest that the Synoptic Gospels present a liturgical account rather than a historical account and the identification of the Last Supper with Passover is theologically motivated.¹⁷¹ Then

---

166. Strack and Billerbeck, *Kommentar zum Neuen Testament*, 2.847–53; Higgins, *Lord's Supper*, 16; Marshall, *Last Supper*, 71–72.

167. Pickl, *Messiaskoenig Jesus*, 247; see the summary of his argument in Jeremias, *Eucharistic Words*, 9.

168. Cf. Burkitt, "Last Supper," 295.

169. The use of ἄρτος instead of ἄζυμα (unleavened) for bread. The mention of the common as opposed to individual cups, the lack of mention of Paschal lamb and bitter herbs are telling objections to the Passover theory. Also the accounts fail to mention the recitation from the kiddush. Instead of drinking from four cups of wine, only one is used. In addition, women and children, who are normally involved in both the meal and the intermittent dialogue, are absent. Cf. Clark, *Approach*, 41; Dix, *Shape of the Liturgy*, 50; Kodell, *Eucharist in the New Testament*, 66; Schweizer, *Lord's Supper*, 29–32; Lietzmann, *Mass and Lord's Supper*, 172; Wainwright, *Eucharist and Eschatology*, 158–59; Feeley-Harnik, *The Lord's Table*, 72–73; Burkitt provides some compelling evidences against the Lord's Supper as a paschal meal, "Last Supper," 291–96; Xavier Leon-Dufour, *Sharing the Eucharistic Bread*, 306–8 claims that although there was a Passover atmosphere, the Last Supper should be properly called the Passover of Jesus, not a Jewish Passover.

170. Cf. Mark 14:1, 2 // Matt 26:1–5; Theissen cites the resolve of the authorities as the principal evidence that the tradition prior to Mark agreed with the Johannine chronology. He further indicates that Simon of Cyrene would not travel to Jerusalem on the day of Passover itself (Mark 15:21), and that the day of preparation mentioned in 15:42 may originally have been understood as for Passover, not the Sabbath. Moreover, the trial of Jesus indicates that it was not a feast day, since no judicial proceedings could be held on that day, likewise the motive for removing Jesus from the cross and burying him before sundown would not make sense if it were already the day of Passover. Theissen, *Gospels in Context*, 166–67.

171. Chilton claims that it is the work of the evangelists who were trying to incorporate Jesus' movement fully within the cultic worship of Judaism, which was the program of James. Chilton, *Feast of Meanings*, 95, 151; Instone-Brewer comments that Mark desired to give the Eucharist an origin in the Passover. "Tractate *Pesachim*," 20; Robbins demonstrates the redactional nature of the Last Supper narrative, including such details

Fellowship Meals in Corinth: The Abuse at the Lord's Supper

the "wish" of Jesus to eat the Passover meal in John 22:15–16 remained an unfulfilled desire.[172]

Rather there is an emerging consensus that it was an ordinary fellowship meal which was held earlier than the Passover meal. If it was indeed a Passover meal Paul could have mentioned it and the celebration would have taken place only annually.[173] But in any case, the Last Supper certainly carried paschal significance from the very beginning. Paschal ideas were bound to have been present in the minds of the gathering in the upper room, owing to the proximity to the Passover feast. Therefore Raymond Brown comments that the Last Supper was not a Passover in the strict sense but a meal that had "Passover characteristics."[174] So the Passover gave added meanings to the supper but inference was drawn from other meal practices as well.[175] Paul would have appealed to the fellowship meal traditions and their significance in a diverse context like Corinth to develop his theology of the Lord's Supper. At the same time Passover and other meals were merely variations of the generic fellowship meal culture practised rigorously by all.

So in all probability the Last Supper was a common fellowship meal which Jesus held with his disciples. Along with the usual significance associated with fellowship meals, the Last Supper was unique in the fact that Jesus gave his own interpretation to the elements and action during the meal.[176] Therefore instead of concentrating on the origin of the Last Supper in a narrow manner as most previous studies have done, on whether it was a Passover meal or some other meal for that matter, the study should be based on a broader understanding of fellowship meal practices in the ancient world. The Passover was also a fellowship meal adapted for a specific

---

as the Passover setting in Mark; Robbins, "Last Meal," 21–40.

172. Cf. Burkitt and Brooke, "St Luke xxii. 15, 16," 569–72; Burkitt, "But though they could not eat Passover together there was yet time for a farewell supper." "Last Supper," 295.

173. 1 Cor 5:7 also suggests that Christ was crucified when the paschal lambs were being slain, and 1 Cor 15:20 suggests that he rose from the dead on Nisan 16th, when the first sheaf of barley was offered. This is supported by Jewish (Babylonian Talmud Sanhedrin 43a-"They hanged him on the eve of Passover") and perhaps by early Christian tradition. Cf. Higgins, *Lord's Supper*, 24–25.

174. Brown, *Gospel According to John, I-XII*, 556.

175. Although the Lord's Supper was not derived from the meals of the Hellenistic cults and mysteries, it would not have grown in the manner it did without Hellenistic influence. Klauck, *Herrenmahl*, 163–65.

176. Cf. Schweizer, *Lord's Supper*, 29–32.

purpose. Since fellowship meals played an important role in society and had important implications for the growth of the church, Paul continued in promoting the fellowship meal practices based on the practice and teaching of Jesus.

The Saying over the Bread (v. 24)

Paul then relates the institution of the breaking of the bread, where Jesus gave thanks and broke bread. Jeremias and others see this as referring to the Jewish practice of the household head giving the blessing.[177] But saying prayer or grace at fellowship meals has been a regular feature in all cultures.[178] Here Jesus as the host of the fellowship meal takes the role as the "master" of ceremony.

In many cultures food played an important role as "boundary marker" for the community and in associating the community with their own identity and values.[179] Likewise here "breaking bread" can be understood as having both a social and religious meaning.[180] Jesus probably used a common symbol to define the community and to bring social cohesion and

177. Jeremias, *Eucharistic Words*, 104–5. Fee, *First Epistle*, 505.

178. Also Thiselton, *First Epistle*, 871 who clarifies that it means "*blessing God for his gifts, not* 'blessing' *the gifts*. . . . Such modern versions of 'grace' as 'bless this food . . .' are not only alien to the meaning conveyed by giving thanks to God, whether in the context of Jerusalem, Jesus, or Paul but also risk imposing at the earliest stage an overly explicit overtone of eucharistic 'consecration.'"

179. Douglas, "Deciphering a Meal," 61–81.

180. Some have claimed that "to break bread" does not occur outside of biblical Greek and so it played no significant role in the Greco-Roman meal. Berger, *Manna, Mehl und Sauerteig*, 97; cf. Blomberg, *Contagious Holiness*, 94–95. Conzelmann also consider this as a common Jewish rite. At the same time he states that breaking of bread is found outside Judaism, though without a ceremonial sense. E.g., Quintus *Historia Alexandri* 4.2.14; Diodorus Siculus *Bibliotheca historica* 17.41.7; Conzelmann, *1 Corinthians*, 197n49. But this view can be questioned on the basis of the usage of bread in the Mysteries. Maccoby and Cumont note that in the mysteries of Attis and in Mithraism, consecrated bread representing the body of the god was consumed. Maccoby further writes that: "In Latin poetry, it is a commonplace to speak of eating Ceres (meaning bread) or drinking Bacchus (wine), and this is not just a poetical trope, but the poetical residue of sacraments in which these food stuffs were regarded as divine." Maccoby, *Paul and Hellenism*, 125; Cumont, *Mysteries of Mithra*, 158; There are also instances in Greco-Roman meal tradition where breaking bread also has a symbolic role. Xenophon describes that tradition among the Greek Thracian households: "He took up the loaves of bread which lay beside him, broke them into little pieces and tossed them to those whom it pleased him, likewise also the meat" Xen. *Anab*. 7.3.22.

Fellowship Meals in Corinth: The Abuse at the Lord's Supper

bonding as in other groups.[181] Paul now relates that aspect with the church in Corinth (cf. 10:16). Further the religious connotation of this symbolic act is clearly seen in the following words: "This is my body, which is[182] for you; do this in remembrance of me."[183]

The act of Jesus at the supper then seems to have been a normal rite, practised regularly in common. But the remarkable thing that Jesus did was to reinterpret the meaning of the bread, in terms of his own body and which was given over to death for the restoration of the new community.[184]

There is lot of discussion in the usage of the term "body," whether it meant "himself" or his "flesh"?[185] Fee comments "Most likely it means neither, but refers to his actual body, which was about to be given over in death."[186] It is argued that the Corinthians considered the bread as a mere ordinary food and had abolished the concept that it represented the body of

---

181. "Paul uses the symbolism of the Supper ritual not only to enhance the internal coherence, unity, and equality of the Christian group, but also to protect its boundaries, vis-à-vis other kinds of cultic association." Meeks, *First Urban Christians*, 160. Since food was used as a primary boundary marker, we can assume that the food at the supper symbolically reminded the members of the congregation of their identity as a group. On the role of bread as a "boundary marker" among the Pharisees which was eaten symbolically on the evening of Sabbath see Instone-Brewer and Harland, "Jewish Association," 9.

182. The Old Latin and Syriac traditions, followed by the Majority Text, add "broken"; the Vulgate, Coptic, and Ethiopic versions add "given" from Luke 22:19. It is missing in P46 ℵ* A B C* 6 33 1739* Origen Cyprian. Fee holds that the diversity of traditions in itself indicates that the words are not original. Cf. Fee, *First Epistle*, 545.

183. In general the religious connotations of fellowship meals have been noted. Moule also comments: "For a devout Jew there was no meal that was not sacred." *Worship in the NT*, 19.

184. We should also note that the demonstrative τοῦτο is neuter and hence cannot, grammatically or in thought, refer to ἄρτος which is masculine. It then refers to the "gift which Christ extends to his disciples." Or as Luther puts it: "It is no longer mere bread of the oven but bread of flesh or bread of body, that is, bread which is sacramentally one with Christ's body." Lenski, *First and Second Epistles to the Corinthians*, 466.

185. See the discussion in Marshall, *Last Supper*, 86. Conzelmann, *1 Corinthians*, 211 n7, 8; notes the widespread use of the metaphor of the body and its parts in popular and philosophical literature, especially as a metaphor for political relationships, and has collected pertinent evidence. Also see on its usage in the Mystery and pagan meals in Maccoby, *Paul and Hellenism*, 125.

186. Fee, *First Epistle*, 550; cf. Schrage, *Der erste Brief*, 3:35–37. Those who see the Last Supper as based on the Passover meal tend to interpret the body symbolism here along the lines of the Passover Haggadah. Jeremias, *Eucharistic Words*, 41–62; Thiselton, *First Epistle*, 877.

Christ.[187] So Paul had to remind them of the significance of sharing in the bread during the supper. Along with its focus on sharing at the fellowship meal, Paul uses this term metaphorically in a number of ways to define the relationship and unity between Christ and the church, and to explain the unity in diversity (cf. 12:4–6, 27).

The phrase "which is for you" is found only in the Pauline-Lukan account. Whether it is an addition or belonged originally to the tradition is disputed.[188] Higgins sees it as a secondary Hellenization of the tradition by Paul, as it cannot be retranslated into Aramaic. It is possible that their presence is due to their being more suitable in worship and more intelligible to Hellenistic communities than the Semitic phrase, "which is poured out for many" in Mark.[189] Fee and others see in this phrase a reference to the suffering Servant of Isa 53:12, who "bore sin for many."[190] Paul must have understood that the breaking of the bread by Jesus at the Last Supper was a symbolic action about his impending death, foretold by the prophets, and now sharing in it means to partake in the "meaning and benefits of that death."[191] Already in 5:7 Paul has regarded Jesus as the new Christian Passover; he seems to make the same point here. Christ has effected deliverance through his crucifixion and death (cf. 1:23; Rom 3:25) and this is represented in the Supper. It is in this sense that the body of Jesus is *for you*.[192]

Paul's and Luke's accounts also bear a distinctive version of the bread saying, namely the command to repeat the action: "Do this in remembrance

---

187. Bornkamm, *Early Christian Experience*, 126.

188. In favor, see the discussion in Marshall, *Last Supper*, 46–51, although Marshall himself finally takes a position of uncertainty. Against this view see Jeremias, *Eucharistic Words*, 166–68. Fee suggests that it seems more probable that they were added in the tradition known by Paul and Luke under the influence of the cup saying, as a way of bringing the two into parallel. *First Epistle*, 551n35.

189. Higgins, *Lord's Supper*, 28–30; Cf. Clark, *An Approach to the Theology*, 37.

190. Fee, *First Epistle*, 551; also Hays, *First Corinthians*. 198; Schrage, *Der erste Brief*, 3.29–35. Some see here the reference to other OT texts; Hofius and Wolff, include texts like Lev 5:8 (cf. 9:8) and Deut 28:23 that speak about sin offering and the removal of curses. Hofius, "τὸ σῶμα τὸ ὑπὲρ ὑμῶν, 1 Kor 11: 24," 80–88; Wolff, *Der erste Brief*, 266.

191. Cf. Fee, *First Epistle*, 551.

192. It is worthwhile to note that there is no reference to the theme of 10.17; Paul could see more than one line of interpretation in the Supper. Barrett, *First Epistle*, 267. Hofius reiterates that while "my body" promotes the theme of sharing, participation, or identification; "for you," explains the "*expiatory death* of Jesus Christ" on our behalf to achieve the "forgiveness of sins and communion with God." Hofius, "Lord's Supper," 98, 99.

Fellowship Meals in Corinth: The Abuse at the Lord's Supper

of me." These words are missing from Mark/Matthew accounts, letting some to question their authenticity.[193] Fee's explanation is that: "The words may have been omitted in the tradition available to Mark for the very reason it was unknown to him or that such a command is implicit in the continuation of the Supper itself."[194] Reasons have been advanced for the belief that the second command to repeat was Paul's addition, while the first was in his tradition.[195] Perhaps Paul here makes explicit what was implicit in the Last Supper tradition, so what he did was in harmony with Jesus' intention on that occasion.[196]

Some scholars have tried to explain the term ἀνάμνησις on the basis of ancient and Hellenistic commemorative meals for the dead.[197] Memorial feasts were a common feature of Greek and Roman life. One of the most striking being from the testament of Epicurus, who made provision for an annual celebration "in memory (εἰς τὴν μνήμην) of us (i.e., me) and

---

193. Jeremias, *Eucharistic Words*, 168; Barrett, *First Epistle*, 267.

194. Cf. Fee, *First Epistle*, 551–52. Jeremias suggests that the earlier tradition did not contain this clause, and it is probable that its formulation owes much to Hellenistic custom. Jeremias, *Eucharistic Words*, 82.

195. See Higgins, *Lord's Supper*, 44.

196. W. D. Davies understands Paul's formulation here as "a Rabbinization of the tradition." Therefore Paul's account here is not the *ipsissima verba* of Jesus. *Paul and Rabbinic Judaism*, 250.

197. This was advocated by H. Lietzmann. He suggested that the Pauline form of the Eucharist, which displaced the Jerusalem form and prevailed everywhere concentrated on the death of Christ rather than on the joy of fellowship and eschatological anticipation. According to him, Paul was influenced by the contemporary Hellenistic practice of the holding of feasts in memory of the dead by relatives and friends on the anniversary of their death, or more frequently. He drew the conclusion that the use of the formula "in remembrance of me" was evidence for the fact that the Lord's Supper was "shaped on the analogy of these memorial meals" in hellenistic Christian circles, *Mass and Lord's Supper*, 148–49, 182. Reitzenstein also sees it in terms of the Mysteries. He points a "corresponding narrative, from about the time of Paul, in a magical text in which Osiris gives to Isis and to Horus his blood to drink in a cup of wine, so that after his death they will not forget him, but must search for him with longing and lamentation, until brought back to life, and is re-united with them"; Cf. Reitzenstein, *Hellenistic Mystery-Religions*, 77. Bultmann also conceived the Eucharistic meal as a representational rite like the "acted rites" of the mysteries; the ceremony acts out the death of the Lord. According to him, the repeated instruction "do this in memory of me" are apparently attributed to the fact that the Lord's Supper was conceived in analogy to Hellenistic memorial-ceremonies, for in the deeds of bequest for such ceremonies similar formulas occur. See Bultmann, *Theology of the New Testament*, 1.149. Cf. Lietzmann and Kümmel, *Briefe des Apostels Paulus*, 162–63.

Metrodorus."[198] On the other hand some argue that this tradition is derived from the Old Testament and Judaism. So it has to be interpreted against this background, specifically the Passover Feast.[199] But fellowship meals in memory of the death or funerary banquets were all part and parcel of the ancient customs and practices.[200] Moreover the "remembrance motif" was not uncommon and had religious significance in many of the religious rites and ceremonial meals. Given that Paul is now dealing with a diverse gathering in a Gentile setting, in all probability he was making an appeal based on a broader context, rather than confining himself to a particular concept or tradition.

Another issue in relation to this term ἀνάμνησις is whether it is used in reference to God or humans. Some see this as a call to God, to "remember" the atoning death of Jesus and likewise act upon the people.[201] Some see this as a call upon human beings to "remember" all about the sacrifice and death of Jesus.[202] Both the arguments put forward have strong contention, but in the light of the context in which Paul is writing to the Corinthians the human-ward reference seems to be more relevant as they have abused the Lord's Supper because of their selfish concern for honor, status, and position at the expense of and disregard for others. Thus Paul's great

---

198. Diogenes Laertius 10.18.

199. Jeremias, *Eucharist Words*, 237–255; Higgins, *Lord's Supper*, 56–58. Fee also indicates that it must be understood in the light of Jewish meals, namely the Passover which was itself a memorial rite (cf. Exod 13:9). Moreover the meal in honor of Jesus was not for a "dead hero" but for the Risen Lord. *First Epistle*, 552. Hofius adds, that such "remembrance" and "participation" is not confined to the Passover alone. On Sabbaths and even in daily prayer "the memory of the foundational saving event . . . has its firm place" ("Lord's Supper," 105).

200. While there is no direct evidence that the Christian community provided provision for burials like the other associations, Meeks rightly observes that "in the face of the sort of sentiment expressed in, say 1 Thess 4:13—5:11 or the enigmatic reference to 'baptism for the dead' in 1 Cor. 15:29, that these groups made appropriate provision for the burial of deceased Christians." Meeks, *First Urban Christians*, 78.

201. This is the position of Jeremias. He interprets the word *memorial*, with the intention that God shall *remember* his Messiah by bringing about the *parousia*. *The Eucharistic Words*, 118. Contra Conzelmann: "This interpretation is in contradiction to the plain wording . . . in remembrance of me." *1 Corinthians*, 199.

202. Conzelmann, *1 Corinthians*, 199; G. Fee also sees that the primary referent is a "man-ward" one. That is why he describes it as "my remembrance." Though, he also does not exclude the possibility that Jesus "reminded" God of their need of his forgiveness based on his sacrifice; Fee, *First Epistle*, 553. See a further analysis of this concept in Thiselton, *First Epistle*, 879.

concern in repeating these words was to remind them of the implications of this "remembrance" in the observance of the Lord's Supper. It should remind them of the love and sacrifice that Jesus has made on their behalf. This redemptive event should transform their identity as individuals as well as a corporate body and prompt them to act correspondingly towards others (cf. 1 Cor 12.)

At the same time, as Thiselton put it: "it is also to 'remember' in the sense of pleading guilty, and pleading the body and blood of Christ under the weight of judgment and the glory of promise. Only in this derivative sense of 'pleading the blood (body) of Christ' is it also directed toward God."[203] It was indeed a multiplicity of meanings seen in a single action.[204] Moreover this concept has to be understood in the biblical sense, which suggests that it is more than a mental exercise, but a realization of what is to be remembered and to live out that message in the community.[205]

The Saying over the Cup (v. 25)

Paul's and Luke's accounts of the tradition mark the transition to the cup at the Lord's Supper by the phrase "after supper." The tradition indicates that in the early church as well as in Corinth, the partaking of the bread and the wine was interrupted by the meal itself.

This format of the Lord's Supper is very similar to the Greco-Roman fellowship meals, where the transition from the meal to the symposium (or first and the second table) was marked by a wine ceremony (usually the mixing of the first jug of wine) accompanied by libation or blessing.[206] This division of the fellowship meal also followed at Corinth can be seen

203. Thiselton, *First Epistle*, 881.

204. Dix, *Shape of the Liturgy*, 236–37.

205. Bruce, *Corinthians*, 110; D. Jones has shown that the four instances of the use of the word ἀνάμνησις in the LXX, together with Heb 10:3 indicate that the word in biblical usage, is a ritual and liturgical term. "ἀνάμνησις in the LXX," 183–91. Conzelmann goes on to propose that the word "is more than mere commemoration; it means a sacramental presence." *1 Corinthians*, 198; For a more recent discussion on this motif see Thiselton, *First Epistle*, 879.

206. Cf. Smith, "Meals and Morality," 323–25. The reference to cup instead of wine implies that the interpretation is not attached to the elements as such, but "to the act of administration." Conzelmann, *1 Corinthians*, 199. Likewise "the formulation 'do this in remembrance of me' (11:24) supports the reading that, not the element of the bread, but the liturgical *act* of blessing and breaking the bread is what is interpreted in 11:24." Lampe, "Eucharist," 43.

Exclusion and Judgment in Fellowship Meals

as a contributing factor to the conflict. It is probable that some members of the church thought it necessary to follow the prevalent customs during the first part of the meal and then to accommodate the rest into the fellowship during the second or sacramental part of the meal.

Paul's and Luke's accounts not only differ from Mark/Matthew (Matt 26:27-28; John 14:24; John 22:20), but in the second part, Paul and Luke differ from each other. Though both show that Jesus identifies the cup with the establishment of the covenant, it is difficult to assess which tradition represents the more primitive form.[207] Mark's version shows that the cup saying is put in a parallel form with the bread saying.[208] In Paul's account of the tradition the cup is linked directly with the covenant, moreover it is linked with the "new covenant" of Jer 31:31, but nonetheless referring to the Old Covenant implicitly. However, Mark's version refers to the old covenant of Exod 24:8 explicitly and then to the new covenant implicitly.[209] In both accounts, the idea expressed is the same; the cup of wine signifies Jesus' blood poured out in death, which ratified the new covenant. It is the sign and pledge of a share in the new covenant and in the kingdom. Here Paul makes a strong emphasis on the eschatological dimension of the Lord's Supper by the use of the word καινή. The participants by sharing the cup enter into covenant with God by means of Christ's blood.[210] Gardner is of the view that this text should be understood in a wider covenant framework than that of the Lord's Supper as a Christian Passover meal alone: "it

---

207. Fee, *First Epistle*, 554.

208. The phrase "my blood of the covenant" in Mark is taken to be an allusion to Exod 24:8, where blood was sprinkled over the people to ratify the covenant. Serious objection has been raised to the phrase "my blood of the covenant" in Mark, especially from the Jewish side, to its meaning and to the possibility that Jesus enjoined the drinking of wine as in some sense representing his blood. This has led to the view that the Markan form of this saying originated in a non-Jewish community, and that the Pauline form is the earlier. Cf. Higgins, *Lord's Supper*, 28–30; Maccoby, *Paul and Hellenism*, 124.

209. Paul's version differs from Mark and Luke as it does not allude to Isa 53: "which is poured out for many." Fee, *First Epistle*, 555. Also see Koester, "Promise and Warning," 45.

210. Those who see this as a Passover meal identify the cup with the third cup at the Passover meal—the cup of blessing, some to the fourth cup. Jeremias, *Eucharistic Words*, 45; Héring, *First Epistle*, 94; Wolff, *Der erste Brief*, 228; Conzelmann, *1 Corinthians*, 171n13; Cohn-Sherbok, "A Jewish note," 704–9; Hofius, "Lord's Supper," 82–83; Thiselton, *First Epistle*, 756–60: "Whatever the details concerning the third or fourth cup, however, an implicit allusion to the covenantal blood of the Passover provides the most convincing and constructive context within which to understand τὸ ποτήριον τῆς εὐλογίας." 760.

Fellowship Meals in Corinth: The Abuse at the Lord's Supper

is upon covenant rather than upon the Passover meal as such that emphasis derived from the sharing of *the cup of blessing* falls primarily."[211]

It is probable that Paul is reminding the Corinthians of the new status they have received through Christ. The Supper presents the promise of belonging to God and to God's people through Christ. In fact this new-found status was in faithfulness to the covenant that God has made. This should motivate them to do away with the social status and other selfish interests they are after at the fellowship meal. As they enter into a covenantal relationship with God, it also reminds them of their commitment and responsibility to God, which entails that they follow his statutes in all matters and in their relationship with others. It also meant living a life excluded from allegiances to other gods and goddesses found in their diverse religious environment (cf. 10.14–22). Their actions now are a contradiction to their beliefs and status as those who are redeemed and accepted by God.

Paul's account again contains the command "Do this in remembrance of me" which is unique, with the addition "as often as you drink" suggesting a repeated action in honor of the Lord.[212] The phrase ὁσάκις ἐὰν πίνητε is clearly Paul's emphasis on the words of command.[213] This is clearly seen in 11:26, where he uses the same language along with an explanatory γάρ in order to reinforce his reason for citing the whole tradition in the first place. The repetition of the command shows Paul's concern in interpreting the Lord's Supper tradition and observing the meal correctly in Corinth, i.e., in "remembrance" of the salvation that his death had obtained for them.

The Proclamation at the Lord's Supper (v. 26)

The tradition of the Lord's Supper received by Paul ended at verse 25. He now adds a further sentence underlining the connection between the Supper and the death of Jesus, and indicating the sense he gave to the words, "Do this in remembrance of me."[214] The explanatory γάρ introduces his

211. Gardner, *Gifts of God*, 159–72.

212. The command is absent in Luke's account, nonetheless it may be implicit; Jeremias, *Eucharistic Words*, 138–203; Marshall, *Last Supper*, 51–53.

213. Fee suggests here that Paul has redacted the tradition to a certain extent; *First Epistle*, 555.

214. This is Paul's intent, is supported by many evidences: the change of person, from first to third; the explanatory γάρ; the word order, which puts the emphasis on his death, the fact that he picks up the precise language of the final repetition command ὁσάκις γὰρ ἐὰν . . ., which in turn picks up the ἐσθίητε τὸν ἄρτον τοῦτον so as to include both parts

reason for repeating the tradition at this point in the argument. It is not because they have forgotten the words, nor because they have abandoned the practice of the Lord's Supper. Rather, it is because their practice of the Lord's Supper has distorted its original meaning.[215] He explains that the bread and cup of this meal together signify the death of the Lord; and "as often as they do this," in his remembrance they are to be reminded through proclamation of the salvation that was accomplished through that death. Paul's concern lies here, as the Corinthians were obviously overlooking this aspect through their action.[216] Hofius argues that lack of hospitality and sharing contradicts the principle of proclaiming the cross of the Christ who died for the sake of others.[217]

According to some scholars the verb καταγγέλλειν implies that during the meal there was a homily or verbal proclamation of Christ's death.[218] Some argue that the Corinthians were under no obligation of proclaiming at the table, rather they proclaimed by the very fact that they gather together in his name and participated in the meal.[219] For the meal they participated in represented the sacrifice of Christ as the seal of the New Covenant.[220] Engberg-Pedersen believes that Paul is emphasising the *actions* during the meals, whenever they partake in the Supper they proclaim

---

of the meal in the explanation; and the emphasis that both the bread and cup proclaim Christ's death. Cf. Fee, *First Epistle*, 556; Barrett, *First Epistle*, 267.

215. Fee, *First Epistle*, 556.

216. Thiselton clearly elucidates Paul's concern here: "The sharing of the meal points above all to the 'for others' of the Lord's death, the very reason why the community celebrates the LS at all. Like apostleship, 'remembering' and 'showing forth' the Lord's death is a matter of conduct and lifestyle, not simply of words and ecclesial ritual." *First Epistle*, 851.

217. Hofius, "Herenmahl," 371–408.

218. Conzelmann asserts that "There is no such thing as a sacrament without accompanying proclamation." *1 Corinthians*, 201; Cf. Schweizer, *Lord's Supper*, 267; Fee, *First Epistle*, 557; Barrett, *The First Epistle*, 270; Ridderbos, *Paul*, 422; Bornkamm, *Early Christian Experience*, 141;, Neunzeit, *Das Herrenmahl*, 132; Jeremias, *Eucharistic Words*, 106–7; Käsemann, *Essays on New Testament Themes*, 201–21; Wolff, *Der erste Brief*, 274–5. Martin, *Worship in the Early Church*, 127.

219. Lietzmann, *An die Korinther,* 58; Smith, *From Symposium*, 199: "In other words, when the meal takes place in its proper form, then that in itself is a 'proclamation of the Lord's death.' . . . when the community eats with unity and equality, that is when they proclaim the death of the Lord."

220. Léon-Dufour, *Sharing the Eucharist*, 224–25; Talbert, *Reading Corinthians*, 78.

Fellowship Meals in Corinth: The Abuse at the Lord's Supper

the Lord's death. But because of their actions he now says that it ceases to become the Lord's Supper.[221]

It is possible that since the fellowship meal at Corinth was part of their worship and given the symbolic nature of the Supper, it meant both the proclamation of the word during the Supper and their participation in the symbolic representation of the Christ event.[222] Paul's emphasis on the "remembrance motif" is further described by these words. It is not merely a subjective recalling to mind, but an active manifestation of the continuing and actual significance of the death of Christ. Thus καταγγέλλειν in this respect has a prophetic, declaratory significance. As often as the church observes the supper, the proclamation of the redemptive act of Christ's death goes out from it, and this has an abiding significance; it is a proclamation "till he comes."[223]

Paul clearly shows the eschatological character of the meal by tracing it back to its first setting.[224] They now have a new beginning through Christ's death. Thus at the meals they are to proclaim the Lord's death until

---

221. Engberg-Pedersen, "Proclaiming the Lord's Death," 116.

222. Lampe shows how the proclamation of Christ's death at the Lord's Supper is intimately related with ethics. Christ died not only for the richer Christians in Corinth but also for the weak ones; therefore, the strong Christians in Corinth are not allowed to look down on or to offend the weak and poorer fellow Christians (8:11; 11:22; Phil 2:7–8; Rom 6:2–8). Christ's self-denial for the benefit of others is made present in the sacrament. Therefore the richer Christians cannot ignore the hunger of the poorer ones in an egocentric way. Moreover the sacramental representation of Christ's death means that Christians die with Christ in the sacrament. Such a cross-existence includes self-denial and active love for others (4:11–15). "Eucharist," 44–45. Thiselton sums it up as: "Proclaiming it in word, sacrament, attitude, and life." *First Epistle*, 870.

223. The Greek phrase ἄχρις οὗ with the aorist subjunctive, and without the particle ἄν always introduces the prospect of the attainment of the eschatological goal: Rom 11:25; 1 Cor 15:25; Luke 21:24; Barrett, *First Epistle*, 270. Léon-Dufour comments that the phrase can mean nothing but the looking forward to the future, to "the real" presence of the Lord himself; *Sharing the Eucharist*, 225. Some see this as a purpose clause ("in order that he might come"), where the supper reminds God of his promise and urges to hasten the coming of Jesus. Jeremias, *Eucharistic Words*, 249–55. Again there are other suggestions like whether it was inserted to address "over-realised eschatology." Collins, *First Corinthians*, 434; or "to add a 'not-yet' to their eschatological 'already,'" Witherington, *Conflict and Community*, 251; or reduce a sacramental enthusiasm based on an exaltation Christology, Conzelmann, *1 Corinthians*, 202; or "to lessen to some extent, the harsh idea of proclaiming the Lord's death," Engberg-Pedersen, "Proclaiming the Lord's Death," 116.

224. On the eschatological character of the Lord's Supper see Wainwright, *Eucharist and Eschatology*, 72–73.

he comes. Through this proclamation the participants are to be reminded of their essentially eschatological existence and the anticipation of its fulfilment "until he comes."[225] The promised future has not yet arrived, but it will be fulfilled at the *parousia*. The Lord's Supper will find its final fulfilment when the Lord himself will partake in the heavenly banquet together with the faithful. So instead of gratifying their own desires they are to proclaim the essential character of the Lord's death to which their existence is intimately linked. This eschatological character of the meal may have given the early church the impetus that participation in the meal was an anticipation of the table fellowship with the Lord at the Messianic banquet. And Paul by using this eschatological motif seems to be reminding the Corinthians to think and act with a broader perspective in mind. For the Lord's Supper has a deeper ramification, it points beyond this world to a deeper reality which would be fulfilled in the coming of the Lord. This understanding would help them to lay aside their zeal for human approval and status.

The situation at Corinth which Paul was horrified to see, particularly the social hierarchies and prejudices that were allowed to infiltrate the central act of worship, led him to present the tradition of the Lord's Supper. Paul in all sincerity attributed the tradition he received to the Lord himself, at the same time he interpreted and interpolated into the tradition, though not in a sense contrary to its original meaning which he also attributed to the Lord and to the Apostolic tradition.[226] The reason why Paul cites the tradition was to reform the Lord's Supper celebration by reminding the Corinthians of the significance of the meal, in order that they would see the deeper meaning of their fellowship and thus change their selfish and disruptive behavior. Right behavior and action towards the community should be the logical outcome of the participation in the Lord's Supper.[227] Paul's interpretation of the Lord's Supper clearly was in comparison to prevailing meal practices as this would make sense to the community to whom the fellowship meals played a dominant socio-religious role.

---

225. "By these final words Paul is reminding the Corinthians of their essentially eschatological existence. They have not yet arrived (4:8); at this meal they are to be reminded that there is yet a future for themselves, as well as for all the people of God." Fee, *First Epistle*, 557.

226. Cf. Higgins, *Lord's Supper*, 28.

227. See Thiselton's review of Erikson's work on the validity of this argument. *First Epistle*, 870; Erikson, *Traditions as Rhetorical Proof*, 110–14, 199–231.

Fellowship Meals in Corinth: The Abuse at the Lord's Supper

Paul follows this up with the practical advice to the Corinthians (vv. 33–34), which shall be considered with his other instructions on the Lord's Supper observance in the next chapter.

CONCLUSION

Paul's teaching on the Lord's Supper was necessitated by the conflict within the community; and the need to restore a community which was founded in a city that played an important role in the Mediterranean world as well as in the mission of the Early Church. Probably some of members of the church reported to Paul about the situation which they were disturbed to see as it was in contradiction with the apostle's teaching. Perhaps his commendation in the beginning of the chapter (11:2) implies that they had observed his instruction but only to a certain extent.

The fellowship meal as a powerful social institution with its ability and power to create bonds and define boundaries and identities had been utilised by Jesus. Paul has continued with this teaching of Jesus and has reinforced this institution by infusing the Gospel tradition as the underlying principle. In the process he reinterprets the whole system, bringing some innovative changes, as well as reinforcing some of the values inherent in the traditions. What was socially and culturally accepted was no longer acceptable in certain cases or they have to be modified keeping in mind the Gospel principle and the welfare of others.[228]

The Corinthians through their actions show that they have lost touch with the meaning of the Supper itself. Paul suggests equality, selfless love, and concern as the theme of their coming together for the commemoration of Jesus' death. The words of the institution are repeated to remind them of why they celebrate such a meal in the first place, a reason that goes back to Jesus himself. Paul takes them back to the Last Supper so that they will have the right understanding and restore the actual meaning of observing the Lord's Supper. The existence of different accounts and the different theologies associated with the tradition indicate that meal traditions were appropriate vehicles to propagate ideologies and beliefs, something that the early communities would understand and relate to.[229] Thus Paul employs them in his theological formulation and interpretation of the Christ event.

---

228. See, for instance, the issue of eating meat offered to idols; Lampe, "Corinthian Eucharistic Dinner Party," 6.

229. As Perrin puts it: "Further, it is evident that the meals themselves were the

Exclusion and Judgment in Fellowship Meals

Paul strongly emphasized the aspect that the bonding created by eating together should not merely be spiritual unity but also a social unity. This should be expressed at the Lord's Supper which is a foretaste and anticipation of the heavenly banquet. At the same time stratification based on race, gender, status or ideology has no place in this new inclusive community. He had stood against it in Antioch (Gal 2:11–14), and now when he heard about the situation in Corinth Paul strongly rebukes them. The conduct of the Corinthians was by no means exceptional in its socio-historical context. It was a normal procedure for some people to be given better quality and quantity of food and priority in sitting, so as to reinforce the social structure in the community. All these factors were part of the fellowship meal ideology. Most scholars interpret the situation at Corinth on this basis. But the situation in Corinth was not solely socially based. This is revealed when we take into consideration the other functions of the fellowship meal and the ideology that lies behind their customs and practices. The already brewing *schism* among the participants based on their individual theologies and allegiance to certain leaders contributed to the situation at hand. The people who had recently become Christians might have brought with them their own socio-religious worldview which had affected and influenced the community in interpreting their faith and practices.

The problems in Corinth reflect a society in the Greco-Roman world holding on to the societal norms and practices but also in a process of transition. It is a struggle between societal expectation based on social standards and a community whose core value is now based on love and sacrifice. Paul's action also reflects some voices in the Greco-Roman world who protested against such practices in the society, who wanted to see a transformed and idealized society beginning from the fellowship meals.

Scholars have tried to interpret the Lord's Supper either against Jewish or some other Hellenistic cultic meals. But the characteristics of the Supper show that it was not based on a particular meal but on the generic fellowship meal practices. Its significance comes from the general meal culture, at the same time other meal interpretations have been incorporated into its meaning and understanding. For the Jewish audience Paul relates the Passover theology and for the Gentile audience he employs the cultic

---

important thing and not a theological purpose which they might be said to serve. The existence of such different theological emphases as those connected with the 'Lord's Supper' in the New Testament (1 Cor 11) is an indication that the occasion has called forth the theologies, not the theologies the occasion." *Rediscovering the Teaching of Jesus*, 104.

Fellowship Meals in Corinth: The Abuse at the Lord's Supper

significance of fellowship meal practices.[230] The uniqueness of the Lord's Supper was the interpretation given to the common bread and wine at the table in terms of the sacrifice on the cross.

In the fellowship meals both secular and sacred character were present, Paul sees both as equally important, each contributing to the body of Christ. Paul clearly saw the powerful role of the fellowship meals so that he equates the participation of the community in it with the proclamation of the Lord's death. It was not merely a symbolic act of a reality but becomes more than that. It furthermore bestows identity upon the community that partakes in it. This is shown in the usage of the 'body' metaphor where the believers are united with the Lord and with one another. This new identity entails existential consequences that should reproduce Christ-like behavior. In Paul's thinking, theology and ethics are inseparable and this is reflected in his Lord's Supper theology. When they come to the table to celebrate what has been sacrificed "for you" they must likewise do to others.[231] So trying to gain advantage and status by humiliating and mistreating others is totally contrary to the Gospel and the fellowship meal that is held in honor of the Lord. Paul's strong rebuke that it is no longer the Lord's Supper suggests that the sanctity of the table was disturbed. His use of the term shows he upheld the meal with a deeper significance. It was not only to nourish but to bring about deeper fellowship and unity among the believers and with the risen Lord. This aspect is clarified when he associates the fellowship meal with eschatological judgment and consequences.

In Paul's response one can see the possibility that if the fellowship meal and the Lord's Supper were observed correctly, it would bring about unity within the church and solve the bitter issues of division and factions in the church.

---

230. Thus Broneer comments: "For Paul, more than any other of the early founders of the church, was in position to draw authoritatively from both pagan and Jewish sources and to combine what he has observed in his own presentation of the new faith that he had come to propagate." Broneer, "Paul and the Pagan Cults," 187.

231. "What is done at the table must take cognizance of all those who have gathered at the table—what they have and do not have, how they are treated, and how they are made to feel." Garland, *1 Corinthians*, 535.

CHAPTER 4

Judgment at the Lord's Supper in Corinth

INTRODUCTION

THIS CHAPTER CONTINUES TO investigate Paul's verdict on the situation created at the celebration of the Lord's Supper. In the previous chapter we have seen his rebuke to the Corinthians for their behavior and his theological exposition on the significance of the Lord's Supper. Based on that explanation Paul now directs them as to how the Lord's Supper should be observed. In doing so, Paul presents the most crucial part of his theological teaching on the Lord's Supper in the whole letter. Improper or inappropriate participation in the Lord's Supper can even lead to consequences of a fatal nature. This has been open to different interpretations, with some going to the extreme of even associating natural calamities and mishaps in this world with being disrespectful to the Lord's Supper.[1] Based on this association of judgment with the Lord's Supper, for centuries the church has been affected by how it approaches and administers the Lord's Supper. This chapter explores how and why Paul connects judgment in the commu-

---

1. For example, Calvin states: "Now, we administer the Supper in its purity, after it has been restored to us as though it had come back from exile. But even among us how much irreverence there is! How much hypocrisy there is in the case of many people! . . . And still we wonder what is the reason for so many wars, so many plagues, so many failures of the harvest, so many disasters and calamities, as if the cause was not in fact as plain as a pikestaff. And we certainly cannot look for an end to misfortunes, until we have removed their cause by correcting our faults." Calvin, *Commentary*, 255.

nity with the unacceptable behavior of the Corinthians. Then it will explain what should be the correct interpretation of the whole passage in the light of the socio-cultural background of Corinth.

Judgment in Corinth

Judgment is an important motif throughout the first letter of Paul to the Corinthians.[2] In the letter, Paul straightaway tackles the issue of division in the church, and in the process relates their actions to the judgment of God. In chapter 3:10–17, using imagery and the metaphor of a building, Paul warns the believers against strife and division in the church in the light of the eschatological judgment. Everybody will be judged according to their own work or contribution in relation to the Body of Christ. The seriousness and gravity of the situation is made clear in terms of eschatological punishment (v. 17).[3] This section in a way builds up to the judgment theme in the Lord's Supper in chapter 11, as the context and Paul's admonition are consistent and similar in pattern. In chapter 5:1–11, Paul again talks of judgment in the context of the fellowship meal.[4] Here he deals with the issue of immorality and commands the church "not even to eat with such a one." We have noted that eating together had a wider implication of acceptance in ancient cultures, so Paul clearly warns the community to disassociate with these people. Since fellowship meals were used as boundary markers, the implication is that they were to be excommunicated from the church.[5] Paul's concept of judgment is closely tied up with his ecclesiology and eschatological understanding. The judgment he expects is generally in the framework of the church with the involvement of the community at large, as an individual sin can affect the whole body.[6] Accordingly, the church as the body of Christ has the prerogative to be an agent of divine judgment.[7]

---

2. On the judgment theme in Corinthians see Roetzel, *Judgment in the Community*.

3. Fee indicates that Paul's warning in vv. 10–15 and in v. 17 are addressed to the same audience and not to different groups. *First Epistle*, 148.

4. For the whole range of discussion on 1 Cor 5:5 see Smith, "Hand This Man Over"; Roetzel, *Judgment in the Community*, 120–21.

5. Excommunication is "a sign of the loss of the realities symbolized and anticipated in the Church's life." Hein, *Eucharist and Excommunication*, 54. Cf. 2 Thess 3:15 where excommunication does not refer to private fellowship as such.

6. 1 Cor 5:3, 11; 6:2–3.

7. 1 Cor 6:2–3. Cf. Roetzel, *Judgment in the Community*, 131–32.

Exclusion and Judgment in Fellowship Meals

This judgment motif comes into play again in chapter 11 specifically in relation to the Lord's Supper incident. From the beginning of the section, Paul indicates that judgment is taking place in the community. Apart from the weakness, illness, and death, even the division in the community shows that the community was already involved in the processes of eschatological judgment. This is implied in the usage of δεῖ, "it is necessary" (v. 19), which most commentators understand as that necessity which is rather "divine, eschatological" in nature.[8] Justin Martyr has even associated these divisions with sayings of Jesus about false prophets recorded in Matt 7:15; 24:11, 24.[9] This eschatological interpretation goes hand in hand with the understanding that Paul sets the conflict at the Lord's Supper into a larger symbolic universe by making them part of an "eschatological drama."[10] As Theissen puts it, the Lord's Supper is "a zone under taboo, in which violation of norms had as its consequence incalculable disaster."[11] Paul highlights the wider implications by stressing that through these divisions those who are "genuine" will be revealed. The root meaning of δόκιμος, meaning "testing" is not specifically forensic, but the verb cognate, δοκιμάζειν is used as a technical term for official testing. Thus, the court of the Areopagus is said to be made up of "those who have won approval" (τῶν δεδοκιμασμένων).[12] However, the context of 1 Cor 11 implies that the term is used forensically,

---

8. The necessity of division is understood in the light of an eschatological judgment by Kümmel in Lietzmann, *An Die Korinther*, 185; Barrett, *First Epistle*, 261–62; Conzelmann, *I Corinthians*, 194; Schrage, *Der erste Brief*, 3:21–22; Lang, *Die Briefe an die Korinther*, 148; Hays, *First Corinthians*, 195; Murphy-O'Connor, "First Letter to the Corinthians," 809; Fitzmyer, *I Corinthians*, 433; Fee, *First Epistle*, 538. On the necessity of division in v. 19 see the discussion in Thiselton, *First Epistle*, 858–859; Murphy-O'Connor, *Keys to First Corinthians*, 218–21. Or is Paul speaking as someone "resigned," to the situation? For instance Murphy-O'Connor on the other hand suggests that "Its value was to show the positive side of what could be an unpleasant experience. . . . When v. 19 is read in this perspective, there is no need to think in terms of eschatology or apocalyptic or unknown dominical sayings. It is simply a proverbial summary of the way things are" (221). But taking into consideration Paul's theological outlook, it is more likely that an eschatological connotation was part of the message here.

9. *Dial. Tryph.* 35.3.

10. This view is elucidated in the discussion on judgment in the fellowship meal which is seen as having eschatological significance. The participation in fellowship meals mirrors the events that transcend the time-space continuum.

11. Theissen, "Soziale Integration" 312.

12. Xen. *Mem.* 3.5.20. Similarly, when one dishonored one's parents "the state. . .rejects him as unworthy of office" (ἀποδοκιμάζουσα), Xen. *Mem.* 2.2.13. Grundmann, "δόκιμος," *TDNT*, 2.255–60.

Judgment at the Lord's Supper in Corinth

e.g., note the legal terminology at 11:27–31: ἔνοχος (v. 27), δοκιμάζειν (v. 28), κρίμα (v. 29), διακρίνειν (vv. 29, 31), κρίνειν (vv. 31, 32), κατακρίνειν (v. 32).[13] Here the term is probably used by Paul to contrast with those who are "guilty" (ἔνοχος, v .27). The situation in Corinth was a sad and unavoidable reality in the church he has founded. But Paul hopes that those who are "genuine" to the gospel will be manifested. Hays terms it as "presumably necessary in the divine plan" in order to distinguish between the genuine members and those who are not genuine, in the light of God's judgment.[14]

The Corinthian context suggests that Paul is using the term "genuine" as a reference to position and status. In traditional fellowship meals, judging a person based on social position in order to assign rank and place at a table was a common practice. In practice the status of a person was revealed at the fellowship meal. For example, in the Greco-Roman context, status was measured according to social and cultural conventions. Paul's use of δόκιμοι reflects that kind of practice but now the term refers to eschatological acceptance or in similar terms an eschatological ranking assigned by God (cf. 2 Cor 10:18). Paul's disapproval of the conflict at the fellowship meal is clearly indicated by showing the gravity of the situation in the light of eschatological judgment. One can also notice Paul's continuous use of the rhetorical style, here in the form of irony.[15] The δόκιμοι are those judged by God to be "genuine," and not those who claim a position for themselves in the community. For the true ranking is one that is assigned by God and not by humans.[16] The term is eludicated more in the following verses, where Paul speficies that the δόκιμοι are the ones who have tested themselves (δοκιμαζέτω ἑαυτόν v. 28), discerned the body (διακρίνων v. 29), and judged themselves (διεκρίνομεν v. 31).

Along with the eschatological connotation Paul furnishes some practical insights here. If they are to be reckoned as "genuine" then they are to

---

13. On this see Käsemann, "Pauline Doctrine," 108–35. Also see the usage of forensic terminology in fellowship meal context in Greco-Roman writings, e.g., Plut. *Quaest. conv.* 616C.

14. Hays, *First Corinthians*, 195. The use of the term δόκιμος (11:19) and the reference to present σχίσματα and αἱρέσεις (11:18, 19), prefigure the eschatological separation of the wheat and the tares. See further, Fee, *First Epistle*, 538, 539 with n. 38. This recalls also the warning of Paul in his farewell speech at Miletus (Acts 20:29–30).

15. So Lietzmann, *An Die Korinther*, 56; Collins, *First Corinthians*, 436; Garland, *1 Corinthians*, 538; Fee, *First Epistle*, 528, also sees it as an anticipation of Paul's later allusion to judgment in 11:28–32.

16. Cf. Smith, "Meals and Morality," 328–29.

shun schism at the meal.[17] Rather than judging one another and create divisiveness they must promote oneness and the communal nature of the fellowship meal (ἀλλήλους ἐκδέχεσθε v. 33).[18]

The usage of this term reiterates the view that Paul considers the fellowship meal as an important act in the life of the community. To participate in it with the right attitude and motive is of utmost importance as this has further implications. They are to shun the prevalent social and cultural practices that would undermine the Gospel. For Paul, a person's standing in the community or anything for that matter should be in accordance with the values and standard set by the gospel.

JUDGMENT IN THE LORD'S SUPPER

Based on the theological exposition of the Lord's Supper tradition, Paul then goes on to define why judgment takes place at their gathering in vv. 27–32, and how their actions incur God's judgment. Paul employs the literary device of paronomasia particularly in this pericope to emphasize judgment in the community by using a string of juridical and near-juridical terms in connection with the Lord's Supper.[19] Six cognate words from the root κρίν appear in vv. 29–32 (κρίμα, διακρίνων, διεκρίνομεν, ἐκρινόμεθα, κρινόμενοι, κατακριθῶμεν).[20] Similar terms with judicial connotation are used to reinforce this judgment theme: ἀναξίως, ἔνοχος, δοκιμάζειν, παιδεύειν.[21]

---

17. Most commentators have argued that here the issue is "economic" based, but as we have seen earlier, the motive behind the abuse of the "have-nots" was primarily based on ideological reasons. See the discussion in chap 3, 127–30, 133-35.

18. Similar appeals can be seen in fellowship meal practices in Greco-Roman context. E.g., the rules of conduct for the Guild of Zeus Hypsistos, where the proscription against schisms (σχίσματα, line 13) not only includes restrictions about forsaking the community (line 14), but also prohibits various disagreements among the members (lines 15–19) including disagreements over their relative status (line 15). Cf. Smith, "Meals and Morality," 329.

19. See Blass et al., *Greek Grammar*, 488, 1b; Mattern, *Das Verständnis Gerichtes bei Paulus*, 99.

20. The usage of different words with the same root complements the rhetorical composition of the letter. Collins stresses that "Paul's reflection recall the rhetorical topos of judgment, the *iudicatio*, in which judgment is made by the gods, men of repute, or judges (see [Aristotle], *Rhet. ad Alex.* 1422a.25–28)." Collins, *First Corinthians*, 436.

21. δοκιμάζειν denote the act of judging or determining by applying one's critical faculties. ἀναξίως and ἔνοχος characterize the failure to apply one's critical faculties and thus come under judgment. Paul uses παιδεύειν to denote God's judgment of the Corinthians.

Judgment at the Lord's Supper in Corinth

The intricate connection between judgment and the Lord's Supper is spelled out clearly at the beginning of v. 27, that judgment is associated with their participation in the meal: Ὥστε ὃς ἂν ἐσθίῃ τὸν ἄρτον ἢ πίνῃ τὸ ποτήριον τοῦ κυρίου...[22] Paul's use of διὰ τοῦτο (v. 30) clearly emphasizes the relationship between the situation at Corinth (vv. 30–32) and the behavior of the Corinthians in the preceeding verses. Paul now measures their action at the meal against the theological basis of the meal he has pointed towards earlier. The division created at the fellowship meals was contrary to the gospel that was preached, and this was undermining the whole purpose of them coming together for fellowship. Here Paul specifically demonstrates why judgment takes place in the community.

ἀναξίως

First of all he indicates it by summing up the whole behavior of the Corinthians with a single word: ἀναξίως.[23] The adverb refers to doing something in contrast with the character or nature of something.[24] The adverb, which has been interpreted "unworthily" or "in an unworthy manner" has been a point of contention for centuries. It is generally taken to imply the self-worthiness or righteousness of the person participating in the Lord's Supper.[25] This led the text to be subjected to various interpretations and likewise various theologies.[26]

Cf. Volf, *Paul and Perseverance*, 99.

22. The connective ἢ translated as "or" has been stressed by some to justify the Eucharistic theology of *sub una specie*, while others opt for "and," as some codices also have it. Some interpreters also use this to support the view that there was an interval—the Agape meal, between the breaking of the bread and the cup. Cf. Lenski, *First and Second Epistle to the Corinthians*, 475–476. We can note here the earlier discussion that Paul's concern was not on the elements of the supper, and he considered the whole meal as equally important. So the interpretation of the connective here does not make any difference to the interpretation of the text.

23. ἀναξίως is a NT hapax legomenon, but it is added to v 29 in later MSS (א2, C3, D, F, G, Ψ, 1881) probably derived from v. 27. On the textual criticism see Metzger. *Textual Commentary*, 496. Metzger states that there is no reason to question the authenticity of the shorter text.

24. Cf. Eph 4:1; Phil 1:27; Col 1:10; 1 Thess 2:12; Garland, *1 Corinthians*, 550.

25. A good example is the interpretation of John Calvin. He states that Paul is speaking of "every kind of fault" including complacency or carelessness, and depending on the degree of unworthiness the Lord inflicts punishment. Calvin, *Commentary*, 251.

26. Different interpretations include: with a bad conscience, and without repentance;

This was as a result of the text being read out of the context. The following v. 28 was also interpreted in like manner, and was understood as a call for intense introspection. Based on this interpretation many were conditioned to abstain from the Lord's Supper, in the belief that they would be found wanting in their moral standing before God and would come under judgment.[27] The table of grace became more of a table of self-condemnation, which has been an obstacle for many to come and experience the fullness of the Lord's Supper.

Paul gives no indication in the letter nor does the context suggest, that he was calling for that kind of self-introspection.[28] On the other hand, there is also the tendency to interpret it as a purely social and ethical issue based on the reference to the "have-nots" (v. 22).[29] But our reading of the text in its socio-cultural context has shown that the conflict was not merely socio-economic. In the passage ἀναξίως, beyond all doubt, refers to the attitude and actions of some of the members that has created a party spirit and division which also manifested during the fellowship meal (v. 21).[30] The social setting points to ideological and theological motives as the reason behind the conflict. It was a struggle for power and dominance in the community.

Their behavior was totally in contradiction with the nature and purpose of the meal.[31] Whilst for Paul participation in the Lord's Supper is not based on a person's social achievement or status, or moral worthiness, nevertheless, in practice he demands that a person's motive and attitude to the Lord's Supper needs to be scrutinized.[32]

---

without self-examination, not realizing the real presence; without faith in the words; without contemplation of the crucified body of Christ, with any form of sin in one's life, etc. See the list in W. Ellis, "On the Text," 45 and Godet, *First Epistle*, 163. Likewise "sacrilege" by Weiss, *Erste Korintherbrief*, 290.

27. Similar concerns have been raised by Barrett, *First Epistle*, 273; Fee, *First Epistle*, 560 and 560, n. 10; Hays, *First Corinthians*, 200.

28. The text refers to the manner of participation, not the ethical state of the participant. Cf. Klauck, *Herrenmahl*, 324; F. Lang, *Die Briefe*, 154; Kremer, *Der Erste Brief*, 252; Aalen, "Das Abendmahl als Opfermahl im NT," 144–45.

29. Similarly E. Schweizer interprets this unworthily (in light of 8:11–12) as primarily a disregard for the poor and weak members of the community; *Lord's Supper*, 6. Barrett explains unworthily as "factiousness and greed," *First Epistle*, 272.

30. Käsemann lists it as "inappropriately," "Pauline Doctrine," 122; Wolff describes it as "inappropriate" or "unsuitable" attitude, *Der erste Brief*, 277. Martin rightly puts it as "fracturing the body of Christ." *Corinthian Body*, 194.

31. So Meyer, *Critical and Exegetical Handbook*, 1.346.

32. As Lampe puts it: "Those whose behaviour does not correspond to Christ's

Judgment at the Lord's Supper in Corinth

In v. 28, though Paul uses the phrase, "eat the bread and drink the cup of the Lord," the context makes it clear that it means simply to participate in the meal known as the Lord's Supper. So in that sense, ἀναξίως is related to the whole meal. As has been discussed earlier, the whole supper and not only the elements of the bread and the cup are in view here. Therefore he makes no connection between the cup and the blood, but with the new covenant.[33]

Once again we can notice the rhetorical style in Paul's usage of the word. When one does not treat others according to their worth as equal human beings, one becomes unworthy in the sight of God. Likewise, to be accepted as worthy before God one has to treat others worthily. Paul's emphasis is that because of their motives and behavior as ἀναξίως, there is judgment in the community.

ἔνοχος

The second term that Paul puts up in connection with ἀναξίως to show why judgment takes place is ἔνοχος. Paul now warns them that those who eat ἀναξίως will be guilty of a terrible sin. The severity of one's action at the supper is made clear in the following phrase, that they will be "guilty" of the body and blood of the Lord in whose memory they are partaking in the supper in the first place. The adjective ἔνοχος, "guilty" in the NT is a technical legal term to express liability.[34] Paul's verdict is that they will be "held accountable" for whatever sins they have committed against Christ, through their actions at the meal.[35]

---

death for others eat the sacrament in an unworthy way (I Cor. 11:27). . ." Lampe, "The Eucharist," 46.

33. Cf. Fee: "The reason for spelling it out in this way is related to the reason for reiterating the words of institution in itself: to remind the Corinthians of what this meal is all about, namely a time for experiencing and proclaiming, their common salvation in Christ through his 'body and blood,' i.e., his death 'for us.'" Fee, *First Epistle*, 559.

34. It occurs in Matt 5:21, 22 (three times); 26:66; Mark 3:29; 14:26; Heb 2:15; Jas 2:10. In genitive constructions it can denote either the person sinned against or the crime itself. So here it can mean either "guilty of sinning against the Lord," or "to be held liable for his death." Fee, *First Epistle*, 560–61. See a detailed discussion on the different interpretations on ἔνοχος in Thiselton, *First Epistle*, 889; Hanse, "ἔχω," *TDNT*, 2.828. It is a judicial term, which means that the Corinthians are answerable to God at the final judgment. Engberg-Pedersen, "Proclaiming the Lord's Death," 119–20

35. BDAG, 338–39; Fee, *First Epistle*, 561; Barrett, *First Epistle*, 273; Conzelmann, *1 Corinthians*, 202.

Exclusion and Judgment in Fellowship Meals

What are they guilty of? Are they guilty of profaning the table? Those who emphasize the sacred nature of the elements tend to interpret this word as referring to sinning against the Lord in terms of the Lord's Supper by desecrating it or profaning it.[36] The body and the blood of the Lord is seen as the object here and in sinning against the object they sin against the Lord himself.[37] Likewise Neyrey has argued that the selfish behavior of the Corinthians polluted the Lord's Supper and rendered it ineffective, it lost its holiness and thus rendered the people unclean and barred from God's presence, making them liable for condemnation.[38]

But in the text Paul does not give any indication to that end. Though he identifies the bread with the body of Christ, he does not identify the wine directly with the Lord's blood. Therefore some have even argued that even the bread refers only to the benefits of the Lord's sacrifice on the cross and the reference to σῶμα that occurs in the text, is not to be understood physically as "flesh," but describes the personhood.[39] Hence Fee also puts it: "His concern is not with the bread and cup in themselves, but with how through these the participants 'remember' Christ."[40] The probable explanation is that Paul does not make an explicit connection between the elements and the Lord's body because of the quasi-magical association some of the members had for the elements of the Lord's Supper. Therefore for Paul the issue was not a matter of *"sacrilege against the elements of the Lord's Supper but of answerability or being held accountable for the sin against Christ."*[41]

Consequently, Paul makes a strong connection between the Corinthians' setting and the historical event of the cross. He does that by indicating that the Corinthians are also liable as those responsible for the Lord's death in the first place. By going after their own interest and thereby mistreating

---

36. Thus the RSV rendering of v. 27 (not the NRSV) speaks of "profaning the body and blood of the Lord"; the NEB of "desecrating the body and blood of the Lord." So Grosheide, *First Epistle to the Corinthians*, 273–74; Héring, *First Epistle*, 120.

37. Godet writes: "for to sin against the object which has been solemnly consecrated and recognized as the sign of a thing, is to sin against the thing itself. He who tramples the crucifix under foot, morally tramples under foot the crucified Himself." Godet, *Commentary*, 164–65.

38. Neyrey, *Paul in Other Words*, 124.

39. I.e., the Person of Christ. Konradt, *Gericht und Gemeinde*, 418. Thiselton's examination of the word ἔνοχος confirms Konradt's view: "in Koine Greek [ἔνοχος with the genitive] came to denote the person against whom the crime is committed." Thiselton, *First Epistle*, 889.

40. Fee, *First Epistle*, 561.

41. Thiselton, *First Epistle*, 890.

Judgment at the Lord's Supper in Corinth

others, the Corinthians commit the same sort of sin that made the death of Christ necessary.[42] Thus, to be guilty of offending the body and blood of the Lord is to be responsible for the death of the Lord, on whose behalf they are celebrating the Supper in the first place.

So, the problem is not the desecration of the elements *per se*, but by creating divisions at the Supper and mistreating others, they sin against Christ. Eating the Lord's Supper in that manner defeats the purpose, nature, and principle of the Supper and makes one "liable" for the death of the Lord. They are now in the same category as those who killed Jesus. Jesus died for this cause; he was killed by those who were against his teaching, so to be against Jesus' teaching signified in the Supper they identify with those who killed him. In that sense, they are as guilty as those who killed Jesus in the first place. A very harsh warning, indeed, to those who profess to believe in the Lord, for they are the very ones who are responsible for his death through their actions. This explains how the behavior at the Supper is so closely associated with God's judgment. This word reflects back to what Paul has said in v. 26, that the Lord's Supper is a proclamation of the death of the Lord, but now through their behavior they become a party with those who were responsible for his death.[43] The logic is that when they proclaim the gospel message without conforming to it, then they are on a par with those who were responsible for the death of Christ.[44] Therefore, the afflictions experienced in the community were a sign of God's judgment on the guilty members.[45]

The argument that Paul is here charging the guilty Corinthians of false profession of Christian faith seems questionable.[46] This reading seems to

---

42. See also 8:12, where to sin against a brother is to sin against Christ. Also Heb 6:6; 10:29; Barrett, *First Epistle*, 273; Conzelmann, *1 Corinthians*, 202; Hays, *First Corinthians*, 201; Watson, *First Epistle*, 125. Fee, *First Epistle*, 561; Murphy-O'Connor, *Becoming Human Together*, 191.

43. It becomes an occasion of murder. So Murphy-O'Connor, *Becoming Human Together*, 191-92.

44. They "align themselves with the rulers of this present age who crucified the Lord" (1 Cor. 2:8; cf. Heb 6:5). Garland, *1 Corinthians*, 550.

45. With Bruce, *Corinthians*, 115; Synofzik, *Die Gerichts- und Vergeltungaussagen bei Paulus*, 52; Robertson and Plummer, *First Epistle of St. Paul to the Corinthians*, 254; Moule, "Judgment Theme," 473; Schlatter, *Paulus*, 329; Lampe, "Church Discipline," 347-48. Similarly, in the context of the meal and the betrayal of Jesus by Judas, Judas's unnatural death was an act of God's judgment (Acts 1:18).

46. Cf. Bruce, *Corinthians*, 114, 115: "Such 'unworthy' eating or drinking was possible only for a Christian whose behaviour belied his profession." Similarly, Fee, *First*

Exclusion and Judgment in Fellowship Meals

be unlikely because though their actions were contrary to what Paul expected of them, the context does not show that the Corinthians have a false profession of faith. We also note here the fellowship meal tradition, where the meal functioned as a boundary marker, so to participate in a meal implied that the members accepted and identified with the ideology of the community. So it is unlikely that those who partook in the Lord's Supper in Corinth would be those who opposed the gospel. Though their actions at the Supper were in contraction with the gospel, it was not an outright rebellion against it. Paul considered their behavior, rather, as zealous and misplaced devotion to certain leaders or groups in the church. This is in contrast to his earlier demand to expel the guilty ones in chapter 5:9–13. In like manner, the judgment upon the community is because they are being disciplined as children of God (11:32). And he continues to address the whole church as ἀδελφοί μου (11:33).[47]

Paul's serious charge against the Corinthians made explicit here in v. 27 indicates that the abuse at the Supper of fellow members was in fact related to the Lord himself. The term σῶμα here clearly refers to the body of the Lord.[48] But suggestions that the allusion to the church is ruled out by the reference to the blood, is mistaken.[49] Paul clearly connects the action against a member of the community as against Christ in chapter 8:11–12. The situation here in chapter 11 also would mean that sinning against the body and blood of the Lord also extends to the church. The unity between Christ and believers is so intimate that when one is affected the other is affected too and vice versa. So, though the primary reference is Christological, the ecclesiological nuance should not be omitted.

The use of ἔσται with ἔνοχος clearly indicates its connection with the eschatological judgment; the effect of the present situation will be disclosed on the Last Day. The judgment motif, which is inherent in the situation at Corinth becomes all the more important as it is linked with the final judgment. This would have enforced the significance of the Lord's Supper for the Corinthians which was considered as part of, and also anticipation of, the heavenly banquet.[50] Thus, Paul's argument is that judgment happens in

---

Epistle, 562, 538, 539.

47. So Volf, *Paul and Perseverance*, 104–5.

48. Among many, Klauck, *Herrenmahl*, 325; Grosheide, *First Epistle*, 275.

49. For instance, Barrett thinks that it makes no reference to the church in this verse, *First Epistle*, 272–73.

50. Just as in chapter 15, where the day of ἀνάστασις has already dawned. Cf.

the community as a result of some members being guilty of sinning against the Lord during the supper.

CAUSALITY AND THE LORD'S SUPPER

Having seen the reasons, we now look at how the behavior of the Corinthians during the Lord's Supper brought judgment upon the community. Different theories have been proposed to account for the cause-effect of judgment. The earliest explanation comes from the Church Fathers who considered the elements of the Lord's Supper as having some supernatural effects.[51] Thus the Corinthians were affected because of their misbehavior at the meal, and as a result of the ingestion of the sacramental elements unworthily.[52] The elements of the Lord's Supper, instead of healing them now cause negative and toxic effects on them because food was considered to acquire or transmit divine qualities.[53] The view of Ignatius and others, though strange in modern thought, can hardly be surprising in the ancient world where the concept of food having potency was prevalent.[54] So, for Paul's readers, the belief that something 'real' happens to the body through partaking in the Lord's Supper would have been intelligible and

---

Käsemann, "Pauline Doctrine,"122.

51. E.g., Ignatius of Antioch who considered the Lord's Supper as φάρμακον ἀθανασίας; Ign. *Eph.* 20.2. A similar idea is promoted by Gregory of Nyssa and Irenaeus of Lyons; Gregory of Nyssa, *Great Catechism*, 37, 504–5; Irenaeus, *Against Heresies*, V.2.2, 59, 435. Likewise modern commentators, e.g., Weiss who considered the elements as "solidly sacramental, magical, and miraculous" that has the potency for physical damage or benefit. Weiss, *Earliest Christianity*, 2.648.

52. Stuart, "Lord's Supper," 531; Martin, *The Corinthian Body*, 191–94.

53. So John Calvin: "which is otherwise beneficial, will be turned into poison and cause the destruction of those who eat unworthily." Calvin, *Commentary*, 253. Similarly by Lietzmann, *An Die Korinther*, 59; Weiss, *Der erste Korintherbrief*, 290–91; Héring, *La première épître*, 104. Also Martin, *The Corinthian Body*, 191: "By portraying the consumed body of Christ as a pharmakon that brings disease and death to the one who eats it unworthily, Paul bizarrely makes the body of Christ the invading agent of disease. . . . The logic of invasion is still at work: one eats one's sickness."

54. For example in the cult of Dionysus, see Euripides *Bacch.* 64–168; *m. Sot.* 1:1— 4:3: When she has "finished drinking," "the suspected adulteress" who is being "tested" or "judged" by "drinking the water" either shows immediate signs of serious illness (yellow complexion, bulging eyes, swelling veins) or "if she has any merit this holds her punishment in suspense. . ." (*m. Sot.* 3:4). Cf. Danby, *Mishnah*, 293–98, with Danby's notes on the text. Also Pliny the Younger *Ep.* 10.96.

credible.⁵⁵ Even modern commentators have followed that line of thought. Dunn comments that when the unacceptable behavior of the Corinthians infringed upon the holy character of the sacraments its effective power for wholeness turns into a "power of destruction."⁵⁶

Based on the prevalent belief in the ancient world regarding the potency of food, some of the Corinthians probably had upheld that view in the Lord's Supper. But there is nothing in Paul to indicate that he considered the elements as having numinous quality. Paul rejects outright the quasi-magical view, that the meals guaranteed them salvation and insurance against apostasy or against divine rejection (chapter 10).⁵⁷ From the outset Paul's emphasis is on the very act of participating in the meal, and the effects it has on the participants. The concern for Paul was on what the meal stands for and signifies and not on the elements.⁵⁸

Since Paul relates the cup with the new covenant, some understand the afflictions in terms of a curse. For instance, Hays links the passage to the prophetic tradition where curses and misfortunes fall upon Israel when they disregard the covenant that God has made with them.⁵⁹ So in the Lord's Supper when they mistreat others, they injure the body of Christ by breaking up the unity of the partnership. And when they do that they go against the very covenant that the meal signifies (v. 25) of which they are a part. Though there is a close link between the Lord's Supper and the covenant, Paul never refers to the judgment at the Lord's Supper as a "curse" in that sense. Likewise, some try to link the reference to death with

---

55. Cf. Nock, *Early Gentile Christianity*, 131; Martin, strongly argues that "It is anachronistic to attribute to Paul the notion that the Eucharist had a "merely" metaphorical or, in the modern sense of the term, "spiritual" effect on the Christian. . . . (10:14–22). The bodily ingestion of idol meat could mean the dangerous ingestion of the daimonic realm; the parallel with the Eucharist is simply assumed by Paul: normally it would constitute the ingestion of the body of Christ, which would of course be positive, even soteriological." *The Corinthian Body*, 190–191.

56. Dunn, *1 Corinthians*, 78.

57. So Higgins, *Lord's Supper*, 72; Käsemann, *Essays on New Testament Themes*, 116–117; Bornkamm, "Lord's Supper," 150, correctly points out that Paul's statement cannot be inverted: he does not say that those who receive the body of Christ worthily will be preserved from dying. Also see Gundry's argument, ΣΩMA *in Biblical Theology*, 237, 238; Léon-Dufour, *Sharing the Eucharistic*, 219.

58. With Gundry, ΣΩMA, 67 and Conzelmann, *1 Corinthians*, 203, who argue that Paul stresses the manner of participation in the Lord's Supper, not the nature of the elements. Against Lietzmann, *An die Korinther*, 59.

59. Hays, *First Corinthians*, 205–6.

the event in Exodus, as Paul cites in 10:1–6: that although all had received "the same spiritual food and drink," all were not therefore pleasing to God; many of them fell into idolatry and were struck dead in the wilderness. Though there are typological similarities with the OT events, the context in chapter 10 is rather different in which Paul was trying to do away with certain misconceptions on the part of the Corinthians.

Some have attributed the problems to natural causes or as a result of over indulgence at the fellowship meals.[60] But there is no concrete evidence for this interpretation. Moreover, Paul makes it clear that the affliction the community is experiencing was not a result of natural causes, but divine judgment.[61] It is unlikely therefore, that Paul would have provided an explanation had it been due to natural causes.

All these explanations as to why judgment takes place at the Lord's Supper are speculative and do not give proper and full explanation to the query; one thing that we can deduce from the letter is that Paul makes it clear that it is the result of a divine intervention which was to discipline them (11:32).

Meal Traditions and Judgment in the Lord's Supper

How do we then explain Paul's theology of judgment at the Lord's Supper? Why does Paul associate judgment with the Lord's Supper? The above attempts show that they do not completely explain the concept of judgment at the Lord's Supper, or the socio-religious background of it. Based on the notion that the Lord's Supper is based on a Jewish meal, scholars have tried to explain certain aspects of the judgment according to Jewish eschatological and apocalyptic traditions. But as we will discover there are inadequacies in this approach, as there are discrepancies with Paul's theology of judgment at the Lord's Supper.

We have already noted that the Lord's Supper was a fellowship meal and the situation at Corinth can be best explained on the basis of fellowship meal practices in ancient cultures. As already intimated the fellowship meal traditions were a prominent influence in the Jesus tradition and also

---

60. "It is possible that the excess in drinking may have led in some cases to illness" Robertson and Plummer, *First Epistle*, 253; Likewise gluttony for Bruce, *Corinthians*, 115; Morris, *First Epistle*, 164; Thiselton, *First Epistle*, 894.

61. Cf. 1 Thess 4:13–14, where no explanation is offered for some Christians having "fallen asleep."

on Paul. Hence even when it comes to the judgment motif our endeavor to explain it will be most appropriately done when it is based on the fellowship meal traditions.

In our analysis of the fellowship meal traditions we have seen that judgment was an integral part of the fellowship meals. It was associated at both the social and religious level. First, we have noticed that since fellowship meals functioned as boundary markers in various ways, communities and individuals judged one another based on their own socio-cultural values. Thus to be part of a fellowship meal was a sign of acceptance within the group. Conversely, when rules and regulations of the community were violated members could be ostracized or even expelled from the fellowship meals as a form of judgment. This was the practice in many of the religious cults and association both in the Greco-Roman and Jewish society. This form of judgment had further social and religious repercussions, as fellowship meals represented a bigger reality in the ancient worldview.[62]

Since the Lord's Supper was a fellowship meal, similar concepts and significance were associated with it. Paul and the early church considered it as a means of defining and associating the believers with their new identity and community. Thus, Paul teaches that the consequence of being incorporated into the body of Christ means exclusion from all other social and religious connections that are detrimental to that unity and existence. The fellowship meal sets this boundary for the church.[63] Meeks rightly stresses that: "Paul uses the symbolism of the Supper ritual not only to enhance the internal coherence, unity, and equality of the Christian group, but also to protect its boundaries vis-à-vis other kinds of cultic associations."[64] To be part of the Lord's Supper was a sign of acceptance into the community and that means being judged by the community as one amongst them; it also denotes one's acceptance of that judgment.[65] This judgment motif was part of the fellowship meal tradition and is thus carried over and reflected in the Lord's Supper tradition.

---

62. See the discussion in ch. 2.

63. Cf. 1 Cor 10:17–21; 12:12–20.

64. Meeks, *First Urban Christians*, 159–60.

65. Similar interpretation has been advocated by Moule, though from a different perspective. Therefore "the Eucharist is an occasion of judgment—either of voluntary self-judgment, in acceptance of God's verdict on fallen man, or else of unwilling liability to God's judgment as it falls upon those who, in the blindness of selfish secularism, side against the Lord Jesus." Moule, "Judgment Theme," 472.

Judgment at the Lord's Supper in Corinth

Just as in the fellowship meals the participants judged one another on the basis of ideological and social criteria, so too was the situation in Corinth. Now Paul turns their practice around and calls the Corinthians to instead scrutinize themselves, to really judge themselves (vv. 28, 31). Paul demands that the criteria for judging themselves are to be based on the Christian foundation of the fellowship meal itself. The new community has been founded on the one event that has brought them together. The participation in the meal in itself was a sign of their acceptance into that one body of Christ, a sign of their newfound corporate identity of acceptance before God. So they are now called to scrutinise themselves on the basis of what it means to be part of the body.

Secondly, as we have seen in chapter 2 section 2.8.1, fellowship meals were closely linked with divine judgment based on the popular belief that humans and gods interacted through the meals. Fellowship meals were seen as the means to achieve bonding and develop relationship with the deities, and as such they became the medium of executing judgment both in the form of divine blessings or punishments. Thus, there was a notion that judgment and participation in fellowship meals go hand in hand.

Now Paul here talks about judgment because he makes a similar connection between the Lord's Supper and the other fellowship meal traditions in the ancient world.[66] Hence Paul emphasizes the presence of the risen Lord in the Lord's Supper.[67] Paul rightly names the meal as the Lord's Supper, for he is the Lord at the meal which is in honor of him. The reality of the presence is highlighted in Paul's response to the Corinthians, that they would fall under judgment unless they are careful with how they conduct themselves at the Supper. Being present at the Lord's Supper with his saving grace and power, the Lord is at the same time a judging Lord.[68] As Käsemann puts it, every partaker "experiences the κρίμα to this extent, that he is

---

66. Cf. 1 Cor 10:18–22.

67. Most commentators understand the Eucharistic texts especially 10:16 and 11:27 in that manner; Lampe who puts emphasis on the presence at the Supper states: "There is no doubt that, for Paul and the Corinthians, the risen Lord Jesus Christ, with his saving power, was personally present at the Eucharist as the host of the ritual. . . . The risen Lord is present; his saving power is inherent in the sacramental act (1 Cor 15:29; 10:1–13);"'The Eucharist" 43. Cf. also Klauck, "Presence," 69–70.

68. We are not going into the details of how this presence is affected. As Lampe writes: "For Paul, the ethical implications of the Eucharist were far more vital than the later intricate theological discussions of *how* Christ might be present in the Lord's Supper. The fact *that* Christ is present matters for Paul; and the *function* in which Christ is present (saving *and* judging) is of importance . . ." Lampe, "Eucharist," 43.

confronted with the Judge of all."⁶⁹ Judgment itself is a further attestation to the presence of the Lord at the Supper (v. 32). Just as fellowship meals were considered as a primary means of association with the divine, the Lord's Supper at Corinth was also considered important for the believers in their relationship with the risen Lord. This is why for Paul the Supper represents and symbolizes the members' unity with the risen Lord.⁷⁰ Consequently, owing to the dynamic nature of the Lord's Supper which is identification with Christ and his community, when one partakes in the Supper, it signifies one's acceptance of the judgment of the cross and so appropriates its victory over the world. So there is an inherent eschatological character of the present judgment experienced by them. At the same time, Paul integrates the notion that one's social matters are connected to one's relationship with the sacred. This understanding is well supported by his theology of "the body of Christ," which he employs to explain the new community, the church. This view is again very much connected with the fellowship meal traditions where the social and sacred dimensions are always integrated.

Similarly, Paul understood the Lord's Supper at Corinth in the sense of creating bonding. It brought about unity between the participants and the Lord. This is indicated in the usage of the word κοινωνία in chapter 10.⁷¹ In chapter 10, Paul warns them not to partake in pagan meals as one cannot partake in the meal of the Lord and of demons at the same time.⁷²

---

69. Käsemann, "Pauline Doctrine of the Lord's Supper," 126. Likewise Aune, "The Eucharist in early Christianity was but one salvific epiphenomenon of the realisation of the presence of God." Aune, "Presence of God," 459.

70. Klauck, *Herrenmahl*, 265. Cf. Schweitzer, *Die Mystik des Apostels Paulus*, 262.

71. Generally the word group κοινων implies "fellowship or sharing with someone or in something." Friedrich Hauck, "κοινωνός," *TDNT*, 3.797; While κοινωνία expresses the notion of sharing, it differs from the other cognate words, and expresses the sense of an "inward union." George V. Jourdan, "κοινωνία in 1 Corinthians 10.16," *JBL* 67 (1948): 111. Cf. Best, *One Body in Christ*, 90; Seesemann, *Der Begriff* ΚΟΙΝΩΝΙΑ, 34–56. See more on the etymology and meaning of the word in Powers, *Salvation through Participation*, 171–72. Powers indicates that the Greek form of the Old Testament never employs the word group κοινων for the relationship between humanity and God. So the concept behind Paul's usage of the word κοινωνία in the Lord's Supper comes from the Hellenistic notion in which fellowship is established between the deity and the participants through the fellowship meal.

72. For more discussion on chap 10 on food offered to idols see Willis, *Idol Meat in Corinth*, 204–9. Willis argues against "sacramental" character of the pagan meals, whereby the participants become one with the deity. Rather κοινωνία expresses primarily the association of the participants with each other and the social obligation, which arise from their common association (167–209). Contra Powers, *Salvation through*

Judgment at the Lord's Supper in Corinth

It was not simply a coming together for food and worship but for Paul, the meal indicates genuine union and fellowship with the Lord and with one another.[73] The meal symbolizes and actualizes the unity they now have as children of God. So participating in the meal itself was a judgment, because it means a person was now part of the chosen community who now participates in the meal looking forward to that final consummation. The Lord's Supper then is the repeated projection of assurance of judgment, pardon and acceptance by God.[74]

Owing to the understanding of the divine presence in the fellowship meal, we have also noticed that for the ancients, fellowship meals were considered to transcend the time and space continuum. In similar manner, we can see how the motif of the Messianic banquet inherent in the ministry of Jesus was associated with the fellowship meals.[75] This is carried on and strongly projected in the understanding of fellowship meals as having eschatological characteristics by the early church.[76] This eschatological reality of the Lord's Supper is affirmed in its association with judgment.

Participation, 172–73. Rightly he argues that κοινωνία stands for both social fraternity of the members and the sacred fraternity as well.

73. So Powers, he states that, although Paul talks about the salvific effect of Jesus' death in non-eucharistic contexts, e.g., 1 Cor 15:3; Rom 4:25; 8:32, 34; Gal 1:4; 2:20; "But in the Lord's Supper, Paul sees the believers' salvation through Jesus' death as now being actualized." It represents and symbolizes the unity they already have. It makes it "visible and experiential." Powers, *Salvation through Participation*, 186, 191. See also Heil, *Meal Scenes in Luke Acts,* 297 who argues on the importance of fellowship meals in Acts of the Apostles. Salvation through meal fellowship or participating in fellowship meals signifying salvation is a major theme: "The community of those being saved experienced, celebrated, and demonstrated their salvation in and through their communal sharing of meal fellowship (2:42–47)."

74. See Moule, "Judgment Theme," 464–68.

75. The idea that Jesus' meal signified the eschatological meal is widely recognized. Priest, "Note on the Messianic Banquet," 222–38. Priest concludes that there is a close association of the eschatological meal with Jesus' meal and the early Christian Eucharist, 234–237. See also Smit, *Fellowship and Food*, 4. Bernd Kollmann concludes that Jesus both preached and enacted the eschatological/messianic banquet, which was as such also received in the meal praxis of the early Christian communities; Kollmann, *Ursprung und Gestalt*, referred from Smit, *Fellowship and Food*, 6.

76. See Smit, *Fellowship and Food*, 2–10 on the survey of literature done on the study of eschatological meals; Koenig who focuses primarily on the NT evidence for eschatological meal within the context of what he understands to be "eucharistic meals" in the NT, interpreting them as one of the foremost early Christian missionary vehicles. *The Feast for the World's Redemption*, 165–214; Also scholars who note the significance of meals as having an eschatological significance: Albert Schweitzer, *Die Mystik des Apostels*

Based on the divine connection and the eschatological character and nature of the fellowship meals, communities enacted their own laws and regulations to safeguard them from internal and outside interference. It was grounded on the belief that disturbance to the harmony of fellowship meals would have consequences for the community. Paul probably made that connection here in his admonishment to the Corinthians, indicating clearly that judgment was an integral part of their fellowship meals. So when the nature of the meal was disturbed judgment was the outcome, which affected the whole community.[77] By participating in the Lord's Supper, believers were transported to an eschatological context.[78] In that way a connection is made between fellowship meal, sin, and judgment, which is now specified in 1 Cor 11, which is why one's action at the Lord's Supper becomes all the more important, as Paul reminds them.

Our analysis reveals that Paul's concept of judgment in the Lord's Supper was based on the fellowship meal tradition. Since judgment was considered as an integral part of the fellowship meal tradition, and the Lord's Supper being part of that tradition, we can see how Paul considers judgment as an integral part of the Lord's Supper. Consequently, he considers the Lord's Supper as the vehicle of dominical judgment. Thus, the primary explanation for Paul's theology of the Lord's Supper should be based on the fellowship meal traditions.

ἈΣΘΕΝΕῖΣ, ἌΡΡΩΣΤΟΙ, AND ΚΟΙΜῶΝΤΑΙ

Paul's teaching on judgment at the Supper is further elaborated by indicating that signs of judgment were now visible in the community. The divisions in the community created by their behavior had led to consequences of a fatal nature. The judgment has concretized in the different forms of problems that have struck the community. Hence some of them had been chastised by sickness and infirmities, and even "death": ἐν ὑμῖν πολλοὶ ἀσθενεῖς καὶ ἄρρωστοι καὶ κοιμῶνται ἱκανοί (11:30).[79] Paul clearly makes

---

Paulus; Wainwright, *Eucharist and Eschatology*, 1–17, 72–73; McCormick, *The Lord's Supper*, 99–105.

77. We can also underline the betrayal of Jesus by Judas at the last supper in that sense (Matt 26:23; Mark 14:20; Luke 22:21; John 13:18). Judas's action brought about judgment on all.

78. Cf. Léon-Dufour, *Sharing the Eucharistic*, 219.

79. Paul indicates that judgment has already begun. Note the present and imperfect

the connection between their actions and the afflictions in the community by using διὰ τοῦτο (v. 30).⁸⁰ The afflictions that he mentions are "material consequences of guilt" for defiling the Lord's Supper.⁸¹ He goes on to show that these consequences are a result of God's judgment. The Greek passive ἐκρινόμεθα (v. 31) implies that God is the judge.⁸²

The suggestion that Paul is speaking of metaphorical sickness and death here does not have much basis.⁸³ Most scholars understand that it is a reference to physical sickness and death or else Paul's argument about the threat of punishment loses its strength. By the way Paul puts it, one would assume that the readers could readily identify those who were sick or had died in the community.⁸⁴

Garland has suggested that those physically weak are those who are denied food. This implies that the remark about illnesses in Corinth "may not be a warning threat but an appeal for them to share with the poor."⁸⁵ He argues this on the basis of Winter's and others' contention that Corinth was undergoing a famine.⁸⁶ But this goes against the whole argument of Paul that the guilty were being punished by God.⁸⁷

Why did Paul associate sickness and illness with God's judgment at the Supper? We have seen that the concept of sickness and divine judgment

---

indicatives, ἐκρινόμεθα v. 31 and κρινόμενοι v. 32, show, it is a judgment which has already begun and continues to strike the Corinthian community. Cf. Wolff, *Der erste Brief*, 95.

80. See the discussion on διὰ τοῦτο in Fee, *First Epistle*, 565: "it can point either backward or forward, that is, it can draw an inferred conclusion on the basis of what has been said, or it can anticipate a reason that will be given in what follows." In this case the former description fits the context of Paul's argument.

81. Conzelmann, *1 Corinthians*, 203. Similarly Synofzik, *Gerichts- und Vergeltungaussagen*, 52; Smith, "Hand this Man Over," 168.

82. Schnabel, *Der erste Brief*, 667.

83. Schneider "Glaubensmängel in Korinth," 3–19, suggested a metaphorical or spiritual interpretation; noted by Fitzmyer, *I Corinthians*, 447. Fitzmyer rightly argues that "The 'weak' are hardly the same as those 'weak' in conscience of 8:10, because the second adj., 'infirm,' makes it clear that they are physically weak; and that is supported by the following words about the dying. Hence these terms are scarcely to be understood only in a spiritual sense, as 'weak in faith,' 'spiritually ill,' or 'spiritually asleep.'"

84. So Allo, he points that there was a "terrible realism" concerning physical illness and death in Corinth. Allo, *Saint Paul*, 283, noted by Marshall, *Kept by the Power of God*, 115. Cf. Garland, *1 Corinthians*, 553.

85. Garland, *1 Corinthians*, 553–54.

86. Winter, "Secular and Christian Response," 86–109; Blue "House Church," 221–39.

87. Fee also recommends that ἄρρωστοι, which literally means "powerless" has taken on the more specific meaning of "being sick or ill" in this case. Fee, *First Epistle*, 565.

in the ancient world was directly linked with the fellowship meal traditions. Since Paul is writing to the Corinthians in a similar context involving meal practices, we can see that he makes similar connections here. Now, in the case of the Corinthians Paul also attributes the afflictions to the divine judgment of God.[88] But Paul does not specify whether those infirmities directly come from God. Some have argued that Satan is the one who causes malevolent consequences, including physical human suffering. However those malevolent deeds can "unwittingly work for righteous—and even salvific— purposes."[89] A good example is seen in the OT story of Job where Satan is allowed to test Job's loyalty to God, and does so by inflicting him with sores (Job 2:6). In the New Testament more emphasis is made on the moral aspect of Satan's work,[90] nonetheless he is also considered as the author of disease and suffering.[91]

Barrett envisages a similar role for physical suffering in 1 Cor 11:30: by abusing others at the Lord's Table they expose themselves to the power of demons, who were taken to be the cause of physical disease.[92] This notion that people are afflicted because the protection of the gods had been withdrawn in judgment relates with the fellowship meal traditions. This has a direct link with the fellowship meals because people believed that they were bonded with the gods through the fellowship meals and thus were granted protection from diseases and other misfortunes.[93] Conversely, they believed that sickness and other forms of maladies were due to divine anger, jealousy or intervention.[94] Thus breaking rules and regulations at fellowship meals through unacceptable behavior were considered as serious matters which could provoke the gods to anger causing these afflictions.

---

88. See Smith, "Hand this Man," for a study on Paul's understanding between human sin and physical suffering/destruction in Corinthians. "For example, in 1 Cor 3, he speaks of the one whose "work" is destroyed as suffering the "loss" of his "work": (v 15). In vv. 16-17, he talks metaphorically of the "destruction" of the community (*naos*) through unholiness. As such, Paul links sin with physical suffering (by which death is not precluded)." Smith, "Hand this Man," 119.

89. In this regard see the argument in Smith, "Hand this Man," 159.

90. Rom 16:19-20; 1 Cor. 7:5; 2 Cor 2:11; 11:14; 1 Thess 2:18; 2 Thess 2:9; Rev 12:9.

91. Luke 13:16; 2 Cor 12:7-8 probably; Travis, *Christ and the Judgment*, 79-80.

92. Barrett, *First Epistle*, 275; cf also 1 Cor 5:5; Murphy-O'Connor, *1 Corinthians*, 114, 115; Smith, "Hand this Man," 33.

93. This belief also is reflected in 1 Cor 5:5, 11 where Paul tells them to hand over the offending member to Satan and to avoid eating with such a person.

94. Livy 41.16.1-2; Ath. *Deipn*. 552.

This was based on the belief that the gods were the protectors as well as the agents of maladies or destruction.[95] Paul's contention here is very similar to the way ancient cultures associated sickness or other forms of maladies with one's behavior at the fellowship meals. Though Paul does not specify this clearly in the text, by attributing the physical affliction to God's judgment the same underlying concept is present.[96]

Paul's understanding of physical suffering (including death) as a consequence of sin was anchored in the prevalent beliefs. However, Paul interprets this punishment within the context of the fellowship meal tradition. As such, neither the physical suffering, nor death is directly salvific, but it is part of the process to bring about restoration. Paul in a context like Corinth, has appealed to ideas that could be understood by all his readers. Since fellowship meals were a platform for human and divine interaction, one of the main reasons why people did appeasements at the fellowship meals was to seek protection from these kinds of mishaps. So this association of diseases and illness and their conduct at the table make sense in its socio-religious context.

Restricted or Universal Judgment

Is Paul's teaching on judgment at the Lord's Supper applicable only to the case of the Corinthians, or is it applicable to every Lord's Supper observance? Did the physical afflictions affect the Corinthians randomly or specific members of the community?

There is the suggestion that this teaching of Paul is an *ad hoc* reflection to some recent calamities in Corinth.[97] It is based on the speculation that probably there was some recent epidemic or plague in Corinth which Paul is now trying to relate to their behavior at the Lord's Supper. Murphy-

---

95. See the discussion in chapter 2, pp. 97-107. Cf. Hom. *Il.* 1.9-10, 43-44; 9.530-38; Hom. *Od.*10.64; 5.396; Plato *Phaedr.* 244 d-e; Cl. Al. *Strom.* VI, 3, 31, 1; Plut. *Sera.* 12.161; Livy 2.36.5; 9.29.11; Tac. *Ann.* 14.22; Hesiod *Op.* 100-105. Also see Martin, *The Corinthian Body*, 153-54.

96. "This is not of course to say that Paul believed the faithful were totally immune from sickness (cf. 2 Cor 12:7-9; 2 Tim 4:20); but that there is relative protection." Travis, *Christ and the Judgment*, 79-80.

97. According to Fee, this is a prophetic insight of Paul linking the attitudes of self-indulgence during the Lord's Supper to the afflictions. Fee, 565; Cf. Klauck, *Herrenmahl*, 327. While Conzelmann understands the effect as "causal" rather than as an act of "punishment." Conzelmann, *1 Corinthians*, 203.

Exclusion and Judgment in Fellowship Meals

O'Connor points out that there is nothing unusual about illnesses in a port city like Corinth, as they would be endemic especially among the lower classes.[98] The point of interest is the usage of ἱκανοί which indicates that an "abnormal"[99] or "quite enough"[100] number of people must have died. The Christian community in Corinth was probably searching for answers to the cause of these afflictions, prompting Paul to interpret it as divine punishment. He associates the cause of the afflictions to the abuse at the Lord's Supper and in the process, justifies his teaching on the Lord's Supper and judgment being part of it.

It also appears that even in chapter 10 where Paul deals with the issue regarding food offered to idols, there is an implicit threat of judgment (v. 22). In that sense, the signs of judgment may not be the same as has been the case in chap. 11. But Paul's intention was to show that judgment was indeed taking place.[101] So in retrospect, for Paul this was not an offshoot incident but a general reality for Christians.[102] More theological arguments can be seen in support of this view. For instance, based on the decretal-like style of Paul in 1 Cor. 11:27, Käsemann suggests that Paul here is formulating general rules for the church and its approach to the Lord's Supper.[103] The early Church Fathers and the liturgies were also of the opinion that every Lord's Supper is the occasion of dominical judgment.[104] Käsemann further elaborates that since the Lord's Supper is founded on the basic principle in Christ where he is both the Savior and the Judge, judgment is always part of it.[105] Whenever one encounters the risen Christ at the Lord's Supper, one

---

98. Murphy-O'Connor, *Keys to First Corinthians*, 228–29.

99. Allo, *Première Épître*, 283.

100. Garland, *1 Corinthians*, 553.

101. Trompf, "On Attitudes Toward Women," 198–201 correctly points to the connections between 10:1—11:2 and 11:17–34.

102. "And when Paul says that they are being punished because of eating unworthily, he is certainly not hazarding a guess, but is asserting something of which he is very well aware." Calvin, *Commentary*, 254.

103. See Käsemann, "Anliegen und Eigenart," 23.

104. E.g., Chrysostom, *Gospel of Matthew*, 684–86. Cf. Wainwright, *Eucharist and Eschatology*, 102–3.

105. Käsemann: "We do not, by our own disrespect, render his gift ineffective or make the presence of Christ unhappen.... Where the Saviour is despised, the universal Judge remains present and shows himself in that very place as the one from whose presence there is no escape ... The sacramental coming of the Lord always sets men in the perspective of the Last Day and therefore itself bears the mark of what God will do at the Last Day. It is a kind of anticipation, within the church, of the Last day." "Anliegen und

Judgment at the Lord's Supper in Corinth

also encounters him as the Judge.[106] As one is reminded and experiences the benefits of Christ's work in every participation, so is the reality of judgment applicable to all occasions. So, the view that Paul's teaching on judgment at the Lord's Supper is restricted only to the case of the Corinthians may be refuted. For the reality of Christ as judge and his judgment is always present when one participates in the Lord's Supper.

Again we are not certain about the extent of the affliction that has occurred in the community. Did it strike randomly or were specific individuals affected by it? Some are of the opinion that Paul is stating that the affliction is on the whole community for tolerating the abuse at the Lord's Supper and not on guilty individual members.[107] In that sense, the suffering of individual members is not related to whether one is guilty or right at the celebration, but denotes that the church is guilty and hence there is judgment on the whole community.

But the context does not support such a reading; Paul does not suggest that the whole community was responsible for the present afflictions.[108] Moreover, his earlier comment in v. 19 shows how the situation distinguishing the δόκιμοι from the ἀδόκιμοι indicates that the whole community was not part of the problem.[109] Unlike chapter 5, where Paul reprimands the whole community, here in chapter 11, he specifically addresses those who have done wrong.[110]

Nonetheless, though the judgment affected certain individuals, their suffering must have affected the community as a whole, re-enforcing the

---

Eigenart," 25-26. Cited from Wainwright, *Eucharist and Eschatology*, 102-3.

106. Davies, *Bread of Life*, 97.

107. So Delling, "Das Abendmahlsgeschehen nach Paulus," 330; Conzelmann, *1 Corinthians*, 203, n. 115; Bornkamm, "Herrenmahl und Kirche bei Paulus," 170; Wolff, *Der erste Brief*, 95; Fee, *First Epistle*, 565; Schrage, *Der erste Brief*, 54; Konradt, *Gericht und Gemeinde*, 442.

108. With Volf, *Paul and Perseverance*, 104-5.

109. The δόκιμοι can already be distinguished from the ἀδόκιμοι, even before the final judgment. With Fee, *First Epistle*, 538, 539n37.

110. See more on the comparison between chap 5 and 11 in Volf, *Paul and Perseverance*, 104-5. Volf concludes that Paul's warning in chap 11 was not directed to the whole community. "The second person plural in 11:22 refers obviously to the offenders only. Contrast 5:1-5, where Paul considers the whole community guilty of pride (πεφυσιωμένοι, 5:2) for tolerating the sexual offender. Yet even there God's judgment does not fall on the community at large. How much less likely, therefore, that the sicknesses and death in chap. 11 represent God's judgment on the whole community, whose general guilt is not even implied."

teaching of Paul about the "body." Moreover this idea of corporate identity was very much associated with the judgment motifs in fellowship meal traditions. So, though some are affected more it has a positive effect on the whole community as it serves as a warning against committing the same mistakes and so saves them from final judgment.[111] So the church may suffer as a result of some members being afflicted but it does not mean that the whole community was guilty of the sins. But the bonding that they had in Christ and was reinforced through fellowship meals meant that all were affected.

But again we cannot claim that all who were sick and had died were transgressors,[112] or that sickness is necessarily a sign of God's judgment on human misbehavior.[113] Nor does the text imply that sickness always occurs because of the Lord's Supper[114] or that physical affliction should be considered as the norm of every judgment.[115] Many things are left unsaid in this passage so one cannot assume that all those who are sick have misbehaved at the Supper. But we can see a strong probability that many who had committed the errors were being affected in some sense. The main emphasis of Paul here was to show that judgment was taking place in the community.

THE LORD'S SUPPER AND FINAL JUDGMENT

The nature of this judgment in Corinth has created a lot of discussion in relation to the wider eschatological situation. How is this present judgment at the Lord's Supper related to the final condemnation of the world? What implications does judgment at the Lord's Supper have for their final salvation?

The judgment in Corinth as Paul describes it is a judgment that strikes in the here and now.[116] Some are of the opinion that κρίμα refers to eternal

---

111. Fascher, *Der erste Brief*, 95: the community as a whole suffers, but some are affected more. Also see 1 Cor 6:1–11 where Paul indicates that strife between individuals "carries the gravest implication not only for the individuals concerned, but for the whole church." Roetzel, *Judgment in the Community*, 131–32.

112. Fascher, *Der erste Brief*, 95.

113. Schnabel, *Der erste Brief*, 667.

114. Schrage, *Der erste Brief*, 54.

115. Travis along with Synofzik comment that since Paul interprets a Christian's suffering as divine judgments only in 1 Cor 5 and 11, we cannot come to a general conclusion that Paul considered suffering as God's standard judgment on sin. Travis, *Christ and the Judgment*, 83. Cf. Synofzik, *Gerichts- und Vergeltungsaussagen*, 52.

116. Verses 29 and 34: ἵνα μὴ εἰς κρίμα συνέρχησθε. On συνέρχησθε εἰς as introducing

judgment rather than judgment in the present time, since Paul uses κρίμα for the last judgment in other instances (Rom 2:2, 3; 3:8).[117] Similarly ἔνοχος ἔσται in 11:27 is taken to presuppose a future eschatological judgment.[118] However, the context of the letter indicates that Paul is talking about the present judgment as some of the Corinthians were already "guilty" and were disciplined for their behavior.[119] And this is Paul's subsequent advice to avoid judgment. Moreover, some are of the opinion that Paul's other usage of κρίμα for the last judgment are arthrous, whereas it is anarthrous in 1 Cor 11:29, 34, implying that the connotation here is not the same.[120] Also the use of ἔσται here, is to be considered as intensive.[121] Based on these evidences the primary reference of ἔνοχος ἔσται is to the present situation at Corinth and κρίμα likewise to the present judgment.[122] Hence, it is clear that Paul is writing about the present judgment as he further distinguishes this present ongoing judgment from the future eschatological judgment which was yet to come.[123]

Nevertheless, Paul's admonishment to the Corinthians in relation to the present judgment that has affected them also relates to the final judgment.[124] This is because what response a person makes in the present time

---

a result, see BDAG, 969–70, s.v. συνέρχομαι, 1.a.

117. So Delling, "Abendmahlsgeschehen," 329; Theissen, "Soziale Integration," 290–317, 312.

118. So Käsemann, "Anliegen und Eigenart," 23; Delling, "Abendmahlsgeschehen," 329; Neuenzeit, Das Herrenmahl, 228; Grosheide, First Epistle, 274.

119. Käsemann tries to explain the shift from the eschatological future (ἔνοχος ἔσται, v. 27) to the fact that the Corinthians are *already* eating and drinking judgment to themselves (vv. 29–30) by saying that: "In the sacrament, what is revealed on the Last Day becomes in a certain way already a present reality" "Anliegen und Eigenart," 23–24; trans. from Wainwright, Eucharist and Eschatology, 102–3.

120. Cf. Volf, Paul and Perseverance, 100; Wolff, Der erste Brief, 94, 95.

121. So Conzelmann, 1 Corinthians, 202; Wolff, Der erste Brief, 94; Volf, Paul and Perseverance, 100: "Thus it seems best to take ἔνοχος ἔσται as a proclamation of incurred guilt with a *futurum intensivum*." Cf. BDF, 362.

122. Correctly, Wolff, Der erste Brief, 94; So also Hofius, "Herrenmahl und Herrenmahlsparadosis," 371–408, 374, n. 20; Synofzik, Gerichts- und Vergeltungaussagen, 82; Conzelmann, 1 Corinthians, 203; Klauck, Herrenmahl, 326; Morris, First Epistle, 164; Robertson and Plummer, First Epistle, 252; Schnabel, Der erste Brief, 665.

123. 1 Cor 11:32; cf. 2 Cor 5:10.

124. Mattern, Verständis, 102, observes that Paul's intention is not to contrast between present and future judgment, but between the judgment of chastening upon the community (with a view to averting of final destruction) and the judgment of annihilation upon the world.

Exclusion and Judgment in Fellowship Meals

has consequences for the future.[125] There is a clear connection between the two realms. The statement παιδευόμεθα, ἵνα μὴ . . . κατακριθῶμεν indicates the inter-connectiveness between the present pedagogical judgment (i.e., disciplinary) and the final condemnation.[126]

We see a juxtaposition of the ideas of present judgment and ultimate deliverance.[127] Paul's argument here can be understood in the light of the eschatological tension where Paul emphasizes both the "already" aspect at the Lord's Supper but at the same time the "not yet" aspect when it will culminate at the *parousia*. Judgment takes place at the Lord's Supper but only in the light of the final eschatological judgment.[128]

Paul does not suggest that Corinthian Christians will reap the judgment of condemnation for their wrong behavior at the Lord's Supper.[129] At the same time the present pedagogical judgment is not a guaranteed protection against future condemnation. But the implication of his statement is that it all depends on how the believers respond to their present situation so that they can escape the final condemnation. This conclusion would be in line with why Paul admonishes the Corinthians in the first place: so that they can avoid the final condemnation by responding positively to the temporal judgment placed upon them.

---

125. So Käsemann, "Anliegen und Eigenart," 25, 27. According to Käsemann, Paul develops a dialectical interpretation of the Lord's Supper in 1 Cor 11:27–32 evoking judgment in both its future and present forms.

126. Some see the present and future judgment in Paul as two different categories. So Volf, who sees judgment as strictly referring to the present temporal judgment; and the present and final judgment as "mutually exclusive categories." She claims that Paul juxtaposes the present and future judgment as diametrically opposed. *Paul and Perseverance*, 102, 107. But Paul makes a clear connection between the present and final judgment. When Paul says that the present judgment is experienced so that they will be saved on the final judgment, it clearly indicates the link between the two. Moreover the present judgment is of little value if that was not the case.

127. Similar ideas can be seen in 5:1–5 where the church is to pronounce a sentence upon the offender not only in order to preserve itself as church but to preserve and ensure the person's deliverance on the day of the Lord.

128. Volf, to the contrary, asserts that the presence of God's discipline implies that those receiving it will be exempt from final condemnation. She states that God does not discipline those whom God may end up finally condemning. She understands Paul to say that we are then disciplined in the present *because* we will not be condemned in the future; *Paul and Perseverance*, 106–7. Contra VanLandingham, *Judgment and Justification*, 197. Volf's reading of this passage is nearly the opposite of what the text actually says.

129. Conzelman explains that here the final judgment is not "seen as a process of separation between the accepted and the damned, but only as execution of 'wrath.'" Conzelmann, *1 Corinthians*, 203.

REPENTANCE AND THE LORD'S SUPPER

The discussion on judgment leads to another issue that revolves around Paul's description that the present affliction, especially death, becomes a means to escape the final judgment. As Paul explains in 11:32, this has often been understood to imply that the present affliction is pedagogical through which one can avoid the condemnation at the final judgment.[130] So how does it become pedagogical judgment? What implications does this have on Paul's teachings on salvation, death, and the final judgment?

As noted, Paul does not say that it is a guarantee that all those who suffer will escape the final judgment. Did Paul mean to imply that it is pedagogical in the sense that he anticipated repentance and change on the part of the afflicted person? Or did Paul envisage a "sentence" of death which continues to take effect even if the preceding illness provokes repentance, which means that the person who dies escapes the condemnation at the final judgment?[131] Then does repentance from the guilty members becomes a prerequisite to save them from the final judgment? The general understanding is that it is a chastisement but unless it is followed by repentance there would be the final condemnation.[132] So though it is disciplinary judgment, it does not automatically protect them from the final condemnation. If they do not act on the disciplinary action then they are in danger of the final judgment and of being excluded from the eschatological salvation.

If so, what happens to those who have already died without having the opportunity to repent? Perhaps those who died as a result of God's discipline in 11:30 did not receive an opportunity for repentance, as was the case for the Israelites whose history Paul recounts in 10:1–12. Does death represent the ultimate stage in an unsuccessful process of discipline? This seems to be the case in Acts 5:1–11 where Ananias and Sapphira experienced God's condemning judgment. Death then can be equated to eternal condemnation for those who died unrepentant. So in effect, if the person

---

130. That it is disciplining judgment, is generally accepted. Gk. παιδευόμεθα (cf. 2 Cor 6:9 and 1 Tim 1:20). Inherent in this usage is the idea of "correcting by discipline." On the use of the word in the Greco-Roman world and the NT, see Bertram, "παιδεύω," *TDNT*, 5.596–625; D. Fürst, *NIDNTT* III, 775–80. Cf. Morris, *First Epistle*, 164; Bornkamm, "Herrenmahl und Kirche bei Paulus," 170; Konradt, *Gericht und Gemeinde*, 447–48, 451.

131. Travis, *Christ and the Judgment*, 82; Lampe, "Church Discipline," 348

132. Godet, *Commentary*, 165–67; Schnabel, *Der erste Brief*, 668; Konradt, *Gericht und Gemeinde*, 447–48; VanLandingham, *Judgment and Justification*, 198. Judgment in the community with an aim to bring about repentance can also be seen in other texts: "In II Thess. 3:14–15 ἵνα ἐντραπῇ is clearly a synonym for repentance. See also II Cor. 2:5–11 where repentance is implied." Roetzel, *Judgment in the Community*, 124, 132–33.

repented, he recovered from his sickness; if not the person died and this physical death was a sign of his spiritual death as well. But Paul does not show that the people who died were in "the ultimate stage in an unsuccessful process of discipline" and so are "definite examples of people who 'fell asleep' and thus forfeited their salvation."[133]

To explain away these difficulties some suggest a post-mortem repentance.[134] So if a person fails to repent, death represents judgment in its totality. Some have noted the possibility of a death-bed repentance.[135] Similarly, Lampe suggests that: "Paul envisages a divine sentence of death which continues to take effect even after illness has induced the offender to come to a better mind."[136] Some have suggested that the afflictions and death are not to be considered as atoning but they prevent the possibility of future sinning; and death brings finality to it.[137] But all these suggestions are highly speculative in nature and do not hold much ground.

Sanders and others have tried to explain this aspect of Paul's theology based on the concept of judgment in Judaism.[138] In Judaism, long life was considered a special blessing of God;[139] and death was sometimes thought of as the means of atonement for sins not dealt with by the Day of Atonement.[140] Proponents of this view associate Paul's usage of the word

---

133. Marshall, *Kept by the Power*, 115–16. Mattern, *Verständnis*, 103, and Roetzel, *Judgment in the Community*, 139, consider the possibility that the church fails to repent through chastisement and thereby joins the world in going to a destiny of condemnation.

134. So Weiss, *Der erste Korintherbrief*, 292. Contra Mattern, *Verständnis*, 101: "has no basis in Paul"; so also, Filson, *St. Paul's Conception*, 87.

135. Allo, *Première Épître*, 283, noted by Marshall, *Kept by the Power*, 115.

136. Lampe, "Church Discipline," 337–61, 348.

137. Smith, "Hand this Man," 177.

138. Sanders, *Palestinian Judaism*, 516, 517; Robertson and Plummer, *First Epistle*, 253; Collins, *First Corinthians*, 436; Hays, *First Corinthians*, 195; Yinger, *Paul, Judaism and Judgment*, 256–57.

139. See Exod 20:12; Ps 128:5–6.

140. See, e.g., *m. Sanh.*6. 2, where even the criminal about to be executed is instructed to say, "May my death be an atonement for all my sins." *Mekilta* II, 278; *m. Abot* 5:23, "Ben He-He [a disciple of Hillel] said: according to the suffering so is the reward." For the atoning value of chastisement in Judaism, see Sanders, *Palestinian Judaism*, 168–72. Roetzel further explains that in rabbinic Judaism judgment was both a future prospect and a present reality. "Illness or even death might follow some sin (*b. Shabbath*, 153–54). Natural disasters, war, etc. were also linked to individual or corporate sin. Cohen, *Everyman's Talmud*, 119–20. Suffering in this world was often considered punishment for sin, but it was also believed to contain redemptive powers." Roetzel, *Judgment in the Community*, 58–59.

παιδεία (11:32) with the Jewish tradition as it occurs frequently in Judaism describing pedagogical judgment. The general idea prevalent was that discipline accepted in this life brings deliverance from punishment in the next.[141] Based on this word παιδεία they explain that judgment in Corinth was disciplinary and it is not only the legitimate expression of love, but it is also for testing and refining. It is to prevent worse from happening for those who are the elect. Discipline is a privilege for the people of God, it has its goal to protect the elect from final judgment. For others, God waits for the accumulation of sins and the final day to destroy them. But for the people of God he acts beforehand through disciplinary judgment.[142] One of the main issues here is that as Sanders points out, this chastisement prevents future condemnation because the chastisement itself is purifying. So for those who have died they will not be condemned at the final judgment because their death is accorded atoning value.[143] This view does not give any room for repentance in the whole process.[144]

So the main argument is that Paul could not have attributed atoning value to the present affliction as in Judaism, as this would lead to theological inconsistency in his thought.[145] For Paul atonement is not through sickness

---

141. 2 Macc 6:12; 2 *Bar.* 13:4-11; 78:6; 83:8; *Pss. Sol.* 10:1-3; Jer 31:18, 19. On suffering as educative punishment since the time of the Maccabees, see Bertram, "παιδεύω," *TDNT*, 5.610, 621; See the definition and many references in BDAG, 748-49; Moore, *Judaism in the First Centuries*, 2.252, 255. See also Str-B 3.445.

142. Konradt, *Gericht und Gemeinde*, 444.

143. Sanders understood Paul's concept of judgment in term of Jewish covenantal nomism. He argues that salvation is by grace, but within the soteriological framework there is reward for good deeds and punishment for iniquity. Based on passages such as 2 Cor 5:10 and 1 Cor 3:10-15 he contends that one may be punished for transgression but still be saved. Sanders, *Paul and Palestinian Judaism*, 515-18. Also Roetzel, *Judgment in the Community*, 117 "Ample precedent exists, therefore, for viewing present affliction or death as God's righteous action to protect the integrity of his covenant with his people. The new element in Paul, however, is his belief that the *final* vindication has already begun."

144. See the critique by Travis, *Christ and the Judgment*, 62: "Paul's doctrine of salvation by grace and judgment according to works do not (as Sanders's scheme suggests) operate on parallel lines which never meet. Sanders does not do justice to the eschatological finality of Paul's doctrine of justification, in which justification is a real (though not irreversible) anticipation of God's final judgment (Rom 5:9; 8:1, 30-34; 1 Thess 5:9). Works express this new relation to God; at the final judgment they will be the evidence that a man's faith and justification are real, and so his destiny to salvation will be confirmed."

145. Sin cannot be atoned for by the physical death as in Judaism as this is contrary to Paul's teaching about salvation. Marshall, *Kept by the Power*, 115.

or death, but through Christ's death.¹⁴⁶ And there is no other instance in the New Testament of the idea that a person's death affects atonement for sin. It is the death of Christ, not humans, which atones.¹⁴⁷ Moreover the judgment Paul describes is not in terms of atonement but corrective chastening.¹⁴⁸ Roetzel also notes that:

> Although Paul shares the viewpoint of the Old Testament, apocalyptic, and rabbinic materials, he naturally differs in the particular way he places his materials in Christocentric focus. In the apocalyptic and rabbinic materials deliverance from the eschatological visitation of death and destruction remains future, whereas for Paul these powers are under attack and are being overcome in the present time.¹⁴⁹

Similarly, Gundry Volf concludes that Paul's concept runs parallel to the Jewish tradition of divine παιδεία. But it also differs in that the divine παιδεία is applied corporately in the OT-Jewish tradition, whereas in Paul it applies to individuals.¹⁵⁰ Furthermore, even within Jewish thought there are discrepancies.¹⁵¹ So owing to the many differences between Paul's un-

---

146. Travis argues that even in Judaism such atonement was not possible unless the death was *owned* as punishment for sin. That repentance is necessary for forgiveness is a basic assumption of Judaism and the New Testament (cf. 2 Cor 12:20–21). Travis, *Christ and the Judgment*, 81.

147. Barrett, *First Epistle*, 126–27; also Yinger, *Paul, Judaism and Judgment*, 257, ". . . an atoning suffering (apart from Christ's) is not attested elsewhere in the NT, whereas the corrective chastening is (cf. Heb 12:5–12; Titus 2:11–12; 1 Tim 1:20)." Cf. Roetzel, *Judgment in the Community*, 124n4.

148. Also VanLandingham, *Judgment and Justification*, 198: "When Paul says that Christians are disciplined so that they may avoid condemnation, he shows that repentance, not atonement for sin, is the objective of the discipline."

149. He further reiterates that "Paul differs from Jewish apocalyptic at those points where his Gospel dictates a change in emphasis. Men receive condemnation in the judgment not because they are Gentiles or apostate Jews, but because they reject 'Christ crucified.' In the universal judgment God is no respecter of persons. No man can appeal to his ancestry, and no man is excused by his ignorance. Unlike the apocalyptic literature, Paul sees the judgment as proleptically present; no longer is it a future prospect only." Roetzel, *Judgment in the Community*, 90.

150. Cf. Volf, *Paul and Perseverance*, 107–11 on comparison between Paul and divine chastisement in the OT-Jewish thought.

151. Again Roetzel points the difficulties in connecting sin, punishment, and atonement even in Judaism "It is significant that the rabbis realized, however, that a direct tie could not always be made between individual suffering and sin; consequently in a later period considerable space is given over to explaining why the guilty are left unpunished in this world while the righteous continue to suffer. (Cohen, *Everyman's Talmud*,

Judgment at the Lord's Supper in Corinth

derstanding and the Jewish view, the concept of judgment in Judaism cannot be a primary basis for understanding Paul's theology here.

Further examination also reveals that Paul does not make any distinction between the afflictions in Corinth; all are categorized as part of the disciplinary judgment, including death. Moreover, death is not the finality in the sense of eternal condemnation, as is seen in Paul's usage of the verb κοιμᾶν.[152] So in the context of the Lord's Supper, Paul does not give the impression that the death of certain members here does not entail an eschatological or spiritual death.[153] But he equates it with the other physical afflictions in the community, which were all part of the pedagogical judgment. So the term Paul uses here to indicate death in the community does not have the same connotation as his other usages.[154] This reiterates Paul's statement that the judgment in its different physical manifestation in the community is pedagogical.

The conclusion we can derive is that this divine chastising judgment does not automatically preserve them from final condemnation. But at the same time, as Paul indicates, its function is to avert them from the final

---

121–23.)" Roetzel, *Judgment in the Community*, 58–59; also VanLandingham, *Judgment and Justification*, 197–198. He also asserts that there are "no Jewish texts that discuss discipline/punishment and then separate the purifying/atoning aspects of discipline from its corrective aspects. (See, e.g., *Pss. Sol.* 10:1–3. Of course when God kills a person, it is hard to find a corrective aspect. Such a death need not be purifying, but can still avert further punishment. See *T. Ab.* 14.15 [Recension A]). Second, the term *paideuo* means 'to treat as a child.' As its root suggests, the term is normally used in an educative or corrective sense, not in a cultic sense."

152. For the NT reserves this term for the death of those who will be raised to new life and whose physical deaths are thus—not just euphemistically—a "falling asleep." 1 Thess 4:13–15; 1 Cor 15:6, 18, 20, 51; John 11:11; Matt 27:52; Acts 7:60; 13:36; 2 Pet 3:4. See also *Herm. Sim.* 9.16.3, 5–7; Ign. *Rom* 4.2; 2 Macc 12:45. Unclear, 1 Cor 7:39. So Bruce, *Corinthians*, 116; Robertson and Plummer, *First Epistle*, 253. For the concept of *thanatos* in Paul see Barrosse "Death and Sin," 449–50; Black, "Pauline Perspectives," 413–433; Roetzel, *Judgment in the Community*, 86–88; Travis, *Christ and the Judgment*, 71: "Certainly Paul gives no formal definition of death. What he does do frequently is to contrast it often with (eternal) *life* (Rom. 5:17, 21; 6:23; 7:10; 8:2, 6; 1 Cor 15:22; 2 Cor 2:16), *salvation* (2 Cor 7:10), *justification* (Rom. 6:16), *the Spirit* (2 Cor 3:7). Thus it is clear, in the absence of a definition of *thanatos*, that Paul viewed it primarily as the negation of life."

153. So Volf, *Paul and Perseverance*, 106–10; Konradt, *Gericht und Gemeinde*, 440. Against Marshall, *Kept by the Power*, 115, 116; Lampe, "Discipline," 348; Grosheide, *First Epistle*, 276; Roetzel, *Judgment in the Community*, 124n4.

154. Note the use of ἵνα v. 32. Though they are judged, even to the extent of causing death, the punishment is not for their destruction but to save them from final destruction.

judgment.¹⁵⁵ The present judgment is a sign of God's grace on the erring members, so that they can avoid condemnation. Judgment has been carried on them to prevent them from becoming one with the world which is destined for condemning judgment.¹⁵⁶ Had they acted correctly even the disciplinary judgment could have been avoided. Disciplinary judgment is a privilege but it should not be taken lightly. Though repentance is not mentioned by Paul as a prerequisite to escape the final judgment, since he does not attribute atoning value to the afflictions, it is implied that repentance becomes part of the equation. As Moule states, "it depends upon the person's response to that situation whether it proves to be remedial and to be a judgment which will prepare him for salvation at last, or whether it plunges him further into a condition of fatal self-concern."¹⁵⁷ So when a person responds appropriately to the divine grace, and in this case judgment through "the sacramental verdict," it leads to an "entry beyond judgment into the life of the age to come."¹⁵⁸

To understand this positive outlook of Paul regarding the judgment at the Lord's Supper, we again need to understand the socio-religious background that motivated his response. Again, the context of the fellowship meal tradition outlined in chapters 1 and 2 above provides the best explanation to understand Paul's thought. Here we can see that Paul's concept is in parallel with the fellowship meal tradition and ideology. Fellowship meals signified the bonding of relationships and unity between members as well as with the deities. Eating together was an expression of intimacy and fellowship, and sharing and accepting an invitation suggested restoration of relationships. By coming together for a meal, we have seen how identities were formed and maintained. So the fellowship meals became an integral part of their socio-religious existence. Likewise, relationships and covenants between people and with deities were ratified and strengthened by having fellowship meals. Examples can be seen in both the social and religious context of fellowship meals in the Greco-Roman world, as well as in Judaism.¹⁵⁹ The bonding that happened at the table was considered sig-

155. So Lietzmann, *An die Korinther*, 60; Similarly, Wolff, *Der erste Brief*, 9; Lampe, The Eucharist," 46, Fee, 566; Horsley, *1 Corinthians*, 162–63; Konradt, *Gericht und Gemeinde*, 441; Mattern, *Verständnis*, 99.

156. Ibid., 103.

157. Moule, "Judgment Theme," 481.

158. Ibid., 481.

159. Cf. 2 Kgs 25:27–30 = Jer 52:31–34; Jos. *Ant.* 19.321; see Jeremias, *New Testament Theology*, 115. That it also had this meaning in everyday life is illustrated vividly by Luke

nificant in the sense of creating unity in a tangible way. This in turn affects how relationship between the participants and the patron gods would work out. Here we are also reminded of the tradition where the host had the responsibility to protect and save his guest, once he has shared food.[160] It was not simply a coming together for food, but in the ancient world it went far beyond; it had far wider ramification in its socio-religious life. Fellowship meal traditions also show that divine judgment was associated not only in the future but was a present reality.

This tradition is also carried over in Paul's understanding of the Lord's Supper in Corinth. The fellowship meal, namely the Lord's Supper, represented the table of grace. So when Paul relates it with judgment, he follows the fellowship meal tradition in saying that it is only disciplinary judgment for their own good. For in participating at the table they have gained new identity and life. This new status gains prominence and exerts influence in all walks of life, so much so that Paul expects the Corinthians to respond positively to his advice and warning. Though they are disciplined through physical ailments and death, the text does not indicate that they are impenitent till the end. His understanding of the fellowship meal tradition and practices is a contributing factor in how judgment is meted out on the Corinthians. It has influenced his positive outlook on the Corinthians' future. Paul here takes for granted that the people who are disciplined would not renounce their faith. The main reason being, that by participating in the fellowship meal a member expresses one's personal commitment and relationship with the risen Lord. Especially in the religious traditions participation in the fellowship meal was considered as a kind of membership into the cults. One would not partake or be permitted to partake unless one accepted the ideology or belief of the group. The Corinthians who have partaken in the Supper were thus considered by Paul as having come to attain certain status and position in relation to faith. Their status as Christians was confirmed by their participation in the fellowship meal, which gave Paul the impetus to claim that even those who have died are saved from the final judgment. So even though a person may be guilty at the Supper, Paul is positive that once they realize that they are being judged, they will be

---

15:23–24.

160. A similar idea is expressed but in the context of covenantal relationship by Volf. She is of the view that though repentance is the goal of chastisement, it does not appear to limit the effects of their punishment. "Rather, election prevents God's punishment of God's children from resulting in annihilation deserved for transgressions." Volf, *Paul and Perseverance*, 111.

penitent, as their participation at the meal indicates a person's conviction and commitment and disposition to the gospel.

The scope of chastisement which was to safeguard them from the final judgment can be seen as the design of the gospel which Paul has proclaimed from the very beginning—a gospel of love and forgiveness, whose message is now enforced by the fellowship meal tradition. They are judged as God's children based on their new gained status that is embodied in their participation of the Supper.[161] The Lord's Supper actualizes the covenantal relationship between the Corinthians and the risen Lord. Thus, this disciplinary or chastising judgment also becomes a kind of affirmation of the new bonding and status that the Corinthians have achieved through the risen Lord.

Thus, the fellowship meal tradition can be understood as the basis behind Paul's theology of judgment at the Lord's Supper. His teaching exhibits that he upholds the values of the culture of that time. At the same time he calls for radical change in their world view. The Corinthians' earlier worldview has to be transformed according to the Gospel values and norms, which was embodied in the very fellowship meal they were celebrating. In all these we see fellowship meal practices and ideology at work in formulating Paul's theology.

Nonetheless, Paul's positive expectation does not omit the alternative possibility, i.e., in case a person fails to respond positively. This tension can be seen in his warning that the danger of the final judgment or condemnation still remains.[162] So for Paul, the present judgment is a preventive measure to preserve them from the final judgment, provided they respond positively. Therefore Paul in the following sections spells out what attitude or behavior a person should have while partaking in the Lord's Supper, to avoid sinning against the Lord, and to avoid judgment.

---

161. Similarly, Bruce, *Corinthians*, 116: "[As in Wis 11:10], so here the fact that the people warned are chastened is a token of their being true children of God." In a similar tone, Volf: "Paul does not make repentance from a sin for which a Christian incurs temporal judgment pivotal for escape from final condemnation. Rather, Christians' relation to God as God's children is here presented as definitive for their final destiny." Volf, *Paul and Perseverance*, 112.

162. So Roetzel: "If, however, in spite of the chastisement the church persists in its stubborn and defiant ways surely *katakrima* is a real possibility for the church. The sacraments do not guarantee salvation no matter how culpable the community may be." *Judgment in the Community*, 139.

ORDINANCES FOR THE LORD'S SUPPER

On the basis of his theological exposition of the significance of the Lord's Supper and its implications on the Corinthians, Paul now sets some remedial steps and guidelines for proper conduct at the Lord's Supper so that judgment can be avoided.

δοκιμαζέτω (v. 28)

How does a person participate worthily at the supper? Firstly, Paul calls them to test or examine themselves before God.[163] Again a lot of discussion revolves around what kind of self-examination Paul refers to. It has been understood by some that Paul is calling for moral self-evaluation in terms of one's merit or worthiness to partake in the Lord's Supper.[164] Some call for introspection in terms of the elements of the Supper.[165] But Paul does not give any indication in the letter that he was calling for that kind of personal assessment in terms of moral self-righteousness and worthiness before partaking the Supper,[166] neither in terms of the sacramental bread and wine. The context rather calls for an introspection of one's attitude and

---

163. δοκιμαζέτω δὲ ἄνθρωπος ἑαυτόν, 11:28. On δοκιμάζω, see BDAG, 255–56, *"to put to test, examine;"* but esp. with reference to the *result* of the examination, e.g., *"proving the genuineness of gold by testing*; hence *to accept as proved, to approve."*

164. Unfortunately for centuries this has been the understanding of the church and many commentators. E.g., As a "moral exercise . . . to judge of his feelings as to the person of Jesus," Godet, *Commentary*, 165. Morris, *First Epistle*, 163; Stuart, "The Lord's Supper," 531.

165. Similarly Conzelmann: "The object of this self-examination is not one's inner state in general, but one's attitude to the sacrament, that is, the propriety of the participation, whether one 'distinguishes' the body of the Lord. It is the criterion of existence in the community." Conzelmann, *1 Corinthians*, 202.

166. Also Foerster: It "does not denote a moral quality but an attitude determined by the Gospel." Foerster, "ἄξιος," *TDNT*, 1.380; Fee, *First Epistle*, 562; Hays, *First Corinthians*, 200. Again there is a tendency to interpret this solely in terms of social ethical concern. For instance Bruce: "The context implies that his self-examination will be specially directed to ascertaining whether or not he is living and acting 'in love and charity' with his neighbours." Bruce, *Corinthians*, 114–15; Also Motyer, *Remember Jesus*, 89. "Reconciliation takes priority over worship! Paul would say: because worship is *impossible* without it, and the Lord's Supper is *dangerous* without it." Social-ethical concerns were important for Paul but the study has shown that social-ethical concerns were the side effects of their ideological differences.

motive at the Supper, and then one's action towards fellow members in the community.¹⁶⁷

It is directly related to vv. 19–21 where abuse and schisms had taken place. The situation in Corinth and Paul's response to it indicates that the call to self scrutiny is an invitation to the Corinthians to consider their motive and how they relate to other members during the fellowship meal.¹⁶⁸ The issue here is whether one's priority in participating in the meal is to recollect the sacrifice made for them and the redemption sought for them, or whether one is participating in it to promote one's interest and position.

The priorty of some Corinthians at the table was to promote their own group for position and honor. The effect was that they treated the other members as no longer equals but relegated them to a lower status. Now, instead of upholding the oneness of the body, they have rather fragmented it by creating schisms. In short, they have come to the Lord's Supper not to observe its signifcance and its effects, but to achieve one's selfish agenda. Though the division has taken place along social and ideological lines, Paul's words indicate that the division in Corinth is more serious than it appears. Those who humiliate others take the side of those who have put to death the Lord. On that basis, Paul calls for self-evaluation, for one's motive and behavior are intricately connected to the "body."

Therefore, by examining themselves before partaking in the meal, they could avoid God's judgment both in the present and the future.¹⁶⁹ The judgment in the form of physical afflictions is in a way God's examination of them in the present, which has found them wanting and so exposed them to the physical frailties. Paul's usage of the verb δοκιμάζω also links it thematically with the cognate adjective δόκιμοι in v. 19.¹⁷⁰ By judging themselves in the right manner the end result is that they will be the ones who are found approved or genuine.¹⁷¹

---

167. Wolff, *Der erste Brief*, 89 correctly takes the admonishment to self-examination to concern behavior associated with the Lord's Supper.

168. The call here is very similar to the fellowship rules in the Greco-Roman context. E.g., The Guild of Zeus Hypsistos, which had rules prohibiting schisms, and disagreement at the meal. A similar concept can be seen in the Gospel; cf. Matt 5:23–26. *Didache* reflects this when it declares: "let none who has a quarrel with his fellow join in your meeting until they are reconciled, lest your sacrifice be defiled" (14:2).

169. Fee, *First Epistle*, 561–62; Fascher, *Der erste Brief des Paulus*, 94.

170. Cf. Barrett, *First Epistle*, 273; Thiselton, *First Epistle*, 891.

171. Fee points out that though the verb is not strictly a forensic term, the context of the text gives it that forensic connotation. *First Epistle*, 561–62.

Judgment at the Lord's Supper in Corinth

The verb δοκιμάζειν also indicates a positive outcome. The result of this examination will be good since when a person undergoes this self examination he will sift out the errors and will come out as one who is genuine and "proved."[172] So in no way did Paul intend that people should abstain themselves from the Lord's Supper. This reiterates Paul's advice in v. 33 that they should wait for one another at the meal. Unfortunately, misinterpretations of this text have made many over the centuries abstain from the Lord's Supper over the fear that one's unworthiness or lack of faith would incur judgment. Rather Paul's words here indicate that he expected the occasion to be used by all participants for putting all things into proper perspective leading to a positive outcome for which the Lord's Supper was meant to serve. In fact, if the unworthy participation at the Supper can work indirectly for the good of the member, how much more will it work for the common good of the church and the individual member when it is rightly celebrated.[173]

As noted above, Paul's call for self-examination has no reference to personal introspection of moral worthiness before one partakes in the Supper. The self-reflection that Paul seeks is in regard to one's motive and interest of partaking in the Supper, whether that interest conforms to the gospel message that they proclaim through partaking in the Supper. This in turn will ultimately affect their relationship with other members of the body.

διακρίνων (v. 29)

Paul's call for self scrutiny is taken further in v. 29 when he indicates that those who do not discern the σῶμα of the Lord, eat and drink judgment. So then they are called to recognize or discern what the body is all about. The verb διακρίνειν has a wide variety of usages in the NT. It basically means "to differentiate by separating" and then "to estimate or judge correctly or to recognize."[174]

Many discussions have been occasioned by Paul's use of the word σῶμα in this context.[175] In the light of v. 27, some early Church Fathers

---

172. Grosheide, *First Epistle*, 274–75.

173. Cf. Wainwright, *Eucharist and Eschatology*, 103–4.

174. BDAG, 231; Grimm-Thayer, 138–39. Also cf. Barrett, *First Epistle*, 274–75 on its usage in Paul.

175. Conzelmann, 1 *Corinthians*, 211nn7–8; based on a number of bits of evidence he notes the widespread use of the metaphor of the body in popular and philosophical

like Justin and Augustine followed by other commentators think that the σῶμα here means the risen body of Christ and understand the verse to refer to the failure to discern the sacramental presence of Christ in the elements, i.e., a failure to discern between the bread and wine of the Lord's Supper and the common food.[176] This interpretation does not fit the context of the letter, moreover Paul does not indicate that the Corinthians have disregarded the sacrament. Rather some observe that the Corinthians were "supersacramentalists"[177] or "sacramentalists"[178] and so Paul was trying to convince them that it is not an automatism. It is the death of the Lord, not the ritual that saves (10:2-5, 12). Paul's concern from the outset has been their failure to see the significance of the whole meal, in the sense that they were using it to promote their personal agendas. The context points to a failure on the part of the Corinthians to have a right estimate of the significance of the fellowship meal based on their cultural disposition.

Some have even suggested that the σῶμα is to be understood as referring to one's self that should be "separated from" the process of judgment that takes place at the table.[179] But there is nothing in Paul to suggest that he referred to this kind of reading.[180]

---

literature, especially as a metaphor for political relationships. Also see Fraine, *Adam and the Family of Man*, on semitic idea of the word. On the multi dimensional meaning of the term "body" in Paul see Martin, *The Corinthian Body*, 194-95; Smith, "Meals and Morality," 329; Robinson, *The Body*, 9; E. Schweizer, "σῶμα," *TDNT*, 7.1067-69; Leon-Dufour, *Sharing the Eucharistic*, 212; also see the discussion in Thiselton, *First Epistle*, 768.

176. Justin *Apology*, 1.66; Augustine *On John*, sect. 62; Godet, *Commentary*, 167; Weiss, *Der erste Korintherbrief*, 291; Lietzmann, *An die Korinther*, 59; Allo, *Première Épître*, 253; Héring, *First Epistle*, 120; Weiss, *Earliest Christianity*, 646-47; Contra Barrett, *First Epistle*, 274; Roberston and Plummer, *First Epistle*, 252; Schrage, *Der erste Brief*, 3.51 and n. 587.

177. See 10:1-13; 15:29; cf. von Soden, "Sakrament und Ethik bei Paulus," 1-40. Rpt. in *Urchristentum und Geschichte*, 239-75. Abridged and trans. as "Sacrament and Ethics in Paul," in *The Writings of St. Paul*, 257-68; Watson, *First Epistle*, 124.

178. Lampe, "Eucharist," 43.

179. Ehrhardt, "Holy Sacrament and Suffering," 259; also by Martin, *The Corinthian Body*, 195 who argues for the same view that σῶμα here points to one's own body, about which care must be taken to keep it from the judgment of disease and possibly even death, also the body of one's Christian neighbor, i.e., paying attention to the bodily needs of other Christians.

180. See the critique by Barrett on this view, *First Epistle*, 275. Also by Dunn on Martin's view of σῶμα as referring to one's own body. "it is unlikely that 'discerning the body' included thought of 'taking proper account of one's own bodily state.'" Dunn, *Theology of Paul*, 612-13.

Judgment at the Lord's Supper in Corinth

Again there are those who interpret it in terms of the body of Christ, in relation to vv. 24 and 27. They uphold the view that the crucified Lord is represented by the elements in the meal, and this adds significance to the fellowship meal. To discern the body means to recognize this uniqueness that the elements represent Christ's death for human kind, who is now present in the elements. As Earle Ellis claims, the same logic and realism underlie Paul's concern about prostitutes and the Lord's Supper: "The body of Christ is no metaphor, nor a simple theological conception, but is at least as real as any other body."[181] In a similar tone, but not necessarily in terms of "substance" of the elements, some view σῶμα as a Christological reference.[182] The main argument against this is that since Paul refers to "body" and not to "blood," many think that he does not have in view the sacramental elements but the church as Christ's body, as he asserts in 10:16–17: though they are many, they are one body.[183] So by mistreating others at the table they commit an offense against Christ. Therefore, they are to discern not the bread but the "body" at the table, which is the church. As noted, fellowship meals functioned in order to create shared identity for the participants, at Corinth that process of identification as belonging to the new community which happened at the fellowship meal is reinforced by the usage of the word σῶμα.

So taking into consideration the context of the Corinthians' situation, the issue was division and the failure to consider others, that they all belonged to one body, the body of Christ—the church. Paul's call for diserning the σῶμα primarily refers to the church as the body of Christ or Christ's presence represented in the fellowship among his people.[184] The call would

---

181. Ellis, *Sōma* in First Corinthians," 140–41. Also Wolff, *Der erste Brief*, 279;Kamp, "With Due Honor," 38–42; Schrage, *Der erste Brief*, 3.52; Fitzmyer, *I Corinthians*, 446. For extended discussion and references see Thiselton, *First Epistle*, 891–94.

182. Without any ecclesiological reference. So Kondradt, *Gericht und Gemeinde*, 418; Also Barrett, *First Epistle*, 273; Grosheide, *First Epistle*, 275.

183. So Fee, *First Epistle*, 563: "Most likely the term 'body,' even though it comes by way of the words of institution in v. 24, deliberately recalls Paul's interpretation of the bread in 10:17, thus indicating that the concern is with the problem in Corinth itself, of the rich abusing the poor. All the evidence seems to point in this direction." See his argument regarding the difference between "body" in vv. 27 and 29: "(a) the absolute use of 'the body,' without a genitive qualifier, and (b) the absence of the heretofore parallel mention of the cup."

184. Similarly, Kümmel in Lietzmann, *An die Korinther*, 186, Bornkamm, *Early Christian Experience*, 148–49; Neuenzeit, *Das Herrenmahl*, 38–39; Käsemann, *Essays on New Testament Themes*, 130–32; Fee, *First Epistle*, 564; Porter, "An Interpretation,"

then mean that when they eat together, they are to remember and exhibit the new corporate identity that they have with the risen Lord and with one another. This new corporate identity as belonging to one body has been achieved on the basis of that broken body, now signified and characterized by the fellowship meal.[185] The Corinthians must have understood that even the act of coming together for a meal in itself was an achievement to this effect as Paul goes on to remind them in 10:17: "Because there is one bread, we who are many are one body, for we all partake of the one bread." So Paul here specifies that the kind of unity they have achieved according to their social norms was not the kind of unity he had envisaged.

The act of coming together and sharing food created bonding among members and this was a common theme in the ancient world.[186] The fellowship meal was the tangible representation of that unity and belongingness. Paul strongly upholds this principle and even concludes with emphasis on this aspect in 11:33, when he tells the Corinthians to wait for one another. For Paul the realization of this truth was the solution to the cause of divisions in the church.

Though the primary reference of σῶμα is ecclesiological in this verse, nonetheless, the Christological reference is also implicit, since there is a very close association between these two meanings and Paul uses σῶμα interchangeably to refer to both.[187] One can safely conclude that Paul is referring to both ecclesiological and Christological concerns here in v. 29. The call then is to discern that the σῶμα is different, a σῶμα that has come into existence because of the σῶμα that was broken in sacrifice on their

---

39–40; Horrell, *Social Ethos*, 153; Hays, *First Corinthians*, 200–201; Murphy-O'Connor, *1 Corinthians*, 123; Collins, *First Corinthians*, 439; Watson, *First Epistle*, 125; Klauck, *Herrenmahl*, 325–27; Best, *One Body in Christ*, 107–9; Furnish, *Theology of 1 Corinthians*, 86; Klinghardt, *Gemeinschaftsmahl und Mahlgemeinschaft*, 316; Witherington, *Conflict and Community*, 252; Bruce, *Corinthians*, 115; Higgins, *Lord's Supper*, 72–73.

185. Cf. For the importance of the term "body" in Paul's Eucharistic theology see Bornkamm, *Early Christian Experience*, 123–60, esp. 143–49.

186. Plut. *Quaest. conv.* 660B.

187. Scholars who view that the term σῶμα is a reference to both the body of Christ and the church are: Marshall, *Last Supper*, 114; Hofius, "The Lord's Supper," 114; Engberg-Pedersen, "Proclaiming the Lord's Death," 121–22; Schrage, *Der erste Brief*, 51–52; Passakos, "Eucharist in First Cor.," 202; Koester, "Promise and Warning," 50–51; Watson, *First Epistle*, 125; Moule, "Judgment Theme," 473; Koenig, *The Feast of the World's Redemption*, 115: He finds the double meaning in 10:16–17; 11:24–29; and 12:12–27. Also "there is a transition from a Christological use of "body" in v. 27 to a primarily ecclesiastical use in v. 29. But this has an exact parallel in 10:16–17. Indeed, 10:17 can be seen as an anticipation both of the present passage and of chapter 12."

behalf. These two meanings belong together.[188] So in a primary sense it refers to the community and then to the person of Jesus who they have been incorporated into. Paul's usage of σῶμα reveals a rhetorical word play to bring out the interconnectiveness between the sacramental body of Christ and the ecclesiastical body.

Through this, Paul shows that their action at the Supper is closely related with their relationship with the Lord and with one another. The two entities are closely linked, when one is affected, the other one suffers as well.[189] Thus, he claimed that the factions at the Corinthian church become an assault on Christ.[190] Paul's intention is that the unity experienced in baptism, in which divisions of role and status are replaced by their bonding with one another, ought to be visible, in the Supper.[191] Therefore to discern the σῶμα indicates a call to properly grasp the significance of the Lord's death, now being celebrated in the Lord's Supper, and through which the community has come into existence. A proper understanding of the significance of the meal should change their attitude and behavior towards others. This coming together at the meal signifies that unity in that "body" and makes them responsible for each other (10:17).[192] As indicated earlier, Paul's concern here transcends socio-economic lines to encompass all aspects of life. Though many commentators tend to make socio-economic

---

188. Lampe, "Church Discipline," 346, rightly says, "It is particularly hard to tell whether 'the body' which the unworthy do not 'discern' is the community as body of, or in, Christ, or the body of Christ whose death is proclaimed in the Supper, or, as is probable, the two are so closely interrelated as to be indistinguishable from each other in this context. A man who eats and drinks unworthily is guilty of the body and blood of Christ. This suggests that to violate the solemn fellowship of Christ's people . . . is to become implicated in responsibility for the death of Christ."

189. For the same viewpoint see Conzelmann, *1 Corinthians*, 202n104: "We offend against the Lord because we offend against his body, the community." Among other scholars who hold this position are Bornkamm, "Lord's Supper," 149; Klauck, "Eucharistie und Kirchengemeinschaft," 7; Barton, "Paul's Sense of Place," 241–42; Murphy-O'Connor, "Eucharist and Community," 370–85 and 56–69; Furnish, *Theology of the First Letter to the Corinthians*, 86; Wainwright, *Eucharist and Eschatology*, 101–2; Neuenzeit, *Das Herrenmah*, 38–39. Cf. Acts 9:4, Paul's conversion experience could have been a significant catalyst to his thinking about the identification of Christ with the Church. Wenham, *Paul and Jesus*, 148–49.

190. So Klauck, "Eucharistie," 7; Barton, "Paul's Sense of Place," 241–42.

191. Meeks, *First Urban Christians*, 159.

192. Likewise in 12:12–27 Paul uses the "body" metaphor to develop his theology and to stress the unity of the church.

reasons the basis of division,[193] the division in Corinth was not solely based on socio-economic status but theological and ideological reasons played a major role.

Paul's call and the emphasis on unity at the Lord's Supper indicate a failure on the part of the Corinthians to discern the mission and meaning of the cross. Since their gathering makes a concrete expression or visible reality of the Body of Christ, they are called to likewise live out that reality in thought and action.[194] Through their participation in the fellowship meal they are to realize that they are entering into an eschatological and soteriological reality through the broken body which is firmly associated with the activity of the Holy Spirit.[195] The act of sharing in a meal then depicts their participation in the salvific process of Christ corporately. To discern means to acknowledge one's unity with the risen Lord in the church. This entails responsibility to maintain the unity both in terms of belief and action. Now in present time the foremost outward manifestation is through one's relationship with other members.[196] If they were able to understand the full significance of that unity, they would honor "its wholeness in the person of each individual member."[197] When division occurs, the unity of that body ceases to exist. By their abuse they were heightening the division among the members and thereby showing a flagrant disregard for the "body." The death of Christ now celebrated in the meal epitomized humility and sacrifice for others. Likewise the Corinthians are called to do so with one another, by leaving aside all personal interest, motives, and prevalent cultural norms, to build up the body. Indeed their participation at the Lord's Supper should be the beginning of transformation of relationships and structures in societies.[198] More importantly celebrating the Lord's Supper as it should

---

193. For example, among many, Lampe, "Eucharist," 45: stresses that to discern/judge correctly means to understand that Christ died for all, even for the poorer Christians, so the richer ones should not ignore them. So Garland, *1 Corinthians*, 551.

194. Thus Paul says they are the "body of Christ." For Paul the "body of Christ" is obviously a concrete entity, and not only a metaphor. 6:12–20; 12:27. Cf. Meeks, *First Urban Christians*, 159–160; Conzelmann, *1 Corinthians*, 211.

195. Cf. 2 Cor 13:13; Zizioulas, *Being as Communion*, 130–31.

196. This basic message of unity with Christ and partnership with one another becomes the guiding principle in chapters 12–14 when he instructs them on diversity and mutuality of spiritual gifts. Cf. Koenig, *New Testament Hospitality*, 69.

197. Koenig, *New Testament Hospitality*, 69.

198. Similar calls for transformation in society beginning from the fellowship meals can be seen in Greco-Roman context; e.g., Plut. *Quaest. conv.* 613F; Lucian *Sat.* 13; Passakos, "Eucharist in First Corinthians," 210.

be celebrated is the key to escaping the final judgment.¹⁹⁹ Their action at the Supper is very closely tied to the eschatological judgment and so whatever they do, should be done in anticipation of the final judgment.

διεκρίνομεν (v. 31)

Thirdly Paul calls for self-judgment, which would then make it unnecessary for them to come under divine condemnation at the final judgment. The Corinthians are called to confine their judgment to themselves and not to judge and rank others disparagingly, because a far more serious judgment awaits them (v. 34).

It is "fundamental blindness" that brings judgment to self.²⁰⁰ So an understanding of one's self in relation to the Lord's Supper and in relationship to the community is important for one to escape the divine examination.²⁰¹ This is similar to the demand of v. 28 for self-examination putting emphasis on the need for self-scrutiny. There is also a close association with v. 29. Discerning the body and judging themselves are two sides of a coin in this context.²⁰² Recognizing the real significance of the body demands that one also recognize one's place and responsibility in the whole set-up. Basically, it is about right judgment about one's self in regard to one's position before God, which in turn affects one's place in the church among members. This would entail that those Corinthian members would stop judging others and relegating to inferior status those who were not in agreement with their views. This also relates with what Paul says with 4:5 and 5:11–12 about judging others.²⁰³ But does it mean that they should never judge others at all, because elsewhere Paul again calls the members to judge other members in the community for wrong doings, as well as settle disputes?²⁰⁴ Paul rather is against wrong judgments for wrong reasons, like "litigious judging" and

---

199. Cf. Dunn, *Theology of Paul*, 622–23.

200. Moule, "Judgment Theme," 473.

201. John Calvin sees it in terms of condemning oneself: "In a word, believers forestall the judgment of God by penitence, and the only remedy by which they can obtain acquittal in the sight of God is by voluntarily condemning themselves." Calvin, *Commentary*, 255.

202. See also the discussion in Thiselton, *First Epistle*, 897.

203. Matt 7:1.

204. Cf. 2:15; 5:3, 11; 6:2–3.

other judgments made out of selfish interest, or "lack of genuine eschatological perspective."[205]

They should first see themselves from the perspective of the cross, as those who have already passed under the judgment of God and are now part of the chosen community. Paul's call for judging themselves aims to point out the errors and mishandling at the table and thus provides the remedy for conducting themselves properly. Paul's conclusion is that when they judge themselves rightly they can escape the final judgment for they pass on themselves "God's verdict."[206] Paul's call for self-judgment gains importance only against the background of eschatological judgment, which is of upmost importance.

The Corinthians have judged others regarding allegiance, position and status in the community; but at the same time they were judging themselves in the process. In some way, their actions were "repudiating" the judgment pronounced on sin.[207] Now this self-judgment is a self-recognition and condemnation of that kind of behavior.[208] So the call for voluntary judgment implies that they accept the indictment of the Lord's death on their behalf.[209] Since the Supper is a meal of remembrance, it should remind them of their first state and to conform to a lifestyle that is according to what the Lord's Supper now represents.

All along the way we can notice Paul's use of word play and rhetorical style to emphasize the motif of judgment. Here we can see the irony of judgment: they have judged others but they themselves were being judged by the Lord who is the judge. But if they judge themselves they will not be judged and condemned with the world.

---

205. Fee, *First Epistle*, 163, 226.

206. "Ideally, we ought voluntarily to anticipate the Lord's judgment; but if we fail to do so, he will himself judge us, but judge in order to save . . . (vv. 31, 32)." Moule, "Judgment Theme," 477; Pannenberg. *Systematic Theology*, 2.326; Thiselton, *First Epistle*, 898.

207. The Corinthians have already accepted the validity of this judgment on sin at their baptism. Wainwright, *Eucharist and Eschatology*, 101–2.

208. Also note the force of the imperfect tense διεκρίνομεν that Paul uses here indicating that it should be an ongoing practice on the part of the church.

209. In the context of eschatological judgment, Moule sees self-judgment as to "plead guilty" and thereby escape the divine judgment. "Judgment Theme," 472.

ἐκδέχεσθε (vv. 33–34)

Finally on the basis of his theological exposition of the Lord's Supper tradition, Paul, with a personal appeal, offers them a simple and practical solution.[210] His response to the Corinthians suggests that if they are hungry and are unable to wait for others then they are to satisfy their hunger at their homes before coming to the fellowship meals. In this way all can have an equal share of food and more importantly fellowship together without any discrimination or hindrance. Most commentators interpret this solution in sociological terms where he was responding to a potential excuse by those who were humiliating the "have-nots."[211]

Based on this some interpreters suggest that Paul wanted to separate the Lord's Supper ritual from the fellowship meal.[212] The problem with this perspective is that, it does not deal with the core issue at Corinth. If Paul wanted to transform the attitude and action of the Corinthians this does not offer a permanent solution. We have noted that the Corinthians were acting in the manner described by Paul to assert their social status and identity, it was a stratification which was based on economic, theological and ideological factors. So eating food to satisfy their hunger was not the issue but their ulterior motive in going ahead with the dinner. Hence if Paul had meant that they should eat at home, i.e., behave according to their own wishes in their private homes, then Paul would be advocating double standards for the church.

---

210. This is one of only three occurrences of his more personal note with the vocative in this letter (1:11; 14:39), Fee, *First Epistle*, 567n3.

211. For instance, Theissen sees Paul's response as a compromise, where he asks the wealthy to have their private meal (ἴδιον δεῖπνον) at home, so that in the Lord's Supper (κυριακὸν δεῖπνον) the norm of equality can prevail; Theissen, "Soziale Integration," 312; Likewise Lampe interprets it as: "If you have difficulty waiting because you are hungry, then eat something at home before you go to the congregational meeting. But once you are there, wait before unpacking your food basket until all fellow Christians have arrived." "The Eucharist," 41; Conzelmann comments: "If they satisfy their hunger at home, they can celebrate the Supper together," *1 Corinthians*, 203; Hofius also understands it as a directive to differentiate between private meals with the Lord's Supper; "Lord's Supper," 94–95. Fee interprets it as: "Paul does not suggest that all should eat the privileged portions of the well-to-do; rather, he implies that in community the well-to-do should eat what the others do." Fee, *First Epistle*, 567; Talbert, *Reading Corinthians*, 74.

212. Theissen and Klauck have commented that Paul wanted just bread and wine at the fellowship meeting and not the complete *eranos* meal. Theissen, *Social Setting*, 145–168. Klauck, *Herrenmahl*, 294, 371.

Moreover, if Paul really intended them to eat at home then he would be doing a great disfavor for those who had less to eat.[213] Furthermore his emphasis on the selfless giving of the Christ event in the Lord's Supper tradition would not be relevant if the wealthy people had to eat at home and not share with others. Garland rightly comments that this:

> . . . misses the entire point. How can they eat the Lord's Supper with a full belly in the presence of those who are starving? He is not giving them license to indulge themselves and to ignore poor brothers and sisters so long as they do not do it in front of them at the Lord's Supper and humiliate them. Nor is he advising them that if they are worried that there might not be enough food to go around if they have to share with everyone, they should dine first at home. He does not believe that they can retreat from the demands of the gospel in their homes. This command to eat at home connects to this first warning that they are worse off for having gathered together (11:17). If they are intent only on indulging their appetites, then they should stay home. If the church's gathering is to be meaningful, it has to be an expression of real fellowship, which includes sharing.[214]

Again if Paul wanted the poor and hungry members to eat only the bread and wine at the fellowship when the rich had their food at their private homes, the whole idea of having fellowship becomes meaningless.[215] So Paul clearly indicates that he wanted all believers to participate in a fellowship meal during their gathering by telling them: "when you come together to eat, wait for one another."[216]

---

213. Paul's action would be in total contravention with the social convention as fellowship meals were also seen as a way of economic redistribution in the society. Also during these meals portions of food or gifts were given to the diners to take away depending on their status as reported by Suetonius *Vesp.* 19, 21; Petron. *Sat.* 56; Pliny the Younger *Ep.* 2.6 and reflected in *Acts of Peter* 19–29. This was an encoded social ritual that acted out hierarchy and social dependency; cf. White, "Regulating Fellowship," 182–84.

214. Garland, *1 Corinthians*, 555.

215. Cf. Lampe, "Corinthian Eucharistic Dinner Party," 8, 9.

216. Moreover the Greek term *deipnon* (11:20, 25) that he uses does not refer to the bread alone but to a complete meal. This was also true for the Jewish understanding, where the blessing of the bread implied the blessing of all foods on the table. *m. Ber.* 6:4 and 6:5 C; cf. Zahavy, *Mishnaic Law*, 84–85. So when Paul talks about the Lord's Supper it was a complete meal, which included the blessing of the bread and the cup. For this reason, the Lord's Supper tradition in 11:23–25 specifically had to refer to the blessing of the bread. Smith rightly states: "it appears unlikely that Paul would quote a liturgy in which a meal intervened between the bread and cup unless it were being practiced in that

Judgment at the Lord's Supper in Corinth

His advice then has to be understood as a rhetorical admonishment as his previous statements have been in the beginning.[217] So when Paul tells them to wait it does not simply mean to eat together. It has a bigger implication. It lays responsibility on them to care for one another and to do away with all selfish interest and schisms. They have to leave behind those social and cultural values and norms that contradict the Gospel, demean others, and are detrimental to the fellowship and unity of the church. Certainly such practices are no longer relevant and have no place in the community of God. It is another matter altogether if they do not want to give up those practices, they can do it in the comfort of their own houses (11:22, 34).[218] The specific words that he uses here advising them to eat at home are chosen because the issue of status, identity, and unity were all intimately related with food and fellowship meal practices.

Likewise his advice "to wait" has to be interpreted in similar manner; as it would not make sense if they had to wait but do not share the food with others.[219] Winter argues that one should look at words within their semantic field. In the context of dinner, the verb means "to welcome."[220] Hofius also point outs that the command can be translated "Care for one another!" "Receive one another warmly!" "Grant one another table fellowship!" "Show hospitality to one another!"[221] So Paul recommends the Corinthians "to receive one another," without any condition or agendas, which at a feast includes sharing food with others. This particular teaching of Paul fits in with the fellowship meal culture which functioned to create social

---

form by the Corinthian church;" "Meals and Morality," 325 n. 19.

217. On the importance of rhetoric in Greco-Roman culture and in Paul's letters see Witherington, *Conflict and Community*, 39–48; he also provides an extensive bibliography on the subject, 48–67.

218. Here also we can see Paul's use of irony. Since it was a status related issue, he forbids them in pursuing it by telling them to practise (eat) at their private homes where it becomes totally irrelevant.

219. "If everyone was to wait before unpacking his or her own food basket, it stands to reason that the contents of these would have been shared on common platters. Otherwise the waiting, which is supposed to prevent some from remaining hungry, would be senseless." Lampe, "Eucharist," 42.

220. Cf. 3 Macc 5:26; Josephus *J.W.* 2.14.7 §297; 3.2.4 §32; *Ant.* 7.14.5 §351; 11.8.6 §340; 12.3.3 §138; 13.4.5 §104; 13.5.5 §148; Winter, *After Paul left Corinth*, 151–52.

221. He cites a case in Philo (*Post. Cain* 41 §136) where it means "receive as a host." Hofius, "Lord's Supper," 94; Also Fee, *First Epistle*, 568; Witherington, *Conflict and Community*, 252; Hays, *First Corinthians*, 202–3; Horsley, *1 Corinthians*, 163; Geert Hallbäck, "Sacred Meal and Social Meeting," 170.

bonding and obligation.²²² As noted, an integral function of the fellowship meal institution was to create an opportunity for the wealthy members of the community to share with the poorer members. To participate in the fellowship meal and the Lord's Supper which was an integral part of it, Paul states that they have to be genuinely concerned with the needs of everyone.²²³ Thus Paul's advice to share food during the Lord's Supper should not be understood as once a week practice, but a regular affair in all matters of life. Paul's main concern is the significance of the Lord's table *vis à vis* their unity in Christ.²²⁴

Basing on Paul's response, the Lord's Supper sequence in Corinth should have been:

1. The gathering of the whole congregation; an extended process since some believers (e.g., slaves, apprentices, and dependent members of non-believing households) would have limited personal control over their time.

2. The preparation of food and drink for a common meal. Most of this would be donated by wealthier members of the congregation inasmuch as the poor had little or "nothing" to spare.

3. The utterance by a leader of Jesus' last supper words over the bread. This liturgical act would mark the beginning of a full meal utilizing the donated food.

---

222. Cf. Smith who strongly argues that Paul's social ethics depends on the Greco-Roman banquet tradition; *From Symposium*, 175; Lampe also comments: "Paul's practical advice thus aims in the same direction as Socrates's actions described by Xenophon: An *eranos* only becomes a truly communal meal once the foods brought by the participants are shared. And only that can be shared which has not been eaten beforehand." "The Eucharist," 41; Xen. *Symp.* 2.1; Plut. *Quaest. conv.* 613F.

223. Even by the time of the *Didache* (10.1) fellowship meal was part of the Lord's Supper celebration. The only evidence that the agape meal became separated from the sacramental meal is seen from the time of Hippolytus (AD 170–235). The main reasons were because of the development of Church halls or buildings from the house settings, and the increase in the number of believers making fellowship meal practices impractical. Still then the agape meal continued to have religious connotation. The *Apostolic Traditions* which probably comes from the time of Hippolytus portrays the agape meal as having the same significance as the Lord's Supper. Moreover the customs associated with the fellowship meals continued in the early church in a different form under ecclesiastical control. Instead of the patrons, now the bishop emerged "as the ultimate mediator of the patronal benefits of the church." For the points here see White, "Regulating Fellowship," 180–81; Cf. *Apostolic Tradition*, 27–28; *Acts of Peter*, 19–29.

224. Fee, *First Epistle*, 544.

Judgment at the Lord's Supper in Corinth

4. The words over the wine, followed by the drinking of wine in common, followed by the worship activities of 1 Cor 14:26–32.[225]

Some scholars have raised the question over whether the Corinthians had deviated from this sequence, so that the act of breaking the bread had been moved to the end of the meal and associated with the sharing of the cup. Klauck and others think that the church in Corinth would not have followed the order: breaking of bread, communal meal and the drinking of the cup, because those who came late would have joined only in the cup.[226] So a change was made to enable those members of the community who could not count on getting to its gatherings on time, to participate in the most significant part of the occasion. Therefore the meeting constituted of two sections, a fellowship meal followed by the sacraments and worship.[227]

Paul has clearly attested to the importance of the fellowship meal from the beginning. In fact he gives equal importance to both the sacramental meal and the fellowship meal. So certainly the issue with Paul was not with the sequence of the meal but in the way it was conducted. The important thing for Paul was to see that the Lord's Supper included both the fellowship meal and the sacrament. We have seen that in the fellowship meal practices the sacred and secular dimension were both present. The Corinthians seemed to have drawn a distinct line between these two in their meetings. Paul strongly considered that this distinction should not be allowed to exist, as both are intimately connected both in life and in the fellowship meal gatherings.

Paul's advice appears to be specifically directed towards the wealthy members who were the patrons and hosted the fellowship meals for the church. They were probably owners of the houses and therefore the heads

---

225. Cf. Theissen, *Social Setting*, 151–63; Lampe, "Corinthians," 7–9. Hofius asserts: "the Lord's Supper *paradosis* handed on by Paul in 1 Cor 11:23b-25, presupposes, as the words μετὰ τὸ δειπνῆσαι clearly attest, a meal between the bread rite and the cup rite. . . ..Historically, there cannot be the slightest doubt about the existence of a Lord's Supper celebration at which a full meal took place between the bread rite and the cup rite" ("Lord's Supper," 88).

226. Klauck, "Presence," 65–66; So Bornkamm, *Early Christian Experience*, 26–28; Jeremias, *Eucharistic Words*, 121; Schweizer, *Lord's Supper*, 5; Conzelmann, *1 Corinthians*, 194 n. 18, 195 n. 23; Watson, *First Epistle*, 11; Neuenzeit, *Das Herrenmahl*, 71–72, holds that the fellowship meal preceded the eucharist and was no longer part of it.

227. But Theissen and others add that there is no sufficient evidence to support this view. The only evidence that one can find from the letter is that the commemorative acts were performed in conjunction with a communal meal. Theissen, *Social Setting*, 152–53; Garland, *1 Corinthians*, 546n11; Fee, *First Epistle*, 541n52.

of the households.²²⁸ Nonetheless it was for all the church members who were trying to create schism in the fellowship, as it was addressed to all the members of the congregation.

Paul concludes with the words "I will give further instruction." Paul still has unfinished business with the Corinthians but none can be certain of what other issues these were or how he wanted to continue with the further instructions.²²⁹

CONCLUSION

The analysis of Paul's theology here indicates that Paul appeals to his readers on terms that they were familiar with, namely the fellowship meal traditions. Paul uses popular culture and ideology to explain the significance of the Lord's Supper to a diverse community that Corinth represents. Thus, Paul's concept of judgment was greatly influenced by the understanding of judgment in the fellowship meal tradition. And we can see his association of judgment with the Lord's Supper comes from that background. So the fellowship meal tradition gives us better insights into his theological formulation and meanings associated with it and this should be the primary basis for understanding his theology of judgment in the Lord's Supper.

At the same time his encounter with the risen Lord becomes the overpowering influence in his understanding and dealing with the different issues confronting the church. So while he is sensitive to the different cultures and communities he has come in contact with and likewise appeals to them using prevalent social-religious ethos, his interpretation of the social-religious customs was based on the Gospel message he now proclaims.

The fellowship meal was an important event which the Corinthians were trying to utilize for their own personal gain. They had carried over their customary social convention creating division in order to achieve their power-based demands. Hence, they were passing judgment on others on the basis of their theological, ideological or parochial biases. In the process they were using socio-economic factors to achieve their superiority over the opposing factions. Paul sets out to correct this misunderstanding

---

228. Coutsoumpos, *Paul and the Lord's Supper*, 115.

229. Winter suggests that these matters are difficult and "perhaps touch the very social structures of Corinthian society." He thinks that this instruction serves as an interim ethic. What the "haves need to do for the poor, he will deal with later." Winter, "Lord's Supper," 80.

of the Corinthians because it was their ideology that was dictating their action at the fellowship meals. Paul gives a new and proper interpretation of the Lord's Supper, in that they can no longer be governed by their old social, cultural and religious norms and values that contradict the Gospel.

They are called to discern that the meal they have is different from the other fellowship meals. It was founded on the sacrifice of Christ and so it is based on a different fellowship meal ideology which they needed to follow. Now, in this fellowship meal founded by Christ, they can no longer follow the normal social conventions. As they are now united and bonded into the body of Christ, it means living and dining according to the principles founded by Christ. It means removing anything that will be detrimental to the body. This can be clearly seen in Paul's dealing with the Corinthians in chapter 10, where he warns them of association with other religious practices. In summary, acceptance into the new community means a total revamp of one's socio-religious and moral orientation and transformation. Based on the fellowship meal tradition, Paul also demonstrates that the church is precisely the body of Christ, therefore the Corinthians' sin against one another has a Christological dimension.

There is no direct mention of judgment at the Last Supper as in 1 Corinthians 11, but we can make a similar connection there based on Jesus' use of fellowship meals as the embodiment of the Gospel message. Just as Paul made explicit the concept of "remembrance" in the Lord's Supper, Paul's teaching on judgment here is not an exclusive category, but he makes explicit the concept of judgment, and based on the fellowship meal traditions brings out a better understanding of judgment in the Lord's Supper.

In ancient cultures participating in a fellowship meal represented life. Here Paul advocates that principle at the Supper. Thus Paul presents to them that the Lord and his judgment is not something that is destructive. Though it appears to be seemingly so, the reason for doing so is for disciplinary and redemptive purpose and not for condemnation. Here he follows the motif of identity and bonding common with fellowship meals. Paul's teaching here is not purely exclusive to the Lord's Supper context but applicable to the church in all situations. Here we can have a clearer understanding on judgment as elucidated by the fellowship meal tradition. The unique ideology behind Paul's promotion of the fellowship meal in Corinth was its Christocentric approach which differed from the contemporary understanding of judgment.

Final Conclusion

THIS STUDY REVEALS THE importance of fellowship meal as an important socio-religious institution in the ancient world. It was connected with social and religious identity and had manifold functions in the communities. There was a feature in all the traditions that was universally recognized and accepted in forging relationships. It contained social codes and was associated with the morality and ethics of a community. But the values and meanings associated with it differed from one culture to another according to the different cultural interpretations. The traditions originated independently, but in the process of development, cultures adopted and adapted from each other. The influence of the Greco-Roman practices on other cultures was part of the process. The response to the Hellenistic influences depended on the group's ideology and outlook.

This study reveals the correlation between this wider fellowship meal tradition and the Lord's Supper theology. Jesus also used the fellowship meals prominently in his ministry and his Gospel was embodied in his meal practices. It is against this background that the Lord's Supper was instituted. It also reveals that the antecedent of the Lord's Supper was based on the common fellowship meal practices in the ancient world and not on a particular meal. The importance of fellowship meals indicates that the last supper of Jesus was as important as any other meal practice; nonetheless the connection with the Passover gave added meanings to the Lord's Supper.

The Lord's Supper which was part of the fellowship meal tradition continued in the early church, and it became an important means of defining the community in terms of identity and belief. An analysis of the Corinthian situation reveals that the fellowship meal tradition played an important role in the church. The church in Corinth included people from different backgrounds and consequently the meal practices were also a culmination of different traditions. More importantly, the different fellowship

Final Conclusion

meal traditions contributed to the overall significance and meaning of the Lord's Supper interpretation.

An examination of the situation reveals the core issue in the church in Corinth. It reveals that the socio-economic factors were just part of a bigger problem. The explanation is that the leaders of the different groups representing different theologies or ideologies were using the Lord's Supper as a means to promote themselves in order to gain influence or dominance in the church.

Paul's response to the situation in Corinth reveals that he upheld the fellowship meal tradition of Jesus. The Lord's Supper tradition that he interprets reveals that he understood the fellowship meal practices as having an important significance for the believers and an important means of continuing the tradition and teachings of Jesus. Based on the fellowship meal tradition, Paul reaffirms that not only the elements of bread and wine, but rather the whole meal was sacramental. Accordingly it meant that the social concern for the members of the community was an integral part of the Lord's Supper. The Corinthians' actions needed to be in harmony with the Lord's Supper celebration. So Paul's intention was that if they are reminded of what the Lord's Supper is all about then it should spur them to appropriate behavior. The emphasis on the whole meal as sacramental on the basis of the fellowship meal tradition reveals the greater social-ethical implication and responsibility for the church.

The study shows that in the process Paul also redefines some of the concepts associated with the fellowship meal tradition. He rejects the notion that the elements of bread and wine carried extra quasi-magical significance. He clarifies the fact that it is the act of coming together to share and participate in the meal that is beneficial and denotes the genuine observance of the Lord's Supper.

Likewise Paul explains the situation in Corinth in terms of judgment. Paul reminds them of the implications their action and behavior at the Supper have in the context of eschatological judgment. The recent sickness and death indicate failure on their part in observing the Lord's Supper properly which has led to judgment here and now. Consequently, the proper observance of the Lord's Supper will help them to avoid the present judgment. Paul's theology is understood better in relation with judgment motifs in the fellowship meal traditions. He reaffirms judgment in the community in accordance with the fellowship meal tradition. At the same time Paul's positive outlook in interpreting judgment in the community now was partly because of the gospel message.

The study elucidates the right interpretation of terms and motifs associated with the Lord's Supper in its proper socio-historical context. Unworthy participation at the Supper that entails judgment is no longer to be understood as based on a person's moral and ethical standards. Likewise the call to participate worthily denotes a call for self-introspection in terms of one's intention of participation at the Lord's Supper. Whether one participates in the Lord's Supper for some agendas like in other meal practices or one participates in order to promote the Body of Christ, becomes the deciding factor for a worthy participation.

Consequently the rules for conduct at the Lord's Supper show that Paul again re-defines the fellowship meal customs and practices. The Corinthians are directed to do away with the practices that are contrary to the gospel. Their actions may be acceptable in the society but they are no longer relevant in the new community, as their behavior distorts the "body" they represent. Hence, status, division, and other popular customs that do not contribute to the larger community have to be eradicated. Rather he calls for a reversal of those practices by the call for self-judgment in the light of God's final judgment.

Finally, Paul, as a contextual theologian, is selective in his approach to the fellowship meal tradition by rejecting those customs and practices that were detrimental to the community. At the same time he reaffirms and accommodates the positive aspects of different cultures in order to make the gospel relevant to all people.

Bibliography

PRIMARY LITERATURE

Aeschylus. *Persians. Seven against Thebes. Suppliants. Prometheus Bound.* Edited and translated by Alan H. Sommerstein. LCL. Cambridge, MA: Harvard University Press, 2009.

Apuleius, Lucius. *The Golden Ass: Being the Metamorphoses of Lucius Apuleius.* Translated by W. Adlington and revised by S. Gaselee. LCL. Cambridge, MA: Harvard University Press, 1989.

Aristides, Publius Aelius. *Aristides.* 4 vols. Translated by C. A. Behr. LCL. London: Heinemann, 1973.

Aristophanes. *Acharnians. Knights.* Edited and translated by J. Henderson. LCL. Cambridge, MA: Harvard University Press, 1998.

———. *Clouds, Wasps, Peace.* Translated by J. Henderson. LCL. Cambridge, MA: Harvard University Press, 1998.

Aristotle. *The Nicomachean Ethics.* Translated by D. P. Chase. London: EML Dent, 1934.

Artemidorus. *The Interpretation of Dreams: Oneirocritica.* Translated by Robert J. White. Noyes Classical Studies. Park Ridge, NJ: Noyes, 1975.

Athenaeus. *The Deipnosophists.* Translated by C. B. Gulick. 7 vols. LCL. London: Heinemann, 1957–61.

Bate, H. N., ed. *The Sibylline Oracles, Books III-V.* Translations of Early Documents; Hellenistic-Jewish Texts. London: SPCK, 1918.

Celsus, Aulus Cornelius. *On Medicine.* 3 vols. Translated by W. G. Spencer. LCL. Cambridge, MA: Harvard University Press, 1960–61.

Charles, R. H., ed. *The Apocrypha and Pseudepigrapha of the Old Testament in English.* 2 vols. Oxford: Clarendon, 1913.

Cicero. *Cicero: On Duties.* Translated by Walter Miller. LCL. London: Heinemann, 1947.

———. *Letters to Atticus.* 4 vols. Translated by D. R. Shackleton Bailey. LCL. Cambridge, MA: Harvard University Press, 1999.

———. *Letters to Friends.* 3 vols. Edited and translated by D. R. Shackleton Bailey. LCL. Cambridge, MA: Harvard University Press, 2001.

———. *The Orations of Cicero Against Catiline.* Translated by C. D. Yonge. London: G. Bell & Sons, 1919.

Bibliography

———. *The Orations of Cicero in Defence of Lucius Murena*. Translated by C. D. Yonge. London: G. Bell & Sons, 1905.

———. *Orations: Philippics 1-6*. Edited and translated by D. R. Shackleton Bailey, revised by John T. Ramsey and Gesine Manuwald. LCL. Cambridge, MA: Harvard University Press, 1999.

———. *Orations: Pro Caelio, De Provinciis Consularibus, Pro Balbo*. Translated by R. Gardner. LCL. Cambridge, MA: Harvard University Press, 1958.

Cohen, A. *Everyman's Talmud*. London: J. M. Dent & Sons, 1932.

Danby, Herbert, trans. *The Mishnah. Translated from the Hebrew with Introduction and Brief Explanatory Notes*. London: Oxford University Press, 1933.

Demosthenes. *Orations*. 7 vols. Translated by J. H. Vince et al. LCL. Cambridge, MA: Harvard University Press, 1926-1949.

Dessau, Hermann, *Inscriptiones Latinae Selectae*. 3 vols. Berlin: Apud Weidmannos, 1892-1916.

Dio Cassius. *Roman History*. 9 vols. Translated by Earnest Cary and Herbert Baldwin Foster. LCL. Cambridge, MA: Harvard University Press, 1914-27.

Dio Chrysostom. *Discourses*. 5 vols. Translated by H. L. Crosby and J. W. Cohoon. LCL. Cambridge, MA: Harvard University Press, 1932-1939.

Diodorus Siculus. *Library of History*. 12 vols. Translated by C. H. Oldfather et al. LCL. Cambridge, MA: Harvard University Press, 1933-67.

Diogenes Laertius. *Lives of Eminent Philosophers*. 2 vols. Translated R. D. Hicks. LCL. Cambridge, MA: Harvard University Press, 1925.

Dittenberger, Wilhelm, ed. *Sylloge Inscriptionum Graecarum*. 4 vols. Leipzig: Hirzel, 1915-24.

Epstein, Isidore, ed. *The Babylonian Talmud*. 18 vols. London: Soncino, 1948-52.

Euripides. *Bacchae. Iphigenia at Aulis. Rhesus*. Edited and translated by David Kovacs. LCL. Cambridge, MA: Harvard University Press, 2003.

———. *Suppliant Women. Electra. Heracles*. Edited and translated by David Kovacs. LCL. Cambridge, MA: Harvard University Press, 1998.

Eusebius. *Ecclesiastical History*. 2 vols. Translated by Kirsopp Lake and J. E. L. Oulton. LCL. Cambridge, MA: Harvard University Press, 1926-32.

The Greek New Testament. Edited by Kurt Aland et al. 4th rev. ed. Stuttgart: United Bible Societies, 1994.

Grenfell, B. P., and A. S. Hunts, eds. *The Oxyrhynchus Papyri*. London: Egypt Exploration Fund, 1889-1916.

Hatzfeld. J. "Inscriptions de Panamara." *Bulletin de Correspondance Hellénique* 51 (1927) 57-122.

Homer. *Iliad*. 2 vols. Translated by A. T. Murray, revised by W. F. Wyatt. LCL. Cambridge, MA: Harvard University Press, 1924-25.

———. *Odyssey*. 2 vols. Translated by A. T. Murray, revised by George E. Dimock. LCL. Cambridge, MA: Harvard University Press, 1919.

Horace. *Odes and Epodes*. Translated by Niall Rudd. LCL. Cambridge, MA: Harvard University Press, 2004.

———. *Satires. Epistles. The Art of Poetry*. Translated by H. Rushton Fairclough. Cambridge, MA: Harvard University Press, 1926.

Jones, I. H. *The Apocrypha*. Epworth Commentaries. Werrington: Epworth, 2003.

Josephus. *Jewish Antiquities*. 9 vols. Translated by H. J. Thackeray. LCL. Cambridge, MA: Harvard University Press, 1930-65.

Bibliography

———. *The Jewish War*. 3 vols. Translated by H. J. Thackeray. LCL. Cambridge, MA: Harvard University Press, 1927–28.

Justin Martyr. *The Dialogue with Trypho*. Translated by A. L. Williams. Translation of Christian Literature. London: SPCK, 1930.

Juvenal. *Satires*. In *Juvenal and Persius*. Edited and translated by S. M. Braund. LCL. Cambridge, MA: Harvard University Press, 2004.

Livy. *The History of Rome*. Translated by Canon Roberts. New York: E. P. Dutton, 1912.

Lucian. *Lucian*. 8 vols. Translated by A. M. Harmon et al. LCL. Cambridge, MA: Harvard University Press, 1913–67.

Martial, *Epigrams*. 3 vols. Edited and translated by D. R. Shackleton Bailey. LCL. Cambridge, MA: Harvard University Press, 1993.

Ovid. *Fasti*. Translated by James G. Frazer. LCL. Cambridge, MA: Harvard University Press, 1931.

Pausanias, *Description of Greece*. 5 vols. Translated by W. H. S Jones and H. A. Ormerod. LCL. Cambridge, MA: Harvard University Press, 1918–35.

Petronius, *The Satyricon*. Translated by Alfred R. Allinson. New York: Panurge, 1930.

Philo. *The Works of Philo*. Translated by C. D. Yonge. Peabody, MA: Hendrickson, 1993.

Philonenko, M. *Joseph et Aséneth: Introduction, Texte Critique, Traduction et Notes*. SPB 13. Leiden: Brill, 1968.

Pindar, *The Odes of Pindar: Including the Principal Fragments*. Translated by John E. Sandys. LCL. London: Heinemann, 1919.

Plato. *Laws*. 2 vols. Translated by R. G. Bury. LCL. Cambridge, MA: Harvard University Press, 1926.

———. *Lysis. Symposium. Gorgias*. Translated by W. R. M. Lamb. LCL. Cambridge, MA: Harvard University Press, 1925.

———. *Republic*. 2 vols. Translated by Paul Shorey. LCL. Cambridge, MA: Harvard University Press, 1930–35.

———. *Theaetetus. Sophist*. Translated by Harold North Fowler. LCL. Cambridge, MA: Harvard University Press, 1921.

Plautus. *The Comedies of Plautus*. Translated by Henry Thomas Riley. London: G. Bell and Daldy, 1912.

Pliny the Younger. *The Letters of the Younger Pliny*. Translated by Betty Radice. London: Penguin, 1963.

Plutarch, *Lives*. 7 vols. Translated by Bernadotte Perrin. LCL. Cambridge, MA: Harvard University Press, 1914–26.

———. *Moralia*. 15 vols. Translated by Frank Cole Babbitt et al. LCL. Cambridge, MA: Harvard University Press, 1927–2004.

Polybius. *The Histories*. 6 vols. Translated by W. R. Paton. LCL. Cambridge, MA: Harvard University Press, 1922–27.

Porphyry. *On Abstinence from Animal Food*. Edited by Esme Wynne-Tyson. Translated by Thomas Taylor. New York: Barnes & Noble, 1965.

Quintus Curtius. *History of Alexander*. 2 vols. Translated by John C. Rolfe. LCL. London: Heinemann, 1946.

Strabo. *Geography*. 8 vols. Translated by Horace Leonard Jones. LCL. Cambridge, MA: Harvard University Press, 1917–32.

Suetonius. *Lives of the Caesars*. 2 vols. Translated by J. C. Rolfe. LCL. Cambridge, MA: Harvard University Press, 1914.

Tacitus. *Annals*. 2 vols. Translated by John Jackson. LCL. Cambridge, MA: Harvard University Press, 1937.
———. *Histories*. 2 vols. Translated by Clifford H. More and John Jackson. LCL. Cambridge, MA: Harvard University Press, 1925–31.
Vermes, Geza. *The Dead Sea Scrolls in English*. Harmondsworth: Penguin, 1962.
Xenophon. *Anabasis*. Translated by Carleton L. Brownson, revised by John Dillery. LCL. Cambridge, MA: Harvard University Press, 1998.
———. *Hellenica*. 2 vols. Translated by Carleton L. Brownson. LCL. Cambridge, MA: Harvard University Press, 1918, 1921.
———. *Memorabilia. Oeconomicus. Symposium. Apology*. Translated by E. C. Marchant and O. J. Todd. LCL. Cambridge, MA: Harvard University Press, 1923.

SECONDARY LITERATURE

Aalen, S. "Das Abendmahl als Opfermahl im Neuen Testament." *NovT* 6 (1963) 128–52.
Adderley, James. "Sacrament and Unity." *The Hibbert Journal* 12 (1913/14) 756–65.
Allison, Dale C. "The Pauline Epistles and the Synoptic Gospels: The Pattern of the Parallels." *NTS* 28 (1982) 1–32.
Allo, E. B. *Saint Paul: Première Épitre aux Corinthiens*. Études Bibliques. 2nd ed. Paris: Gabalda, 1956.
Alon, Gedalyahu. *Jews, Judaism, and the Classical World: Studies in Jewish history in the times of the Second Temple and Talmud*. Jerusalem: Magnes, 1977.
Anderson, Gary A. *Sacrifices and Offerings in Ancient Israel: Studies in their Social and Political Importance*. Harvard Semitic Monographs 41. Atlanta, GA: Scholar, 1987.
Andrews, Herbert T. "The Place of the Sacraments in the Teaching of Paul." *The Expositor* 12 (1916) 353–72.
Angus, S. *The Mystery-Religions and Christianity: A Study in the Religious Background of Early Christianity*. London: J. Murray, 1925.
Argetsinger, Kathryn. "Birthday Rituals: Friends and Patrons in Roman Poetry and Cult." *Classical Antiquity* 11 (1992) 175–93.
Arthur, B. G., ed. *The Interpreter's Dictionary of the Bible*. Vol. 2. Nashville, TN: Abingdon, 1990.
Ascough, R. S. "Forms of Commensality in Greco-Roman Associations." *Classical World* 102 (2008) 33–45.
Augustine. *Tractates on the Gospel of John* in *The Fathers of the Church: St. Augustine Tractates in the Gospel of John 1–10*. Translated by John W. Rettig. Washington DC: The Catholic University of America Press, 1988.
Aune, D. E. "The Presence of God in the Community: The Eucharist in its Early Christian Cultic Context." *SJT* 29 (1976) 451–59.
———. "Septem Sapientum Convivium (Moralia 146B–164D)." In *Plutarch's Ethical Writings and Early Christian Literature*, edited by Hans D. Betz, 51–105. Leiden: Brill, 1978.
Avramidou, Amalia. *The Codrus Painter: Iconography and Reception of Athenian Vases in the Age of Pericles*. Wisconsin: University of Wisconsin Press, 2011.
Bacon, B. W. "The Gospel Paul 'Received.'" *The American Journal of Theology* 21 (1917) 15–42.

———. "The Lukan Tradition of the Lord's Supper." *Harvard Theological Review* 5 (1912) 322–48.
———. "Reflections of Ritual in Paul." *Harvard Theological Review* 8 (1915) 504–24.
Badia, L. F. *The Dead Sea People's Sacred Meal and Jesus' Last Supper*. Washington: University Press of America, 1979.
Bahr, Gordon J. "The Seder of Passover and the Eucharistic Words." *NovT* 12 (1970) 180–202. Reprinted in *Essays in Greco-Roman and Related Talmudic Literature*, edited by Henry A. Fischel, 473–94. New York: KTAV, 1977.
Baillie, D. M. *The Theology of the Sacraments and Other Papers*, edited with a biographical essay by John Baillie. London: Faber and Faber, 1957.
Balch, David L. "Paul, Families, and Households." In *Paul in the Greco-Roman World: A Handbook*, edited by P. J. Sampley, 258–92. Harrisburg: Trinity Press International, 2003.
———. "Rich Pompeiian Houses, Shops for Rent, and the Huge Apartment Building in Herculaneum as Typical Spaces for Pauline House Churches." *JSNT* 27 (2004) 27–46.
Baldwin, J. G. *Daniel*. Leicester: InterVarsity, 1978.
Balsdon, J. P. V. D. *Life and Leisure in Ancient Rome*. New York: McGraw-Hill, 1969.
Banks, Robert. *Paul's Idea of Community: The Early House Churches in their Historical Setting*. Rev. ed. Peabody, MA: Hendrickson, 1994.
Barclay, John M. G. "Thessalonica and Corinth: Social Contrasts in Pauline Christianity." *JSNT* 47 (1992) 49–74.
Barrett, C. K. *The First Epistle to the Corinthians*. BNTC. London: A & C Black, 1971.
———. *The New Testament Background: Selected Documents*. London: SPCK, 1956.
———. "Sectarian Diversity at Corinth." In *Paul and the Corinthians. Studies on a Community in Conflict: Essays in Honour of Margaret Thrall*, edited by Trevor J. Burke and J. K. Elliott 287–302. NovTSup 109. Leiden: Brill, 2003.
Barrosse, T. "Death and Sin in St. Paul's Epistle to the Romans." *CBQ* 15 (1953) 438–59.
Bartchy, S. Scott. *First-Century Slavery and the Interpretation of 1 Corinthians 7:21*. SBLDS 11. Atlanta, GA: Scholars, 1973.
———. "The Historical Jesus and Honor Reversal at the Table." In *The Social Setting of Jesus and the Gospels*, edited by W. Stegemann, B. J. Malina and G. Theissen, 175–83. Minneapolis, MN: Fortress, 2002.
———. "Table Fellowship." In *Dictionary of Jesus and the Gospels*, edited by Joel B. Green, et al., 796–800. Downers Grove, IL: InterVarsity, 1992.
Barton, George A. "The Origin of the Discrepancy between the Synoptists and the Fourth Gospel as to the Date and Character of Christ's Last Supper with His Disciples." *JBL* 43 (1924) 28–31.
Barton, Stephen C. "Paul's Sense of Place: An Anthropological Approach to Community Formation in Corinth." *NTS* 32 (1986) 223–46.
Batey, Richard. "Paul's Interaction with the Corinthians." *JBL* 84 (1965) 139–46.
Bauer, W. et al. *A Greek-English Lexicon of the New Testament and Other Early Christian Literature*. 3rd ed. Chicago: University of Chicago Press, 1999.
Baumgarten, Joseph M. "Sacrifice and Worship among the Jewish Sectarians of the Dead Sea (Qumran) Scrolls." *Harvard Theological Review* 46 (1953) 141–59.
Beall, Todd S. *Josephus Description of the Essenes Illustrated by the Dead Sea Scrolls*. Cambridge: Cambridge University Press, 1988.
Beck, Norman A. "The Last Supper as an Efficacious Symbolic Act." *JBL* 89 (1970) 192–98.

Bibliography

Becker, W. A., and H. Göll. *Charikles: Illustrating the Private Life of the Ancient Greeks*. 8th ed. London: Longmans, 1889.
Belkin, Samuel. "The Problem of Paul's Background." *JBL* 54 (1935) 41–60.
Berger, Klaus. *Manna, Mehl und Sauerteig*. Stuttgart: Quell, 1993.
Best, Ernest. *One Body in Christ: A Study in the Relationship of the Church to Christ in the Epistles of the Apostle Paul*. London: SPCK, 1955.
Betz, Hans D. "The Mithras Inscriptions of Santa Prisca and the New Testament." *NovT* 10 (1968) 62–80.
―――, ed. *Plutarch's Ethical Writings and Early Christian Literature*. Leiden: Brill, 1978.
Betz, Johannes. *Die Eucharistie in der Zeit der griechischen Väter*. 2 vols. Freiburg: Herder, 1955/1961.
Betz, Otto. "The Dichotomized Servant and the End of Judas Iscariot." *Revue de Qumran* 5 (1964) 43–58.
Bilde, P. "The Common Meal in the Qumran-Essene Communities." In *Meals in a Social Context: Aspects of the Communal Meal in the Hellenistic and Roman World*, edited by Inge Nielsen and Hanna Sigismund Nielsen, 145–66. Aarhus Studies in Mediterranean Antiquity 1. Aarhus: Aarhus University Press, 1998.
Black, C. C. "Pauline Perspectives on Death in Romans 5–8." *JBL* 103 (1984) 413–33.
Black, M. *The Scrolls and Christian Origins: Studies in the Jewish Background of the New Testament*. London: T. Nelson, 1961.
Blakiston, Herbert E. D. "The Lucan Account of the Institution of the Lord's Supper." *JTS* 4 (1903) 548–55.
Blass, F., A. Debrunner, and R. W. Funk. *A Greek Grammar of the New Testament and Other Early Christian Literature*. Chicago: University of Chicago Press, 1961.
Blenkinsopp, J. *Isaiah 1–39*. AB. New York: Doubleday, 2000.
Blomberg, C. L. *Contagious Holiness: Jesus' Meals with Sinners*. Leicester: InterVarsity, 2005.
Blue, Bradley B. "The House Church at Corinth and the Lord's Supper: Famine, Food Supply, and the Present Distress." *Criswell Theological Review* 5 (1991) 221–39.
Blümner, H. *The Home Life of the Ancient Greeks*. New York: Cooper Square, 1966.
Bogle, A. N. "1 Corinthians 11:23–34." *ExpTim* 12 (1900–1901) 479.
Boismard, Marie-Émile. *Synopse Des Quatre Évangiles*. Vol. 2. Paris, Éditions du Cerf, 1972.
Bokser, Baruch M. *The Origins of the Seder: The Passover Rite and Early Rabbinic Judaism*. Berkeley, CA: University of California Press, 1984.
Bookidis, Nancy. "Ritual Dining in the Sanctuary of Demeter and Kore at Corinth." In *Sympotica: A Symposium on the Symposium*, edited by Oswyn Murray, 86–94. Oxford: Clarendon, 1990.
Booth, Roger P. *Jesus and the Laws of Purity: Tradition History and Legal History in Mark 7*. JSNTSup 13. Sheffield: JSOT, 1989.
Borg, Marcus J. *Conflict, Holiness and Politics in the Teachings of Jesus*. Studies in the Bible and Early Christianity 5. Lewiston, NY: Edwin Mellen, 1984.
―――. *Jesus: A New Vision: Spirit, Culture and the Life of Discipleship*. London: SPCK, 1993.
Bornkamm, Günther. *Early Christian Experience*. The New Testament Library. New York: Harper & Row, 1969.
―――. "Herrenmahl und Kirche bei Paulus." In *Studien zu Antike und Christentum*. BEvT 28, 138–76. München: Kaiser, 1959.

———. *Jesus of Nazareth*. London: Hodder & Stoughton, 1960.
Bowie, A. M. "Thinking with Drinking: Wine and the Symposium in Aristophanes." *JHS* 117 (1997) 1–21.
Bowker, John. *Jesus and the Pharisees*. Cambridge: Cambridge University Press, 1973.
Box, G. H. "The Jewish Antecedents of the Eucharist." *JTS* 3 (1902) 357–69.
Bradshaw, Paul F. *The Search for the Origins of Christian Worship: Sources and Methods for the Study of Early Liturgy*. London: SPCK, 1992.
Bradshaw, Paul F., and Lawrence A. Hoffman, eds. *The Making of Jewish and Christian Worship*. Notre Dame, IN: University of Notre Dame, 1991/2.
Branick, Vincent. *The House Church in the Writings of Paul*. Zaccheus Studies: New Testament. Wilmington, DE: Michael Glazier, 1989.
Breech, James. *The Silence of Jesus: The Authentic Voice of the Historical Man*. Philadelphia, PA: Fortress, 1983.
Bremmer, Jan N. "Adolescents, Symposion and Pederasty." In *Sympotica: A Symposium on the Symposium*, edited by Oswyn Murray, 135–48. Oxford: Clarendon, 1990.
Brilioth, Y. *Eucharistic Faith and Practice: Evangelical and Catholic*. Translated by A. G. Hebert. London: SPCK, 1965.
Broneer, Oscar. "Paul and the Pagan Cults of Isthmia." *Harvard Theological Review* 64 (1971) 169–87.
Brown, Collins, ed. *New International Dictionary of New Testament Theology*. 4 vols. Grand Rapids: Zondervan, 1975–1985.
Brown, Raymond E. *The Gospel According to John*. AB. Garden City, NY: Doubleday, 1970.
Brown, Raymond E., et al., eds. *The New Jerome Biblical Commentary*. 2nd ed. London: G. Chapman, 1990.
Bruce, F. F. *1 and 2 Corinthians*. NCB. London: Oliphants, 1971.
Bruit, Louise. "The Meal at the Hyakinthia: Ritual Consumption and Offering." In *Sympotica: A Symposium on the Symposium*, edited by Oswyn Murray, 162–74. Oxford: Clarendon, 1990.
Brumberg-Kraus, Jonathan. "'Not by Bread Alone...': The Ritualization of Food and Table Talk in the Passover Seder and in the Last Supper." *Semeia* 86 (1999) 165–91.
Büchler, A. *Studies in Sin and Atonement in the Rabbinic Literature of the First Century*. Jews College Publications 11. London: Oxford University Press, 1928.
Bultmann, Rudolf. *Theology of the New Testament*. Vol. 1. Translated by Kendrick Grobel. London: SCM, 1952.
Bunn, L. H. "Symbol and Sacrament." *ExpTim* 53 (1941–42) 149–50.
Burchard, C. "The Importance of Joseph and Aseneth for the Study of the New Testament: A General Survey and a Fresh Look at the Lord's Supper." *NTS* 33 (1987) 102–34.
Burke, Trevor J., and J. Keith Elliott, eds. *Paul and the Corinthians. Studies on a Community in Conflict: Essays in Honour of Margaret Thrall*. NovTSup 109. Leiden: Brill, 2003.
Burkert, W. "Oriental Symposia: Contrasts and Parallels." In *Dining in a Classical Context*, edited by W. J. Slater, 7–24. Ann Arbor, MI: University of Michigan Press, 1991.
Burkhart, John E. "Reshaping Table Blessings: 'Blessings ... and Thanksgiving ... to our God' (Rev. 7:12)." *Interpretation* 48 (1994) 50–60.
Burkill, T. A. "The Last Supper." *Numen* 3 (1956) 161–177.
Burkitt, F. C. "The Last Supper and the Paschal Meal." *JTS* 17 (1916) 291–97.
Burkitt, F. C., and A. E. Brooke. "St. Luke xxii. 15, 16: What is the General Meaning?" *JTS* 9 (1907–1908) 569–72.
Burnaby, J. "The Eucharist and St. Paul." *Theology* 27 (1933) 92–94.

Bibliography

Burrows, Millar. *The Dead Sea Scrolls*. London: Secker & Warburg, 1956.

Burton, Ernest De Witt. *Syntax of the Moods and Tenses in New Testament Greek*. 3rd ed. Edinburgh: Clark, 1898.

Cabaniss, Allen. "The Gospel according to Paul." *The Evangelical Quarterly* 48 (1976) 164-67.

Cadbury, Henry J. "The Macellum of Corinth." *JBL* 53 (1934) 134-41.

Calvin, John. *Commentary on the Epistles of Paul the Apostle to the Corinthians*. Vol. 1. Translated by John W. Fraser. Edinburgh: Saint Andrew, 1960.

Cameron, S. W. "The Intention of Jesus' Action at the Last Supper." *Modern Churchman* 2 (1959) 150-57.

Campbell, R. A. "Does Paul Acquiesce in Divisions at the Lord's Supper?" *NovT* 33 (1991) 61-70.

Carmichael, Deborah Bleicher. "David Daube on the Eucharist and the Passover Seder." *JSNT* 42 (1991) 45-67.

Carney, T. F. *The Shape of the Past: Models and Antiquity*. Lawrence, KS: Coronado, 1975.

Carter, Timothy L. "'Big Men' in Corinth." *JSNT* 66 (1997) 45-71.

Case, Shirley Jackson. "Christianity and the Mystery Religions." *The Biblical World* 43 (1914) 3-16.

Chesnutt, Randall D. *From Death to Life: Conversion in Joseph and Aseneth*. JSPSup 16. Sheffield: Sheffield Academic Press, 1995.

Childs, Brevard S. *Isaiah*. OTL. Louisville, KY: Westminster John Knox, 2001.

Chilton, Bruce. *A Feast of Meanings: Eucharistic Theologies from Jesus through Johannine Circles*. NovTSup 72. Leiden: Brill, 1994.

———. "The Purity of the Kingdom as Conveyed in Jesus' Meals." In *Society of Biblical Literature 1992 Seminar Papers*, edited by E. H. Lovering, 473-88. SBLSP 31. Atlanta, GA: Scholars, 1992.

———. *The Temple of Jesus: His Sacrificial Program Within a Cultural History of Sacrifice*. University Park, PA: Pennsylvania University Press, 1992.

Chow, John K. *Patronage and Power: A Study of Social Networks in Corinth*. Sheffield: Sheffield Academic Press, 1992.

Chrysostom, John. *The Homilies of S. John Chrysostom, Archbishop of Constantinople: On the Gospel of St. Matthew*. Library of Fathers. Oxford: John Henry Parker, 1843.

Clark, Neville. *An Approach to the Theology of the Sacraments*. SBT 17. London: SCM, 1958.

Clarke, Andrew D. *Secular and Christian Leadership in Corinth: A Socio-historical and Exegetical Study of 1 Corinthians 1-6*. Leiden: Brill, 1993.

Clement of Alexandria, *The Writings of Clement of Alexandria*. 2 vols. Translated by William Wilson. Ante Nicene Christian Library. Edinburgh: T. & T. Clark, 1909.

Clements, R. E., et al. *Eucharistic Theology Then and Now*. SPCK Theological Collections 9. London: SPCK, 1968.

Coats, R. H. "Sacraments and Unity." *The Hibbert Journal* 12 (1913-1914) 496-508.

Coffin, C. P. "Two Sources for the Synoptic Account of the Last Supper." *The American Journal of Theology* 5 (1901) 102-16.

Cohn-Sherbok, D. "A Jewish Note on τὸ ποτήριον τῆς εὐλογίας." *NTS* 27 (1981) 704-9.

———. "Some Reflections on James Dunn's: The Incident at Antioch (Gal. 2:11-18)." *JSNT* 18 (1983) 68-74.

Cole, R. Lee. *Love-Feast: A History of the Christian Agape*. London: Charles H. Kelly, 1916.

Collins, A. Yarbro. *The Combat Myth in the Book of Revelation.* HDR 9. Missoula, MT: Scholars, 1976.
Collins, Raymond F. *First Corinthians.* Sacra Pagina Series. Collegeville: Liturgical, 1999.
Conzelmann, Hans. *Acts of the Apostles: A Commentary on the Acts of the Apostles.* Translated by James Limburg et al. Hermeneia Commentary Series. Philadelphia, PA: Fortress, 1987.
———. *1 Corinthians: A Commentary on the First Epistle to the Corinthians.* Translated by James W. Leitch. Hermeneia Commentary Series. Philadelphia, PA: Fortress, 1975.
Corley, Kathleen E. "Jesus' Table Practice: Dining with 'Tax Collectors and Sinners,' including Women." In *Society of Biblical Literature 1993 Seminar Papers,* edited by E. H. Lovering, 444–59. SBLSP 32. Atlanta, GA: Scholars, 1993.
———. *Private Women, Public Meals: Social Conflict in the Synoptic Tradition.* Peabody, MA: Hendrickson, 1993.
———. "Were the Women around Jesus Really Prostitutes? Women in the Context of Greco-Roman Meals." In *Society of Biblical Literature 1989 Seminar Papers,* edited by David J. Lull, 487–521. SBLSP 28. Atlanta, GA: Scholars, 1989.
Cotter, W. E. P. "St. Paul's Eucharist." *Expository Times* 39 (1927–1928) 235.
Coutsoumpos, Panayotis. *Paul and the Lord's Supper: A Socio-historical Investigation.* SBL 84. New York: Peter Lang, 2005.
Coyle, J. Timothy. "The Agape/Eucharist Relationship in 1 Corinthians 11." *Grace Theological Journal* 6.2 (1985) 411–24.
Craig C. T., and John Short. "The First Epistle to the Corinthians." In *Interpreter's Bible.* Vol. X, edited by George Arthur Buttrick, 3–262. Nashville, TN: Abingdon, 1953.
Cross, Frank Moore. *The Ancient Library of Qumran and Modern Biblical Studies.* Garden City, NY: Doubleday, 1958.
Crossan, John Dominic. *The Historical Jesus: The Life of a Mediterranean Jewish Peasant.* San Francisco: Harper, 1991.
Crossan, John Dominic, and Jonathan L. Reed. *In Search of Paul: How Jesus' Apostle Opposed Rome's Empire with God's Kingdom: A New Vision of Paul's Words and World.* London: SPCK, 2005.
Cullmann, O. "Kyrios as Designation for the Oral Tradition Concerning Jesus." *SJT* 3 (1950) 180–97.
Cullmann, O., and F. Leenhardt. *Essays on the Lord's Supper.* Translated by J. G. Davies. Ecumenical Studies in Worship 1. London: Lutterworth, 1958.
Cumont, Franz. *The Mysteries of Mithra.* New York: Dover, 1956.
———. *Oriental Religions in Roman Paganism.* New York: Dover, 1956.
Custer, James. "When is Communion Communion?" *Grace Theological Journal* 6.2 (1985) 403–10.
Dahl, N. A. "Paul and the Church at Corinth according to 1 Corinthians 1.10—4.21." In *Christian History and Interpretation: Studies Presented to John Knox,* edited by W. R. Farmer, et al., 313–35. Cambridge: University Press, 1967.
D'Arcy, C. F. "Slaves at Roman Convivia." In *Dining in a Classical Context,* edited by W. J. Slater, 171–84. Ann Arbor, MI: University of Michigan Press, 1991.
———. "St. Paul on Life and Immortality." *The Expositor* 5 (1902) 428–34.
D'Arms, John H. "Control, Companionship, and Clientela: Some Functions of the Roman Communal Meal." *Echoes du Monde Classique/Classical Views* 28 (1984) 327–48.
———. "The Roman Convivium and the Idea of Equality." In *Sympotica: A Symposium on the Symposium,* edited by Oswyn Murray, 308–20. Oxford: Clarendon, 1990.

Bibliography

Davies, Horton. *Bread of Life and Cup of Joy: Newer Ecumenical Perspectives on the Eucharist*. Grand Rapids: Eerdmans, 1993.
Davies, Philip R. "Food, Drink and Sects: The Question of Ingestion in the Qumran Texts." *Semeia* 86 (1999) 151–63.
Davies, W. D. *Paul and Rabbinic Judaism: Some Rabbinic Elements in Pauline Theology*. 3rd ed. Philadelphia, PA: Fortress, 1980.
Davies, W. D., and D. Daube, eds. *The Background of the New Testament and its Eschatology: Studies in Honour of C. H. Dodd*. Cambridge: Cambridge University Press, 1964.
Deissmann, A. *Light from the Ancient East*. Translated by L. R. M. Strachan. 1927. Repr., Grand Rapids: Baker, 1965.
———. *The New Testament in the Light of Modern Research*. London: Hodder & Stoughton, 1929.
Delling, Gerhard. "Das Abendmahlsgeschehen nach Paulus." In *Studien zum Neuen Testament und zum hellenistischen Judentum: Gesammelte Aufsätze 1950–1968*, edited by Ferdinand Hahn et al., 318–35. Göttingen: Vandenhock & Ruprecht, 1970.
Delorme, J., et al. *The Eucharist in the New Testament: A Symposium*. Translated by M. Stewart. Baltimore: Helicon, 1964.
Dembitz, L. N. "Seder." In *The Jewish Encyclopedia*. Vol. 11, edited by Isodore Singer, 142–47. New York: Funk & Wagnalls, 1901.
Dentzer, Jean-Marie. "Aux origines de l'iconographie du banquet couché." *RAr* 2 (1971) 215–58.
———. *Le motif du banquet couché dans le proche-oriet et le monde grec du VIIe au IVe siècle avant J.-C*. Bibiothèque des écoles françaises d'Athènes et de Rome 246; Rome: École française de Rome, 1982.
deSilva, David A. *Honor, Patronage, Kinship and Purity: Unlocking New Testament Culture*. Downers Grove, IL: InterVarsity, 2000.
Dockx, S. *Chronologies néotestamentaires et vie de l'Eglise primitive: recherches exégétiques*. Gembloux: Duculot, 1976.
Donfried, Karl P. "Justification and Last Judgment in Paul." In *Paul, Thessalonica and Early Christianity*, Karl P. Donfried, 253–278. London: T. & T. Clark, 2002.
Dix, Gregory. *The Shape of the Liturgy*. Westminster: Dacre, 1945.
Donahue, John F. *The Roman Community at Table during the Principate*. Ann Arbor, MI: University of Michigan Press, 2004.
Douglas, Mary. "Atonement in Leviticus." *Jewish Studies Quarterly* 1.2 (1993–94) 109–30.
———. "Deciphering a Meal." *Daedalus* 101 (1972) 161–81.
———. "The Forbidden Animals in Leviticus." *JSNT* 59 (1993) 3–23.
———. *Implicit Meanings: Essays in Anthropology*. London: Routledge, 1975.
———. *Purity and Danger: An Analysis of Concepts of Pollution and Taboo*. New York: Praeger, 1966.
Duff, J. Wight. *Roman Satire: Its Outlook on Social Life*. Berkeley, CA: University of California, 1936.
Dunbabin, Katherine M. D. *The Roman Banquet: Images of Conviviality*. Cambridge: Cambridge University Press, 2003.
Dunn, James D. G. *1 Corinthians*. Sheffield: Sheffield Academic Press, 1995.
———. "The Incident at Antioch (Gal. 2:11–18)." *JSNT* 18 (1983) 3–57.
———. *Jesus, Paul and the Law: Studies in Mark and Galatians*. London: SPCK, 1990.
———. "Jesus, Table-Fellowship and Qumran." In *Jesus and the Dead Sea Scrolls*, edited by James H. Charlesworth, 254–72. New York: Doubleday, 1992.

———. *The Theology of Paul the Apostle*. Grand Rapids: Eerdmans, 1998.
Dupont-Sommer, A. *The Essene Writing from Qumran*. Oxford: Blackwell, 1961.
Dutch, Robert S. *The Educated Elite in 1 Corinthians: Education and Community Conflict in Graeco-Roman Context*. JSNTSup 217. London: T. & T. Clark, 2005.
Easton, Burton Scott. "The Pauline Theology and Hellenism." *The American Journal of Theology* 21 (1917) 358–82.
Edwards, O. C. "Sociology as a Tool for Interpreting the New Testament." *Anglican Theological Review* 65 (1983) 431–46.
Ehrhardt, A. "Holy Sacrament and Suffering." In *The Framework of the New Testament Stories*, edited by A. Ehrhardt, 256–74. Manchester: Manchester University Press, 1964.
Ehrman, Bart D. "The Cup, the Bread and the Salvific Effect of Jesus' Death in Luke-Acts." In *Society of Biblical Literature 1991 Seminar Papers*, edited by E. H. Lovering, 576–91. SBLSP 30. Atlanta, GA: Scholars, 1991.
Elert, Werner. *The Lord's Supper Today*. Translated by Martin Bertram and Rudolp F. Norden. St. Louis, MO: Concordia, 1973.
Ellis, E. Earle. "*Sōma* in First Corinthians." *Interpretation* 44 (1990) 132–44.
Ellis, William. "On the Text of the Account of the Lord's Supper in 1 Cor. 11:23–32 with some Further Comment." *ABR* 12 (1964) 43–51.
Engberg-Pedersen, Troels. "Proclaiming the Lord's Death: 1 Corinthians 11:17–34 and the Forms of Paul's Theological Argument." In *Society of Biblical Literature 1991 Seminar Papers*, edited by E. H. Lovering, 592–617. SBLSP 30. Atlanta, GA: Scholars, 1991.
Eriksson, Anders. *Traditions as Rhetorical Proof: Pauline Argumentation in 1 Corinthians*. ConBNT 29. Stockholm: Almqvist, 1998.
Farmer, W. R. "Peter and Paul and the Tradition Concerning 'The Lord's Supper' in 1 Corinthians 11: 23–26." In *One Loaf, One Cup: Ecumenical Studies of 1 Cor 11 and other Eucharistic Texts*, edited by B. F. Meyer, 35–55. The Cambridge Conference on the Eucharist, August 1988. New Gospel Studies 6. Macon, GA: Mercer, 1993.
Farmer, W. R. et al., eds. *Christian History and Interpretation: Studies Presented to John Knox*. Cambridge: University Press, 1967.
Farnell, L. R. *The Cults of the Greek States*. 5 vols. Oxford: Clarendon, 1896–1909.
———. "Sacrificial Communion in Greek Religion." *The Hibbert Journal* 2 (1903–1904) 306–22.
Farner, Donald. "The Lord's Supper Until He Comes." *Grace Theological Journal* 6.2 (1985) 391–401.
Farrer, Austin. "The Eucharist in 1 Corinthians." In *Eucharistic Theology Then and Now*. R. E. Clements et al., 15–33. SPCK Theological Collection 9. London: SPCK, 1968.
Fascher, Erich. *Der erste Brief des Paulus an die Korinther, Erster Teil*. THKNT 7/1. Berlin: Evangelische Verlagsanstalt, 1975.
Fee, Gordon D. "εἰδωλόθυτα Once Again: An Interpretation of 1 Corinthians 8–10." *Biblica* 61 (1980) 172–97.
———. *The First Epistle to the Corinthians*. NICNT. Grand Rapids: Eerdmans, 1987.
Feeley-Harnik, Gillian. *The Lord's Table: Eucharist and Passover in Early Christianity, Symbol and Culture*. Philadelphia, PA: University of Pennsylvania Press, 1981.
Ferguson, Everett. *Backgrounds of Early Christianity*. 2nd ed. Grand Rapids: Eerdmans, 1993.
Ferguson, W. S. "The Attic Orgeones." *Harvard Theological Review* 37 (1944) 61–140.
Filson, F. V. *St. Paul's Conception of Recompense*. Leipzig: Hinrichs, 1931.

Bibliography

———. "The Significance of Early House Churches." *JBL* 39 (1939) 105–7.

Finger, Reta Halteman. *Of Widows and Meals: Communal Meals in the Book of Acts*. Grand Rapids: Eerdmans, 2007.

Fischel, Henry A., ed. *Essays in Greco-Roman and Related Talmudic Literature*. New York: KTAV, 1977.

Fisher, Nicholas R. E. "Greek Associations, Symposia, and Clubs." In *Civilization of the Ancient Mediterranean: Greece and Rome*, edited by Michael Grant and Rachel Kitzinger, 2.1167–97. 3 vols. New York: Charles Scribner's, 1988.

———. "Roman Associations, Dinner Parties, and Clubs." In *Civilization of the Ancient Mediterranean: Greece and Rome*, edited by Michael Grant and Rachel Kitzinger, 2.1199–1225. 3 vols. New York: Charles Scribner's, 1988.

Fitzmyer, Joseph A. *Essays on the Semitic Background of the New Testament*. London: Chapman, 1971.

———. *1 Corinthians: A New Translation with Introduction and Commentary*. The Anchor Yale Bible. New Haven, CO: Yale University Press, 2008.

Flusser, David. "The Dead Sea Sect and Pre-Pauline Christianity." In *Aspects of the Dead Sea Scrolls*, edited by Chaim Rabin and Yigael Yadin, 215–66. ScrHier 4. Jerusalem: Magnes, Hebrew Univeristy, 1965.

Fortna, R. T., and Beverly R. Gaventa, eds. *The Conversation Continues: Studies in Paul and John in Honor of J. Louis Martyn*. Nashville, TN: Abingdon, 1990.

Fotopoulos, John. *Food Offered to Idols in Roman Corinth: A Social-rhetorical Reconsideration of 1 Corinthians 8:1—11:1*. WUNT 2:151. Tübingen: Mohr Siebeck, 2003.

Fraine, J. De. *Adam and the Family of Man*. Translated by D. Raible. Staten Island, NY: Alba, 1965.

Freedman, D. N., ed. *The Anchor Bible Dictionary*. 6 vols. New York: Doubleday, 1992.

Frymer-Kensky, Tikva. "Pollution, Purification, and Purgation in Biblical Israel." In *The Word of the Lord Shall Go Forth: Essays in Honor of David Noel Freedman in Celebration of his Sixtieth Birthday*, edited by Carol L. Meyers and M.O'Connor, 399–414. ASOR Special volume series 1. Winona Lake, IN.: Eisenbrauns, 1983.

Fuller, Reginald H. *Christ and Christianity: Studies in the Formation of Christology*. Edited by Robert Kahl. Valley Forge, PA: Trinity, 1994.

———. "The Double Origin of the Eucharist." *Biblical Research* 8 (1963) 60–72.

Fung, Ronald Y. K. "Revelation and Tradition: The Origins of Paul's Gospel." *The Evangelical Quarterly* 57 (1985) 23–41.

Furnish, Victor Paul. *The Theology of the First Letter to the Corinthians*. Cambridge: Cambridge University Press, 1999.

Gager, John G. *Kingdom and Community: The Social World of Early Christianity*. Englewood Cliffs, NJ: Prentice-Hall, 1975.

———. "Review of M. Grant, *Early Christianity and Society: Seven Studies*; Abraham J. Malherbe, *Social Aspects of Early Christianity*; and G. Theissen, *Sociology of Early Palestinian Christianity*." *RelSRev* 5 (1979) 174–80.

Gardner, E. A. "Food and Drink, Meals, Cooking, and Entertainments." In *A Companion to Greek Studies*, edited by Leonard Whibley, 541–46. Cambridge: Cambridge University Press, 1905.

Gardner, P. D. *The Gifts of God and the Authentication of a Christian: An Exegetical Study of 1 Corinthians 8–11*. Lanham, MD: University Press of America, 1994.

Garland, David E. *1 Corinthians*. BECNT. Grand Rapids: Baker Academic, 2003.

Bibliography

Garnsey, P. *Food and Society in Classical Antiquity.* Cambridge: Cambridge University Press, 1999.

———. *Non-Slave Labour in the Greco-Roman World.* Cambridge Philological Society Supplement 6. Cambridge: Cambridge University Press, 1980.

Gärtner, Bertil. *The Temple and The Community in Qumran and the New Testament.* SNTSMS. Cambridge: Cambridge University Press, 1965.

Gavin, F. *The Jewish Antecedents of the Christian Sacraments.* London: SPCK, 1928.

Gese, Hartmut. "The Origin of the Lord's Supper." In *Essays in Biblical Theology.* Translated by Keith Crim, 117–40. Minneapolis, MN: Augsburg, 1981.

Gill, David. "Trapezomata: A Neglected Aspect of Greek Sacrifice." *Harvard Theological Review* 67 (1974) 117–37.

Godet, F. L. *Commentary on the First Epistle of St. Paul to the Corinthians.* 2 vols. Translated by A. Cusin. Edinburgh: T. & T. Clark, 1886/1893.

Goodenough, E. R. *Jewish Symbols in the Greco-Roman Period.* 13 vols. New York: Pantheon, 1953–1968.

Goody, J. *Cooking, Cuisine and Class: A Study in Comparative Sociology.* Cambridge: Cambridge University Press, 1982.

Goudge, H. L. *The First Epistle to the Corinthians.* Westminster Commentaries. 4th ed. London: Methuen, 1915.

Gowers, Emily. *The Loaded Table: Representations of Food in Roman Literature.* Oxford: Clarendon, 1993.

Grant, Robert M. *Early Christianity and Society.* London: W. Collins, 1978.

———. *Paul in the Roman World: The Conflict at Corinth.* Louisville, KY: Westminster, 2001.

Gregg, David. *Anamnesis in the Eucharist.* Grove Liturgical Study 5. Nottingham: Grove, 1976.

Gregory of Nyssa. *The Great Catechism.* In *A Select Library of the Nicene and Post-Nicene Fathers of the Early Church,* edited by Philip Schaff and Henry Wace, 471–509. Series 2, vol. 5. Grand Rapids: Eerdmans, 1956.

Grimm, Carl Ludwig Wilibald. *A Greek-English Lexicon of the New Testament: Being Grimm's Wilke's Clavis Novi Testamenti.* 4th edn. Translated by, revised and enlarged by Joseph Henry Thayer. Edinburgh: T. & T. Clark, 1914.

Grosheide, F. W. *Commentary on the First Epistle to the Corinthians.* NICNT. Grand Rapids: Eerdmans, 1953.

Gulick, Charles Burton. *The Life of the Ancient Greeks with special reference to Athens.* New York: D. Appleton, 1902.

Gundry, R. H. ΣΩΜΑ *in Biblical Theology with Emphasis on Pauline Anthropology.* SNTSMS 29. Cambridge: Cambridge University Press, 1975.

Hallbäck, Geert. "Sacred Meal and Social Meeting: Paul's Argument in 1 Cor 11:17–34." In *Meals in a Social Context: Aspects of the Communal Meal in the Hellenistic and Roman World,* edited by Inge Nielsen and Hanna Sigismund Nielsen, 167–76. Aarhus Studies in Mediterranean Antiquity 1. Aarhus: Aarhus University Press, 1998.

Hamilton, Victor P. *The Book of Genesis.* 2 vols. NICOT. Grand Rapids: Eerdmans, 1990, 1995.

Harland, Philip A. *Associations, Synagogues and Congregations: Claiming a Place in Ancient Mediterranean Society.* Minneapolis, MN: Fortress, 2003.

Harrington, Hannah K. "Did the Pharisees Eat Ordinary Food in a State of Ritual Purity?" *JSJ* 27 (1995) 42–54.

———. *The Impurity Systems of Qumran and the Rabbis: Biblical Foundations.* SBLDS 143. Atlanta, GA: Scholars, 1993.

Harris, Rendel, *Eucharistic Origins.* Cambridge: W. Heffer & Sons, 1927.

Haupt, Paul. "The Last Supper." *JBL* 40 (1921) 178–80.

Havener, I. "A Curse for Salvation—1 Corinthians 5.1–5." In *Sin, Salvation, and the Spirit: Commemorating the Fiftieth Year of the Liturgical Press*, edited by D. Durken, 334–44. Collegeville, MN: Liturgical, 1979.

Hays, Richard B. *First Corinthians.* Interpretation: A Bible Commentary for Teaching and Preaching. Louisville, KY: John Knox, 1997.

Heawood, Percy J. "The Time of the Last Supper." *The Jewish Quarterly Review* 42 (1951) 37–44.

Heil, John Paul. *The Meal Scenes in Luke-Acts: An Audience-oriented Approach.* SBLMS 52. Atlanta, GA: SBL, 1999.

Hein, Kenneth. *Eucharist and Excommunication: A Study in Early Christian Doctrine and Discipline.* European University Studies: Series 23, Theology 19. 2nd ed. Frankfurt: Peter Lang, 1975.

Henderson, Suzanne Watts. "'If Anyone Hungers . . .': An Integrated Reading of 1 Cor. 11:17–34." *NTS* 48 (2002) 195–208.

Hengel, Martin. *The Charismatic Leader and His Followers.* Translated by James C. G. Greig. Edinburgh: T. & T. Clark, 1981.

———. *Judaism and Hellenism: Studies in their Encounter in Palestine during the Early Hellenistic Period.* 2 vols. Translated by John Bowden. Philadelphia, PA: Fortress, 1974.

———. *Property and Riches in the Early Church: Aspects of a Social History of Early Christianity.* Translated by John Bowden. London: SCM, 1974.

Henrichs, Albert. "Changing Dionysiac Identities." In *Jewish and Christian Self-definition.* vol. 3: *Self Definition in the Greco-Roman World*, edited by Ben F. Meyer and E. P. Sanders, 137–60. Philadelphia, PA: Fortress, 1982.

Henzen, Wilhelm, and Fratres Arvales, eds. *Acta Fratrum Arvalium quae supersunt.* Berlin: G. Reimeri, 1874.

Héring, Jean. *The First Epistle of Saint Paul to the Corinthians.* Translated by A. W. Heathcote & P. J. Allcock. London: Epworth, 1963.

———. *La première épitre de Saint Paul aux Corinthiens.* CNT 7. Neuchâtel: Delachaux & Niestlé, 1949.

Herrmann, P., and K. Z. Polatkan, *Das Testament des Epikrates und Andere Neue Inschriften aus dem Museum von Manisa.* Österreichische Akademie der Wissenschaften; Philosophisch-Historische Klasse, Sitzungsberichte 265; Vienna: Hermann Böhlaus, 1969.

Hesiod. *The Homeric Hymns and Homerica.* Translated by H. G. Evelyn-White. London: Heinemann, 1914.

———. *Theogony. Works and Days. Testimonia.* Translated by Glenn W. Most. LCL. Cambridge, MA: Harvard University Press, 2007.

Higgins, A. J. B. *The Lord's Supper in the New Testament.* SBT 6. London: SCM, 1952.

Hoffmann, David Z. *Das Buch Leviticus.* 2 vols. Berlin: M. Poppelauer, 1905–1906.

Hofius, Otfried. "The Lord's Supper and the Lord's Supper Tradition: Reflections on 1 Corinthians 11: 23b-25." In *One Loaf, One Cup: Ecumenical Studies of 1 Cor. 11 and other Eucharistic Texts,* edited by B. F. Meyer, 75–115. The Cambridge Conference on the Eucharist, August 1988. New Gospel Studies 6. Macon, GA: Mercer, 1993. In

German: "Herrenmahl und Herrenmahlsparadosis. Erwägungen zu 1 Kor 11: 23b-25." *ZTK* 85 (1988) 371–408.

———. "τὸ σῶμα τὸ ὑπὲρ ὑμῶν, 1 Kor 11: 24." *ZNW* 80 (1989) 80–88.

Holmberg, Bengt. *Sociology and the New Testament: An Appraisal*. Minneapolis, MN: Fortress, 1990.

Holper, J. Frederick. "As Often as You Eat This Bread and Drink the Cup." *Interpretation* 48 (1994) 61–73.

Hook, Norman. *The Eucharist in the New Testament*. London: Epworth, 1964.

Hopper, R. J. "Ancient Corinth." *Greece and Rome* 2 (1955) 2–15.

Horrell, David G., ed. *Social-Scientific Approaches to New Testament Interpretation*. Edinburgh: T. & T. Clark, 1999.

———. *The Social Ethos of Corinthian Correspondence: Interests and Ideology from 1 Corinthians to 1 Clement*. Edinburgh: T. & T. Clark, 1996.

Horsley, G. H. R. *New Documents Illustrating Early Christianity, Vol. 5: Linguistic Essays*. North Ryde: The Ancient History Documentary Research Centre, Macquarie University, 1989.

Horsley, Richard A. *1 Corinthians*. ANTC. Nashville, TN: Abingdon, 1998.

Houlden, J. L. "A Response to James D. G. Dunn." *JSNT* 18 (1983) 58–67.

Howard, J. K. "'Christ our Passover': A Study of the Passover-Exodus Theme in 1 Corinthians." *Evangelical Quarterly* 41/2 (1969) 97–108.

Hunter, Archibald M. *Paul and his Predecessors*. New rev. ed. London: SCM, 1961.

Hurd, John C. *The Origin of 1 Corinthians*. London: SPCK, 1965.

Instone-Brewer, David. "Tractate Pesachim: Passovers." Unpublished work. Cambridge, Tyndale, 2007.

Instone-Brewer, David and Philip A. Harland. "Jewish Associations in Roman Palestine: First Century Evidence from the Mishnah." Unpublished work. Cambridge, Tyndale, 2008.

Irenaeus. *Against Heresies*. In *The Writings of Irenaeus: Ante-Nicene Christian Library Translations of the Writings of the Fathers down to AD 325, Part 5*. Translated by Alexander Roberts and James Donaldson. Edinburgh: T. & T. Clark, 1869.

Jabbur, Jibrail S. *The Bedouins and the Desert: Aspects of Nomadic Life in the Arab East*. Translated by Lawrence I. Conrad. Albany, NY: State University of New York Press, 1995.

Jameson, Michael H. "Sacrifice and Ritual: Greece." In *Civilization of the Ancient Mediterranean: Greece and Rome*, edited by Michael Grant and Rachel Kitzinger, 2:959–79. 3 vols. New York: Charles Scribner's, 1988.

———. "Theoxenia." In *Ancient Greek Cult Practice from the Archaeological Evidence. Proceedings of the Fourth International Seminar on Ancient Greek Cult, organized by the Swedish Institute at Athens, 22–24 November 1991*, edited by Robin Hägg, 35–57. Stockholm: Svenska Institutet I Athen, Paul Aströms Förlag, 1994.

Jaubert, A. *The Date of the Last Supper*. Translated by Issac Rafferty. Staten Island, NY: Alba, 1965.

Jenks, A. W. "Eating and Drinking in the Old Testament." In *ABD*. Vol. 2, edited by D. N. Freedman, 250–54. New York: Doubleday, 1993.

Jeremias, J. *The Eucharistic Words of Jesus*. Translated by Norman Perrin. New York: Scribner's, 1966.

———. "The Last Supper." *ExpTim* 64 (1952/3) 91–92.

———. *New Testament Theology: The Proclamation of Jesus*. Translated by J. Bowden. London: SCM, 1971.
———. *The Parables of Jesus*. Translated by S. H. Hooke. London: SCM, 1963.
———. "This is My Body." *ExpTim* 83 (1972) 196–203.
Jewett, Robert. "Paul, Shame, and Honor." In *Paul in the Greco-Roman World: A Handbook*, edited by P. J. Sampley, 551–74. Harrisburg, PA: Trinity Press International, 2003.
Johnson, Edwin. "The Table of Demons: 1 Cor. 10:21." *The Expositor* 8 (1884) 241–50.
Jones, Douglas. "ἀνάμνησις in the LXX and the Interpretation of 1 Cor. 11: 25." *JTS* 6 (1955) 183–91.
Jones, Paul H. *Christ's Eucharistic Presence: A History of the Doctrine*. New York: Peter Lang, 1994.
Jourdan, G. V. "κοινωνία in 1 Corinthians 10. 16." *JBL* 67 (1948) 111–24.
Judge, E. A. "The Social Identity of the First Christians: A Question of Method in Religious History." *JRH* 2 (1980) 201–17.
———. *The Social Pattern of the Christian Groups in the First Century*. London: Tyndale, 1960.
Juengst, S. C. *Breaking Bread: The Spiritual Significance of Food*. London: WJKP, 1992.
Just, Arthur A. *The Ongoing Feast: Table Fellowship and Eschatology at Emmaus*. Collegeville, MN: Liturgical, 1993.
Kamp, C. H. "With due Honor to the Lord's Body: An Exegetical Study on 1 Cor. 11:29." *Reformed Review* 10.3 (1957) 38–42.
Kane, J. P. "The Mithraic Cult Meal in its Greek and Roman Environment." In *Mithraic Studies: Proceedings of the First International Congress of Mithraic Studies*, edited by John R. Hinnells, 2.313–51. 2 vols. Manchester: Manchester University Press, 1975.
Karris, R. J. *Eating your Way through Luke's Gospel*. Collegeville, MN: Liturgical, 2006.
Käsemann, E. "Anliegen und Eigenart der paulinischen Abendmahlslehre." *Evangelische Theologie* 7 (1947–48) 263–83.
———. *Exegetische Versuche und Besinnungen*. 2 vols. Göttingen: Vandenhoeck & Ruprecht, 1960–64.
———. *Essays on New Testament Themes*. Translated by W. J. Montague. SBT 41. London: SCM, 1964.
———. *New Testament Questions of Today*. Philadelphia, PA: Fortress, 1969.
Keating, J. F. *The Agape and the Eucharist in the Early Church: Studies in the History of the Christian Love-Feast*. London: Methuen, 1901.
Kee, Howard, C. *Christian Origins in Sociological Perspective*. London: SCM, 1980.
———. "The Social-Cultural Setting of Joseph and Aseneth." *NTS* 29 (1983) 394–413.
Kennedy, H. A. A. "St. Paul and the Mystery-Religions." *The Expositor* 3 (1912) 289–305, 420–41.
———. "St Paul and the Mystery-Religions: Sacramental Meals." *The Expositor* 5 (1913) 63–75, 115–26.
Kent, J. H. *Corinth: Results of Excavations conducted by the American School of Classical Studies at Athens*. Vol. 8, part 3: *The Inscriptions 1926–1950*. Princeton, NJ: ASCSA, 1966.
Keohane, Alan. *Bedouin: Nomads of the Desert*. London: Kyle Cathie, 1994.
Kilpatrick, G. D. *The Eucharist in Bible and Liturgy*. The Moorhouse Lectures. Cambridge: Cambridge University Press, 1983.
———. "The Last Supper." *ExpTim* 64 (1952–3) 4–8.

King, Philip. "Commensality in the Biblical World." In *Hesed Ve-Emet: Studies in Honor of Ernest S. Frerichs*, edited by J. Magness and Seymour Gitin, 53–62. Atlanta, GA: Scholars, 1988.

Kittel, G., and G. Friedrich, eds. *Theological Dictionary of the New Testament*. 10 vols. Translated by G. W. Bromiley. Grand Rapids, MI: Eerdmans, 1964–1976.

Klauck, Hans-Josef. "Eucharistie und Kirchengemeinschaft bei Paulus," *Wissenschaft und Weisheit* 49 (1986) 1–14. Repr. in *Gemeinde, Amt, Sakrament: Neutestamentliche Perspectiven*. Würzburg: Echter, 1989, 331–47.

———. *Herrenmahl und hellenistischer Kult: Eine religionsgeschichtliche Untersuchung zum ersten Korintherbreif*. Neutestamentliche Abhandlungen 15. Münster: Aschendorff, 1982.

———. *1 Korintherbrief, Die Neue Echter Bibel*. Kommentar zum Neuen Testament mit der Einheitsübersetzung 7. Würzburg: Echter Verlag, 1984.

———. *Magic and Paganism in Early Christianity: The World of the Acts of the Apostles*. Translated by Brain McNeil. Edinburgh: T&T Clark, 2000.

———. "Presence in the Lord's Supper: 1 Corinthians 11:23–26 in the Context of Hellenistic Religious History." In *One Loaf, One Cup: Ecumenical Studies of 1 Cor. 11 and other Eucharistic Texts*, edited by B. F. Meyer, 57–74. The Cambridge Conference on the Eucharist, August 1988. New Gospel Studies 6. Macon, GA: Mercer, 1993.

Klawans, Jonathan. *Impurity and Sin in Ancient Judaism*. Oxford: Oxford University Press, 2000.

———. "Notions of Gentile Impurity in Ancient Judaism." *AJSR* 20/2 (1995) 285–312.

———. *Purity, Sacrifice, and the Temple: Symbolism and Supersessionism in the Study of Ancient Judaism*. Oxford: Oxford University Press, 2006.

Klinghardt. M. *Gemeinschaftsmahl und Mahlgemeinschaft: Soziologie und Liturgie frühchristlicher Mahlfeiern*. Tübingen: Francke, 1996.

———. "A Typology of the Community Meal." Unpublished paper, SBL Consultation on Meals in the Greco-Roman World. Atlanta, November, 2003.

Knoch, O. "'Do This is Memory of Me!' (Luke 22:20; 1 Corinthians 11:24–25) The Celebration of the Eucharist in the Primitive Christian Communities." In *One Loaf, One Cup: Ecumenical Studies of 1 Cor. 11 and other Eucharistic Texts*, edited by B. F. Meyer, 1–10. The Cambridge Conference on the Eucharist, August 1988. New Gospel Studies 6. Macon, GA: Mercer, 1993.

Kodell, J. *The Eucharist in the New Testament*. Collegeville, PA: Liturgical, 1988.

Koenig, John. *The Feast of the World's Redemption: Eucharistic Origins and Christian Mission*. Harrisburg, PA: Trinity, 2000.

———. *New Testament Hospitality: Partnership with Strangers as Promise and Mission*. Overtures to Biblical Theology. Philadelphia, PA: Fortress, 1985.

Koester, Craig R. "Promise and Warning: The Lord's Supper in 1 Corinthians." *WW* 17 (1997) 45–53.

Kollmann, Bernd. *Ursprung und Gestalt der frühchristlichen Maßfeier*. GTA 43. Göttingen: Vandenhoeck & Ruprecht, 1990.

Konradt, Matthias. *Gericht und Gemeinde: Eine Studie zur Bedeutung und Funktion von Gerichtsaussagen im Rahmen der paulinischen Ekklesiologie und Ethik im 1 Thess und 1 Kor*. BZNW 117. Berlin: Walter de Gruyter, 2003.

Koster, Helmut. *Introduction to the New Testament*. Vol 1: *History, Culture, and Religion of the Hellenistic Age*. Philadelphia, PA: Fortress, 1982.

Bibliography

Kovacs, Judith L., ed. *1 Corinthians: Interpreted by Early Christian Commentators*. The Church's Bible. Grand Rapids: Eerdmans, 2005.

Kreider, E. *Communion Shapes Character*. Scottdale, PA: Herald, 1997.

Kremer, J. *Der Erste Brief an die Korinther*. RNT. Regensburg: Pustet, 1997.

Kugelmann, R. "The First Letter to the Corinthians." In *The Jerome Biblical Commentary*, edited by R. E. Brown et al., 254–75. Englewood Cliffs, NJ: Prentice-Hall, 1968.

Kuhn, Karl G. "The Lord's Supper and the Communal Meal at Qumran." In *The Scrolls and the New Testament*, edited by K. Stendahl. London: SCM, 1958.

Küng, Hans. *The Sacraments: An Ecumenical Dilemma*. Concilium 24. New York: Paulist, 1967.

Kuss, Otto. *Paulus, Auslegung und Verkündigung*. Regensburg: Pustet, 1971.

Kyrtatas, D. J. *The Social Structure of the Early Christian Communities*. London: Verso, 1987.

Lambert, John. "The Passover and the Last Supper." *JTS* 4 (1903) 184–93.

Lampe, George William Hugo. "Church Discipline and the Interpretation of the Epistle to the Corinthians." In *Christian History and Interpretation: Studies Presented to John Knox*, edited by W. R. Farmer et al., 337–61. Cambridge: University Press, 1967.

———. "The Eucharist in the Thought of the Early Church." In *Eucharistic Theology Then and Now*, edited by R. E. Clements et al., 34–58. SPCK Theological Collections 9. London: SPCK, 1968.

Lampe, P. "The Corinthian Eucharistic Dinner Party: Exegesis of a Cultural Context (1 Cor. 11:17–34)." *Affirmation* 4.2 (1991) 1–15.

———. "The Eucharist: Identifying with Christ on the Cross." *Interpretation* 48 (1994) 36–49.

———. "Das korinthische Herrenmahl im Schnittpunkt hellenistisch-römischer Mahlpraxis und paulinischer Theologia Crucis (1 Kor 11, 17–34)." *ZNW* 82 (1991) 183–213.

———. "Paul, Patrons, and Clients." In *Paul in the Greco-Roman World: A Handbook*, edited by P. J. Sampley, 488–523. Harrisburg, PA: Trinity, 2003.

Lang, Bernhard. "The Roots of the Eucharist in Jesus' Praxis." In *Society of Biblical Literature 1992 Seminar Papers*, edited by E. H. Lovering, 467–72. SBLSP 31. Atlanta, GA: Scholars, 1992.

Lang, F. *Die Briefe an die Korinther*. NTD 7. Göttingen/Zurich: Vandenhoeck & Ruprecht, 1986.

Lattey, Cuthbert. "Sacrament and Sacrifice: A Catholic View." *The Hibbert Journal* 40 (1942) 185–88.

Lattimore, R. A. *Themes in Greek and Latin Epitaphs*. Urbana: University of Illinois Press, 1962.

LaVerdiere, Eugene. *The Eucharist in the New Testament and the Early Church*. Collegeville, PA: Liturgical, 1996.

Lenski, R. C. H. *The Interpretation of St Paul`s First and Second Epistles to the Corinthians*. Minneapolis, MN: Augsburg, 1963.

Leon-Dufour, Xavier. *Sharing the Eucharistic Bread: The Witness of the New Testament*. Translated by M. J. O'Connell. New York: Paulist, 1987.

Levine, Baruch A. *In the Presence of the Lord: A Study of Cult and Some Cultic Terms in Ancient Israel*. SJLA. Leiden: Brill, 1974.

Lewis, N., and Meyer Reinhold, eds. *Roman Civilization*. 2 vols. New York: Harper & Row, 1966.

Lieberman, S. "The Discipline in the So-Called Dead Sea Manual of Discipline." *JBL* 71 (1952) 199–206.
Lietzmann, Hans. *Mass and Lord's Supper: A Study in the History of the Liturgy*. Translated by Dorothea H. G. Reeve. Leiden: Brill, 1979.
Lietzmann, Hans, and W. G. Kümmel. *Die Briefe des Apostels Paulus: An die Korinther I, II*. HNT 9. 5th ed. Tübingen: Mohr, 1949.
Lindars, B. "'Joseph and Asenath' and the Eucharist." In *Scripture: Meaning and Method. Essays Presented to Anthony Tyrell Hanson for his Seventieth Birthday*, edited by B. P. Thompson, 181–99. Hull: Hull University Press, 1987.
Lindemann, Andreas. *Der Erste Korintherbrief*. HNT 9/1. Tübingen: Mohr, 2000.
Lissarrague, Francois. *The Aesthetics of the Greek Banquet: Images of Wine and Ritual*. Princeton, NJ: Princeton University Press, 1990.
———. "Around the Krater: An Aspect of Banquet Imagery." In *Sympotica: A Symposium on the Symposium*, edited by Oswyn Murray, 196–209. Oxford: Clarendon, 1990.
Lock, Walter. "St. Paul's Knowledge of the Gospel History." *JTS* 6 (1905) 617–19.
Lohmeyer, E. "Das Abendmahl in der Urgemeinde." *JBL* 56 (1937) 217–52.
———. "Vom urchristlichen Abendmahl." *TRu* 9 (1937) 168–277, 273–312; 10 (1938) 81–99.
Maccoby, Hyam. "Paul and Eucharist." *NTS* 37 (1991) 247–67.
———. *Paul and Hellenism*. London: SCM, 1991.
———. *Ritual and Morality: The Ritual Purity System and its Place in Judaism*. Cambridge: Cambridge University Press, 1999.
MacComb, Samuel. "The Eschatology of Paul." *The Biblical World* 22/1 (1903) 36–41.
Macgregor, G. H. C. "The Concept of the Wrath of God in the New Testament." *NTS* 7 (1960–61) 101–109.
———. *Eucharistic Origins: A Survey of the New Testament Evidence*. London: James Clarke, 1928.
Mack, Burton L. *A Myth of Innocence: Mark and Christian Origins*. Philadelphia, PA: Fortress, 1988.
MacMullen, Ramsay. *Roman Social Relations, 50 BC to AD 284*. New Haven, CT: Yale University Press, 1974.
Magness, J., and Seymour Gitin, eds. *Hesed Ve-Emet: Studies in Honor of Ernest S. Frerichs*. Atlanta, GA: Scholars, 1988.
Malherbe, A. J. *Social Aspects of Early Christianity*. Baton Rouge, LA: Louisiana State University Press, 1977.
Manning, Phili. "Melchizedek's Eucharist." *ExpTim* 3 (2000) 158–60.
Marshall, I. Howard. *Kept by the Power of God: A Study of Perseverance and Falling Away*. Library of Ecumenical Studies. London: Epworth, 1969.
———. *Last Supper and Lord's Supper*. Grand Rapids: Eerdmans, 1980.
Martin, Dale B. *The Corinthian Body*. New Haven, CO: Yale University Press, 1995.
Martin, James Perry. "Belonging to History: A Communion Meditation on 1 Cor. 11:23–26." *Interpretation* 17 (1963) 188–92.
Martin, Ralph P. *Worship in the Early Church*. London: Marshall, Morgan & Scott, 1964.
Martin, Ralph P & Peter H. Davids, eds. *Dictionary of the Later New Testament and its Development*. Leicester: InterVarsity, 1997.
Marxsen, Willi. *The Lord's Supper as a Christological Problem*. Translated by Lorenz Nieting. FBBS 25. Philadelphia, PA: Fortress, 1970.

Bibliography

Massie, John. "I have Received of the Lord: 1 Corinthians 11: 23." *The Expositor* 2 (1885) 206–11.

Matson, D. L. *Household Conversion Narratives in Acts: Pattern and Interpretation.* JSNTSup 123. Sheffield: Sheffield Academic Press, 1996.

Mattern, Liselotte. *Das Verständnis des Gericht bei Paulus.* ATANT 47. Zürich/ Stuttgart: Zwingli Verlag, 1966.

Maurus Servius Honoratus. *Servii Grammatici qvi fervntvr in Vergilii carmina commentarii.* Edited by Georgius Thilo and Hermann Hagen. Leipzig: B. G. Teubner, 1881.

Mayor, J. B. "Gardner on the Origin of the Lord's Supper. Review of Percy Gardner, *The Origin of the Lord's Supper.*" *The Classical Review* 8.4 (1894) 148–52.

McConnell, John F. "The Eucharist and the Mystery Religions." *CBQ* 10 (1948) 29–41.

McCormick. S. *The Lord's Supper: A Biblical Interpretation.* Philadelphia, PA: Westminster, 1966.

McGowan, A. B. *Ascetic Eucharists: Food and Drink in Early Christian Ritual Meals.* Oxford Early Christian Studies. Oxford: Clarendon, 1999.

McKay, Johnston R. "A Feast for the Fallen?" *ExpTim* 116 (2005) 324.

McPartlan, Paul. *Sacrament of Salvation: An Introduction to Eucharistic Ecclesiology.* Edinburgh: T. & T. Clark, 1995.

McQueen, James Milroy. "Note on 1 Corinthians 11:24, 25." *Expository Times* 44 (1932–1933) 384.

Meeks, Wayne A. *The First Urban Christians: The Social World of the Apostle Paul.* New Haven, CO: Yale University Press, 1983.

———. *The Moral World of the First Christians.* Library of Early Christianity. Philadelphia, PA: Westminster, 1986.

———. "The Social Context of Pauline Theology." *Interpretation* 37 (1982) 266–77.

Meier, J. "The Eucharist at the Last Supper: Did it Happen?" *Theology Digest* 42 (1995) 335–51.

Mendels, D. "Hellenistic Utopia and the Essenes." *Harvard Theological Review* 72 (1979) 207–22.

Menoud, P. H. "The Acts of the Apostles and the Eucharist." In *Jesus Christ and the Faith: A Collection of Studies.* Translated by Eunice M. Paul, 84–106. PTMS 18. Pittsburgh, PA: Pickwick, 1978.

Menzies, Allan. "The Lord's Supper: St. Mark or St. Paul?" *The Expositor* 10 (1899) 241–62.

Metzger, Bruce M. "Considerations of Methodology in the Study of Mystery Religions." *Harvard Theological Review* 48 (1955) 1–20

———. *A Textual Commentary on the Greek New Testament: A Companion Volume to the United Bible Societies' Greek New Testament.* 2nd ed. Stuttgart: Deutsche Bibelgesellschaft, 1994.

Meyer, Ben F. "The Expiation Motif in the Eucharistic Words: A Key to the History of Jesus?" In *One Loaf, One Cup: Ecumenical Studies of 1 Cor 11 and other Eucharistic Texts,* edited by B. F. Meyer, 11–33. The Cambridge Conference on the Eucharist, August 1988. New Gospel Studies 6. Macon, GA: Mercer, 1993.

Meyer, Ben F., and E. P. Sanders, eds. *Jewish and Christian Self-definition.* Vol. 3: *Self Definition in the Greco-Roman World.* Philadelphia, PA: Fortress, 1982.

Meyer, H. A. W. *Critical and Exegetical Handbook to the Epistle to the Corinthians.* 2 vols. Translation revised and edited by William P. Dickson. Edinburgh: T. & T. Clark, 1877–1879.

Milgrom, Jacob. "Israel's Sanctuary: The Priestly 'Picture of Dorian Gray.'" *RB* 83 (1976) 390-99.

———. *Leviticus 1-16: A New Translation with Introduction and Commentary*. AB. New York: Doubleday, 1991.

Mitchell, Margaret M. *Paul and the Rhetoric of Reconciliation: An Exegetical Investigation of the Language and Composition of 1 Corinthians*. HUT 28. Tübingen: Mohr, 1991.

Moffatt, James. "Discerning the Body." *ExpTim* 30 (1918-1919) 19-23.

Moloney, Raymond. *The Eucharist: Problems in Theology*. London: Geoffrey Chapman, 1995.

Monks, George Gardner. "The Lucan Account of the Last Supper." *JBL* 44 (1925) 228-60.

Moore, George Foot. *Judaism in the First Centuries of the Christian Era*. 3 vols. Cambridge, MA: Harvard University Press, 1927-1930.

Morgan, W. *The Religion and Theology of Paul: The Kerr Lectures, Delivered in the United Free Church College, Glasgow, during Session 1914-15*. Edinburgh: T. & T. Clark, 1917.

Morris, Leon. *The First Epistle of Paul to the Corinthians: An Introduction and Commentary*. TNTC. 2nd ed. Leicester: InterVarsity, 1985.

Motyer, Steve. *Remember Jesus: A User's Guide to Understanding and Enjoying Holy Communion*. Fearn: Christian Focus, 1995.

Moule, C. F. D. "The Judgment Theme in the Sacraments." In *The Background of the New Testament and its Eschatology*, edited by W. D. Davies and D. Daube, 464-81. Cambridge: Cambridge University Press, 1964.

———. "Punishment and Retribution: An Attempt to Delimit their Scope in New Testament Thought." *Svensk Exegetisk Årsbok* 30 (1965) 21-36.

———. *Worship in the New Testament*. Ecumenical Studies in Worship 9. London: Lutherworth, 1961.

Munck, J. *Paul and the Salvation of Mankind*. Translated by Frank Clarke. London: SCM, 1977.

Murken, Todd B. *Take and Eat, and Take the Consequences: How Receiving the Lord's Supper is an Action that Makes a Difference*. New York: Peter Lang, 2002.

Murphy-O'Connor, Jerome. *Becoming Human Together: The Pastoral Anthropology of St. Paul*. Good News Studies. Wilmington, DE: Michael Glazier, 1982.

———. "Eucharist and Community in First Corinthians." *Worship* 50 (1976) 370-85 and 51 (1977) 56-69.

———. *1 Corinthians*. New Testament Message 10. Wilmington, DE: Michael Glazier, 1979.

———. "The First Letter to the Corinthians." In *NJBC*, 798-815.

———. *Keys to First Corinthians: Revisiting the Major Issues*. Oxford: Oxford University Press, 2009.

———. *Paul, A Critical Life*. Oxford: Clarendon, 1996.

———. *St. Paul's Corinth: Texts and Archaeology*. Good News Studies. Wilmington, DE: Michael Glazier, 1983.

Mylonas, G. E. *Eleusis and the Eleusinian Mysteries*. Princeton, NJ: Princeton University Press, 1961.

Neuenzeit, Paul. *Das Herrenmahl: Studien zur paulinischen Eucharistieauffassung*. Studien zum Alten und Neuen Testaments 1. München: Kösel-Verlag, 1960.

Neusner, Jacob. "The Fellowship (havurah) in the Second Jewish Commonwealth." *Harvard Theological Review* 53 (1960) 125-42.

Bibliography

———. *From Politics to Piety: The Emergence of Pharisaic Judaism*. Englewood Cliffs, NJ: Prentice-Hall, 1973.

———. *The Idea of Purity in Ancient Judaism*, SJLA 1. Leiden: Brill, 1973.

———. *The Rabbinic Traditions About the Pharisees Before 70.* 3 vols. Leiden: Brill, 1971.

———. "Two Pictures of the Pharisees: Philosophical Circle or Eating Club." *Anglican Theological Review* 64 (1982) 525–38.

Newton, Michael. *The Concept of Purity at Qumran and in the Letters of Paul*. SNTSMS 53. Cambridge: Cambridge University Press, 1985.

Neyrey, Jerome H. "Ceremonies in Luke-Acts: The Case of Meals and Table Fellowship." In *The Social World of Luke-Acts Models for Interpretation*, edited by Jerome H. Neyrey, 361–87. Peabody, MA: Hendrickson, 1991.

———. *Paul, in Other Words: A Cultural Reading of His Letters*. Louisville, KY: Westminster/John Knox, 1990.

———, ed. *The Social World of Luke-Acts: Models for Interpretation*. Peabody, MA: Hendrickson, 1991.

Nielsen, Inge, and Hanna Sigismund Nielsen, eds. *Meals in a Social Context: Aspects of the Communal Meal in the Hellenistic and Roman World*. Aarhus Studies in Mediterranean Antiquity 1. Aarhus: Aarhus University Press, 1998.

Nock, Arthur Darby. "The Cult of Heroes." *Harvard Theological Review* 37 (1944) 141–74.

———. *Early Gentile Christianity and its Hellenistic Background*. Harper torchbooks, The Cloister library. New York: Harper & Row, 1964.

Noy, D. "The Sixth Hour is the Mealtime for Scholars: Jewish Meals in the Roman World." In *Meal in a Social Context: Aspects of the Communal Meal in the Hellenistic and Roman World*, edited by Inge Nielsen and Hanna Sigismund Nielsen, 134–44. Aarhus Studies in Mediterranean Antiquity 1. Aarhus: Aarhus University Press, 1998.

O'Carroll, Michael. *Corpus Christi: An Encyclopedia of the Eucharist*. Wilmington, DE: Michael Glazier, 1988.

Oesterley, W. O. E. *The Jewish Background of the Christian Liturgy*. Oxford: Clarendon, 1925.

———. *Sacrifices in Ancient Israel: Their Origin, Purpose and Development*. London: Hodder and Stoughton, 1937.

Oppenheimer, A. *The "am Ha-aretz": A Study in the Social History of the Jewish People in the Hellenistic-Roman Period*. Translated by I. H. Levine. ALGHJ 8. Leiden: Brill, 1977.

Origen, *Contra Celsum*. Translated by Henry Chadwick. Cambridge: Cambridge University Press, 1953.

Oropeza, B. J. "Apostasy in the Wilderness: Paul's Message to the Corinthians in a State of Eschatological Liminality." *JSNT* 75 (1999) 69–86.

Orr, William F., and James Arthur Walter, *I Corinthians: A New Translation*. AB 32. Garden City, NY: Doubleday, 1976.

Oswalt, John N. *The Book of Isaiah*. 2 vols. NICOT. Grand Rapids, MI: Eerdmans, 1986, 1998.

Otto, R. *The Kingdom of God and the Son of Man*. Translated by F. V. Filson and B. Lee-Woolf. Lutterworth Library 9, 2nd edn. London: Lutterworth, 1943.

Otto, W. F. *Dionysus: Myth and Cult*. Translated by Robert B. Palmer. Bloomington, Ind.: Indiana University Press, 1965.

Palmer, Paul. F. *Sacraments and Worship: Liturgy and Doctrinal Development of Baptism, Confirmation and the Eucharist*. Westminster, MD: Newman, 1955.

Panikulam, George. *Koinōnia in the New Testament: A Dynamic Expression of Christian Life*. Analecta Biblica 85. Rome: Biblical Institute Press, 1979.
Pannenberg, Wolfhart. *Systematic Theology*. 3 vols. Grand Rapids, MI: Eerdmans, 1991.
Passakos, D. C. "Eucharist in First Corinthians: A Sociological Study." *RB* 192 (1997) 192–210.
Paul, G. "Symposia and *Deipna* in Plutarch's *Lives* and in Other Historical Writings." In *Dining in a Classical Context*, edited by W. J. Slater, 157–69. Ann Arbor, MI: University of Michigan Press, 1991.
Paulus Orosius, *The Seven Books of History Against the Pagans*. Translated by R. J. Deferrari. Washington: Catholic University Press, 1964.
Pauly, A. F. *Paulys Realencyclopädie der classischen Altertumswissenschaft*. 49 vols. New edn. G. Wissowa. Munich: Druckenmüller, 1894–1980.
Pedersen, J. *Israel: Its Life and Culture*. 2 vols. London: Oxford University Press, 1926, 1940.
Perrin, Norman. *Rediscovering the Teaching of Jesus*. London: SCM, 1967.
Pervo, Richard I. *Luke's Story of Paul*. Minneapolis, MN: Fortress, 1990.
Peters, E. H. "St. Paul and the Eucharist." *CBQ* 10 (1948) 247–53.
Petuchowski, J. J. "Do This in Remembrance of Me: 1 Corinthians 11:24." *JBL* 76 (1957) 293–98.
Pfitzner, V. C. "Purified Community—Purified Sinner: Expulsion from the Community according to Matthew 18:15-18 and 1 Corinthians 5:1–5." *ABR* 30 (1982) 34–55.
Pickl, J. *The Messias*. Translated by A. Green. St. Louis, MO: B. Herder, 1946.
Ploeg, J. van der. "The Meal of the Essenes." *JSS* 2 (1957) 163–73.
Pogoloff, Stephen M. *Logos and Sophia: The Rhetorical Situation of 1 Corinthians*. SBLDS 134. Atlanta, GA: Scholars, 1992.
Polhill, John B. *Acts*. NAC 26. Nashville, TN: Broadman, 1992.
Pope, Marvin H. *Song of Songs*. AB 7C. Garden City, NY: Doubleday, 1977.
Porter, C. L. "An Interpretation of Paul's Lord's Supper Texts: 1 Corinthians 10:14–22 and 11:17–34." *Encounter* 50 29–45.
Porter, David S. "Meals, Sacred." In *The Oxford Classical Dictionary*, edited by Simon Hornblower and Antony Spawforth, 942. 3rd edn. Oxford: Clarendon, 1999.
Powell, Barry B. *Classical Myth: With New Translations of Ancient Texts by Herbert M. Howe*. Englewood Cliffs, NJ: Prentice Hall, 1995.
Powers, Daniel G. *Salvation through Participation: An Examination of the Notion of the Believers' Corporate Unity with Christ in the Early Christian Soteriology*. CBET 29. Leuven: Peeters, 2001.
Price, S. R. F. *Rituals and Power: The Roman Imperial Cult in Asia Minor*. Cambridge: Cambridge University Press, 1984.
Priest, John. "A Note on the Messianic Banquet." In *The Messiah: Developments in Earliest Judaism and Christianity*, edited by James H. Charlesworth, 222–38. The First Princeton Symposium on Judaism and Christian Origins. Minneapolis, MN: Fortress, 1992.
Priest, J. F. "The Messiah and the Meal in 1QSa." *JBL* 82 (1963) 95–100.
Pritchard, Norman M. "Profession of Faith and Admission to Communion in the Light of 1 Corinthians 11 and other Passages." *SJT* 33 (1980) 55–70.
Pryke, J. "The Sacraments of Holy Baptism and Holy Communion in the Light of the Ritual Washings and Sacred Meals at Qumran." *RevQ* 5.20 (1996) 543–52.
Rabin, Chaim. *Qumran Studies*. Scripta Judaica 2. London: Oxford University Press, 1957.

Bibliography

Rahner, Karl, and Angelus Häussling. *The Celebration of the Eucharist*. Translated by W. J. O'Hara. New York: Herder & Herder, 1968.
Ramage, Edwin S. et al. *Roman Satirists and their Satire*. Park Ridge, NJ: Noyes, 1974.
Ramsay, W. M. "The Teaching of Paul in Terms of the Present Day." *The Expositor* 3 (1912) 137–52, 276–88, 354–73, 442–68.
Reicke, Bo C. "The Law and This World According to Paul." *JBL* 70 (1951) 259–76.
Reitzenstein, Richard. *Hellenistic Mystery-Religions: Their Basic Ideas and Significance*. Translated by John E. Steely. PTMS 15. Pittsburgh, PA: Pickwick, 1978.
Reumann, J. *The Supper of the Lord: The New Testament, Ecumenical Dialogues and Faith and Order on Eucharist*. Philadelphia, PA: Fortress, 1985.
Ridderbos, H. *Paul: An Outline of his Theology*. Translated by John Richard De Witt. London: SPCK, 1977.
Ringgren, H. *The Faith of Qumran*. Philadelphia, PA: Fortress, 1963.
Robbins, Vernon K. "Last Meal: Preparation, Betrayal, and Absence (Mark 14:12–25)." In *The Passion in Mark: Studies on Mark 14–16*. Translated by Werner H. Kelber, 21–40. Philadelphia, PA: Fortress, 1976.
Roberts, C. et al. "The Gild of Zeus Hypsistos." *Harvard Theological Review* 29 (1936) 39–88.
Robertson, Archibald, and Alfred A. Plummer. *A Critical and Exegetical Commentary on the First Epistle of St. Paul to the Corinthians*. ICC 33. Edinburgh: T. & T. Clark, 1914.
Robinson, John A. T. *The Body: A Study in Pauline Theology*. SBT 5. London: SCM, 1957.
Roetzel, Calvin J. *Judgement in the Community: A Study of the Relationship Between Eschatology and Ecclesiology in Paul*. Leiden: Brill, 1972.
Rowley, H. H. "Sacrament and Sacrifice: A Protestant View of the Lord's Supper." *The Hibbert Journal* 40 (1942) 181–85.
———. *Worship in Ancient Israel: Its Form and Meaning*. London: SPCK, 1978.
Ryken, L. et al., eds. *Dictionary of Biblical Imagery*. Leicester: IVP, 1998.
Safrai, S. "Home and Family." In *The Jewish People in the First Century: Historical Geography, Political History, Social, Cultural and Religious Life and Institutions*. Vol. 2, edited by S. Safrai and M Stern, 728–92. CRINT. Assen: Van Gorcum, 1976.
Sampley, J. Paul, ed. *Paul in the Greco-Roman World: A Handbook*. Harrisburg, PA: Trinity, 2003.
Sanders, E. P. "Jewish Association with Gentiles and Galatians 2:11–14." In *The Conversation Continues: Studies in Paul and John in Honor of J. Louis Martyn*, edited by R. T. Fortna and Beverly R. Gaventa, 170–88. Nashville, TN: Abingdon, 1990.
———. *Paul and Palestinian Judaism: A Comparison of Patterns of Religion*. London: SCM, 1977.
Sanders, Jack T. "Paul between Jews and Gentiles in Corinth." *JSNT* 65 (1997) 67–83.
Sandmel, Samuel. *The First Christian Century in Judaism and Christianity: Certainties and Uncertainties*. New York: Oxford University Press, 1969.
———. *Judaism and Christian Beginnings*. New York: Oxford University Press, 1978.
Savage, Timothy B. *Power through Weakness: Paul's Understanding of the Christian Ministry in 2 Corinthians*. SNTSMS 86. Cambridge: Cambridge University Press, 1995.
Schiffman, L. H. "Communal Meals at Qumran" *RevQ* 10 (1979) 45–56.
———. *The Eschatological Community of the Dead Sea Scrolls*. SBLMS 38. Atlanta, GA: Scholars, 1989.

―――. *Reclaiming the Dead Sea Scrolls: The History of Judaism, the Background of Christianity, the Lost Library of Qumran*. Philadelphia, PA: Jewish Publication Society, 1994.
Schiffman, L. H., and J. C. VanderKam, eds. *Encyclopaedia of the Dead Sea Scrolls*. 2 vols. Oxford: Oxford University Press, 2000.
Schillebeeckx, E. *The Eucharist*. Translated by N. D. Smith. New York: Sheed and Ward, 1968.
Schlatter, Adolf. *Paulus, der Bote Jesu: Eine Deutung seiner Briefe an die Korinther*. Stuttgart: Calwer, 1969.
Schmemann, Alexander. *The Eucharist: Sacrament of the Kingdom*. Translated by Paul Kachur. Crestwood, NY: St. Vladimir's Seminary, 1988.
Schmithals, Walter. *Gnosticism in Corinth: An Investigation of the Letters to the Corinthians*. Translated by John E. Steely. Nashville, TN: Abingdon, 1971.
Schmitt-Pantel, Pauline. "Sacrificial Meal and Symposion: Two Models of Civic Institutions in the Archaic City?" In *Sympotica: A Symposium on the Symposium*, edited by Oswyn Murray, 15-33. Oxford: Clarendon, 1990.
Schnabel, Eckhard J. *Der erste Brief des Paulus an die Korinther*. HTA, Neues Testament. Wuppertal: Brockhaus; Giessen: Brunnen, 2006.
Schneider, S. "Glaubensmängel in Korinth: Eine neue Deutung der 'Schwachen, Kranken, Schlafenden' in 1 Kor 11:30." *FN* 9 (1996) 3-19.
Scholer, D. M., ed. *Social Distinctives of the Christians in the First Century: Pivotal Essays by E. A. Judge*. Peabody, MA: Hendrickson, 2008.
Schottroff, Luise. "Holiness and Justice: Exegetical Comments on 1 Corinthians 11:17-34." *JSNT* 79 (2000) 51-60.
―――. "'Not Many Powerful': Approaches to a Sociology of Early Christianity." In *Social-Scientific Approaches to New Testament Interpretation*, edited by David G. Horrell, 275-87. Edinburgh: T. & T. Clark, 1999.
Schrage, Wolfgang. *Der erste Brief an die Korinther*. 4 vols. EKKNT 7/1-4. Neukirchen-Vluyn: Neukirchener; Zürich: Benziger, 1991-2001.
Schramm, G. "Meal Customs (Jewish)" In *Anchor Bible Dictionary*. Vol. 4, edited by D. N. Freedman, 648-50. New York: Doubleday, 1993.
Schürer, Emil. *The History of the Jewish People in the Age of Jesus Christ (175 B.C.- A.D. 135)*. 3 vols. Revised and edited by Geza Vermes et al. Edinburgh: T. & T. Clark, 1973-87.
Schürmann, Heinz. *Der Paschamahlbericht, Lk 22, (7-14), 15-18: I Teil einer quellenkritischen Untersuchung des lukanischen Abendmahlsberichtes, Lk 22, 7-38*. NTAbh xix, 5. Münster: Aschendorffsche Verlagsbuchhandlung, 1953.
Schweitzer, Albert. *Die Mystik des Apostels Paulus*. Tübingen: Mohr, 1930.
Schweizer, Eduard. *The Lord's Supper According to the New Testament*. FBBS 18. Philadelphia, PA: Fortress, 1967.
Seesemann, Heinrich. *Der Begriff KOINΩNIA im Neuen Testament*. BZNW 14. Gießen: Töpelmann, 1933.
Segal, J. B. *The Hebrew Passover, from the Earliest Times to A.D. 70*. London Oriental Series 12. London: Oxford University Press, 1963.
Sharon, D. M. "When Fathers Refuse to Eat: The Trope of Rejecting Food and Drink in Biblical Narrative." *Semeia* 86 (1999) 135-48.
Shimoff, S. R. "Banquets: The Limits of Hellenization." *JSJ* 27 (1996) 440-52.

Bibliography

Skehan, Patrick W. *The Wisdom of Ben Sira: A New Translation with Notes.* AB 39. New York: Doubleday, 1987.
Slater, William J., ed. *Dining in a Classical Context.* Ann Arbor, MI: University of Michigan Press, 1991.
———. "Peace, the Symposium and the Poet." *Illinois Classical Studies* 6.2 (1981) 205–14.
Sloyan, Gerard S. "'Primitive' and 'Pauline Concepts of the Eucharist.'" *CBQ* 23 (1961) 1–13.
Smit, Peter-Ben. *Fellowship and Food in the Kingdom: Eschatological Meals and Scenes of Utopian Abundance in the New Testament.* WUNT 2:234. Tübingen: Mohr Siebeck, 2008.
Smith, David Raymond. *"Hand this Man over to Satan": Curse, Exclusion and Salvation in 1 Corinthians 5.* Library of New Testament Studies 386. London: T. & T. Clark, 2008.
Smith, Dennis E. "The Egyptian Cults at Corinth." *Harvard Theological Review* 70 (1977) 201–31.
———. *From Symposium to Eucharist: The Banquet in the Early Christian World.* Minneapolis, MN: Fortress, 2003.
———. "The Historical Jesus at Table." In *Society of Biblical Literature 1989 Seminar Papers*, edited by David J. Lull, 466–86. SBLSP 28. Atlanta, GA: Scholars, 1989.
———. "Meal Customs (Greco-Roman)." In *ABD*. Vol. 4, edited by D. N. Freedman, 650–53. New York: Doubleday, 1993.
———. "Meals and Morality in Paul and His World." In *Society of Biblical Literature 1981 Seminar Papers*, edited by Kent Harold Richards, 319–39. SBLSP 20. Chico, CA: Scholars, 1981.
———. "The Messianic Banquet Reconsidered." In *The Future of Early Christianity: Essays in Honor of Helmut Koester,* edited by A. Pearson, 64–73. Minneapolis, MN: Fortress, 1991.
———. "Social Obligation in the Context of Communal Meals: A Study of the Christian Meal in 1 Corinthians in comparison with Graeco-Roman Communal Meals." ThD diss., Harvard Divinity School, Cambridge, MA, 1980.
———. "Table Fellowship and the Historical Jesus." In *Religious Propaganda and Missionary Competition in the New Testament World: Essays Honoring Dieter Georgi,* edited by Lukas Bormann et al,, 135–62. NovTSup 74. Leiden: Brill, 1994.
———. "Table Fellowship as a Literary Motif in the Gospel of Luke." *JBL* 106 (1987) 613–38.
Smith, Dennis E., and Hal E. Taussig. *Many Tables: The Eucharist in the New Testament and Liturgy Today.* Philadelphia, PA: Trinity, 1990.
Smith, Edgar W. "*Joseph and Asenath* and Early Christian Literature: A Contribution to the Corpus Hellenisticum Novi Testamenanti." PhD diss., Claremont, 1974.
Smith, Gordon T., et al. *The Lord's Supper: Five Views.* Downers Grove, IL: InterVarsity, 2008.
Smith, Morton. "The Dead Sea Sect in Relation to Ancient Judaism." *NTS* 7 (1960/61) 347–60.
———. *Jesus the Magician.* London: Gollancz, 1978.
———. "On the wine god in Palestine (Gen 18, John 2 and Achilles Tatius)," In *Salo Wittmayer Baron Jubilee Volume,* edited by S. Lieberman and A. Hyman, 815–29. Jerusalem: American Academy for Jewish Research, 1975.
———. "Palestinian Judaism in the First Century." In *Essays in Greco-Roman and Related Talmudic Literature,* edited Henry A. Fischel, 183–97. New York: KTAV, 1977.

Smith, Ralph F. "Eucharistic Faith and Practice." *Interpretation* 48 (1994) 5-16.
Smith, William Robertson. *Religion of the Semites*. 2nd ed. New Brunswick, NJ: Transaction, 2002.
Soards, Marion L. *The Speeches in Acts: Their Content, Context, and Concerns*. Louisville, KY: Westminster John Knox, 1994.
Sourvinou-Inwood, Christiane. "What is Polis Religion?" In *The Greek City from Homer to Alexander*, edited by Oswyn Murray and S. R. F. Price, 295-322. Oxford: Clarendon, 1990.
South, James T. *Disciplinary Practices in Pauline Texts*. Lewiston, NY: Edwin Mellen, 1992.
Spens, Will. "The Eucharist." In *Essays Catholic and Critical*, edited by Edward Gordon Selwyn, 425-48. London: SPCK, 1926.
Spitta, Friedrich. "Die urchristlichen Traditionen über Ursprung und Sinn des Abendmahls." In *Zur Geschichte und Literatur des Urchristentums*. 3 vols., 1.207-337. Göttingen: Vandenhoeck & Ruprecht, 1893-1907.
Stambaugh, John E. *The Social World of the First Christians*. London: SPCK, 1986.
Stambaugh, John E., and David L. Balch. *The New Testament in its Social Environment*. LEC 2. Philadelphia, PA: Westminster, 1986.
Steer, S. "Eating Bread in the Kingdom of God: The Foodways of Jesus in the Gospel of Luke." PhD diss., Westminster Theological Seminary, 2002.
Stein, S. "The Influence of Symposia Literature on the Literary Form of the Pesah Haggadah." *The Journal of Jewish Studies* 8 (1957) 13-44. Repr. in *Essays in Greco-Roman and Related Talmudic Literature*, edited by Henry A. Fischel, 13-44. New York: KTAV, 1977.
Stendahl, K., ed. *The Scrolls and the New Testament*. London: SCM, 1958.
Stibbs, Alan M. *Sacrament, Sacrifice and Eucharist: The Meaning, Function and Use of the Lord's Supper*. London: Tyndale, 1961.
Stookey, L. H. *Eucharist: Christ's Feast with the Church*. Nashville, TN: Abingdon, 1993.
Stowers, Stanley K. "Greeks Who Sacrifice and Those Who Do Not: Toward an Anthropology of Greek Religion." In *The Social World of the First Christians: Essays in Honor of Wayne A. Meeks*, edited by L. Michael White and O. Larry Yarbrough, 293-333. Minneapolis, MN: Fortress, 1995.
Strack, Hermann L., and Paul Billerbeck. *Kommentar zum Neuen Testament aus Talmud und Midrasch*. 6 vols. München: C. H. Beck'sche Verlagsbuchhandlung, 1922-1961.
Stuart, M. "The Lord's Supper in the Corinthian Church: Remarks on 1 Corinthians 11:17-34." *BSac* (1843) 499-531.
Swete, H. B. "Eucharistic Belief in the Second and Third Centuries." *JTS* 3 (1902) 161-77.
Synofzik, Ernst. *Die Gerichts- und Vergeltungaussagen bei Paulus: Eine traditionsgeschichtliche Untersuchung*. GTA 8. Göttingen: Vandenhoeck & Ruprecht, 1977.
Talbert, Charles H. *Reading Corinthians: A Literary and Theological Commentary on 1 and 2 Corinthians*. Reading the New Testament. New York: Crossroad, 1987.
Tannehill, Robert C. *The Narrative Unity of Luke-Acts*. 2 vols. Foundations and Facets. Philadelphia, PA: Fortress, 1986.
Taylor, Nicholas. *Paul, Antioch and Jerusalem: A Study in Relationships and Authority in Earliest Christianity*. JSNTSup 66. Sheffield: JSOT, 1992.
Tellbe, Mikael. *Paul Between Synagogue and State: Christians, Jews, and Civic Authorities in 1 Thessalonians, Romans and Philippians*. ConBNT 34. Stockholm: Almquist & Wiksell International, 2001.

Bibliography

Thayer, J. Henry. "Recent Discussions Respecting the Lord's Supper." *JBL* 18 (1899) 110–31.

Theiss, Norman. "The Passover Feast of the New Covenant." *Interpretation* 48 (1994) 17–35.

Theissen, Gerd. *The Gospels in Context: Social and Political History in the Synoptic Tradition*. Translated by L. M. Maloney. Minneapolis, MN: Fortress, 1991.

———. Social Conflicts in the Corinthian Community: Further Remarks on J. J. Meggitt, Paul, Poverty and Survival." *JSNT* 25 (2003) 371–91.

———. *Social Reality and the Early Christians: Theology, Ethics, and the World of the New Testament*. Translated by Margaret Kohl. Edinburgh: T. & T. Clark, 1992.

———. *The Social Setting of Pauline Christianity: Essays on Corinth*. Translated by John H. Schütz. Edinburgh: T. & T. Clark, 1982.

———. "The Social Structure of Pauline Communities: Some Critical Remarks on J. J. Meggitt, Paul, Poverty and Survival." *JSNT* 84 (2001) 65–84.

———. "Soziale Integration und sakramentales Handeln: Eine Analyse von 1 Cor. 11:17–34." *NovT* 16 (1974) 179–206.

———. "Soziale Schichtung in der Korinthischen Gemeinde: Ein Beitrag zur Soziologie des hellenistischen Urchristentums." *ZNW* 65 (1974) 232–72.

Thiselton, Anthony C. "*The First Epistle to the Corinthians*: A Commentary on the Greek Text. NIGTC. Grand Rapids: Eerdmans, 2000.

———. "Realized Eschatology at Corinth." *NTS* 24 (1978) 510–26.

Thurian, Max. *The Eucharistic Memorial*. 2 vols. Translated by J. G. Davies. Ecumenical Studies in Worship 7 & 8. Richmond, VA: John Knox, 1968.

Tod, Marcus N. "Clubs and Societies in Greek World." In *Sidelights of Greek History: Three Lectures on the Light thrown by Greek Inscriptions on the Life and Thought of the Ancient World*, 71–96. Oxford: B. Blackwell, 1932.

Tomson, Peter J. "Jewish Food Laws in Early Christian Community Discourse." *Semeia* 86 (1999) 193–211.

Travis, Stephen. *Christ and the Judgment of God: Divine Retribution in the New Testament*. Foundations for Faith. Basingstoke: Marshall Pickering, 1986.

Troeltsch, Ernst. *The Social Teaching of the Christian Churches*. 2 vols. Translated by O. Wyon. London: Allen & Unwin, 1931.

Trompf, G. W. "On Attitudes Toward Women in Paul and Paulinist Literature: 1 Corinthians 11:3–16 and its Context. *CBQ* 42 (1980) 196–215.

Tuckett, C. M. "1 Corinthians and Q." *JBL* 102 (1983) 607–19.

Tuker, M. A. R. "The Words of Institution at the Last Supper." *The Hibbert Journal* 9 (1910–11) 134–45.

VanderKam, James C. *The Dead Sea Scrolls Today*. Grand Rapids: Eerdmans, 1994.

VanLandingham, C. *Judgment and Justification in Early Judaism and the Apostle Paul*. Peabody, MA: Hendrickson, 2006.

Vermaseren, J. M. *Mithras, the Secret God*. New York: Barnes and Noble, 1963.

Vermes, Geza. *The Dead Sea Scrolls: Qumran in Perspective*. London: Collins, 1977.

———. *Jesus the Jew: A Historian's Reading of the Gospels*. London: Collins, 1973.

Vickers, Michael J. *Greek Symposia*. London: Joint Association of Classical Teachers, 1978.

Volf, Judith M. Gundry. *Paul and Perseverance: Staying in and Falling Away*, WUNT 2:37. Tübingen: Mohr, 1990.

Von Soden, Hans Freiherr. "Sacrament and Ethics in Paul." In *The Writings of St. Paul*, edited by W. A. Meeks, 257–68. New York: Norton, 1972.

Bibliography

Wainwright, G. *Eucharist and Eschatology*. New York: Oxford University Press, 1981.
Watson, Nigel. *The First Epistle to the Corinthians*. Epworth Commentaries. London: Epworth, 1992.
Weiss, Johannes. *Earliest Christianity: A History of the Period A.D. 30–150*. Edited by Frederick C. Grant. New York: Harper, 1959.
———. *Der erste Korintherbrief: völlig neu bearbeitet*. KEK. 9th ed. Göttingen: Vandenhoeck & Ruprecht, 1977.
Wenham, David, ed. *Gospel Perspectives: The Jesus Tradition Outside the Gospels*. Vol. 5. Sheffield: JSOT Press, 1985.
———. *Paul and Jesus: The True Story*. London: SPCK, 2002.
Wernberg-Moller, P., trans. *The Manual of Discipline*. STDJ 1. Leiden: Brill, 1957.
White, L. Michael. "Regulating Fellowship in the Communal Meal: Early Jewish and Christian Evidence." In *Meal in a Social Context: Aspects of the Communal Meal in the Hellenistic and Roman World*, edited by Inge Nielsen and Hanna Sigismund Nielsen, 177–205. Aarhus Studies in Mediterranean Antiquity 1. Aarhus: Aarhus University Press, 1998.
White, L. Michael, and O. Larry Yarbrough, eds. *The Social World of the First Christians: Essays in Honor of Wayne A. Meeks*. Minneapolis, MN: Fortress, 1995.
William, N. P. "The Origin of the Sacraments." In *Essays Catholic and Critical*, edited by Edward Gordon Selwyn. London: SPCK, 1926, 367–423.
Willis, Wendell Lee. *Idol Meat in Corinth: The Pauline Argument in 1 Corinthians 8 and 10*. SBLDS 68. Chico, CA: Scholars, 1985.
Winter, Bruce W. *After Paul Left Corinth: The Influence of Secular Ethics and Social Change*. Grand Rapids: Eerdmans, 2001.
———. "The Lord's Supper at Corinth: An Alternative Reconstruction." *The RTR* 37 (1978) 73–82.
———. *Philo and Paul Among the Sophists: Alexandrian and Corinthian Responses to a Julio-Claudian Movement*. 2nd ed. Grand Rapids: Eerdmans, 2002.
———. "Secular and Christian Responses to Corinthian Famines." *TynBul* 40 (1989) 86–106.
Witherington, Ben. *Conflict and Community in Corinth: A Socio-rhetorical Commentary on 1 and 2 Corinthians*. Grand Rapids: Eerdmans, 1994.
Wolff, Christian. *Der Erste Brief des Paulus an die Korinther*. THKNT 7. Berlin: Evangelische Verlagsanstalt, 1996.
Wood, Irving F. "Paul's Eschatology." *The Biblical World* 38 (1911) 79–91, 159–70.
Wright, David P. "The Spectrum of Priestly Impurity." In *Priesthood and Cult in Ancient Israel*, edited by Gary A. Anderson and Saul M. Olyan, 150–81. JSOTSup 125. Sheffield: JSOT Press, 1991.
Yerkes, Royden Keith. *Sacrifice in Greek and Roman Religions and Early Judaism*. Hale Lectures. London: Adam & Charles Black, 1953.
Yinger, Kent L. *Paul, Judaism, and Judgment according to Deeds*. SNTSMS 105. Cambridge: Cambridge University Press, 1999.
Youtie, Herbert C. "The Kline of Sarapis." *Harvard Theological Review* 41 (1948) 9–29.
Zahavy, Tzvee. *The Mishnaic Law of Blessings and Prayers: Tractate Berakhot*. BJS 88. Atlanta, GA: Scholars, 1987.
Zizioulas, John D. *Being as Communion: Studies in Personhood and the Church*. New York: St. Vladimir's Seminary Press, 1985.

Index of Modern Authors

Aalen, S., 172n
Allo, E. B., 185n, 188n, 194n, 204n
Angus, S., 7n, 65n, 66n, 67n
Ascough, R. S., 7n, 8n, 71n, 81n, 95n, 135n
Aune, D. E. 5n, 8n, 10n, 13n, 14n, 15n, 16n, 17n, 18n, 70n, 94, 127n, 133n, 182n
Avramidou, A., 7n, 105n, 106

Bahr, G. J., 31n
Baldwin, J. G., 78n
Balsdon, J. P. V. D., 10n
Banks, R., 126n
Barrett, C. K., 116n, 117n, 129n, 136n, 137, 138n, 139n, 145n, 147n, 154n, 155n, 160n, 161n, 168n, 172n, 173n, 175n, 176n, 186, 196n, 202n, 203n, 204n, 205n
Barrosse, T., 197n
Bartchy, S. S., 124n, 132n
Barton, S. C., 129n, 142n, 207n
Baumgarten, J. M., 38n
Becker, W. A., 10n, 13n, 16n, 18n, 35n
Berger, K., 152n
Best, E., 182n, 206n
Bilde, P., 42n
Black, C. C., 197n
Black, M., xvn, 59n, 149n
Blass, F., 170n
Blenkinsopp, J., 56
Blomberg, C. L., 22n, 23n, 26n, 35n, 36n, 57n, 78n, 79n, 81n, 110n, 111n, 113n, 124n, 133n, 152n
Blue, B. B., 185n

Blümmer, H., 11n, 15n
Bokser, B. M., 31n, 34n
Borg, M. J., 124n
Bornkamm, G., 115n, 124n, 133n, 141n, 146n, 147n, 148n, 154n, 160n, 178n, 189n, 193n, 205n, 206n, 207n, 215n
Bowker, J., 50
Box, G. H., xvn
Branick, V., 126n
Breech, J., 124n, 143n
Brilioth, Y., 149n
Broneer, O., 165n
Brown, R. E., 151
Bruce, F. F., 141n, 157n, 175n, 179n, 197n, 200n, 201n, 206n
Bultmann, R., xvin, 68, 146n, 147n, 155n
Burchard, C., xvn, 21n, 22n, 53, 54n, 57n
Burkert, W., 110n, 111n
Burkitt, F. C., 150n, 151n
Burrows, M., 39n
Burton, E. De W., 141n

Calvin, J., 140n, 166n, 171n, 177n, 188n, 209n
Carney, T. F., 135n
Carter, T. L., 136n, 138n
Charles, R. H., 34n
Chesnutt, R. D., 21n, 50n, 53, 54, 55n
Childs, B. S., 97n
Chilton, B., 60n, 124n, 150n
Chow, J. K., 116n, 136n, 138n, 139n
Chrysostom, D., 188n

251

Index of Modern Authors

Clark, N., 149n, 150n, 154n
Clarke, A. D., 136n
Clements, R. E., 144n
Cohen, A., 194n
Cohn-Sherbok, D., 158n
Cole, R. L., 94
Collins, A. Y., 58n
Collins, R. F., 135n, 136n, 161n, 169n, 170n, 194n, 206n
Conzelmann, H., 115n, 136n, 137, 141n, 145n, 147n, 152n, 153n, 156n, 157n, 158n, 160n, 161n, 168n, 173n, 175n, 178n, 185n, 187n, 189n, 191n, 192n, 201n, 203n, 207n, 208n, 211n, 215n
Corley, K. E., 70nn
Coutsoumpos, P., 12n, 116n, 118n, 120n, 121n, 123n, 128, 147n, 216n
Craig, C. T., 117n
Cross, F. M., 41, 58
Crossan, J. D., 4n, 8n, 74n, 83n, 95, 96n, 104n, 124n, 135n, 145n
Cullmann, O., 144n, 146, 147n, 148n
Cumont, F., 67n, 68n, 152n
Custer, J., 140n

Danby, H., 177n
D'Arms, J. H., 11n, 70n, 80n
Davies, H., 189n
Davies, W. D., 144n, 155n
Deissmann, A., 116n, 117n, 118, 120
Delling, G., 189n, 191n
Delorme, J., 144n
Dembitz, L. N., 30n
Dentzer, J.-M., 11n
deSilva, D. A., 75n
Dix, G., xvn, 149n, 150n, 157n
Donahue, J. F., 7n
Douglas, M., xviin, 2, 22n, 107, 108n, 110n, 152n
Duff, J. W., 86n
Dunbabin, K. M. D., 7n
Dunn, J. D. G., 45n, 49n, 79n, 178, 204n, 209n

Edwards, O. C., 122n
Ehrhardt, A., 204n
Ellis, E. E., 205n

Ellis, W., 172n
Engberg-Pedersen, T., 129n, 160, 161n, 173n, 206n
Epstein, I., 48n
Erikson, A., 162n

Farnell, L. R., 65
Fascher, E., 190n, 202n
Fee, G. D., 116n, 117n, 118n, 127, 129n, 136n, 137n, 138n, 140n, 141n, 142n, 144n, 146, 148, 152n, 153, 154, 155, 156n, 158n, 159n, 160n, 162n, 167n, 168n, 169n, 172n, 173n, 174, 175n, 185n, 187n, 189n, 198n, 201n, 202n, 205n, 210n, 211n, 213n, 214n, 215n
Feeley-Harnik, G., xvn, 22n, 23n, 26, 27n, 57n, 59n, 78, 110n, 150n
Ferguson, E., 7n, 8n, 68n
Filson, F. V., 121, 126n, 194n
Finger, R. H., 80n, 135n
Fischel, H. A., 84n
Fisher, N. R. E., 2n, 3n, 4, 7, 8n, 10n, 11n, 14n, 16n, 17n, 20n, 70n, 71n, 72n, 76, 81n, 82n, 90n, 91n, 92n, 94n, 106n, 111n, 112n
Fitzmyer, J. A., 138n, 168n, 185n, 205n
Flusser, D., 40n
Fraine, J. De, 204n
Furnish, V. P., 206n, 207n
Furst, D., 193n

Gager, J. G., 119n, 121n, 131n
Gardner, P. D., 159n
Garland, D. E., 129n, 136n, 141n, 165n, 169n, 171n, 175n, 185, 188n, 208n, 212, 215n
Garnsey, P., 135n
Gill, D., 65n
Godet, F. L., 172n, 174n, 193n, 201n, 204n
Goodenough, E. R., 34n, 57n
Goody, J., 2
Goudge, H. L., 115n
Gowers, E., 17n
Grenfell, B. P., 66n

252

Index of Modern Authors

Grosheide, F. W., 174n, 176n, 191n, 197n, 203n, 205n
Grundmann, W., 168n
Gulick, C. B., 15n
Gundry, R. H., 178

Hallback, G., 141n, 213
Hamilton, V. P., 24n
Harrington, H. K., 49n, 101n
Hatzfeld, J., 66n
Hauck, F., 182n
Hays, R. B., 136n, 138n, 143n, 148n, 154n, 168n, 169, 172n, 175n, 178n, 194n, 201n, 206n, 213n
Heil, J. P., 124n, 183n
Hein, K., 79n, 167n
Hengel, M., 35n, 119, 120, 124n
Henrichs, A., 103n
Héring, J., 146n, 147n, 158n, 174n, 177n, 204n
Hermann, P., 99n
Higgins, A. J. B., xvn, 144n, 146n, 148n, 150n, 151n, 154, 155n, 156n, 158n, 162n, 178n, 206n
Hofius, O., 146n, 154n, 156n, 158n, 160, 191n, 206n, 211n, 213, 215n
Holmberg, B., 118n, 120, 121n, 122n
Horrell, D. G., 114n, 116n, 118, 121n, 122n, 127n, 137n, 138n, 139n, 206n
Horsley, G. H. R., 68, 69n
Horsley, R. A., 145n, 198n, 213n
Hunter, A. M., 146n, 147n
Hurd, J. C., 136n

Instone-Brewer, D., 30, 32n, 49n, 50n, 52n, 64n 82n, 126n, 150n, 153n

Jabbur, J. S., 3n
Jameson, M. H., 66n
Jaubert, A., 149
Jenks, A. W., 22n
Jeremias, J., xvn, 21, 22, 50, 53, 57n, 70n, 71n, 124n, 143n, 145n, 147n, 148, 149n, 150n, 152, 153n, 154n, 155n, 156n, 158n, 159n, 160n, 161n, 198n, 215n
Jones, I. H., 107n
Jones, P. H., 144n
Jourdan, G. V., 182n
Judge, E. A., 119, 121n, 122n
Juengst, S. C., 22n

Kamp, C. H., 205n
Kane, J. P., 8n
Käsemann, E., 137n, 140, 160, 169n, 172n, 177n, 178n, 181, 182n, 188, 191n, 192n, 205n
Kee, H. C., 55n, 121n
Kilpatrick, G. D., 53n
King, P., 22
Klauck, H.-J., 98n, 122n, 129n, 142n, 151n, 172n, 176n, 181n, 182n, 187n, 191n, 206n, 207n, 211n, 215
Klinghardt, M., 6n, 10n, 109, 206n
Kodell, J., 149n, 150n
Koenig, J., 124n, 126n, 183n, 206n, 208n
Koester, C. R., 68n, 158n, 206n
Kollmann, B., 183n
Konradt, M., 129n, 174n, 189n, 193n, 195n, 197n, 198n
Koster, H., 206n
Kreider, E., 125n
Kremer, J., 172n
Kuhn, K. G., 40, 41n, 53, 54, 58n, 149n
Kung, H., 144n
Kyrtatas, D. J., 123

Lampe, G. W. H., 142n, 157, 161, 172n, 173n, 175, 181n, 193n, 194, 197n, 198, 204n, 207n, 208n, 211n, 213n, 214n
Lampe, P., xvin, 14n, 114n, 127, 128n, 129n, 163, 212n, 215n
Lang, F., 168n, 172n
Lattimore, R. A., 56n
Lenski, R. C. H., 153n, 171n
Leon-Dufour, X., 149n, 150n, 160n, 161n, 178n, 184n, 204n
Lewis, N., 83n, 92n
Lieberman, S., 38
Lietzmann, H., xv, xviii, 9n, 138n, 144n, 146n, 147n, 149n, 150n, 155n, 160n, 168n, 169n, 177n, 178n, 198n, 204n, 205n

253

Index of Modern Authors

Lindemann, A., 138n, 148n
Lohmeyer, E., 124n, 147n

Maccoby, H., xvin, 140n, 144n, 145n, 146n, 147n, 152n, 153n, 158n
Mack, B. L., xvin
MacMullen, R., 117n, 131n
Malherbe, A. J., 120, 126n, 131n
Marshall, I. H., xvn, 129n, 143n, 144n, 146n, 147n, 148n, 149n, 150n, 153n, 154n, 159n, 185n, 194n, 195n, 197n, 206n
Martin, D. B., 99n, 100n, 172n, 177n, 178n, 187n, 204n
Martin, R. P., 160n
Marxsen, W., 144
Mattern, L., 170n, 191n, 194n, 198n
McCormick, S., 184n
Meeks, W. A., 74n, 114n, 115n, 120, 123n, 125n, 126n, 131, 136n, 153n, 156n, 180, 207n, 208n
Meier, J., 145n
Metzger, B. M., 171n
Meyer, H. A. W., 172n
Mitchell, M. M., 136n
Moore, G. F., 195n
Morris, L., 116n, 179n, 191n, 193n, 201n
Motyer, S., 201n
Moule, C. F. D., 145n, 153n, 175n, 180n, 183n, 198, 206n, 209n, 210n
Munck, J., 136n
Murphy-O'Connor, J., 73n, 115n, 116n, 117n, 126n, 136, 139n, 168n, 175n, 186n, 188n, 206n, 207n
Mylonas, G. E., 68n

Neuenzeit, P., 191n, 205n, 207n, 215n
Neusner, J., 40n, 48, 49, 50, 51
Newton, M., 39, 40n, 41n, 42n, 43n
Neyrey, J. H., 124n, 125n, 174
Nock, A. D., 9, 65, 66n, 67n, 98n, 178n
Noy, D., 30n

Oesterley, W. O. E., xvn, 27
Oppenheimer, A., 51n
Orr, W. F., 117n, 118n
Oswalt, J. N., 107n

Otto, R., xvn, 149
Otto, W. F., 15n

Palmer, P. F., 144n
Pannenberg, W., 210n
Passakos, D. C., 130, 137n, 206n, 208n
Pedersen, J., 27n
Perrin, N., 124n, 163n
Philonenko, M., 55n
Pickl, J., 150
Pogoloff, S. M., 131
Pope, M. H., 58n
Porter, C. L., 205n
Powers, D. G., 182n, 183n
Price, S. R. F., 6, 95, 97n
Priest, J., 183n
Priest, J. F., 42n
Pryke, J., 41n

Rabin, C., 38, 43n
Ramage, E. S., 86n
Reitzenstein, R., xvin, 155
Ridderbos, H., 160n
Ringgren, H., 39n, 40n
Robbins, V. K., 151n
Roberts, C., 76n, 77n, 83n, 95n, 96n
Robertson, A., 175n, 179n, 191n, 194n, 197n, 204n
Robinson, J. A. T., 204n
Roetzel, C. J., 100n, 167n, 190n, 193n, 194n, 195n, 196, 197n, 200n
Rowley, H. H., 64n
Ryken, L., 3n, 29

Sanders, E. P., 49, 194, 195
Savage, T. B., 116n
Schiffman, l. H., 41n, 42n, 44n
Schlatter, A., 175n
Schmithals, W., 136
Schmitt-Pantel, P., 1n, 4n, 70n, 76n, 91n, 94n
Schnabel, E. J., 185n, 190n, 191n, 193n
Schneider, S., 185n
Schottroff, L., 125n, 144n
Schrage, W., 121n, 145n, 148n, 153n, 154n, 168n, 189n, 190n, 204n, 205n, 206n
Schramm, G., 22n

Schürer, E., 45n, 100n
Schweitzer, A., 146n, 182n, 183n
Schweizer, E., xvi, 144n, 150n, 151n, 160n, 172n, 204n, 215n
Seesemann, H., 182n
Sharon, D. M., 25n
Shimoff, S. R., 111
Slater, W. J., 93n
Smit, P.-B., 183n
Smith, D. E., xviii, 2n, 3n, 4n, 5n, 6n, 7n, 8n, 9n, 10n, 11, 12n, 13n, 14n, 20n, 31n, 35n, 36, 44, 47n, 56n, 57n, 58n, 66n, 67n, 69n, 72n, 73n, 77n, 79n, 82, 83n, 84n, 85n, 86n, 87n, 90, 95n, 96n, 109, 110n, 111, 124n, 125n, 126n, 130n, 131, 132, 133, 144n, 157n, 160n, 167n, 169n, 170n, 204n, 212n, 214n
Smith, D. R., 167n, 185n, 186n, 194n
Smith, E. W., 55n, 56
Smith, M., 34n, 48, 49, 124n
Smith, W. R., 3, 24, 27
Spitta, F., xv
Stambaugh, J. E., 116n, 123n
Steer, S., 22n, 23n, 25n, 26n, 27n, 28n, 29n
Stein, S., 5n, 11n, 19n, 31n, 37n, 71n, 84n, 88n, 94n, 110n, 111n
Strack, H. L., 150n
Stuart, M., 177n, 201n
Synofzik, E., 175n, 185n, 190n, 191n

Talbert, C. H., 116n, 146n, 160n, 211n
Theissen, G., 114, 115n, 116n, 121n, 122n, 126n, 127n, 128, 129, 130, 131, 136n, 141n, 142n, 150n, 168, 191n, 211n, 215n
Thiselton, A. C., 115n, 136n, 137n, 140n, 142n, 143n, 148n, 152n, 153n, 156n, 157, 158n, 160n, 161n, 162n, 168n, 173n, 174n, 179n, 202n, 204n, 205n, 209n, 210n
Travis, S., 186n, 187n, 190n, 193n, 195n, 196n, 197n
Troeltsch, E., 119
Trompf, G. W., 188n

van der Ploeg, J., 41n
Vanderkam, J. C., 37n
VanLandingham, C., 192n, 193n, 196n, 197n
Vermaseren, J. M., 68n
Vermes, G., 39n, 124n
Volf, J. M. G., 171n, 176n, 189n, 191n, 192n, 196, 197n, 199n, 200n
Von Soden, H. F., 204n

Wainwright, G., 103n, 124n, 150n, 161n, 184n, 188n, 189n, 191n, 203n, 207n, 210n
Watson, N., 175n, 204n, 206n, 215n
Weiss, J., 100n, 140n, 144n, 146n, 172n, 177n, 194n, 204n
Wenham, D., 207n
Wernberg-Moller, P., 39n, 43n
White, L. M., 80n, 99, 125, 212, 214
Willis, W. L., 182n
Winter, B. W., 135, 136, 138, 185, 213, 216
Witherington, B., 116n, 123, 138, 141n, 142, 161, 206, 213
Wolff, C., 146n, 148, 154, 158, 160, 172, 185, 189, 191, 198, 202, 205

Yerkes, R. K., 9n
Yinger, K. L., 194n, 196
Youtie, H. C., 67n

Zahavy, T., 212n
Zizioulas, J. D., 208n

Index of Ancient Sources

OLD TESTAMENT
Genesis
1:29	25
2:9	106n
3:14	102n
3:17	102n
9:3–4	25
14:18–20	23n
14:18–19	23n
18:2–8	23n
18:4	22n
19:1–11	22n
19:1–3	23n
19:2	22n
21:8	23n
24:23–25	22n
24:32	22n
26:26–31	23n
26:30–31	24, 69n, 91n
26:30	22n
26:54	91n
27	24
27:33	24, 69n
29:22	23n
29:27–28	23n
31:44–46	23n
31:51–54	23n
31:54	22n, 24, 69n
32:3–21	24
40:20	23n
43:1–11	24
43:16–24	22n
43:24–34	24, 91n
43:32	78n
43:34	24n

Exodus
2:20	80n
3:8	26
12:14	23n
12:47	27
13:9	156n
13:18	30
15:26	101n
16:1–17:7	57n
18:12	23n, 27n
19:6	49
20:12	194n
23:14	28n
24:8	158
24:9–12	27, 69n
24:9–11	103n
25:30	26
28:43	40n
30:17–31	40n
34:15	23n
39:35	28n
40:31–32	40n

Leviticus
2:13	28n
3:1–16	27n
4:3–4	104n
5:8	154n
5:14–15	104n
6:1–5	43n
6:24–25	104n

257

Leviticus (continued)

7:12–15	149
7:16	49n
7:19	101n
9:8	154n
11:38	43n
11:40	101n
17:15	101n
19:16	43n
21:17–23	40
22:3–4	101n
22:6	40n
23:22	82n
23:40	27n
24:8	26
24:42–43	29
26:3–5	26n

Numbers

9:1–14	28n, 82n
11:4–6	26n
11:7–9	57n
18:19	28n
20:2–13	26n, 57n
21:4–5	26n
25:1–3	26

Deuteronomy

7:12–15	101n
8:7–10	26n, 97n
12:12	27n
12:15	97n
12:17–18	27n
13:–14	78
14:2	78
14:22–26	64n
14:26	27n
15:1–17	28n
16:11	27n
16:15	27n
26:5	30n
28:23	154n
28:58–69	101n

Joshua

2:1–6	22n
5:10–12	28
8:30–35	28
8:33–35	82n
9:3–15	23n
24:1–28	28

Judges

9:26–28	23n
9:27	25, 64n, 91n
14:10–17	23n
14:10	23n
16:23	23n
19:21–22	22n

1 Samuel

1:1–18	23n
7:2–14	23n
9:–10	23n
9:6–7	24n
13:1–15	23
14:1–46	23
15:1–33	23
16:1–13	23n
20:1–42	23
20:34	25n, 91n
28:3–25	23

2 Samuel

3:1–21	23n
3:20	23n
6:1–19	23n
6:19	23n
9	70n
9:7	23n
9:10–11	23n
11:1–17	23
12:1–25	23
13:1–22	23
13:23–29	23
13:23–27	23n
15:1–12	23
16:1	24n

Index of Ancient Sources

1 Kings

1:9	23n, 24n, 91n
1:19	24n, 91n
1:25	24n, 91n
1:39–41	23n
1:41	24n, 91n
1:49	24, 91n
2:7	70n
4:7–23	24n
8:10–13	40n
8:62–66	28n, 69n
13:1	25
13:7–10	25
13:11–32	25n
14:1–3	24n
19:19–21	23

2 Kings

6:22–23	22n
6:23	25, 91n
23:21–23	29
25:27–30	198n, 70n

1 Chronicles

12:38–40	23n, 24n, 57n
29:22	23n

2 Chronicles

7:1–10	28n
13:5	28n

Ezra

6:6–22	28

Esther

1:9–22	25n
2:8	35
9:22	23n
14:17	35n

Job

2:6	100n, 186
42:11	23
42:7–9	23

Psalms

22:26–29	26n
23:5	103, 26n, 3n
36:8–9	26n
36:8	26n
41:9	25n
78:15–31	26n
78:25	103n, 57n
104:14–15	26n
104:15	32
104:21	26n
104:27–28	26n
113:–118	31
128:5–6	194n
136:26	26n
145:15–16	26n
147:9	26n

Proverbs

9:1–18	26
9:1–6	103n
9:1–5	23n
15:17	23n, 26n
17:1	23n, 26n

Ecclesiastes

2:24–25	26n
9:7	26n
10:19	26n

Song of Solomon

5:1	103n

Isaiah

1:11–17	101n
3:17	102n
5:11–12	101n, 111n
5:22–23	101n, 111n
7:21–22	102n
9:19–20	102n
22:13	111n
23:18	104n

259

Index of Ancient Sources

Isaiah (continued)

24:7–11	102n
25:6–8	26
25:6	56
28:7–8	101n
30:23	104n
32:10	102n
33:15–16	104n
48:21	107n
49:9–10	107n
53:12	154
54:2–8	58n
54:4–8	58n
54:5–55:5	58n
55:5	107n
65:4	78n
65:13–14	56
65:13	102n, 107n
65:25	107n
66:3	78n
66:17	78n

Jeremiah

5:1–34	198n
8:13	103n
14:3–6	103n
14:13–16	103n
16:5–9	23n
24:10	103n
29:17–18	103n
31:5	104n
31:12–14	104n
31:18–19	195n
31:31	158
32:2	103n
34:17	103n
44:12–14	103n
52:31–34	70n

Ezekiel

4:9–17	101n
4:12–13	102n
16:7–8	58n
24:1–14	102n
24:16–17	23n
33:25	78
34:13–31	107n
34:23–24	56n
39:17–20	102n, 107n
41:22	22n
43:24	28n

Daniel

1:8	78
5:1–4	64n

Hosea

2:1–23	58n
2:9	103n
2:12	103n
2:22	26n
4:8–16	103n
5:7	103n
5:12	103n
7:4–14	103n
8:7–13	103n
9:2–16	103n
9:3	78
13:5–6	104n
14:7	104n

Joel

1:15–20	102n
2:24–26	58n
2:24–27	104n
3:18	26n, 58n

Amos

2:6–8	101n
5:21–24	101n
6:4–7	101n, 111n
7:12	24n
8:10	103
9:13–15	104n
9:13b	26n
1:7	25n

Micah

3:5	24n
4:3–4	104n

5:2–4	56n	15:3	103n
6:14–15	102n	18:32	34n
7:14	104n	18:37	36n
		19:1–3	36n
Habakkuk		24:19–21	103n
		29:21–23	36n
2:15–16	102n	29:22	34n
3:17	102n	31:12–42	111n
		31:12–18	36n
Zephaniah		31:15–17	36n, 36n
1:7	104n	31:15–30	82n
3:17–18	104n	31:19–22	36n
		31:23–30	36n
Zechariah		31:25–30	36n
8:19	26n	32:1–2	35, 36n
9:17	107n, 56n	32:3–6	36n
		32:3–4	36n
		32:5–6	36n
		32:7–9	36n
APOCRYPHA		32:11	36n
Tobit		33:4–6	36n
1:6–12	35n	34:9–12	36n
4:17	35n	37:16–26	36n
		37:27–31	36n
Judith		37:29–31	34n
		39:4	35n
10:5	107n, 35n	39:8	36n
10:10–13	107n, 35n	40:20–21	36n
11:11–15	107n	41:19	36n
12:5–9	107n, 35n		
16:20	34n	**1 Esdras**	
		1:122	34n
Wisdom		4:63	34n
2:24	100n	5:51–55	34n
11:10	200n	7:10–15	34n
16:20	103n, 34n, 57n	8:85	34n
		9:50–55	34n
		1:17–23	34
Ben Sira			
6:19	103n	**1 Maccabees**	
9:9	34n	1:62–63	35n
9:15–16	36n		
12:12	35	**2 Maccabees**	
13:8–13	34n, 36n	6:12	195n
13:21–23	36n	6:18—7:42	35n
14:10	34n	12:45	197n

261

4 Ezra

1:19	103n, 34n, 58n
6:52	57n
8:52–54	34n
8:52	57n
9:19	58n

PSEUDEPIGRAPHA

2 Baruch

13:4–11	195n
29:1–4	58n
29:4–8	57n
29:5	34n
29:8	34n
78:6	195n
83:8	195n

1 Enoch

24:4—25:7	103n, 58n
60:24	57n
62:12–14	57n
62:13–14	5719n
62:14	34n

2 Enoch

42:5	57n, 58n

3 Enoch

48:10	57n
48:A:9–10	58n

Joseph and Aseneth

7:1	56n
8:5–7	54
8:5	53n
8:7	56n
8:9	53n
15:5	53n
16:14	57n, 106n
16:16	53n
19:5	53n
21:21	53n

Jubilees

6:35b	35n
10:1–13	101n

3 Maccabees

3:2–5	35n
5:26	213n

4 Maccabees

5–18	35n

Psalms of Solomon

10:1–3	195n

Sibylline Oracles

4:24–30	21n

Testament of Levi

18:11	103n, 58n

QUMRAN

Damascus Document (CD)

5:6–7	39n
20:22	39n
22:3	43n

1QH

3:21–22	39n
6:13	39n

1QM

7:4–6	42n
7:6	39n
12:1ff.	39n

1QS

1:11–12	42
3:1	42n
3:4	40n

Index of Ancient Sources

3:8–9	43n	4QFl	
3:9	40n	1:4	39n
4:10	42n		
5:19–20	39n	4QMa	
5:24—6:1	44n		39n
5:7	44n		
5:13–14	42n, 44n	11QT	
5:13	38, 38n, 43n	45:12–14	42n
6	38n		
6:1–6	41n		
6:1–4	44n		
6:16–17	38n		
6:20	38n	**RABBINIC WORKS**	
6:22	42n, 44n	Babylonian	
6:24–25	43n	*Avodah Zarah*	
6:25–27	43n	8a–b	79n
6:2–6	38n		
6:5	43n	*Bava Batra*	
6:8–13	44n	74b	57n
7:3	43n		
7:4–5	43n	*Berakhot*	
7:5	43n	46a	51n
7:15–16	43n	55a	48, 60n
7:16	43n		
7:18–20	43n, 44n	*Pesahim*	
7:18	43n	108b	31n
8:5–6	39n	116a	31n
8:16–17	44n	8:1	31n
8:17	43n		
8:21–24	43n	*Rosh HaShanah*	
11:7–9	39n	29a–b	51n

1QSa		Jerusalem	
	41	*Pesahim*	
2:3–10	42	37b	31n
2:11–22	41, 75n, 98n	10:8	32
2:11–12	44n		
2:17–22	41n	Mishnah	
2:17–18	43n	*Avodah Zarah*	
		5:5	79n
4QCD			
	42n	*Avot*	
		3:3	22n
4QDb			
	39n		

Index of Ancient Sources

Avot (continued)
5:23	194n

Berakhot
6:4	212n
6:5	32n
6:5C	212n
6:6	52n
7:1	79n
7:5b	32n

Eruvim
6:6	50n

Hagigah
2:5	61n

Pesahim
1:1	32
7:3	82n
8:7	50n
9:5	30n
10:1–9	29n
10:1	32, 73n, 82, 89n
10:2	30n
10:6	31, 32n
10:7	30n
10:8	32n, 50n

Sanhedrin
6:2	194n

Sheqalim
3:3	82n

Sotah
1:1—4:3	177n
3:4	177n

Tosefta

Pesahim
10:1	32
10:4	32n
10:9b	32n

NEW TESTAMENT

Matthew
5:21–22	173n
5:23–26	202n
7:1	209n
7:15	168
9:10–11	113n
9:15	58n
11:16–19	14n
22:1–14	58n
22:1–10	10n
23:25	49n
24:11	168
24:24	168
25:1–14	58n
26:23	184n
26:27–28	158
26:66	173n
27:52	197n

Mark
2:1–12	100n
2:19–20	58n
3:29	173n
7	49n
7:1–15	49n
7:3	61n
14:1–2	150n
14:20	184n
14:24	158
14:26	173n
15:42	150n

Luke
5:34–35	58n
7:31–35	14n
7:44–46	61n
11:38	49n
13:10–17	100n
13:16	186n
14:1–24	75n
14:7–11	58n
14:16–24	10n
15:23–24	198n
21:24	161n

Index of Ancient Sources

22:15–16	151
22:19–20	144n
22:19	153n
22:20	158
22:21	184n

John

1:1–11	58n
2:1–2	61n
3:29	58n
3:39	58n
9:1–2	100n
11:11	197n
13:18	184n

Acts

1:18	175n
2:42–47	183n
5:1–11	194
7:60	197n
9:4	207n
11:14–18	120
11:29–30	135n
13:36	197n
13:43	120
13:50	120
15	80
15:20	125n
15:29	125n
16:14	120
16:15	120
17:4	120
17:17	120
18:1–17	117
18:1–8	118n
18:4	116n
18:7	120
18:17	122n
18:24	118
19:1	118
20:7	132n
20:29–30	169n
21:25	125n

Romans

2:2–3	191
3:8	191
3:25	154
4:25	183n
5:9	195n
5:17	197n
5:21	197n
6:2–8	161n
6:16	197n
6:23	197n
7:10	197n
8:1	195n
8:2	197n
8:6	197n
8:30–34	195n
8:32	183n
8:34	183n
11:25	161n
14:1—15:13	125n, 132n
15:7	141n
16:19–20	186n
16:22	122n
16:23	118n

1 Corinthians

1:1	122n
1:10–17	118n
1:10–12	138n
1:10	136, 138n, 138n
1:11	117n, 211n
1:12	118, 118
1:23	154
1:26–28	119n, 121
1:26	121
2:8	175n
2:15	209n
3:1–4	138n
3:3	138
3:4–9	118
3:10–17	167
3:10–15	195n
3:12	138
3:15–17	186n
3:17	167
3:22	118
4:5	209
4:8–13	121n
4:8	137, 162n

265

Index of Ancient Sources

1 Corinthians (continued)

4:11–15	161n
5	189, 190n
5:1–11	167
5:1–5	189n, 192n
5:1	117n
5:2	137
5:3	167n, 209n
5:5	167n, 186n
5:7	151n, 154
5:9–13	176
5:11–12	209
5:11	125n, 167n, 186n, 209n
6:1–20	118n
6:1–11	190n
6:2–3	167n, 209n
6:12–20	208n
7	137
7:1	117
7:5	186n
7:10	145, 146n
7:21–22	132n
7:39	197n
8–10	138n
8:1—10:22	118n
8:11–12	172n, 176
8:11	161n
8:12	143n, 175n
9:5	118
9:14	145
10–14	133n
10:1—11:2	188n
10	182
10:1–13	137, 181n, 57n
10:1–12	194
10:1–6	179
10:2–5	204
10:12	204
10:14–22	128, 178n
10:14	159
10:15–16	147n
10:16–17	205, 206n
10:16	143, 153, 181n
10:17–21	180n
10:17	126, 139, 142, 154n, 205n, 206, 207
10:18–22	181n
10:21	141
10:22	188
11–14	132
11	184, 189, 190n
11:1	122
11:2	145, 163
11:10–15	167n
11:17–34	xviii, 188n
11:17–22	27
11:17	145, 167n, 212
11:18–19	169n
11:18	117n, 126, 136
11:19–21	202
11:19	136, 168, 189
11:20–21	128
11:20	132n, 133n, 140, 141, 212n
11:21–22	129
11:21	141, 141n, 172
11:22	130n, 131, 142n, 143, 145, 161n, 17, 189n, 213
11:23–26	129, 143
11:23–25	132, 146n, 212n, 215n
11:23	143n, 145, 147, 148n
11:24–29	206n
11:24–25	143n
11:24	152, 157n, 205, 205n
11:25	157, 159, 178, 212n
11:26	143n, 145, 159
11:27–32	170, 192n
11:27–31	169
11:27	143, 169, 171, 173n, 174n, 176, 181n, 188, 191, 203, 205, 205n
11:28–32	169n
11:28	169, 169, 172, 173, 181, 201, 209
11:29–32	170
11:29	169, 169, 171n, 190n, 191, 203, 205n, 206, 209
11:30–32	171
11:30	171, 184, 185, 186, 194
11:31–32	210n
11:31	169, 169, 181, 185, 185n, 209
11:32	169, 176, 179, 182, 185n, 191n, 193, 195, 197n
11:33–34	130, 163, 211
11:33	126, 141n, 142, 170, 176, 206
11:34	190n, 209, 213

Index of Ancient Sources

12–14	126n, 133
12	137, 157
12:2	118, 118n
12:4–6	154
12:12–27	206n, 207n
12:12–20	180n
12:13	118
12:25	136
12:27	154, 208n
14:23	133n
14:26–32	215
14:26	126n
14:39	211n
15:1–58	118n
15:3–4	146n
15:3	145n, 183n
15:5	118
15:6	197n
15:12–19	137
15:18	197n
15:20	151n, 197n
15:22	197n
15:25	161n
15:29	156n, 181n
15:51	197n
16:3	122
16:7	117
16:8	118
16:15	118n
16:17	122n

2 Corinthians

2:5–11	193n
2:11	186n
2:16	197n
3:7	197n
5:10	191n, 195n
6:9	193n
7:10	197n
8:1–2	123n
8:14	123n
10:18	169
11:2	58n
11:14	186n
12:7–9	187n
12:7–8	186n
12:20–21	196n
13:13	208n

Galatians

1:4	183n
1:12	146n
1:18	147n
2:11–14	125n, 164
2:11–12	132n
2:11	141n
2:20	183n

Ephesians

4:1	171n
5:23–32	58n

Philippians

1:27	171n
2:7–8	161n

Colossians

1:10	171n

1 Thessalonians

2:12	146n, 171n
2:18	186n
4:1	146n
4:13–5:11	156n
4:13–15	197n
4:13–14	179n
5:9	195n

2 Thessalonians

2:9	186n
3:6	146n
3:14–15	193n
3:15	167n

1 Timothy

1:20	193n, 196n

2 Timothy

4:20	187n

Titus
2:11–12	196n

Hebrews
2:14	100n
2:15	173n
6:5	175n
6:6	175n
10:29	175n
12:5–12	196n

James
2:10	173n

2 Peter
3:4	197n

Revelation
2:7	57n
12:9	186n
19:7–9	58n
21:2	58n
22:2	57n
22:14	57n
22:17	58n
22:19	57n

EARLY CHRISTIAN WRITINGS

Acts of Peter
19–29	214n

Clement of Alexandria
Stromata
VI 3.31.1	102n, 187n

Didache
9:3–4	21
10:1	125n
10:1	214n
14:2	202n

Eusebius
Historia ecclesiastica
5.21.1	120n

Hippolytus
The Apostolic Tradition
27–28	214n

Ignatius
To the Ephesians
20.2	177n

Justin Martyr
Dialogue with Trypho
35.3	168n

Odes of Solomon
6:8–18	57, 106n
11:7–8	57n, 106n
30:1–7	57n, 106n

Origen
Contra Celsum
3.48	121n
158	119n

GRECO-ROMAN WRITINGS

Aeschylus
Supplices
26–27	102n

Apuleius
Metamorphoses
10	73n

Index of Ancient Sources

11	67n, 116n
11.21–24	67n
11.21	102n, 106n

Aristophenes
Acharnenses

1085–1149	10n

Vespae

1122–23	91n
1216	11n

Aristotle
Ethica Nichomachea

8.9.5	7n

Politica

1274b 17–18	18n
1311b	92n
1311b 23–24	18n
1336b 20–24	12n

Artemidorus Daldianus
Onirocritica

2.39	102n
5.82.7	64n

Athenaeus
Deipnosophistae

1.4	9n
1.11–12	11n
1.15e	94n
1.18a	12n
2.36	17n
2.38c–d	15n
2.39	16n
2.58c	14n
2.479	16n
3.101	15n
3.109de	13n
4	17n
4.31	89n
4.129	13n, 15n
4.131	15n
4.134	16n
4.140	94
4.150	15n
4.173	94
5.149	94
5.178	14n
5.179	94
5.183c–186b	20n
5.185a	20n
5.186a	20n
5.192	94
8.349	15n
8.362	8n, 13n
8.362	13n
8.363–64	11n
9.377	70n
9.409	15n
9.428b	11n
10.426D	13n
11.462c–d	11n, 13n
12.527	14n
12.534	94
14.640B–F	13n
14.641D–E	13n
14.642A–F	13n
14.643A–D	13n
14.644d	70n
15.631d	94n
15.675b–c	14n
128	81n
149	89n
194c–195f	81n
194c–195f	90n
196a–203d	81n
210c	81n
362E	13n
427d	17n
552	98n, 186n
614e–615a	90n
666d–668e	17n

Aulus Gellus
Noctes Atticae

7.13.1–4	126n
13.11.6–7	13n

269

Index of Ancient Sources

Noctes Atticae (continued)

15.2.	84n

Cicero

De natura deorum

3.38	102n

De officiis

1.134–5	19n

Epistulae ad Atticum

1.16	17n
13.52	91n

Epistulae ad familiars

7.9	72n
7.16	72n
9.24	12n
9.26	71n

In Catalinam

2.33–34	17n

Prationes philippicae

2	17n

Pro Caelio

35	17n

Pro Murena

36.76	20n

Dio Cassius

Historia Romae

40.11	135n
43.50	115n
51.19.7	14n, 94n, 128n
60.6.6	92n

Diodorus Siculus

Bibliotheca Historica

17.41.7	152n

Diogenes Laertius

Lives of Eminent Philosophers

1.110	99n
8.35	63n
10.18	156n

Euripedes

Bachae

64–168	67n, 177n
417–20	103n

Electra

637	98n

Hesiod

Opera et dies

100–105	99n, 102n, 187n

Homer

The Iliad

1.9–10	102n, 187n
1.43–44	102n, 187n
1.468	87n
1.554	87n
1.602	87n
1.707	87n
2.431	87n
2.569–70	115n
5.177–78	98n
5.335–42	106n
7.357	87n
9.68ff.	90n
9.219	104n
9.530–38	102n, 187n
9.533–38	98n
13.664	115n
19.38–39	106n
24.606	98n

The Odyssey

1.225–26	1, 71n
1.226–27	10n, 13n
3.336	65n

INDEX OF ANCIENT SOURCES

4.5ff.	90n
5.1	106n
5.396	99n, 102n, 187n
7.201–4	98n
7.201–3	65n
9.5–10	1, 71n
10.64	99n, 102n, 187n

Horace
Carmina

4.5.31–32	14n, 94n, 128n

Josephus
Jewish Antiquities

3.320–21	135n
7.14.5	213n
11.8.6	213n
12.3.3	213n
13.4.5	213n
13.5.5	213n
14.10.8	92n
18.1–5	40
19.321	198n

Jewish War

2.10	82n
2.14.7	213n
2.129–328	38n
2.130	38n
2.131	38n
2.138–39	79n
2.139	38n
2.143	109n
3.2.4	213n
7.3.3	79n

Juvenal
Satirae

3.81	74n, 129n
3.152–56	74n, 129n
5.152–55	74n, 85n, 129n
5.156–70	74n

Livy
History of Rome

2.36.5	102n, 187n
9.9.3	102n
9.29.11	102n, 187n
22.9.7	98n
41.16.1–2	99n, 186n
41.16.9	99n

Lucian
De parasite

5	14n
15	10n
51	16n

Dialogi deorum

4.3–5	106n

Dialogi meretricii

1–15	16n
15	16n

Lexiphanes

6, 9, 13	10n

Saturnalia

10	88n
10	101n
12	88n
12	101n
13	70n
13	88n
13	208n
17	74n
18	88n
82–83	87n

Symposium

5	9n
5	127n
8	10n, 70n
9	11n, 72n
13	71n
17	17n

271

Index of Ancient Sources

Symposium (continued)
46	17n

Martial

Epigrams
1.20	74n, 129n
3.60	74n, 85n, 129n
4.85	74n, 85n, 129n
6.11	74n, 129n
10.49	74n, 129n
11.31.4–7	14n
60	74n

Ovid

Fasti
4.743ff.	65n

Pausanias

Graeciae description
1.24.4	98n
1.28.10	98n
2.2.3	116n
8.2.4	103n
21.2	115n

Petronius

Satiyricon
26–78	16n, 17n
56	16n, 80n, 212n
59	75n
60	14n, 128n

Philo

De specialibus legibus
1.221	98n

De vita contemplativa
48–50	33n
57	45n
58–59	46n
64	47n

66	46n, 47n
67–72	90n
67	46n, 75n
69	30, 46n
70–71	46n
72	47n
73	47n
74	47n
75–78	9n

In Flaccum
136	17n, 77n

On the Posterity and Exile of Cain
41.136	213n

Pindar

Isthmionikai
6.10	15n

Olympionikai
5.17	102n

Plato

Leges
1.640A	17n
2.671A	17n
2.671C–672A	84n
3	17n
10.910a	105n
10.910a–b	105n

Phaedrus
244d–e	102n, 105n, 187n

Respublica
2.363c–d	56n, 105n

Symposium
118b	98n
174A	10n
175A	11n, 72n
176A	14n, 93n
176E	19n, 20n, 36n

272

177D–E	72n	613	84n
177E	84n	613F	88n, 208n, 214n
213B	72n	614A–B	63n, 85n
223B	18n	614A	19n
		614C	19n
Theaetetus		614D–E	64n, 85n
173d	92n	615–17	73n
		615A	19n, 100n
		615B	14n, 15n, 94n

Pliny the Younger
Epistulae

		615C–D	11n. 75n
		615D	11n, 73n
1.15	16n	615E	74n, 89n
2.17	4n	616C	108n, 169n
2.6	74n, 85n, 129n, 212n	616C–F	89n
10.34–35	92n	616E–F	89n
10.93–94	92n	616F	132n
10.96	125n, 172n	617C	72n
		619B	11n, 73n

Plutarch

		620–622B	15n
		620A–622B	19n, 85n
		622C	16n
		642C	85n, 100n

Alexander

38	17n	643A	63n
52.8–9	17n	643B–E	63n
		643F–644A	141n

Cato Major

25.4	63n	644C	63n, 85n, 128n
		644D	141n
		660A–B	63n

De sera numinis vindicta

12.161	102n, 187n	660B	85n, 206n
		678E–F	63n
		679B–C	63n

De vitioso pudore

		703B	81n
531B	16n	703E	81n
		707A	11n
		708D	6n

Moralia

		709A–E	11n
226E	89n	713A	14n
831a	115n	716D–E	71n
		716F	17n

Quaestiones convivales

		717B	9n, 127n
1.2	74n	734A	14n
2.10.1	98n	761D	17n
4.5	110n		
5.5	16n, 63n	### *Septem sapientium convivium*	
7.6	5n	150D–155E	70n
612D	84n, 85n	150D	13n, 15n
612E–F	13n, 20n		
612F	17n, 70n		

Index of Ancient Sources

Polybius
Histories
26.1.4	18n

Porphyry
De abstinentia
2.10	98n
2.29	98n

Quintus Curtius Rufus
Historiae Alexandri Magni
4.2.14	152n

Strabo
Geographica
8.6.20	115n
8.361	115n
8.377	115n
8.381	115n

Suetonius
Divus Augustus
32	92n
32.1	93n

Divus Claudius
18.2	135n
25.4	92n

Divus Julius
42	92n

Domitianus
7	80n

Vespasianus
19	16n, 80n, 212n
21	212n
488–89	93n

Tacitus
Annales
3–54	20n
12.43	135n
13.17	65n
14.22	102n, 187n
16.16	102n

Historiae
5.4–5	78n

Xenophon
Anabasis
1.8.16	102n
5.3.7–13	67n
6.1.5	94
7.3.22	152n

Hellenica
3.3.4	102n

Memorabilia
2.2.13	168n
2.6.28	17n
3.14.1	10n, 13n, 88n
3.5.20	168n
4.3.16	105n

Symposium
1.8	71n
2.1	14n, 16n, 214n
3.1	16n
3.2–3	20n
3–4	10n
8	17n
9	67n
9	106n
9.2–7	17n
9.3–7	16n

INSCRIPTIONS AND PAPYRI

Inscriptions

IDelos 1520, 1521	71
ILS 2.1.4966	93
ILS 7212, II.25	20
SIG 1025.46	80n
SIG 1026.4	80n
SIG3 1109.73ff.	20n
SIG3, I, 408, 6–7	102
SIG3, II, 589, 26–31	102
SIG3, III, 985, 60–62	102

Papyri

Oxyrhyncus Papyri

110	106n
523	106n
1484	106n

www.ingramcontent.com/pod-product-compliance
Lightning Source LLC
Chambersburg PA
CBHW071236230426
43668CB00011B/1457